"WORK HARD, STUDY . . .
AND KEEP OUT OF POLITICS!"

ALSO BY JAMES A. BAKER, III

The Politics of Diplomacy:
Revolution, War & Peace, 1989–1992 (with Thomas M. DeFrank)

"WORK HARD, STUDY...
AND KEEP OUT
OF POLITICS!"

JAMES A. BAKER, III
with STEVE FIFFER

NORTHWESTERN UNIVERSITY PRESS

Evanston, Illinois

Northwestern University Press
www.nupress.northwestern.edu

Printed in the United States of America

10 9 8 7 6 5 4 3 2 1

Library of Congress Cataloging-in-Publication Data

Baker, James Addison, 1930–
    "Work hard, study—and keep out of politics!" / James A. Baker, III ; with Steve Fiffer. —
Northwestern University Press ed.
        p. cm.
    Includes bibliographical references and index.
    ISBN-13: 978-0-8101-2489-9 (pbk. : alk. paper)
    ISBN-10: 0-8101-2489-0 (pbk. : alk. paper)
    1. Baker, James Addison, 1930– 2. Baker, James Addison, 1930– —Philosophy. 3. Statesmen—
United States—Biography. 4. Cabinet officers—United States—Biography. 5. United States—
Politics and government—1981–1989. 6. United States—Politics and government—1989– 7. Civil
service—United States. 8. United States—Politics and government—Philosophy. I. Fiffer, Steve.
II. Title.
E840.8.B315A3 2008
973.92092—dc22

2008006221

∞ The paper used in this publication meets the minimum requirements of the American National
Standard for Information Sciences—Permanence of Paper for Printed Library Materials, ANSI
Z39.48-1992.

TO THOSE PRESIDENTS OF THE UNITED STATES
WHO GAVE ME THE OPPORTUNITY TO EXPERIENCE
AN UNEXPECTED PUBLIC LIFE

CONTENTS

PREFACE

I WAS IN WASHINGTON, D.C., on January 20, 1953, the crisp, sunny day that Dwight David Eisenhower was inaugurated as our nation's thirty-fourth president. At the time, I was a twenty-two-year-old second lieutenant in the United States Marine Corps, on leave from nearby Quantico, Virginia. My fiancée, Mary Stuart McHenry, of Dayton, Ohio, was in town for a visit before I shipped out. I had joined the Marines' platoon leader officer program the summer after my junior year at Princeton, in part to keep from being drafted before I graduated. The Korean War was raging when I signed up, and I fully expected to be sent there.

Strolling down the street arm in arm on the day before the inauguration, very much in love, Mary Stuart and I were stopped by a well-dressed older gentleman. I was wearing my uniform. "Lieutenant," he said, "thank you for your service. I have a son who is a Marine second lieutenant in Korea. I'm wondering, would you and your lady like two tickets to the inaugural parade tomorrow?"

"Yes, sir," I said to our anonymous benefactor, "and thank you."

Mary Stuart and I showed up early the next day to claim our seats and discovered they were on the lip of Lafayette Park, directly across Pennsylvania Avenue from the White House and only a few yards downstream from the presidential reviewing stand. An estimated 750,000 people attended the inaugural festivities that day, and except for President Eisenhower, Vice President Richard Nixon, and the dignitaries and family members with them, we had some of the best seats in town.

As floats and marching bands streamed by, I clicked away with my 35mm camera. I still have the slides, including one of President Eisenhower and John Foster Dulles, soon to be sworn in as secretary of state, as they drove past, and another of a cowboy roping the president in the reviewing stand.*† Newspaper accounts said the parade lasted about four hours. I can't remember if we stayed until the end, but I doubt it. The dignitaries (and Mary Stuart) all wore heavy overcoats, but I had on only a light uniform jacket. Whatever the weather, however, it was a great experience. Mary Stuart and I had no idea what the months ahead might bring, but that day we were happy and thankful.

Twenty-eight years later another president-elect took the oath of office, this time on the terrace of the west front of the Capitol. I was privileged to attend both the inauguration ceremony and the parade that followed. This time, I didn't sit across from the parade reviewing stand, however; I sat *in* it. I was to be Ronald Reagan's White House chief of staff, charged with helping turn his ideas about the economy and defense into legislative and political realities. To those who knew me my first fifty years, my presence at this 1981 inauguration was as unexpected as my presence at Ike's, and I was just as surprised.

After my two-year tour of active duty with the Marines and three years of law school, I had dedicated myself to a career in a major Houston law firm. In my time away from the demands of the office, I

---

*Nothing like that would happen today, of course. After the assassination of President Kennedy and attempts on the lives of Presidents Ford and Reagan, White House reviewing stands are now enclosed by thick bulletproof glass.

†More than half a century later, my public service and political papers, as well as Dulles's, are stored on the same shelf at Princeton's Seeley G. Mudd Manuscript Library.

was more interested in serving a tennis ball than serving in a government job or a political campaign.

What finally blew my life off its more-or-less conventional course was a deep personal tragedy in early 1970. Afterward, a Republican friend invited me to get involved in my first political campaign—his losing bid for the U.S. Senate that same year. I threw myself into this new and exciting project, and if politics didn't exactly save my life, it certainly helped preserve my sanity. When Ronald Reagan was sworn in as president, that friend, George H. W. Bush, was sworn in as vice president. Later that day, he came up to me, smiling.

"Bake," he said, "who'da thunk it?"

WHO, INDEED?

Few have had the opportunity to serve six American presidents—two in the military and, decades later, three in senior government positions, then one more on several special projects. In my first book, *The Politics of Diplomacy: Revolution, War & Peace, 1989–1992,* I wrote in detail about how the world changed, dramatically and fundamentally, during my four years as secretary of state under the first President Bush. While revisiting some of those events in this second book, my aim here is to tell the story of my journey from Houston, Texas, to Washington, D.C., then around the world, and to share memories of the political campaigns, the presidential administrations in which I served, and the other offices I held.

But I hope to do more. I've now lived more than three-quarters of a century, some in private life, some in public service. I'm more at ease when I'm getting things done in the world of action than in stirring the ashes of the past and writing about what it all meant. Still, I've learned some lessons (often the hard way) and worked out some ideas about politics and public policy. While I'm telling the story of my life, of what happened, I'll also share a few of these lessons and ideas. But what I offer in this book are not grand theories; they are the lessons from one man's hard-won experiences during a long and varied life.

SOON AFTER Mary Stuart and I watched the inaugural parade of one of the great war leaders of the twentieth century, now my commander in chief, I shipped out from Quantico. The Corps sent me to the Mediterranean, not Korea. My months of service with the Sixth Fleet and the reinforced battalion of Marines that the United States maintains in the Mediterranean, even to this day, were not unpleasant and, obviously, were considerably less dangerous than even a few days in Korea. That bloody conflict occupies a hazy zone in our national consciousness between the glory of World War II and the disappointment of Vietnam, and is too often forgotten. It's something I never forget, however, because many of my classmates from Marine Corps Basic School—men I knew—sacrificed their lives on the Korean peninsula. I survived and they didn't, which still triggers a bit of guilt.

We have no say in choosing our parents. I was fortunate to grow up in Houston in a loving home under comfortable circumstances. Having gone away from home for two years of prep school, then on to Princeton, I entered the Marines as an immature young man. I left with more personal discipline and with a greater sense of purpose— the products of military training, of facing up to what it means to prepare for combat in time of war, and of losing young friends whose potential seemed so limitless.

As the old saying goes, "There is no such thing as a former Marine." Early in 1989, after I was sworn in as the sixty-first secretary of state of the United States, the commandant of the Corps paid a courtesy call. When General Al Gray walked into my seventh-floor office at the State Department with his four stars on each shoulder, I had to remind myself that I was no longer a second lieutenant who should stand and salute.

We had a very pleasant visit. "Mr. Secretary, I have a gift for you," the general said as he prepared to depart. He left a stack of small business cards with a military camouflage background. In the center of each card in large letters was, "James A. Baker, III, United States Marine." And under that, in very tiny letters, "and Secretary of State."

While in that office, I participated in the decision to dispatch Marines and other servicemen and -women to fight in the Gulf War. No matter how just the cause, it is a sobering responsibility to send Americans into combat, but it's a responsibility that, at times, must be met. To stand aside when America's core interests are challenged, as the nation was tempted to do after Vietnam, is dangerous.

In his inaugural address, President Eisenhower called for peace, but promised that America would remain strong. When President Reagan took his oath twenty-eight years later, he said the same thing. By then the Cold War had become a seemingly permanent feature of the second half of the twentieth century.

The payoff for four decades of American leadership and resolve came during the presidency of my friend George H. W. Bush. We saw the fall of communism in Eastern Europe and the Soviet Union. With the end of the Cold War, the principles of classical liberalism—personal, religious, and economic freedom, self-government, and the rule of law—prevailed against totalitarian ideology. There were other victories, as well, including the end of apartheid in South Africa and renewed hopes for peace in the Middle East. When those years ended, the United States was (and it remains) the world's sole surviving superpower.

Our geopolitical rival in the Cold War was the expansionist and nuclear-armed Soviet Union. Our adversaries today—transnational terrorist organizations and smaller nations with authoritarian rulers and nuclear ambitions—present different kinds of threats. Certain truths remain, however. As it has since World War II, the source of America's power rests in no small part on our ability to project strength responsibly around the world and our willingness to use that strength when necessary in furtherance of our values and interests.

My full-time career in public service ended with the inauguration of President Bill Clinton in 1993. In the previous thirteen years, I had served as White House chief of staff, secretary of the treasury, and secretary of state, and I had led presidential election campaigns. I was tired, and it was time to do other things—spend time with my family; write my diplomatic memoir; serve as senior partner for Baker Botts, my law firm, and as senior counselor for the Carlyle Group, a Washington-based private equity firm; help establish the James A. Baker III Institute for Public Policy as a first-rate think tank at Rice University; do some public speaking; submit the occasional op-ed piece on topics that interested me; and hunt, fish, and play golf.

In the years after 1993, however, I have been called off the bench several times. Kofi Annan asked me to try to help resolve a lingering dispute in Western Sahara, and candidate George W. Bush asked me to help preserve his 2000 presidential election victory in Florida, then to serve as his envoy or representative on several special projects—in 2003 and 2004, a mission to persuade countries to forgive a substantial share of the debt owed to them by Iraq; a trip to the former Soviet Republic of Georgia in 2004 to encourage my old friend Eduard Shevardnadze to support a free election; service in 2005 as cochairman with President Jimmy Carter of the Commission on Federal Election Reform; and a call later that year to chair the American delegation to Israel on the tenth anniversary of the assassination of my friend, the former prime minister of Israel, Yitzhak Rabin. More recently I agreed to serve as cochair of a bipartisan study group to make a forward-looking assessment of the situation in Iraq.

All but one of those summonses came after I had celebrated my seventieth birthday. All were unsought. None had a salary, except one that earned a dollar a year before taxes.* So why did I take time from my own affairs and the pleasures of private life to accept these commissions?

For several reasons, I suppose. For one, the projects were interest-

---

*However, federal law required that my law firm be paid for its work in the Florida recount effort in 2000.

ing. For another, I thought that each one had a worthy purpose or goal. The biggest reason, however, is that I simply felt a sense of responsibility. For the first few years of my adult life (except for my military service), I had largely left the burdens of public life to others. Then came my friendship with George H. W. Bush, my family's personal tragedy, and my unexpected life in politics and public service. Each of us, I learned, has the capacity to make the world a better place. All it takes is the dedication of some part of our time and talent to public service. This is a small price, really, for the privilege of being a citizen of our great nation. As a young man, I had sat on the sidelines; now I understood the importance of joining the parade.

"We must be willing, individually and as a nation, to accept whatever sacrifices may be required of us," President Eisenhower said in his inaugural address more than fifty years ago. Each citizen "plays an indispensable role," he said. "No person, no home, no community can be beyond the reach of this call," for "whatever America hopes to bring to pass in the world must first come to pass in the heart of America."

My hope is that this book will help the reader gain some appreciation for the importance of participation in public service and its corollary, politics, and also for the satisfaction that comes from giving both one's very best. For it is the promise of such participation by our citizens that is the best hope for our country's future.

ONE

"NUMBER ONE, I DON'T KNOW ANYTHING ABOUT POLITICS"

THE PRESIDENTIAL ELECTION was the tightest in a century. As the results came in, it was apparent that a small number of votes for my candidate or his opponent would swing the contest one way or the other. When I finally went to bed at 3:00 A.M., I was certain I would never see another race for president decided by such a narrow margin. Boy, was I wrong.

The 1976 race between Governor Jimmy Carter and President Gerald Ford was close. If there had been a shift of fewer than 5,600 votes in Ohio and 3,700 in Hawaii, Ford would have retained the presidency, winning the electoral vote while losing the popular election. But '76 now pales in comparison to the 2000 race between Vice President Al Gore and Governor George W. Bush. That one was decided by 537 votes in Florida and a 7–2 margin in the U.S. Supreme Court more than a month after the balloting. As most everyone knows, although Gore won the popular vote, Bush prevailed in the Electoral College.

In 1970, as a forty-year-old Houston corporate lawyer who had little interest and no experience in politics, I could never have imagined that I would be intimately involved in either of these presidential contests, much less both. Nor could I ever have dreamed that I would lead five successive presidential campaigns for three different candidates. At the beginning of 1975, I was still practicing law in my hometown. By that fall, I was in Washington, D.C., second in command at the Department of Commerce. And by the summer of '76, I was campaign chairman for the Ford-Dole ticket. Who'da thunk it?

Before losing narrowly to Carter, we had come back from a double-digit deficit after the conventions. Many observers believe that if Ford-Dole had been Ford-Reagan, we would have won. So why didn't Ford tap Reagan for the second spot and create a dream ticket?

The actor-turned-politician from California was the obvious choice. He had a huge core of supporters, and he was a great campaigner. Moreover, he had just missed getting the nomination himself at what turned out to be the last closely contested national convention in this nation's history.

President Ford was not happy that Governor Reagan had mounted such a strong challenge against a sitting president. But other nominees have chosen runner-ups after bitter contests, particularly if those runner-ups could improve the chances of victory in November. John F. Kennedy picked Lyndon Johnson that way. While the chemistry between Ford and Reagan was not good, that alone didn't impel Ford to bypass Reagan. Most accounts say there was another reason.

Early during President Reagan's first term, when I was his White House chief of staff, he and I discussed this. "You know, Mr. President," I said, as we sat together alone in the Oval Office one day, "if President Ford had asked you to run with him, he would have won, and you might never have been president."

"You're right," the president responded. "But I have to tell you, Jim, if he had asked, I'd have felt duty-bound to run."

"President Ford didn't ask you," I replied, "because we received word from your campaign that you would join him for a unity meeting only on the condition that he *wouldn't* offer you the vice presidency. And besides that, you very publicly shut down the movement by your supporters in Kansas City to draft you for the vice presidential nomination."

"Look," President Reagan said, "I really did not want to be vice president, and I said so at the time. But I don't have any recollection of telling anyone to pass a message to President Ford not to offer me the spot. If he had asked, I would have felt duty-bound to say yes."

I was shocked. How different history might have been. Given the intensity of their primary battle, Ford really didn't want Reagan as his running mate, but the president might have asked if he had thought Reagan would accept. And with a Ford-Reagan ticket in 1976, I think two presidential portraits might be missing from the White House walls today—those of Jimmy Carter . . . and Ronald Reagan.

This conversation about the vice presidency occurred early in President Reagan's tenure and was revisited several times over the years. As anyone who knew him well would attest, Ronald Reagan was completely without guile. What you saw was what you got. I have no reason to believe he wasn't being totally up front with me. Still, I must add here that a few years ago one of his close friends and advisers, former Nevada senator Paul Laxalt, told me that he still believes candidate Reagan made it clear in 1976 that he didn't want to be offered the second spot. But if, as President Reagan told me, he didn't tell anyone to pass on that message to the Ford camp, this would suggest his staff did that on its own. Why? Perhaps they knew he didn't want to be vice president, but would have felt he could not turn down a direct offer from the president. Or perhaps they simply reasoned that if a Ford-Reagan ticket had won, their man would have been too old to run for president in 1980 or 1984. (He wasn't, of course, and ran successfully in both of those years, although without having first served as vice president.)

MY ROLES as presidential campaign chairman and White House chief of staff would not have sat very well with another James Addison Baker, my grandfather. Nor would my view that all Americans should consider public service. A successful lawyer known as the "Captain," he admonished all who joined his firm to "work hard, study, and keep out of politics," which he viewed as a somewhat unseemly undertaking that really good lawyers left to others. He was an imposing figure who helped transform Houston from a regional cotton market and rail hub into a vibrant seaport and the capital of the U.S. oil industry. In the process, he turned a local law practice into a preeminent Texas firm that would later expand worldwide.

With due respect to the Captain, however, *not* keeping out of politics turned out to be one of the best decisions I ever made. Although my unplanned entry into public life was occasioned in part by personal tragedy, I found I had a strong predilection and passion for what the former *New York Times* correspondent Hedrick Smith called "the power game." Over the years, I witnessed the exercise of more power than I would have ever dreamed possible, but was often reminded (sometimes the hard way) to keep a sense of perspective about it all.

No one was better at keeping me humble than my mother, Bonner Means Baker. On my visits to Houston in the late 1980s and early nineties, she invariably asked: "Now, darling, tell me exactly, what is it you do?"

"Mom, I am secretary of state."

"Of the United States of *America?*"

"Yes, Mom."

"You don't mean it!"

Then she would add, "Well, you know, dear, if your father had lived, he would never have let you go to Washington."

My mother lived to the handsome age of ninety-six. She and my dad had tried to have children for thirteen years before I came along, so she doted on me and my younger sister, Bonner, when we finally arrived—me on April 28, 1930, and Bonner some eighteen months later. I talked baby talk until I was three or four years old, and I called my mother "Mamish." She was a warm, spirited, and elegant woman, not indifferent to fashion. I am still not sure whether her affectionate cross-examination of me in her twilight years stemmed from a failing mind or her enduring sense of humor.

Mother was only fifteen when she and my father, James A. Baker, Jr., met at a high school dance in Houston. It was love at first sight, she always said. They were engaged for five and one-half years. My dad wanted to be in a position to support his bride and, eventually, a family, but after he finished Princeton in 1915 and got his law degree at the University of Texas in 1917, World War I intervened. They married on August 4, 1917, about ten months before he shipped out as a young army lieutenant for the trenches of France. I remember Mother telling me that in his absence she comforted herself every day by repeating a verse from the 91st Psalm: "A thousand shall fall at thy side, and ten thousand at thy right hand; *but* it shall not come nigh thee."

Like my mother, Dad had a wonderful sense of humor and loved to joke, but he also had an austere demeanor and was a strict disciplinarian. And like his father, he, too, had a saying: "Prior preparation prevents poor performance." He called this the "Five Ps." It's a simple aphorism, the sort of thing adults tell children, then forget. People are often surprised to hear a man my age recite it, and without embarrassment. But this was a gift from my father that has helped me in one way or another almost every day of my adult life.

Dad was an intercollegiate wrestling champion and fine pole-vaulter while at Princeton. No doubt his training as an athlete and his military service reinforced his views about the importance of discipline and preparation, about doing your best in the fleeting time you are given on this earth.

Dad's fifth-year Princeton reunion book features the photographs of many classmates who never returned from the bloody battlefields of Europe. He came back, however, as an infantry captain and a genuine war hero. He once ordered some in his company to clear out an enemy trench. When they balked, he went in by himself, armed only with his .45-caliber service revolver, and captured two German soldiers. I had that pistol for many years until it was stolen, and I still have his World War I helmet and uniform.

My sister and I always addressed Dad with respect, but behind his back, my friends and I called him "Warden." He expected good manners, hard work, and deference to adult authority, and he regarded corporal punishment as a useful way to help us see the benefits of satisfying those expectations. The culture of the 1930s supported this approach. In those days, children did what their parents asked them to. Sometimes he spanked me. Occasionally, he would throw cold water on me in bed if I didn't get up when I should.

I'll leave it to the child-rearing experts to debate the pros and cons of this sort of upbringing, now considered old-fashioned and too harsh. All I can say is that he was a terrific dad. We had a wonderful relationship, I loved him dearly, and he set me on the right path. Many of my contemporaries had their lives ruined because their parents gave them too much money and too little discipline. That was never a problem in the Baker household.

Dad also loved to hunt and fish. From the time I was six, he and I spent many hours together in duck blinds. They are superb classrooms for teaching other forms of discipline, including the patience necessary to know exactly the right time to pull the trigger. After his love and his emphasis on the Five Ps, sharing his passion for the outdoors was Dad's greatest gift to me.

As a young competitive tennis player, I didn't question my father's orders to stay on the court after matches and practice backhand after backhand. Nor did I question his decision to send me across the country to Pottstown, Pennsylvania, to his alma mater, the Hill School. I didn't even protest when he told me to join his old undergraduate social fraternity at the University of Texas, Phi Delta Theta. Here I was *in law school,* twenty-four years old, just out of the Marine Corps, married with a child, and having to go through a Hell Week hazing in which college kids younger than I was poured raw eggs down my throat and made me sit bare-assed on a block of ice.

I didn't rebel. When I was growing up, our objective was to please our parents. Mother and Dad knew best, and we didn't argue with them. But we certainly didn't always do everything we were told. Like most teenagers, then and now, I broke curfew more than a few times.

One irony in my father's life is that he earned his military rank of captain in the most difficult way possible, but for my grandfather, "Captain" was an honorific title bestowed by a ceremonial Houston militia he joined in the late 1800s. After the Civil War, many prominent men in the South were forever known as "General Smith" and "Colonel Jones." My grandfather's militia was formed, I have heard, to give younger men a way to wear outlandish uniforms, join parades, conduct balls, and (not least) claim military rank of their own—all without the grim necessity of being actual soldiers.

I remember the Captain as a heavyset man who always smelled of cigars. He sat on the boards of many major banks, utility companies, and railroads, and represented them as a lawyer. Well known in Texas, he rose to national prominence in 1900 when he became the central figure in one of the most sensational scandals of his era.

In a New York murder trial, he proved that a butler and an unscrupulous lawyer had poisoned William Marsh Rice, a wealthy Texas merchant, with mercury and chloroform, then claimed Rice's fortune under a forged will. My grandfather had been Mr. Rice's lawyer, and his efforts restored the victim's original will, which endowed William Marsh Rice Institute, a "university of the first class" that Rice had chartered in Houston in 1891. Rice Institute (now Rice University) opened in 1912, and my grandfather served as its first chairman of the board of trustees for fifty years.

The Captain was the second James A. Baker in our family. The first, his father, was born in 1816 near Florence, Alabama, to Elijah and Jane Baker. Family lore says they descended from Scottish immigrants. They were part of the great migration of early Americans out of the thirteen original states to the unsettled forests and plains out west. They were, it seems, a well-educated family. In Alabama, James apprenticed to a lawyer and appeared to have prospects for a good career. In April 1852, however, he abruptly left for Texas, apparently in grief over the sudden death of his bride of less than two years. During the Civil War, he served as a judge. Afterward, he joined a small Houston law firm— the one that to this day bears his name, Baker Botts. He and his second wife, Rowena, are buried in Huntsville, Texas, not far from his friend General Sam Houston.

I will not pretend that I grew up under modest circumstances. My mother's father, J. C. Means, was in the timber, oil, and cotton business. He was not particularly successful, but the Bakers were reasonably well-to-do. Each generation had built on the success of the previous one. We lived in a nice two-story house near Rice University and belonged to two country clubs. The family owned a considerable amount of Houston real estate and made other good investments.

Still, I don't think my parents spoiled me. Dad was quite frugal. He understood that it was easier to spend a dollar than to make it. As a result, we didn't lead the stereotyped bigger-than-life Texas existence. No mansion. No big cars. And no big allowance for me. Dad invested most of his money. Yet he did spend, without hesitation, for his children's education or for things my mother wanted; material possessions for himself or his children were meaningless, something else I inherited from him. But I've become much better as the years have gone by and I have been able to accumulate some means of my own.

There were occasional extravagances in my childhood. Some were outlandish: when I was a young boy, my mother once had me dressed in a pink linen smock for a portrait by a member of the French Academy. Some were just plain fun: when the University of Texas played Texas A&M in football, the Captain often took us to the game in a private rail car arranged through one of his railroad clients.

There was one domain in which my father was willing to give me money. When I was a teenager, he said he would pay me $1,000 if I didn't smoke until I was twenty-one and another $1,000 if I didn't drink alcohol before that age. I didn't collect, though I managed to wait until I was eighteen for my first taste of hard liquor. I was not a habitual smoker until I went into the Marine Corps. At breaks in our training, the drill instructors would always say, "The smoking lamp is lit"—meaning it was okay to smoke. Most everyone did, so I did, too.

It's somewhat remarkable that I didn't start drinking the moment my parents dropped me off at the Hill School. My first year there was tough. I entered as a junior and didn't know anybody. Most classmates had already been there for two years and had established friendships. I was a new boy. All my friends were back in Houston. I even had to wear a beanie, and every time I put it on, it reminded me that I was not a part of the old boys' club.

By senior year, I was much more at ease. I was elected to the student government and captained the tennis team. I also made friendships that continue to this day. My grades were good, but not outstanding. Still, I managed to get into the university I wanted and that my father had attended: Princeton. Two centuries after it was founded by colonial Presbyterian clerics, it was still the destination of choice for many young American men of Scottish heritage, particularly those from the South.

As I said, I didn't really drink until I was eighteen, but I quickly made up for lost time during my first year at Princeton. Liberated from the constraints of prep school, I went wild. I became a member of both Princeton's Right Wing Club—so named because we spent much of our time using our right arms to hoist spirituous beverages—and 21 Club, another social organization with a similar mission. I also used my right arm to play tennis as cocaptain of the freshman team, but the team was loaded with nationally ranked players who were better than I was. The next year I gave up tennis and switched to rugby, in part because the rugby team went to Bermuda for spring break, and the tennis team went only to North Carolina. It was in Bermuda in 1950 that I met the girl I was later to marry, Mary Stuart McHenry, who was there on spring break from Finch College in New York.

My freshman and sophomore year grades reflected my membership in the social clubs. I ignored the Five Ps to such an extent that it is a wonder I didn't get five Fs and flunk out. By junior year, fortunately, I had matured a bit. I studied more, finding the classics (my minor) and history (my major) especially interesting.

My senior thesis covered the conflict within Britain's Labour Party in the 1930s and forties between two powerful members of Parliament, Aneurin Bevan, whom I saw as a "true socialist," and Ernest Bevin, a "social democrat." There was no love lost between these two men. When a British cabinet member declared that Bevan was his own worst enemy, Bevin said, "Not while I'm around."

I argued that the clash between Bevan and Bevin was a clash between idealism and realism. Those who know me will not be surprised that I favored the approach of the realist, Bevin, who served as Clement Attlee's foreign secretary. "Bevin was not interested in theories, but in practicalities," I wrote. "He knew that when men were unemployed they wanted bread and work, not an oration on the coming revolution. . . . Bevin believed in solving the problems of the present before tackling the problems of the future."

I had no interest or talent in science or math, but did have a fair grasp of history—an indicator that I might have an aptitude for the law. More important, however, I'd been brought up with the idea that Baker Botts was everything. I'd sat in my father's office as he worked, and had worked at the firm myself as an office boy.* That was my legacy. That was the history of my family.

"Practicing law is a wonderful lifestyle," Dad told me. "Although you'll never make really big money doing it, it's very satisfying." Still, this career path was not ordained. More than once Dad told me the choice was mine. "I'd never insist you be a lawyer." I even flirted with going to medical school, but that was before I took a job at St. Joseph's Hospital one summer as a teenager. My assignment was to hold the tray while stabbing victims and overdosed drug users threw up. I also had the opportunity to watch a baby being born and observe a surgeon cutting into a patient's chest cavity. All that blood! I quickly realized I didn't have the stomach or the aptitude to become a doctor.

In any event, I didn't have to make a decision by graduation day

---

*Another alumnus of the Baker Botts office-boy pool, hired many years later, was George W. Bush.

in the late spring of 1952. My immediate future was Basic School—the U.S. Marine Corps' officer training program—not law school. The government had started drafting young men out of college when the Korean War broke out in 1950. I wanted to serve, but I wanted to finish school first. It was too late to join an ROTC program at Princeton, and my tendency to motion sickness made it prudent not to consider the Air Force or the Navy.

The CIA seemed a possibility until I had an on-campus interview. "Would you have any problem jumping out of an airplane with a parachute behind enemy lines?" I was asked.

"You bet I would." End of interview.

Then I learned of the Marine Corps platoon leaders program. The deal: go to boot camp for six weeks each summer for two summers, and we'll give you a commission when you graduate. After that you'll have an obligation to serve on active duty for two years. I signed on.

In Basic School at Quantico, I was one of about five hundred second lieutenants. Our commanding officer told us that if we worked hard, we'd get our choice of duty station and military occupational specialty (MOS). I graduated at the top of the reserves in our class—behind a few regular Marine enlisted men picked to become officers. When it came time to hand out MOSs, the commanding officer told me, "We're going to put you where we put our best—platoon leader, MOS 0302—infantry officer."

"Major," I replied, "one reason I worked so hard is because I have a friend who graduated a year ago, and he talked to me about being a naval gunfire spotter, MOS 0840. That's what I really want to do." Spotters went in with the first wave of an amphibious invasion. They had a couple of jeeps, a few men, and some radio equipment, and their job was to deploy forward and direct the fire of naval ships supporting the operation. This was hazardous duty, as was leading a platoon, but I preferred it. I didn't want to be responsible for the lives of forty-four other people.

Although the major wasn't pleased by my request, he honored it. I thought I'd be going to Korea, and fifty-nine of the sixty officers in our class who received artillery MOSs went to Fort Sill, Oklahoma, for two weeks and then on to Korea. The sixtieth—me—ended up with the battalion of Marines the United States had kept deployed in the Mediterranean since the end of World War II. I was on a troop transport ship, the USS *Monrovia,* where the biggest danger was falling overboard as I perpetually heaved over the rail.

I was in the Mediterranean for six months. When I returned in November 1953, Mary Stuart and I were married in her hometown of Dayton, Ohio. After my discharge from active duty in 1954, we moved to a small apartment in Austin, Texas, where I entered law school on the GI Bill. I thought about applying to Harvard, but my father argued that the University of Texas was the best place to learn Texas law and establish connections with others who would be practicing in Texas. Again, I didn't question his counsel, which turned out to have been excellent.

During that initial year in law school, our first son, Jamie, was born. Nothing concentrates the mind like military service and being married with a child. Practicing the Five Ps to exhaustion, I made the law review and graduated with honors, but I wasn't much fun to be around.

We never considered settling anywhere except Houston. My family was there. So, too, was Baker Botts, the law firm where three James A. Bakers before me had hung their shingles.* I would have been happy to follow in their footsteps, but the firm had an ironclad antinepotism rule. My father was still practicing there, so I could not.

Thanks to my academic record and my name, the partnership considered making an exception for me, but eventually decided against waiving the rule. I was disappointed. Baker Botts was all I knew. In the end, however, their decision was the best thing that could have happened to me. Had I succeeded at a firm so closely identified with my father, my grandfather, and my great-grandfather, neither I nor any-

---

*Why am I James A. Baker, III, not IV? Because the numbering didn't start until I came along.

body else would have been able to say with certainty whether my success was based on my skills or my name. Going to another firm gave
me a chance to sink or swim on my own.

That other firm was Andrews, Kurth, Campbell & Bradley. It was a
smaller but also well-respected firm with a blue-chip roster of clients
that included Howard Hughes. When I joined in 1957, the firm had
thirty-five lawyers, and I was only the seventy-eighth to have been
hired in the firm's fifty-five-year history. It was a wonderful place to
work. The philosophy of the practice was collegial, we were proud of
AK and its history, and we were loyal to the firm and one another.

"We're going to assign you to Harry Jones," said Mickey West, the
firm's chief recruiter. "What an opportunity!"

And it truly was. The man who would become my mentor was
warm, gentlemanly, brilliant, and pragmatic, the smartest practitioner
I've ever known. In law school, I had briefed every case so thoroughly
that I often got lost in the details. If not for Harry Jones, I might have
followed the same dead-end path in my practice. He taught me to get
to the heart of the matter.

I would sit across from him in his corner office while he read what
I'd written. "Is there anything more on this?" he would ask in a non-
threatening and professorial voice. The ability to separate the wheat
from the chaff or, less delicately, to cut through the BS in a written
memo or a face-to-face negotiation, not only served me well at the law
firm, but has also been one of my strengths in politics and public service. I owe much of that to Harry Jones, a lawyer's lawyer.

In 1957, the practice of law was not as specialized as it is today. Andrews Kurth was just beginning to establish departments. In law school
they told us that real lawyers tried lawsuits, so I asked to be assigned to
the trial section. I soon found myself sitting second chair down at the
courthouse as one of our lawyers tried a personal injury case. Our
client was an insurance company bound by contract to provide a defense for its policyholder. It seemed obvious to me that witnesses were
lying under oath and that nothing was being done about it. I didn't

want any part of that, so I said goodbye to litigation and hello to a general business law practice—mergers and acquisitions, corporate and securities work, oil and gas, banking, and real estate.

As I approached forty, life was good. Our marriage flourished. Three more boys—Mike, John, and Doug—followed Jamie. We joined a couple of country clubs. And thanks to Mary Stuart, we could be described as a churchgoing family. My father was raised a Presbyterian. Mother had for a while been a Christian Scientist and for one year I went to Sunday school at her church. Dad was not a churchgoer, although he was a man of faith. He was a workaholic who spent Sundays at the office. On his way to work those mornings, and after that first year of Sunday school at Mother's church, he would drop Bonner and me off for Sunday school at First Presbyterian Church near his office in downtown Houston, to learn the hereditary faith of my Scottish forebears. After class, we'd join him at work.

I remember first getting a sense of fulfillment out of religion when I was at the Hill School. We attended chapel every day, and I found myself enjoying the hymns and learning a little how to pray. I was a nonobservant Christian in college and attended church only occasionally in the Marines and during law school.

Mary Stuart was a better Episcopalian than I was a Presbyterian, and when we married, I switched. I didn't think about it at the time, but my ancient Baker ancestors may have turned in their graves when I left the faith they had brought across the ocean from Scotland and went over to the "English" church they had spent so many centuries railing against. In Houston we attended St. Martin's fairly regularly. I found the services rewarding and eventually served on the vestry, the committee of lay members who help manage the parish, but my faith then was not nearly as important to me as it is now.

Like my father, my church on Sundays was often my law office. *Workaholic* is an overworked term, but it describes me during those first twelve years of practice. I made time for tennis and indulged my lifelong desire to escape to the country every once in a while to hunt and fish and clear my head, but Mary Stuart and I took very few real vacations.

Houston was my world, and I never dreamed of living anywhere else or doing anything besides being a lawyer. Politics was not in the picture. The most that can be said of me politically is that I voted . . . in some elections anyway. Oftentimes I did something else instead.

Texas still hadn't forgotten that Republicans were in office during Reconstruction, so like just about everyone else in the state at the time, I was a Democrat. And like many other conservative Democrats in the 1950s, when I voted, I voted for my party's candidates in local and state elections and for the Republican candidate for president. Mary Stuart was different. She came from a long line of Republicans in Ohio, and she remained active in the small Texas branch of her party, even serving as a precinct captain and often as a campaign worker for local candidates.

I sometimes wonder whether, if Mary Stuart had stayed healthy, I would have kept out of politics for my entire life. But in February 1968, she noticed a lump in her breast. Her doctor told her not to worry; the lump was most likely just mastitis, a side effect of being on birth control pills, which were relatively new at the time. "Come back if it persists," he said.

That summer we took a fishing trip into the mountains of Wyoming, camping at the same spot near the headwaters of the Yellowstone River where my father and I had camped to hunt elk twenty-four years earlier. By the end of the trip, Mary Stuart had lost all her stamina. The lump was now hot and red. Not too long after we returned, one of America's best surgeons, our friend Denton Cooley, performed a mastectomy. In the waiting room after the surgery, he didn't say, "She doesn't have a chance," but I sensed he was telling me to prepare for the worst. I was scared and depressed, but hopeful.

We were building a new home. Mary Stuart had designed it, and she continued to watch over construction. As the months passed, however, the cancer spread to her bones, and it was clear that she wasn't going to make it.

From the time I met her in Bermuda in 1950, I never dated anyone else. She was a gorgeous and bright woman, a devoted wife, and a loving mother.

We were close, but—whether out of fear or uncertainty or, more probably, concern for the other—we never talked openly about her real prognosis. She never told me she knew she was dying, and I never told her that I knew she was dying. That knowledge hung over us like a dark cloud in those last months. She did write me a goodbye letter. I found it after her death. Dated November 29, 1969, and addressed to "My dear sweet loving and lovable Jimmy," it reads in part:

> Though my time to die may not be far off, it is not now. I am not afraid. . . . My darling, it has been a beautiful life. We have been fortunate in so many ways. . . . Since the night I kissed you on the beach in Bermuda I have loved you more than anybody could ever love another body. The only thing that makes me sad about dying is leaving you and the boys. I often wonder what they will be like as grown men. Since they are half you they will have some good qualities in them. . . . God and I will watch over you and the boys and keep you safe. . . . Don't be sad. Rejoice and come to me someday.

My instinct from earliest memory has been to keep personal things personal. These few words reveal something about Mary Stuart's spirit that is worth sharing, however, not only for the sake of her children and grandchildren, but also as a model for others of how this young woman's faith gave her the courage to accept her own mortality so serenely.

When the house was just about finished, we took her over the threshold in a wheelchair. She never got to live in it. Within days, she had lapsed into a coma. The boys were ages seven, eight, thirteen, and fifteen. I never told them she was dying—a mistake I now profoundly regret.

Most nights while Mary Stuart was in the hospital, I had slept on a cot in her room. One evening, however, I went home for a shower and some rest in my own bed. The hospital called during the night and said, "You'd better come over here." When I arrived, Mary Stuart was breathing heavily. I held her in my arms, only the two of us, and I told her what a wonderful wife she'd been and how much I loved her. She made a little sound, and I like to think she heard me. She died a few hours later at 11:00 A.M., February 18, 1970. We had been married for sixteen years. The boys and I were devastated.

Eight months earlier, my tennis doubles partner had suggested that I file for the congressional seat he was vacating to run for the Senate. He and his wife were our good friends and had experienced their own tragedy with cancer in 1953, when their three-year-old daughter died of leukemia. I told him I was flattered, but given Mary Stuart's illness, there was no way I could do that.

After Mary Stuart died, that same friend suggested that I work on his senatorial campaign to take my mind off my grief. I thanked him for his concern and said there were two problems with that— "Number one, I don't know anything about politics, and number two, I'm a Democrat."

He chuckled. "We can take care of that second problem."

We did, and he put me in charge of the Houston area. I dotted the i's and crossed the t's, and we carried the county but lost statewide. Still, from that time forward, I was hooked on politics and forever linked with the candidate, George Herbert Walker Bush.

I first met the man I have called "George," "Bushie," "Mr. President," and now *"Jefe"* (the Spanish word for *chief* or *boss*) in 1959, when he moved his family (Barbara and their five children) and his business (Zapata Offshore Company) to Houston from Midland, Texas.

George and I shared a passion for tennis, and we became doubles partners at Houston Country Club—although I still preferred and continued to play singles. We were both extraordinarily weak servers, but George was excellent playing net and volleying, while I had very good ground strokes. We complemented each other nicely and won back-to-back club doubles championships in 1966 and 1967.

George and I would also play pickup games with the club pro,

Hector Salazar, and Hector's recruited partner of convenience. To me it was clear that Hector was playing just hard enough to take the match to three sets and make us believe we were almost as good as he. George was so competitive, so certain that we were elevating our game, however, that I'm not sure he ever quite realized we were being conned. George is genuinely personable, easygoing, and considerate of others— a truly wonderful human being—traits that come through in face-to-face meetings and on television. What sometimes doesn't come through is his competitive spirit and steely determination, which I first encountered on the tennis court and which strengthened him for success in business and politics.

Our friendship on the tennis court carried over to our homes. Mary Stuart and I occasionally entertained the Bushes and were frequent guests at their weekend barbeques. When he ran for office, Mary Stuart worked in his campaigns.

Lone Star Republicans were a lonely lot back in 1960. The state was overwhelmingly Democrat and had not elected a Republican statewide since Reconstruction. Some inroads had been made, however. At the presidential level, native son Dwight Eisenhower had carried the state in 1952 and 1956, thanks in part to a Democrats-for-Eisenhower movement led by Governor Allan Shivers.

Mary Stuart was undaunted by the strength of the opposition party or the weakness of her own. In 1958, she became our precinct's Republican chairperson and held the precinct's first-ever convention in our house. One other guy showed up! I served the two of them drinks while Mary Stuart conducted the meeting and did the paperwork.

Within a few years Republican prospects had brightened. In 1961, an obscure college professor and Democrat-turned-Republican, John Tower, won a special election against several vote-splitting Democrats for the Senate seat vacated by Lyndon Johnson when he assumed the vice presidency.

George Bush entered the fray the following year. Republicans afraid that the ultraconservative John Birch Society might take over the local party asked him to lead the county GOP organization for the Houston area. Two years later, he entered the statewide primary to become the party's candidate for the U.S. Senate. He won the nomination but lost the general election to the incumbent Democrat, Ralph Yarborough, who rode LBJ's long coattails in the 1964 presidential election.

George was undaunted. In 1966 he ran for a seat in the U.S. House of Representatives against a popular local district attorney, Frank Briscoe. In winning he became the first Republican congressman from Houston since Reconstruction.

I was not involved in George's first race for the Senate. In his campaign for Congress, however, I gave him some money, went to a few events, and voted for him. Still, I wasn't ready to call myself a Republican. In fact, I lent my name to the steering committee of a group of attorneys supporting Texas Attorney General Waggoner Carr, the candidate anointed by establishment Democrats in 1966 to recapture LBJ's old Senate seat from John Tower, the upstart professor. Thanks to an election-day boycott by liberal Democrats, however, Tower won again.

My political schizophrenia was often challenged by Mary Stuart and her Republican friends. One of those friends, Susan Winston, was married to a hunting buddy of mine, also a lifelong Democrat. "C'mon, you guys," Mary Stuart and Susan would tell us. "We know you vote Republican in the fall. Things aren't going to change until you get religion and convert to the GOP."

During his first term, George sat on the powerful House Ways and Means Committee. By 1968, he was on the short list of Richard Nixon's potential vice presidential running mates. When Nixon selected Spiro Agnew, George ran for reelection to Congress and won easily. Then, with his eyes on a higher prize, he gave up his safe House seat to run for the Senate again in 1970. This was the race in which I got my feet wet in politics, switching parties and coordinating the Bush campaign in Harris County.

George had backers far more powerful than I. Both President

Nixon and (privately) former President Johnson encouraged him. They sensed that the liberal Senator Ralph Yarborough, an outspoken critic of the Vietnam War, could be defeated by a moderate opponent. They were right, but unfortunately for George, that opponent ended up being Lloyd Bentsen, who beat Yarborough for the Democratic nomination and took the steam out of the "Anybody But Ralph" movement. Lloyd, a fine man who would become a friend of mine in later years, easily defeated George. Ironically, George, who had planned to run as the conservative alternative to the liberal Yarborough, found Bentsen portraying himself as the conservative alternative to an allegedly liberal Bush. George did carry Harris County, where both he and Lloyd lived, with 61 percent of the vote.

When I agreed to help George, I knew nothing about running a campaign organization. With the help of George's skilled campaign manager, Marvin Collins, I quickly learned that the operative word is "organization." The Five Ps proved invaluable.

For some time after Mary Stuart died, I was, quite simply, out of it. In addition to George, many others helped me cope. Harry Jones said, "You just take off whatever time you need." And I did.

Moving into that big house on Greentree Road that Mary Stuart had designed was painful. Less than three months after her death, I marked my fortieth birthday there with many of her friends and their husbands. Later they presented me with a portrait of her.

These same friends helped me find housekeepers. I use the plural because several did not work out. The boys didn't like one of them, and one of them liked me a little too much.

During these difficult months, I would come home from the law firm or the campaign, help the boys do their homework, get them to bed, have a drink to take my mind off things, have a second drink, and then maybe one or two more. I kept thinking that Mary Stuart might have survived if her doctor had diagnosed the cancer on her first visit, even though it was an aggressive malignancy.

Alcoholism runs on both sides of my family. Why didn't I succumb? In part because I always feel nauseated after three or four drinks. In part because I had my work—be it law, politics, or public service—to divert me. And in part because so many of Mary Stuart's friends, the wives of my friends—Fran Lummis, Mary Wilson, Kay Sharp, Susan Winston, Joanne Baker, Dossy Allday, Julia Wallace, and many others—rallied to our side, and were there in so many ways for my boys. Mostly, though, I owed it to those four boys not to succumb.

Susan Winston had her own worries during this period. Her marriage to my friend James (Jimbo) Winston ended, and she and her three young children endured some very dark days. The Winstons divorced, and in 1974 Jimbo died of pancreatitis. He was thirty-eight, the same age as Mary Stuart when I lost her.

About a year after Mary Stuart's death, I began to date. After going out with Susan, I never dated anyone else. Love blossomed out of friendship, and we married in August 1973.

Susan, eight years my junior, is the daughter of Jack and Mary Garrett. Her father, "Whispering Jack," was a well-known Texas rancher and rice farmer, and she grew up on a large ranch near Danbury, a tiny town near the Gulf of Mexico some forty miles south of Houston. He died on Christmas Eve of 2005. Her lovely mother died on January 31, 2004. Susan went to college at the University of Texas at Austin, where she studied a liberal arts program. She is a beautiful woman with great common sense, a wonderful spirit, and unwavering faith.

Susan had been a very close friend to Mary Stuart, but we had much in common beyond our love for Mary Stuart. We were both struggling single parents, and our combined seven children knew one another. We both loved the outdoors. And by this time, we both had an interest in politics—Republican politics. Susan's family had worked for the GOP when it was a dangerous thing to do.

We will always regret our big mistake in the way we went about getting married. We wanted to do it on my mother's birthday, August 6, because she kept encouraging us to marry. It had been a hard year for her. Dad, long incapacitated by Parkinson's disease, had passed away that May. Because Susan was Catholic and divorced, the Episcopal Church to which I belonged (and served on the vestry) refused to marry us. Fortunately, Dad's church, First Presbyterian, was willing. The minister, Jack Lancaster, a real man of God and a wonderful guy, performed the ceremony in the chapel. Only Susan and I were present—no family or friends. We had conspired to bring Susan's mother in from Danbury for lunch at my mother's house. We went there directly from the church to share our surprise. Both moms were ecstatic.

It was a different story with the seven kids. They were shocked. To them, the suddenness and secrecy of our marriage were close to family treason. We should have prepared them in advance. Our failure made the job of blending our families—difficult enough in the best of circumstances—much tougher. It took a while, but thanks to Susan's heroic efforts, we succeeded. My four (Jamie, Mike, John, and Doug) and her three (Elizabeth, Bo, and Will) soon became *our* seven. We added Mary Bonner in 1977. At this writing, Susan and I have seventeen grandchildren. We lost one of Jamie's girls—sweet Graeme, only seven years old—when she drowned in a neighbor's pool in 2002. She was a gift on loan to our family from God. Susan and I treasure the seven years she was with us, and her loss reminded us again how precious is our time with those we love.

At the time of our marriage, I was an acknowledged Republican. Participating in George's campaign for the Senate had awakened a sense of adventure and high challenge that was missing from the daily practice of law. I wasn't ready to quit the practice or run for office, but I was ready for something different. After the election, party leaders asked me to become state finance chairman.

This was, I knew, a thankless job. In trying to raise money for the party, I would be competing against committees seeking funds for two popular reelection candidates, President Nixon and Senator Tower. Candidate money is considerably easier to raise than party money, particularly for a party as weak as the Texas GOP was back then. Still, I accepted. I had to start somewhere.

Actually "somewhere" was everywhere. I had a small paid staff in Austin and many volunteers around the state, but I spent many a day driving to fund-raisers around our huge state and to party meetings in the capital. That's how I first got to know Senator Tower and Anne Armstrong, who had been a counselor for President Nixon and vice chairman of the Republican National Committee.

In 1972, I also coordinated the Nixon reelection effort in the fourteen-county Gulf Coast area of Texas. At George Bush's request, I organized a fund-raiser, and without using notes, the president gave a magnificent *tour d'horizon* on foreign policy. He seemed comfortable while speaking, but was clearly ill at ease in face-to-face meetings at the event. I remember his handshake as brief, formal, perfunctory.

We met a number of other times when I was in the Reagan and Bush administrations, and he periodically wrote me letters with suggestions on campaign strategies and foreign affairs. I was always respectful of him, but I find it hard to forgive him for betraying the country in the Watergate scandal. He lied to the American people, and with the release of his tapes in later years, his reputation fell lower and lower.

Watergate was traumatic, but in a way it demonstrated the strength and resilience of our system. The president's malfeasance was discovered, and within a relatively short time, by history's measure, he was gone. I wish we had just declared victory, thanked the Founders for their foresight, and moved on. Unfortunately, we tried to fix a system that, though imperfect (as all systems are and forever will be), wasn't broken. One thing we got in return was a generation of unaccountable independent counsels who investigated and attempted to criminalize every political controversy, a dreadful idea that was finally allowed to die a well-deserved death in 1999.

Nixon also betrayed the Republican Party and all of us who had worked hard for him, taken his claims of innocence at face value, and defended him in the early months of the scandal. He cost the party, as well as the nation, a great deal. After Watergate, Republicans suffered a political bloodbath. I will never forget my eldest son, Jamie, telling me right after Watergate broke that Nixon was behind it. I told him he and his hippie friends didn't know what they were talking about. The night Nixon announced he was resigning, Jamie called and said, "I told you so. But I'm proud to be an American, because the system worked."

When I was secretary of the treasury, Nixon wrote me to say he was giving up his taxpayer-supported secret service protection and would henceforth assume the cost personally. That was a noble thing to do. He deserves credit for opening relations with China, his serious efforts to disengage from Vietnam with honor, and other accomplishments, but I think his achievements will forever be overshadowed by the fact that he is the only president who has had to resign the office in disgrace.

In 1973, when Vice President Spiro Agnew resigned (also under a cloud), George Bush was on the short list to replace him as VP, a position that went instead to Gerald Ford. At the time, George was chairman of the Republican National Committee. Before that, he had served as our ambassador to the United Nations. Some say he would have preferred that President Nixon name him treasury secretary instead of sending him to the United Nations, but—much to George's disappointment—that job was given to former Texas Governor John Connally, a Democrat and a Nixon favorite.

When Nixon resigned on August 9, 1974, Vice President Ford took the oath of office as president. A poll of Republican officeholders put George on the top of the list to replace Ford as VP. I, along with many others, sent a telegram to Ford extolling my friend's virtues. Ford considered George but chose Nelson Rockefeller. George was asked to head our delegation in China, and he left for Beijing in 1974.

During this period, I decided it was time for me to do something different. The excitement of politics made me restless as a lawyer. I lacked Washington experience, but I had several things going for me. One was enthusiasm. I was ready for new challenges. Another was a work ethic grounded in the Five Ps. My father and the Marines had also taught habits of personal discipline that expressed themselves both in my personal behavior—polished shoes, neat suits, moderation in eating, drinking, and spending—and in my professional work. In addition, Harry Jones had taught me to organize and prioritize my work, to focus on what was achievable. To this day, I make lists—Point 1, Point 2—to organize my thoughts and my labors. I had also developed certain ways of dealing with colleagues and staff that would prove useful. (More about that later.) Finally, I was blessed with good health and stamina, which I always tried to preserve by exercising and getting outdoors as much as possible.

As a lifetime lawyer, my first choice for public service was the Justice Department, where I hoped to serve as assistant attorney general in charge of the civil division. In seeking such jobs, however, you don't call the White House; the White House calls you, and almost always after someone with clout has put in a good word. My interview with Attorney General Richard Kleindienst, scheduled for April 30, 1973, came courtesy of a good word from George Bush (although he never admitted it). The timing couldn't have been worse. Kleindienst resigned that same day, a casualty of Watergate. Goodbye interview. A few weeks later, I got a nibble about serving as the head of enforcement at the Environmental Protection Agency, but I wasn't interested.

Two years passed. I was still in Houston, still practicing law, raising seven children with Susan in the house on Greentree. But, having a close friend playing in the Big Game of politics and public service, I was growing ever more restless.

In June 1975 another opportunity presented itself. Again, thanks to George, I suspect, I was being considered for a high-level position. I met with Rogers Morton, who had recently replaced Fred Dent as secretary of commerce. Cabinet members are generally allowed to pick their own deputies, and Morton was looking for a number-two person with whom he would feel comfortable. Morton—a gentle giant from Kentucky, a wonderful man, and an outstanding public servant—interviewed several candidates for the spot, including some being pushed by the White House. A few days passed. Nothing.

I was on Interstate 10 between San Antonio and Houston, returning home from picking some of our kids up at summer camp. Checking in with my office from a roadside restaurant, I learned that Rogers Morton had called me. To learn my fate, I called the secretary of commerce of the United States from a pay phone outside a Stuckey's restaurant.

TWO

"GOBBLERS AND HENS"

IT'S A PRETTY LONG WAY from a Stuckey's on Interstate 10 between San Antonio and Houston to the Oval Office, but there I found myself in mid-April 1976—not just sitting across from the president of the United States, but offering him advice. Nine months earlier, Rogers Morton had brought me to Washington as under secretary of commerce—the number-two position in the department. Now, President Ford and Ronald Reagan were in the middle of a close, contentious battle for the Republican presidential nomination. I had come to the White House to tell the president that his chances of winning the upcoming primary in my home state could increase dramatically if Secretary of State Henry Kissinger refrained from briefing the White House press before departing on a diplomatic tour of Africa.

The May 1 Texas primary could be pivotal. In the Illinois contest on March 16, Ford had soundly beaten Reagan to take a commanding lead in the delegate count. There was speculation that the challenger—whom I had met only once, four years earlier—might drop out of the race. "He'll survive until Texas," said John Sears, Reagan's campaign manager, "but if he loses there, he's out."

Kissinger was a carryover from the Nixon administration, and President Ford relied on him to maintain a steady course for U.S. foreign policy in the aftermath of Watergate and Vietnam. In 1976, however, he became a target of unhappy conservatives who viewed his policy of détente with the Soviet Union as appeasement, who were concerned about losing U.S. military superiority, and who opposed the Panama Canal Treaty and other initiatives. Reagan repeatedly accused the secretary of state of taking a defeatist posture toward the Soviet Union, of believing that the "day of the U.S. is past and today is the day of the Soviet Union," of "giving away our own freedoms." Real peace, Reagan argued, "does not come from weakness or retreat. It comes from the restoration of American military superiority."

Texas Republicans ate it up.

Kissinger was scheduled to make a two-week tour of Africa in late April and early May. When I learned that he planned to brief the press before leaving, I called Ford's chief of staff, Dick Cheney. "If you want to win Texas, you can't do this." Putting Kissinger on the air just before the primary was guaranteed to stir the political blood of the conservatives back home, I explained.

"Why don't you come over to the White House?" Dick suggested.

"Mr. President, I'm talking to you now as a Texan," I said after being seated in the Oval Office. "This would be devastating in the lead-up to the primary."

The president was rarely without his pipe. "Well, Jim"—puff, puff, puff—"Henry's done an extraordinarily good job"—puff, puff, puff—"and I think it's important that he tell the nation. It's very important to our foreign policy"—puff, puff, puff. "And you know, Jim," he added, "the *thinking* Republicans will understand my position on this."

"Mr. President," I replied, "with respect to this issue, there *are* no thinking Republicans in Texas right now."

Kissinger's pre-Africa press appearance with the president's blessing was probably one of several reasons why Reagan swept all ninety-six delegates in Texas and regained his momentum. It also didn't help that the president had tried to eat a tamale in San Antonio without first removing its corn-husk wrapper—a gastronomical gaffe that won headlines across the state. Or that nothing in Texas law prevented conservative Democrats from voting in the GOP primary. How bad was it? Even Senator John Tower was defeated in his bid to be a Ford delegate.

Shortly before the primary, I accompanied the president on a swing through Texas. On the flight back to Washington, he asked me to leave Commerce to work full-time in the campaign. One week later, I assumed the position of deputy chairman for delegate operations. My job was to keep Ford delegates in the candidate's camp and to win support from uncommitted delegates to the Republican National Convention in August. I took over the duties of Jack Stiles, Ford's longtime friend and congressional campaign manager, who had died in a car crash earlier that month.

In public service, titles are important for both symbolism and prestige, but they do not necessarily reflect the importance of your duties or how much influence you have. Presidents rely upon the people in whom they have the most confidence, regardless of title. Generally, these are the people who have been in the trenches with them—men and women who worked in the campaigns and helped win difficult elections. That's why—often to the dismay of some members of the cabinet with more prestigious titles—campaign workers who move to the White House staff are frequently the most important advisers to the chief executive.

Jockeying for post-election influence begins during the campaign. Titles tend to denote status, and higher-ups in a successful campaign can expect to get better jobs in an administration. The organization had several deputy chairmen, each with different responsibilities, but it was a prestigious title. Still, at first I felt that I was just another campaign hand, a delegate hunter. I would have preferred to stay at Commerce. As Rog Morton's alter ego and stand-in at cabinet meetings (and after he left, acting secretary of commerce for several months), I enjoyed dealing with the interesting and important issues that landed on my desk. Little did I know that the nomination fight would be settled on the floor of the convention and that the fortunes of Gerald

Ford and Ronald Reagan—and Jim Baker, to a certain extent—would eventually rest on who won the uncommitteds.

But remaining at Commerce was not an option. The president had already named Rog as chairman of the President Ford Committee (PFC), a title that *did* reflect Rog's power. He was in charge of the entire campaign. At Commerce, we had worked well together and liked each other. Now he asked the president to reassign me to the PFC. How could I say no to the man who had brought me to Washington in the first place? And even if I could have, I could not say no to the president.

BACK IN JUNE 1975, I received a letter from George Bush, then still in China. "Bake," it began, "I just got a call from Rog Morton querying me on you for under secretary of commerce. The job could be a good one and Morton would be good to work for in my opinion."

George was right on both counts. Rog was a terrific boss, as big-hearted as he was big in stature. Before coming to Commerce, he had served ten years as a congressman from Maryland, two years as chair of the Republican National Committee, and four years as secretary of the interior.

Although I was Rog's first choice for under secretary when he moved from Interior to Commerce at President Ford's request in May 1975, I was not necessarily the White House's. Reasoning that the appointment of a Reagan supporter to the number-two spot at Commerce might win points with conservatives, Don Rumsfeld, then White House chief of staff, lobbied Rog to offer the job to William Banowsky, president of Pepperdine University in California and GOP national committeeman from California. As I understand it, Rog went straight to President Ford and said, "No, Baker's the one I want."*

My visit with the president before the Texas primary was not my

---

*Soon after taking office, the Ford administration tried to head off a possible Reagan candidacy in an even more dramatic fashion, by offering the former California governor the top job at Commerce or Transportation, or the ambassadorship to the Court of St. James's. No luck.

first. Several months after I arrived in Washington, Rog poked his head into my office and said, "Jim, let's go over to the White House." When we got there, Rog instructed me to wait outside the Oval Office. Five or ten minutes passed. I busied myself reading. Finally the door opened. "Jim, come in here for a minute," Rog said.

I don't care how old you are or how much you think you have accomplished, walking into the Oval Office for the first time—or anytime, for that matter—to meet the president of the United States is a heady and humbling experience.

The door was held open by a man some ten years my junior, but far senior in the pecking order—Dick Cheney, Rumsfeld's successor and the youngest White House chief of staff in history. President Ford sat behind his desk. Rog sat in a nearby chair. Dick's chair was empty for the moment. He motioned for me to take it, and I thought, "Golly, the chief of staff is giving me his seat."

Rog introduced me to the president, who said something like, "Jim, we're certainly glad to have you on board." We exchanged a few more pleasantries and then discussed an issue of the day. I can't remember what it was, but I will never forget how gracious Dick was. It's a small thing, but powerful men and women in Washington, D.C., don't give up their seats. And the White House chief of staff, I came to learn, is potentially the second most powerful person in Washington, as long as the holder of that office remembers who is the boss.

First impressions count for a lot in Washington. Dick and I have worked together in several administrations. We do not always agree on policy—who does?—but the seeds of our long-lasting friendship were sown that day. That friendship extends far beyond Washington. Dick taught me everything I know about fly-fishing, and I still don't know half of what he knows.

Dick is an extremely bright, no-nonsense guy. He is very loyal to President George W. Bush, just as he was to the first President Bush and to President Ford. He understands that the people who go out there and take the risks and put their name on the ballot and get elected are the ones who have the right to exercise power.

When I was nominated for the position at Commerce, I told the *Houston Chronicle* that I hoped to help ease the problems that "government regulations and bureaucratic red tape" caused for businesses, particularly small businesses. President Ford had made this a priority. As a business lawyer for eighteen years, I'd seen many of those problems, such as the need to provide duplicate reports to different government agencies. "In some areas," I added, "governmental regulation is totally appropriate." I still believe that. The trick is to find the right balance, and that's never easy.

After I was confirmed by the Senate, Susan and I and five of our seven children moved to Washington. Jamie, my first son, was at Cornell, and Mike, my second, chose to stay in Houston to complete his senior year of high school and keep his place on the school football team.

Mike was a gifted athlete, the star of the Bush-Baker family football games (Turkey Bowls) we played after lunch every Thanksgiving Day. The other kids nicknamed him Conrad Dobler, after a tough offensive lineman ("I only bit one guy!") for the St. Louis Cardinals. Mike's football coach and family stayed with him in the Baker house on Greentree.*

Washington was (and still is) largely a one-industry town, but if you're in power it's a great place to live. While continuing to own our house in Houston, we lived in the northwest section of the District in a house rented from Alex Hufty. We might have preferred to enroll the kids in public school, but the system in the District at that time was in bad shape. As a result we found ourselves paying for private educations on a salary that was considerably lower than what I had earned at Andrews Kurth.

I am not looking for sympathy. It's bad form to ask for a job, then

---

*Mike has made his career with Smith International, a major Houston-based supplier of oilfield equipment and services. He also took on the extraordinarily difficult task of rearing two children as a single parent, something I don't think I could have done.

complain about the size of your paycheck. In addition, public service offers many important nonfinancial benefits. For one thing, the quality of life in Washington back then was better than in Houston—less traffic and less pollution. But many public servants make genuine economic sacrifices when they come to Washington. Fortunately, Susan and I were in a better position than most, in part because about that time, an oil play on a ranch I owned in South Texas provided us with a much-needed financial boost.

In Houston, our social life was organized around get-togethers with lifelong friends. In Washington, a city based on power and the perception of power, we found it more difficult to establish as many true friendships. You are extremely busy with your work and, further, you can never be certain whether people are attracted by your personality and character or by your title. With all the attention ranking public officials receive, it's hard to stay grounded. But you can be sure of this: the people who wouldn't return your phone calls before you went to Washington damn well won't return them after you go home.

Without a circle of old friends like those we had back home, we enjoyed far fewer backyard barbeques and endured far more official functions—where protocol determines almost everything. Your position at the table for an official luncheon or dinner (or for that matter a formal private party) is determined by your position in the government, and people pay attention to whether you are seated above the salt or below it.

Cabinet and subcabinet officials get invited to far more of these dinners and receptions than they can possibly attend. If you want to get all your work done—six and a half days a week at the office in my case—you have to learn to say no to the parties.

Of course, the work is what's important. A few weeks after I arrived at Commerce, I asked two of my top assistants, Frank Hodsoll and Jim Goyette, to present me some ideas for initiatives that might make a difference. I offer the following excerpts from the resulting "eyes only" memorandum because they express a guiding principle of policymaking: don't do anything without being aware of its political impact, especially during an election cycle. Frank and Jim listed five factors to consider in choosing initiatives. The first two are most instructive:

1. Interest in and usefulness of these actions in terms of good government to (a) the president, (b) the secretary, and (c) other key administration officials.
2. Public visibility and political impact of these actions.

At Commerce, I quickly learned that the power game is continually being played between departments within the executive branch. To illustrate, I have one word: *textiles.* In 1976, the State Department argued for the unlimited import of Chinese textiles into the United States. This policy would further former President Nixon's (and Secretary of State Kissinger's) earlier effort to open the door to the People's Republic, State argued. True enough. But the administration believed that our country's best economic interest was to pursue a more balanced approach that contained some protection for domestic textile manufacturers. Clearly, it was also in the best interest of the Ford political operation to avoid alienating the textile manufacturing states where important primaries between the president and Reagan loomed.

In late March the president flew to San Francisco to address the American Textile Manufacturers Institute. An advance draft of his speech was sent for comment to interested departments, including State and Commerce. At Commerce we were happy with language to allay the manufacturers' fears that cheaper Chinese textiles would flood American markets. The president intended to say that he was committed "to ensure that our domestic market is not seriously disrupted."

While we expected State to lobby for the removal of that language, the department had not weighed in when Ford took off for California.

At a meeting of the Economic Policy Board, Bob Ingersoll, the deputy secretary of state, had simply said that he didn't have the secretary's position yet. This was vintage Kissinger. A master at playing the power game, he knew that he who speaks last often speaks loudest. I figured that he would try to get the problematic sentence removed at the last minute—when it would be too late for us to offer a rebuttal. On the day of the president's flight, my suspicion was confirmed by Bob Hormats, an international economics specialist with the National Security Council. Kissinger planned to place a call to the president on Air Force One, Bob said.

I quickly called Cheney on the plane. He told me that Kissinger had already called and that the president had tentatively decided to remove the sentence. After hearing my argument, Dick agreed that at that time, politics should trump policy, and he persuaded the president to restore it.

A few days later, I met Kissinger—for the first time—at a State Department function. "Ah," he said in that distinctive voice of his, "so you're Textile Baker."

I guess that was better than being called "Goodbye-Kissinger Baker." In early April, the campaign asked me to attend a fund-raising event in Oklahoma, another important primary state where Reagan was strong. After my presentation, I was asked what role Kissinger would have if Ford won in November.

We were at a wealthy contributor's home. It was my understanding that no media were present, but just to be safe, I declared my remarks off the record, not for publication. I then said it was hard to imagine that Kissinger would serve in the next Ford administration.

As it turned out, reporters were present from both the *Oklahoma Journal* and the *Daily Oklahoman*. As Denise Donoho, a reporter for the *Journal* later wrote me, "We honored your request of confidence and apparently the *Daily Oklahoman* did not."

When I returned to Washington, I was not aware of this. Nor was I aware that Rog, now President Ford's campaign manager, had made similar remarks in California. Our unorchestrated comments had put the administration on the defensive and forced the president's press secretary, Ron Nessen, to tell the media that the president was not trying to ease Kissinger out of office.

After a ceremony in the White House Rose Garden, I finally learned what had happened. "Before you leave the White House, stick your head in Mr. Cheney's office," said Nell Yates, the president's secretary. The wire services had picked up the *Daily Oklahoman's* story featuring my speculation about Kissinger's future, and a solemn chief of staff showed me the clips. The State Department and the secretary were furious, Cheney reported.

This was my first major blunder on the job. It could have been my last. Presidents should never be forced to explain or correct the statements of those who serve them, particularly one as far down the pecking order as the under secretary of commerce. I told Cheney how sorry I was. "Don't worry," he laughed. "Just make it right with Henry." I called the secretary and begged his forgiveness, which he kindly gave me—but only after I had properly groveled in my apology to him.

Why did Cheney treat me so gently? I later learned that the White House had been impressed by my role in helping the president avoid a potentially big political problem with an issue that was hardly a household phrase: common situs picketing.

Common situs picketing is the picketing by a labor union of multiple employers at a job site because of the union's grievances against one employer at the site. Under federal labor laws, it is generally illegal. In December 1975, however, Congress—its ranks of Democrats swollen by the post-Watergate midterm election of 1974—passed legislation to make it easier for the unions to shut down multi-employer job sites. Now the president had to decide whether to sign or veto.

Within forty-eight hours of the bill's passage, I wrote a memorandum to Rog Morton and a letter to Jim Lynn, director of the Office of Management and Budget, explaining why it was imperative for the president to veto the bill. My eleven-point memo to Rog, which I knew would be forwarded to the White House, outlined the substantive problems with the bill. For instance, it would "strike hardest at small business and nonunion craftsmen and contractors, particularly minorities," I said. But I also laid out the political implications, with point one being this fairly blunt warning: "A failure to veto will be political suicide as far as the nomination is concerned."*

On January 3, 1976, the president vetoed the legislation. "I had hoped that this bill would provide a resolution for the special problems of labor-management relations in the construction industry and would have the support of all parties," he explained. "My earlier optimism in this regard was unfounded." This was the first veto he ever exercised. Secretary of Labor John Dunlop was so disappointed that he resigned and returned to his teaching post at Harvard.

When should a public official leave an administration over differences in policy? This is obviously a question each person might answer differently. One of my predecessors at State, Cyrus Vance, resigned in 1980 after Jimmy Carter authorized a military operation to free American hostages in Iran. Vance not only disapproved of the plan (which failed), but he also (justifiably) believed he had been ignored in the decision-making process. President Carter had made the determination after meeting with other advisers, principally Zbigniew Brzezinski, his national security adviser, while Vance was away for the weekend in Florida.

Although I never came close to resigning over a policy issue when I was at Treasury or State, there are times when it is appropriate to do so—when you can't in good conscience support a policy the administration asks you to carry out, or when, like Vance, you are not con-

---

*I was not alone in my call for a veto. Bill Simon, the treasury secretary, also opposed the bill. He and I were on the same wavelength so often that he once asked the president to let me leave Commerce and serve as his deputy. The president declined to do so. Bill was a true conservative, much admired by that wing of the party. Those conservatives who thought I was too moderate to serve President Reagan always ignored Bill's sense that he and I were in tune ideologically.

sulted about a significant issue in your portfolio. If you do choose to resign, you should do it in a way that is the least detrimental to the president and his administration. The president, after all, has given you the chance to serve.

At Commerce, I briefly worked under someone involved in one of the most spectacular cabinet resignations in history, Elliot Richardson. Elliot became commerce secretary on February 2, 1976. At the same time, Rog moved to the White House as a cabinet-rank counsellor to the president on domestic and economic issues and liaison to the President Ford Committee and the Republican National Committee. As noted, he would later become Ford's campaign chairman.

Immediately before replacing Rog, Elliot had been our ambassador to the United Kingdom. Before that, the Harvard-educated attorney served as secretary of health, education and welfare, secretary of defense, and—most famously—attorney general. In that latter position, he became the first victim of the "Saturday Night Massacre" in October 1973 when he chose to resign rather than to obey President Nixon's order to fire the Watergate special prosecutor, Archibald Cox.

Elliot was a wonderful man. This Boston Brahmin—who couldn't tolerate more than one drink—wasn't as earthy as Rog, but he was just as genuine. He once said that Washington was a city of cocker spaniels, meaning people who would rather be petted and admired than wield power. Maybe we hit it off because he knew I would rather wield power.

He was extraordinarily bright, so cerebral that he was sometimes difficult to understand. He often seemed to talk in riddles. In 1976, he wrote a book called *The Creative Balance: Government, Politics, and the Individual in America's Third Century.* I tried to read it but found it too esoteric to finish.

Politics, as the saying goes, ain't beanbag. It's a blood sport, featuring raw emotion and gutfighting. The intellectual is often at a disadvantage, but some have been successful. Elliot was one. He never considered himself too refined for retail politics and was never reluctant to stump for President Ford, whom he obviously admired.

I worked with Elliot for only three months before I left Commerce, reluctantly, for the PFC. The offices of our campaign headquarters at Eighteenth and L Streets were small and poorly furnished, as they should have been. A well-run campaign spends money on the things that will get its candidate elected, like television, not on amenities for the staff.

At the PFC, I reported directly to Rog, who had succeeded former Secretary of the Army Bo Callaway as chairman. In the weeks between Callaway's departure and Rog's arrival, Stu Spencer ran the PFC. Stu, a first-rate political consultant, had made a name for himself working for presidential candidate Nelson Rockefeller in 1964 and had cemented his reputation in 1966, when he and Bill Roberts helped orchestrate Reagan's win over Pat Brown for the California governorship.

Stu also worked on Reagan's successful campaign for reelection in 1970, but in September 1975, he joined the Ford effort. In time, he was appointed deputy chairman for political organization—the chief political strategist.

Stu was political, but he was not politic. At one point, he told Ford, "Mr. President, as a campaigner, you're no fucking good." The president was taken aback, but laughed it off.

Jack Stiles, my predecessor as delegate hunter, had reported directly to Stu. Although Stu and I worked closely together, I did not report to him. Initially, this was a source of tension. As time went on, however, we forged a strong relationship.

When I came to the PFC, there was no how-to manual on rounding up delegates, so I tracked down some good delegate hunters from past campaigns and picked their brains. Clif White, who engineered Barry Goldwater's remarkable drive for the Republican presidential nomination in 1964, and Dick Kleindienst, Nixon's man in 1968, were the most helpful.

Clif's advice went something like this: "You want to learn everything you can about these delegates. What makes them tick. What are their interests. What issues are important to them. Who are the personalities that are important to them. And then you want to get them to commit to Ford, if possible in a public way, not just tell you, 'I'll be there.' You want them nailed, so that it would be embarrassing for them to change."

Five days after moving to the PFC (and based largely on my conversations with White and Kleindienst), I sent Rog, Stu, and Roy Hughes, the deputy chairman for administration, a six-page, single-spaced memorandum titled "Proposed Delegate Management Operation."

"The primary results of the last ten days make it likely that the president and Reagan will go to the convention with neither having sufficient delegates for a first-ballot victory," I wrote—wrongly, as it turned out. As a result the delegate-hunting operation would be of vital importance and needed to be "promptly and carefully organized and implemented." I proposed that we keep dossiers on each delegate—"ours," "theirs," and "uncommiteds." I also offered a plan to divide the country into eleven regions, each headed by a regional chairman. Each state in the region would also have a chair, who should be a "knowledgeable party politician rather than [an] elected official who normally would be too busy to give us the time required." This is a cardinal rule of politics: party people will work their tails off for a candidate they like; elected officials have divided loyalties (their own careers always come first) and too many other demands on their time.

In the memo, I urged that the chairmen update the campaign two or three times a week on the status of delegates in their region, that the president set aside twenty to thirty minutes a day to call targeted delegates, and that we schedule caucuses with delegations in order to keep them "informed, plugged in, and fired up." "The worst thing that can happen to a politician is not to have someone to talk to," I wrote. "The next worst thing is not to know what is going on. Communication is the answer to both."

Twenty-nine states selected their delegates through primaries, while twenty-one chose them at state conventions. In all, 2,259 delegates would come to Kansas City. The magic number for the nomination was 1,130.

The race seesawed back and forth. After Reagan took Texas to put himself back in contention, Ford still led 232–183. Wins in Indiana, Georgia, and Alabama gave Reagan a brief lead, but by May 25, the count was Ford 732, Reagan 530, uncommitted 184. Ford stayed ahead through the end of the primary season on June 8. By then, however, only eleven of the twenty-one state conventions had been held, and Reagan was better organized in most. After the final state conventions on July 16, the *New York Times* called it 1,102–1,063 for Ford with ninety-four critical votes uncommitted.

Reagan's campaign manager, John Sears, saw it differently. On July 19, he said his man would come to Kansas City with 1,140 delegates, ten more than needed. Such projections, if credible, are important. When delegates perceive that one candidate has the nomination clinched, many will flock to his side. Everybody loves a winner. If Sears's numbers were even close to being accurate and if we couldn't hold those delegates committed to us and win enough of the uncommitteds, Gerald Ford would become the first sitting president to fail to hold his party's nomination since Chester Arthur.

NOT TOO MANY years ago, John Cabaniss, my protégé from the Andrews Kurth law firm in Houston, introduced me for a speech back home. "I realized on one of our spring turkey hunts that Jim Baker was destined for high office," John said. "There just has to be greatness in a man that can distinguish whether a wild turkey you are tracking is a gobbler or a hen by closely examining its droppings."

After the laughter stopped, he added: "The operative word there is *closely*."

I didn't hunt delegates for President Ford exactly like wild turkeys, but almost. I began by sending out biographical questionnaires. Many delegates responded, and we filled in the blanks as best we could on those who did not. Here's an example, excerpts from a three-page, single-spaced bio we compiled on a delegate from the South who eventually committed to Ford.

> Engaged in practice of law continuously since 1951. Served on the Citizens Advisory Committee to juvenile court.... Active in Chamber of Commerce work.... Member of the Propeller Club of the United States.... American Legion, Young Americans for Freedom. Has been and probably would like to continue to be consulted on attorneys named as federal judges in [his state]. Practices extensively in federal courts.

The biography also included a detailed chronology of the delegate's involvement in Republican campaigns and activities, including information about local, state, and national candidates he had supported. For example: "1961, member Goldwater banquet committee which sponsored large and successful banquet honoring Senator Goldwater ... long before Senator Goldwater was considered a presidential candidate."

We also kept a log of our contacts with delegates. In the case of our quarry mentioned above:

> 6/18/76—President sent him a thank you in response to letter of recommendation on behalf of [a candidate] for appointment to vacancy on the U.S. district court.
> 6/22—Per Jim Plummer: Will go for Ford on three conditions: If Ford does not veto the offshore oil revenue sharing bill; the vice presidential candidate is not unacceptable (Brooke/Percy); [and will not go for Ford if Ford challenges] Louisiana and Mississippi delegations [for not having] enough blacks, females, and young.
> 6/24—Baker: He needs lots of attention.

Whether the nomination would go to Ford or Reagan depended on the votes of about 150 swing delegates. Some were truly uncommitted. The rest backed either Ford or Reagan but not firmly. The contest would go to the outfit that did the best job of corralling its own herd while picking off strays from the other side.

It was my job to stalk the uncommitteds. Sometimes, however, they stalked me, and not always appropriately. I doubt that any of these pols were Latin majors, but clearly several of them understood the meaning of *quid pro quo*. If I had taken them up on their proposed deals, I well might have been *in flagrante delicto*. Two examples, and my responses:

> [A delegate from Missouri] offered through Peter Roussel [of the PFC] to deliver the uncommitteds in Missouri who do not like [Governor] Kit Bond if we would assure them they would have final say on patronage in the St. Louis area. I told Roussel not to discuss it with [the delegate]. . . .
>
> Party people had reported [that a delegate from Pennsylvania] wanted a federal job. He called me and asked for an appointment with Art Fletcher, [the deputy] assistant to the president [for urban affairs]. I refused to do it for him.

In all I had at least seventeen questionable contacts with delegates with their hands out. I remember that number because four weeks before the convention, I wrote a memorandum for the file ("Improper Suggestions from Delegates") that listed these incidents and the rest of them. For instance, a congressman from Colorado hinted we could get his vote if we promised to name him to the Federal Communications Commission; a delegate from the Virgin Islands wanted the new federal building named after him; and "a delegate from Brooklyn . . . issued a public statement saying he would sell his vote to the candidate who bids the most for it."

While we were scrupulous about making a record of improper

suggestions (and rebuffing them), we were otherwise plenty aggressive. For instance, we identified and assigned one key person as a "persuader" to approach each targeted delegate. It might be a public official, a party leader, or even a neighbor—anyone with enough personal influence to win or hold a commitment. The president would then follow up with a phone call and, in some instances, a face-to-face meeting.

Candidate Reagan also telephoned and met with key delegates, but Gerald Ford had a big advantage here. Imagine receiving a personal phone call at home from the president of the United States, asking for your help. Or being invited to a state dinner at the White House with President Ford and the leader of a foreign country. Or celebrating the nation's bicentennial on board the USS *Forrestal* in New York Harbor on July 4, 1976, as forty tall ships from around the world sailed past.

President Ford also met at the White House with entire state delegations. He was impressive at these events—gracious, humble, and articulate. No one who actually knew the president ever quite understood Chevy Chase's *Saturday Night Live* impersonation of him as a genial dolt who stumbled over doorsteps and big words. Unfortunately, the caricature—particularly the physical humor—took on a life of its own. Even the slightest misstep was taken as more proof that this graceful and athletic man, who had played on two national championship football teams at the University of Michigan and turned down offers from the pros, was, in fact, a bumbler.

President Ford personified all that is good about America, and he was comfortable with himself, popular with old friends on both sides of the aisle in Congress, admired and respected by his staff, and effective in private sessions with delegates. So why did he fail to win in 1976? The economy and the pardon of Richard Nixon were the principal reasons, but a contributing factor was that he was not television-friendly at a time when television had become the nation's window on politics. The president had a habit of pausing for several beats before he spoke. When the red light on a television camera would come on—

his cue to talk—he would not start speaking right away. This sometimes gave the mistaken impression that he was struggling to find the right words.

TV-friendly or not, this wonderful, lifelong public servant was absolutely the right person at the right time to heal the wounds of Watergate, to restore America's confidence in its government, and to bring the nation out of that terrible period. Pardoning the disgraced Nixon on September 8, 1974, was the right thing to do. The scandal "could go on and on and on, or someone must write an end to it," Ford said. "I have concluded that only I can do that, and if I can, I must. My conscience tells me that it is my duty not only to proclaim domestic tranquility but to use every means that I have to ensure it." By doing the right thing, however, he hurt himself in the polls, the primaries, and—ultimately—the election.

The average American might wonder whether it is proper for a sitting president to entertain delegates at the White House, just as Americans had concerns about President Clinton's inviting donors to stay overnight in the Lincoln Bedroom. After one delegation lunched with President Ford, reporters asked who had paid for the meal. Answer: The president had used personal funds.

Having led presidential campaigns five times from 1976 through 1992—and for three incumbent presidents—I have long been sensitive to these matters. The first rule, clearly, is to follow the law. We always took pains to do so. In late June 1976, I drafted guidelines "in connection with visits to Washington of delegates." We could not use government funds for "entertainment or political meetings or receptions at the White House," I wrote, but it was okay for delegates to attend state dinners and other official events, "as long as their presence does not alter the official nature of the event." Small gifts—cuff links, tie clasps, and the like—were okay if they were not purchased with government funds.

While I spent part of the summer of '76 at the White House with delegates, I spent most of the time at PFC headquarters working the phones and keeping in daily contact with regional and state chairmen, with our "persuaders," and with the delegates themselves. Spencer and I also flew around the country to meet delegates.

When the convention began, the *New York Times* published an article about our delegate operation under the headline, "'Miracle Man' Given Credit for Ford Drive." In Kansas City, the campaign picked up on the headline and gave me the code name "Miracle Man" for our walkie-talkie network. I earned that "sobriquet," the *Times* reported, by "having turned the most crucial phase of the Ford effort—the delegate hunt—from a failure into a success. . . . Others bugged the delegates on behalf of Mr. Ford. But they saved Mr. Baker for the soft sell on the hard cases."

I like recognition as much as the next guy, but delegate hunting is a team sport, and we had a great one—Jackie Fernald, Pete Roussel, Pete McPherson, Paul Manafort, Judy McLennan, Richard Mastrangelo, and others at headquarters, and many more in regional and state operations in the field. By the convention, we had a tremendous organization in place.

In politics, organization is much more important than people think. Texas pols have a term for a disorganized campaign: they call it a "goat rope" (as in roping goats, a figurative term for "chaos"). Without a smoothly functioning presidential campaign apparatus, the chairman would be forced to spend far too much time refereeing battles between players who are on the same team.*

PFC Chairman Rog Morton did have to referee one battle involving me. Some background: In 1966, Godfrey "Budge" Sperling, a Washington-based *Christian Science Monitor* reporter, started hosting breakfasts at which print reporters met for freewheeling on-the-record discussions with political newsmakers. Although Sperling re-

---

*Political operatives use a cruder term, also involving animals, for a campaign in which members of the same team spend most of their time fighting for turf and promoting themselves at the expense of their colleagues. They call that a "rat f—k."

linquished his duties as host in 2001 and retired from journalism in 2005, the breakfasts are now a Washington institution.

In 1976, I was asked to talk about the delegate hunt. I was eager to attend. The battle for the uncommitteds was being played out in the press; this was a chance to talk about our operation and delegate count. But the invitation created a furor within the campaign. Peter Kaye, head of the small PFC press operation, strenuously objected to my going.

Why? He told me I would be eaten alive by the veteran journalists, but I suspect the real reason was turf. The PFC press people wanted to keep tight control of what was said and by whom, but I didn't report to them. I was adamant about going, so I took my case to Rog, who gave his blessing.

The breakfast not only went smoothly but also contributed to our credibility. The Washington press corps certainly can eat you alive, particularly if you are ill-prepared or untruthful. In my early days at the campaign, however, no one seemed anxious to devour me. I was new to the Beltway, I was not a professional politician, and I came with a decent résumé: a successful lawyer in private practice with a good education who had done a respectable job as under secretary of commerce. Maybe they were just giving the new guy the benefit of the doubt.

As the summer progressed, however, the major reason that I had credibility with the press was simple: *I never lied to them.* I never claimed a delegate unless we had something from that delegate—a letter or a public statement, for example—that would support my claim.

Credibility is important in every political campaign, but it was essential in the too-close-to-call '76 nomination fight. Because reporters saw that the delegate counts we announced were accurate, not speculative, they could say, "Looks like Ford's got it," as we headed to Kansas City. This won support for us from some uncommitteds because it's human nature to side with the winner. (I believe the way we handled information about delegates also contributed to my generally positive relationship with the media in the eighties and nineties.)

The other side did not enjoy the same credibility. After Reagan campaign manager John Sears proclaimed on July 19 that his candidate had 1,140 delegates, I accused him of "blowing smoke." Four days later, I reported that we had picked up fifteen delegates from Hawaii and now counted 1,135 in our column—five more than we needed to win. The *New York Times* would later report:

> Some Ford operatives urged Mr. Baker to use razzle-dazzle to toss out numbers without names and claim delegates not yet confirmed and thus create a momentum in fiction that might lead to one in fact. He refused. . . .
>
> Unlike his counterpart in the Reagan campaign, where claims of 1,140 delegates—ten over the nomination—stood for weeks without evidence, Mr. Baker edged along slowly to the magic number, citing three delegates in Virginia or five in Hawaii—and handing out their names and addresses.
>
> The news media canvasses invariably confirmed the switches and, within a few delegates one way or the other, matched the Ford count and rebutted the Reagan count.

As we "edged along slowly," we knew that victory was not assured, even if we did reach the magic number by the beginning of the convention. By state law, some delegates had to vote for a particular candidate on the first ballot, but were free to go their own ways on procedural votes and, in some cases, on subsequent ballots for the nomination. We figured about twenty first-ballot Ford delegates might go Reagan's way on procedural matters.

Why was this important? Because unseating a president from your own party is hard to justify, unless he's perceived as a loser. Beating President Ford on procedural issues, the Reagan team believed, would create doubts in the minds of uncommitted delegates and some of our delegates, too. If Gerald Ford can't control his own convention, how can he defeat Jimmy Carter in November?

On July 26, Reagan made a desperate pitch for these swing delegates by naming a running mate, Senator Richard Schweiker of Pennsylvania. The senator was viewed as considerably to the left of Reagan, and Reagan's strategists believed he would broaden the appeal of the ticket in the general election. More important, they hoped that Pennsylvania delegates committed to Ford would switch to Reagan at the convention to show support for their home-state senator. This was possible but not probable. In football parlance, the Schweiker ploy was a Hail Mary pass.

The man who could make the ploy work or defeat it was Drew Lewis, President Ford's chairman in Pennsylvania. In 1974, he had managed his friend Schweiker's senate reelection campaign, but in 1976, Drew Lewis could not be moved. He not only remained loyal to Ford; he also prevailed on the Ford delegates to honor their commitments. (Drew would later serve as secretary of transportation for President Reagan before becoming CEO of Union Pacific Corporation.)

How confident was I that we had the nomination won when we arrived in Kansas City? Not totally. On the Sunday evening before the convention, I attended church with Susan. "If the count had been 1,250 for Mr. Ford, maybe that wouldn't have been necessary," I joked to the press.

THREE

"THE CLOSEST PRESIDENTIAL ELECTION YOU'LL EVER SEE IN YOUR LIFETIME"

VICE PRESIDENTIAL NOMINEES don't decide presidential elections. Americans vote for the top of the ticket. But it can be reasonably argued that in 1976, at least, the Republican nomination hinged on who the vice presidential nominee was . . . or was not.

As delegates were packing for their trips to Kansas City, Ronald Reagan's campaign strategist, John Sears, asked the party rules committee to force candidates to pick their running mates before the convention voted on a nominee. With Pennsylvania Senator Richard Schweiker already lined up for Reagan, Sears wanted to force Ford's hand. He reasoned that he could pick off some Ford delegates or undecideds who were alienated by whomever President Ford selected as his running mate. Aware of this, we opposed the proposal. So, too, did the rules committee, which we controlled. This forced a floor fight over what came to be known as Rule 16-C.

When the convention began on Monday, August 16, we knew the vote on 16-C would determine the nomination itself. And it did. The final count after the Tuesday night showdown was 1,189 no and 1,060 yes, with 10 abstentions. Sears's make-or-break gambit had failed by only 29 votes.

If I had been advising Reagan, I told reporters after the convention, I would have rolled the dice on a three-word proposal that was ideological, not procedural: "Fire Henry Kissinger!" That would have mobilized the Reagan troops, attracted some undecideds, and, more than likely, won support from a few of the president's supporters.

My suggestion about attacking Henry had nothing to do with my judgment of him or his policies. It was a purely political assessment. It would have been harder for President Ford to have kept his troops in line on a referendum over the controversial secretary of state.

I have always liked Henry and consider him a friend. When I sought his counsel before taking office as secretary of state in 1989, he offered lots of good advice. We come from very different backgrounds, but we are both realists—practitioners of realpolitik—and we generally see eye to eye on foreign policy issues, particularly those that demand national sacrifices. Values are important, of course, but we each realize that the American public will not long support a policy that cannot be explained in terms of hard national interests. We are both good bureaucratic infighters, too.

The vote on the nomination on Wednesday, August 18, was anticlimactic. Everyone knew Ford would win. Overnight, the uncommitteds committed, and a few soft Reagan delegates also joined the winning team. The president won 1,187 to 1,070, a narrow but decisive 117-vote margin.

From 1972 through 1996, I attended all seven Republican conventions. For sheer drama and excitement, 1976 stands alone. It was the last time either party actually picked its candidate on the floor. Candidates prefer to wrap up the nomination early, so they can spend more time and money against their general election opponents. I confess, however, that I am nostalgic for the days when the outcome was not preordained by state primary contests. Each election cycle, it seems, the primaries are earlier than last time, and a few key states always have disproportionate influence. Our system now virtually guarantees that the nominee will be known months before the party convention and that many states will have little or no say in the decision. The

Commission on Federal Election Reform that I cochaired with former President Carter in 2005 recommended having a series of regional primaries after the contests in Iowa and New Hampshire. That would be a good way to permit states that now have little say help decide who runs for our nation's highest office.

I do not suggest a return to smoke-filled rooms, but the modern system deprives us of something important. When the three major television networks first began covering the conventions in earnest in the early 1950s, the box in the living room drew Americans of all ages and political persuasions into the drama of self-governance. Seeing the system at work inspired many Americans to get involved. I wish we could find a way to reinvest major-party conventions with that same meaning and excitement. Nowadays, the selection of sixty-five teams to compete for the NCAA Men's Division I Basketball Championship seems to generate more excitement than the selection of the two nominees for the highest office in the most powerful nation on earth.

When John Kerry picked John Edwards as his running mate before the 2004 Democratic convention, the last vestige of suspense was drained out of the convention. By contrast, when Ford won the nomination in 1976, nobody—including the president himself—knew for sure whom he would select. As noted, he was under the impression that he should not offer the spot to Reagan. My choice, George Bush, was also out of the running.

George was conspicuously absent from politics in 1976. In January, he became director of the Central Intelligence Agency, a position he didn't seek. He hoped to run for president someday, and Langley seemed like a major detour, possibly a dead end, on the path to the White House. Would Americans ever accept a former spy chief as chief executive?

Before voting on the CIA nomination, Senate Democrats wanted President Ford to pledge that he would not ask George to be his running mate in 1976. Both Rogers Morton and I advised George not to take the post. George saw it differently. "It's an important position," he said, "and if the president wants me to do it, I'm gonna do it."*

There was speculation that the CIA appointment was engineered by Don Rumsfeld, then Ford's White House chief of staff. Rummy, who became secretary of defense after Ford fired Jim Schlesinger, was thought to have presidential aspirations of his own. If true, removing George from the scene could only have helped his chances.

After winning the nomination, Ford wisely sought Reagan's advice on possible running mates, among them John Connally, Howard Baker, Bob Dole, Bill Simon, Elliot Richardson, and William Ruckelshaus. Reagan favored Senator Dole, and after talking with his own advisers, Ford tapped the World War II hero as his running mate.

Anne Armstrong, then U.S. Ambassador to the United Kingdom, was also on the list. Had she been chosen, she would have been the first woman nominated by a major party to run on a national ticket. That would have been a big surprise in 1976, especially from our party. The face of the Kansas City GOP convention was largely white and male. While this demographic still predominates at our conventions, we now count considerably more women delegates and delegates of color. This is good for our party and our nation, and—not coincidentally—good politics.

After the convention, Ford advisers and campaign officials, including me, gathered at a retreat in Vail, Colorado, to plan the campaign against Jimmy Carter. In discussions to which I was not privy, a decision was made to replace Rog as chairman of the President Ford Committee (PFC). Rog had made a few mistakes during the primaries. Most notably, when Ford lost in Indiana, Alabama, and Georgia three

---

*In the end, George enjoyed his time as CIA director and did a great job in the office. "You restored America's trust in the CIA and the rest of the intelligence community," President Clinton wrote in 1999 when the Langley compound was named the George Bush Center for Intelligence. The experience also made George a better president, I think, because it enabled him to understand both the importance and the limitations of intelligence-gathering.

days after being humiliated in Texas, Rog had said, "I'm not going to rearrange the furniture on the deck of the *Titanic*." At the same time, he permitted himself to be photographed in front of a row of less-than-full liquor bottles. To be fair to Rog, the press had joined in emptying those bottles. Furthermore, although few knew it, Rog was suffering from cancer.

Rumor had it that John Connally would replace Rog, who would then be given the largely ceremonial title of chairman emeritus. I was shocked when I learned that the president wanted *me* to take over day-to-day control of the campaign.

Chairman of the President Ford Committee was not a position I was seeking. I had been in Washington for less than a year. I really struggled with the question of loyalty to Rog, a wonderful man, now ill, who had been so good to me and had brought me to the capital in the first place.

The situation grew even worse when Rog's wife, Anne, a lovely woman and dear friend, heard about the offer. "Don't take it, Jim," she urged. "Tell him you can't do it."

"But, Anne," I said, "how can I turn down the president?"

If I hadn't thought it would hurt Anne even more, I would have told her that the decision to replace Rog had already been made. Even if I had turned down the president, he would have offered the chairmanship to somebody else. At least I could make certain Rog received the respect he deserved and the responsibility he wanted in his new role as chairman of a blue-ribbon steering committee for the campaign. When we returned to Washington from Vail, I refused to move into the large PFC chairman's office, insisting that Rog remain there.

The Ford-Carter contest in the year of our national bicentennial was historic on many levels. It marked the first chance Americans had to elect a president after Watergate. It was the only time one of the candidates was a sitting president who had not been elected to that office or, for that matter, to the vice presidency. And it was the last election in which Joe Garagiola played an important role.

I am only half-kidding when I mention Joe, the former catcher for the St. Louis Cardinals who parlayed his genial sense of humor into a career as a baseball broadcaster and television celebrity, eventually hosting NBC's *Today* show. His presence on the campaign trail symbolized the increased importance of television. By 1976, TV had not only penetrated our culture—almost every household had one or more sets—but had also begun to change the way most Americans thought about government and politics. The newspaper generation read about Watergate. The TV generation experienced it, through broadcast hearings and press conferences, and finally through the live resignation of a president, right there in the living room.

The post-Watergate campaign laws compounded the power of the tube. In *Marathon: The Pursuit of the Presidency, 1972–1976,* his comprehensive book on the 1976 election,* reporter Jules Witcover called the 1976 presidential race "ordination by television." In part this simply reflected the power of the medium, but it was also an indirect consequence of the new campaign-finance law passed by the Democratic Congress in 1974 in response to the fund-raising abuses of the 1972 Nixon campaign. In theory, both candidates Carter and Ford "voluntarily" accepted public financing of their general election campaigns. In reality, they had no choice, given the new limits on how much individuals and groups could contribute. (This decision had already been made by the time I took over.) Both campaigns got $21.8 million, but in return they could not accept private donations. As Witcover pointed out, this was "roughly one-third of what it had cost four years earlier" for Nixon's campaign against McGovern.

The spending limits forced each campaign to look for low-cost and no-cost strategies to sell its candidate to the public.† Television could

---

*This book, for which I was interviewed extensively, will refresh the memory of anyone interested in revisiting 1976. It refreshed mine.

†It also required us to assign a large tribe of lawyers and accountants to interpret the new law, comply with its detailed rules, and file reports with the Federal Election Commission.

reach millions, so the challenge for both campaigns was to win as much airtime as possible for as few dollars as possible. Twenty-four-hour cable news networks did not exist back then. The evening news on the three major networks—ABC, CBS, and NBC—drove the daily numbers. This begat a simple philosophy: orchestrate events featuring the president that the networks had to cover. If we wanted to emphasize the difference between our farm program and Carter's, for example, then send the president to a farm.

Televised debates—the ultimate reality television—also offered a way to reach tens of millions of Americans at a time. In his convention acceptance speech, the president said, "This year the issues are on our side. I am . . . eager to go before the American people and debate the real issues face-to-face with Jimmy Carter."

Here Ford was breaking the mold. He would be the first sitting president to participate in a broadcast debate with the other party's nominee. Comfortably ahead in the polls and reasoning that they had nothing to gain by giving their opponents a forum and credibility, Presidents Johnson and Nixon had refused to debate.

Free coverage was important, but both camps also recognized the importance of paid political advertising. For the last few days of the campaign, President Ford flew to key venues to do half-hour commercials in a talk-show format, not with his running mate, Bob Dole, but with a TV personality, Garagiola. Stay tuned for more about the "Joe and Jerry Show."

As chairman of the PFC, I appeared on television whenever the networks wanted me. We coveted the opportunity to push the Ford message without having to spend precious dollars. On September 12, 1976, a little less than one month after President Ford had won the nomination, I appeared on *Face the Nation,* where I was grilled on a range of issues (for which I had fastidiously Five P'd). Why was the president pursuing a Rose Garden strategy? Would he win any Southern states? What role would Reagan play in the campaign? And who the heck was James A. Baker, III?

"Do you go through Mr. Cheney to see the president on campaign issues, or do you have direct access?" I was asked by Bob Pierpoint.

"I have all the access to the president that I believe I require, Bob. Anytime I want to see the president, I can see the president."

I wasn't the only one surprised by my new job. On *Agronsky & Co.,* a forerunner of today's cable and network shows that feature pundits commenting on current political events, respected newspaperman Peter Lisagor characterized my appointment as "curious," given how little experience I had in national politics. On the same show, the conservative columnist James Kilpatrick acknowledged that I was a "competent technician" but deemed my ascension "startling." He wished aloud that Ford had brought in John Sears and other Reagan operatives.

The *Washington Post* reported my appointment under the headline: "Former Democrat, Political Neophyte Leads Ford Drive." The article described my style as "extremely low key" and "with an ever-evident sense of humor." Obviously, however, President Ford didn't appoint me because he liked my jokes. "Jim, as you know, was a very accurate counter in the pre-convention process," he said when he named me as chairman. "He demonstrated to me a very outstanding organizational capability."*

In a memo written early in 1975, well before he had even announced his candidacy, organizational ability was one of several characteristics the president had been advised to look for in a campaign manager. Among the other traits outlined in this memo, whose author was not identified: "1) Absolute loyalty to the president, even to exclu-

---

*I was not the only member of the Baker clan working for President Ford. Over the summer, my youngest son, Doug, then fifteen, volunteered as a grunt at PFC headquarters. That's probably where he got the bug for law, politics, and public service. When he grew up, he worked a few years as a lawyer in private practice, then served as executive director for the Houston Sport Authority. He also helped me in the 2000 Florida election dispute. In the first term of the Bush 43 administration, he was deputy assistant secretary at the Commerce Department. In the second term he moved to the White House as a special assistant to the president for homeland security.

sion, if necessary, of his own best interests; 2) the ability to make a decision. Indecisiveness to politicians is disastrous; 3) general knowledge of the political, business, and media worlds; 4) available on a full-time basis; and 5) a 'good guy' with few, if any, deep-seated adversaries."

Looking back from the perspective of five presidential campaigns, I would add one other essential characteristic: the willingness to look your candidate in the eye and give the bad news with the good. This is never easy.

About two weeks before the convention, Stu Spencer and Dick Cheney presented the president with a comprehensive, one-hundred-plus-page strategy notebook they had prepared with the help of a small group, most notably including Mike Duval, a valuable holdover from the Nixon administration. Although ever-changing circumstances prevented us from following it to the letter and the president always had the final say, this manifesto guided the campaign from August until November. My job was to implement it. Looking back on it today, I think it holds up as a good diagnosis of the problems the campaign faced and a good prescription for curing them.

The strategists began by offering a realistic assessment of the president's chances: "You face a unique challenge. No president has overcome the obstacles to election which you will face." In the greatest comeback in recent history, they noted, President Harry Truman trailed Thomas Dewey by only 11 points in August 1948. Ford, they predicted, would trail Carter by almost 20 points after our convention. (He was down by a staggering 33 percent margin—62–29, with 9 percent undecided—in the late July Gallup Poll, three weeks before Kansas City.)

This forecast proved pretty accurate. Thanks in part to a rousing acceptance speech that unified the convention and Republicans across the country, the president actually trailed by only 10 points in the first post–Kansas City Gallup Poll, 49 to 39, with 12 percent undecided. A week later, however, with the convention already fading from memory, the margin was back up to 15 percent.

Why was the president so far behind? In part because of a sluggish economy; in part because of the lingering effects of Watergate and the Nixon pardon; and, in part, according, to our polling, because Ford was frequently perceived as too partisan, particularly on the campaign trail. His national approval rating *declined* when he left the White House during the primary season.

I've learned that you really cannot, and should not try to, present a candidate as something he or she is not. You don't suggest a personality makeover or try to build a strategy around a false image. "Our campaign strategy has been developed around the president's actual strengths and aimed at Carter's actual weaknesses," our strategy document said. "We are not trying to change the president (style and substance); we are trying to change the voter's perception of the president and Carter."

Mistakes could be fatal. To avoid self-inflicted wounds, "the president must establish ironclad control over administration and campaign officials." This proved prophetic. In late September, it was reported that Secretary of Agriculture Earl Butz—a holdover from the Nixon administration—had told an offensive joke shortly after the convention that was derogatory to African Americans. President Ford instructed him to apologize, but did not publicly call for his resignation as many Republicans and Democrats demanded. With the controversy dominating the news and sidetracking the campaign, Cheney, Spencer, and I urged the president to jettison the secretary. The next day, October 4, Butz resigned.

"The president's campaign must be television oriented," said our strategy document. "We must change the perception of literally millions of voters, and this can only be done through the mass media." Many of our strategy points related to television. For example, the president was counseled: "Carefully plan, prepare, and execute all on-camera appearances. The president should be seen on television as in control, decisive, open, and candid." Also: "Use ads and advocates to compare the president's personal characteristics and experience with Carter's."

Other advice from the strategy memo reveals just how carefully a candidate is prepped for the campaign:

- Avoid self-deprecating remarks (I'm a Ford, not a Lincoln) and acts (being photographed with a cowboy hat).
- Avoid symbolic acts such as bill signings, submitting legislation, vetoes, and the like, which simply reinforce the perception of the president as part of the Washington establishment. . . .
- The president must not campaign for GOP candidates. This will seriously erode his support among independents and ticket splitters.
- In order to break the president out of the Washington establishment mold, we should launch an attack on the Democratic majority which has governed Washington for forty of the past forty-eight years.

Traditionally, presidential campaigns kick off after Labor Day, but normally the sitting president does not trail his opponent by double digits in August. After the convention, we had seventy-five days until the November 2 election. Ford did not have the luxury of relaxing for two weeks. He got in a few rounds of golf at Vail, but even that was squeezed into a working vacation.

The first order of business was to reorganize the operation. With the team in place, we could then develop a campaign blueprint based on the strategy notebook, post-convention developments, and the ideas of some campaign newcomers we had signed up. A five-page document, dated August 25 and titled "The President's Campaign," began with an important guiding principle that reflected the impact of Watergate: Pollster Bob "Teeter's data indicate that the 1976 election is a personality contest, not a battle of issues. Issues will be one of the determinants people use in sizing up each man."

Because "each candidate's style as perceived by the electorate [is] all-important," the campaign needed "to project the following characteristics." Reading the list of those characteristics must have transported Ford, the only Eagle Scout ever to serve as president, back to his youth. "Knowledgeable, solid, stable, decisive, compassionate, trust-worthy, future-oriented, experienced, and positive."

In discussing the Ford strategy in 1976, I do not mean to suggest that the campaign was bereft of substance. In fact, we were eager to engage the Democrats on the issues. We worked up a document—"Major Differences in Platform"—that contrasted the two parties' positions on twenty-four topics. On energy, for instance, the Republican platform "eliminates price controls on oil and new sources of natural gas in order to increase the supply of oil and gas." The Democrat platform, on the other hand, "maintains 1975 oil prices and raises price ceilings on natural gas." The president would emphasize this difference, particularly in the oil and gas producing states.

We focused our message on issues of the day. For each, the president would speak at a venue selected to yield coverage on the evening news. His surrogates—Senator Dole, cabinet members, high-profile supporters, members of the First Family, and I—would also push the same issue.

Then, as now, the press loved to play "gotcha" by finding contradictions in a candidate's statements or differences between what he and his surrogates were saying. How did we manage not to contradict one another? I still retain another thick document from the campaign that includes talking points on twenty-one issues of the day, from abortion to tax reform, from amnesty to drug abuse, from the economy to juvenile delinquency. Under "Older Americans," for instance, we said, "In his acceptance speech, the president reconfirmed his concern for the nation's elderly. 'We will ensure the integrity of the Social Security system and improve Medicare.'" Below that, we listed four points about the president's proposals or accomplishments, including: "The president proposed a catastrophic health insurance program to limit the out-of-pocket amount older Americans must pay for medical and physicians' fees each year."

Every campaign with which I have been associated—and, I am confident, every opposing campaign—prepared talking points like these for the candidate and his surrogates. We also developed a dozen guidelines for these spokespersons. They included: "Two days travel per week per cabinet secretary, at least." "Emphasize travel to cities whose TV covers 70 percent of population" and "take it for granted people won't like [being addressed by a low-profile cabinet officer]—so have ready a list of very heavy hitters who aren't scheduled at all—supporters who can plug the perceived holes, and—even more—can nail Carter into a barrel when targets of opportunity arise. Our list of 'attackers' is: Mrs. Ford, Bob Dole, John Connally, Nelson Rockefeller, John Tower, Howard Baker, Rogers Morton."

We would have liked to include Ronald Reagan on this list. It is fair to say, however, that after the convention, the president and many of his supporters were not enamored of Reagan. It had nothing to do with the former governor's personality and everything to do with the fact that he had challenged and almost beaten a sitting president from his own party. At the same time, President Ford recognized that Governor Reagan could help him in some areas of the country.

While the president was at the White House and Dole and others were crisscrossing the United States, I was, for the most part, at the still-spartan PFC headquarters at Eighteenth and L Streets in northwest Washington. As chairman, I oversaw the activities of state chairmen and the deputy chairmen at the PFC, worked with the political people at the White House, and acted as a principal spokesman for the campaign with the print and television media.

There's no such thing as a typical day in a presidential campaign, except one that involves long hours, many meetings, and lots of telephone calls. On most days, I checked in by telephone with our paid state campaign chairs around the country and met in the office with our PFC deputies. Cheney, Spencer, Teeter, and I also devoted a good deal of time to figuring out how to allocate our limited resources and time.

In a race for the presidency, you are not dealing with one election; you are dealing with the electoral votes of fifty states and D.C.—i.e.,

fifty-one separate elections. Teeter's polling and reports from operatives in the field helped us target states for advertising and visits by
Ford or Dole.*

The PFC was theoretically governed by an executive committee
composed of me and other top officers of the campaign. I chaired the
meetings. My outline from one of the very first meetings, at 7:30 A.M.
on September 7, began with this note to myself: "Hold to forty-five
minutes." That was wishful thinking. I had put nineteen topics on the
agenda, among them PFC–White House coordination, campaign material distribution, coordination with Reagan staff, phone-bank operations, state organizations, president's schedule, and Democrats and
independents for Ford. All these and more were under my purview.

One thing we tried to do was create a better working relationship
between the PFC and the White House, which had not always seen
eye to eye during the primary season. Almost every day I would walk
over to the White House for strategy meetings with Cheney. White
House political appointees Mike Duval, Foster Chanock, and Jerry
Jones usually joined us. So did Jim Field, a young Cheney aide from
Rhode Island who served as liaison between Dick and me.

It didn't take long for the press to catch on to this pattern. Journalists began staking out our headquarters, following me with television
cameras on the walk, and peppering me with questions. I liked these
reporters, but the best way to get our message out was under controlled conditions, not impromptu walks down the street with micro-
phones in my face, so I started driving to the White House.

The presidential debates were also a topic of discussion at that

---

*The operatives' reports had to be taken with a grain of salt. During a campaign, everyone
believes the candidate should visit his or her state, yesterday, or the world will end. Everyone is an expert on strategy. Supporters sent the president stacks of letters and telegrams
on how to conduct his campaign. Many were referred to me. One of my favorites—from
a retired alternate delegate from Illinois—began in all caps: "GREAT BALLS OF GREEN
CHEESE, PRESIDENT FORD! WHY DO YOU LET CARTER GET AWAY WITH
HIS STATEMENTS ON UNEMPLOYMENT?"

September 7 meeting. The first ninety-minute Ford-Carter debate, sponsored by the League of Women Voters and moderated by veteran NBC newsman Edwin Newman, was held at the Walnut Street Theatre in Philadelphia on September 23. "The debates will overshadow all other presidential campaign activity," said the Vail campaign strategy document. "This activity must have the priority call on the president's time." And it did. Ford's preparation, led largely by Mike Duval, advertising guru Doug Bailey, and media consultant Bill Carruthers, began long before the first question was asked.

On September 15, Bailey sent Duval a two-page memo with a "debate thesis"—"'Winning the debate' will result from the president's seeing it not as a contest with Carter, but as an opportunity to communicate with the people, regardless of what Carter does—and a "debate strategy"—"The dominant fact of the debate will be that it is not between two candidates but between one candidate and the president." Seven guidelines followed, including these:

> The president should always stand, never using the stool. He should . . . take notes when Carter is making a strong point; ignore the cameras, always assuming they are on him.
>
> He should refer to him as "Mr. Carter." He should avoid any direct conversation with him. . . .
>
> The president should not cite congressional anecdotes. He should always be presidential by referring to the past two years.

A final guideline referred the president to an attached chart listing "seven points to be made, the type of question or comment which can be used to make them, and some memorable summary lines on each." Here is one example:

> Basic message to communicate: "With recovery of peace, economic stability, and trust, we can enter a new generation of freedom."
>
> When to use it: Questions on priorities; issues such as busing, government reorganization, equal rights, crime, education.

Key lines to use: "FDR's Four Freedoms are still valid. But today we must also seek freedom from government restrictions in our lives—freedom from Washington in our lives."

Carter arrived in Philadelphia for the first debate with a commanding 18 percent lead, but—thanks to an article from a most unexpected media source—momentum was beginning to shift our way. Three days before the debate, *Playboy* released a long interview with Carter.

"Christ said, 'I tell you that anyone who looks on a woman with lust has in his heart already committed adultery,'" Carter told his interviewers. "I've looked on a lot of women with lust. I've committed adultery in my heart many times. This is something that God recognizes I will do—and I have done it—and God forgives me for it. . . ."

Carter's statement was the perfect political gaffe. It hurt him with almost every voting group. His fellow Southern Baptists, for instance, were offended that he gave the interview without condemning *Playboy*'s role in what they saw as the coarsening of culture and weakening of traditional sexual morality. Some voters simply thought it was funny (in the sense of odd) for a presidential candidate to talk openly about his lustful thoughts. And others were troubled by what they saw as excessive religiosity. The episode cast doubt on Carter's judgment and political skills. Frank Irwin, a conservative Democrat from Texas, even printed bumper stickers saying, "God doesn't want you to vote for Jimmy Carter."

Meanwhile, we had to decide how to respond. It's inevitable on the painfully long campaign trail that a candidate will, at some point, say something controversial. The opposition then has to figure out whether it will gain more by speaking up or keeping quiet. The determining factor is often whether the press itself can be expected to keep the story alive, and on "lustful thoughts," reporters were doing just fine, thank you very much, without any help from us. Neither the president nor Bob Dole said a thing.

I accompanied the president to Philadelphia for the first debate.

Surprisingly, none of the panelists asked about the *Playboy* interview. Not surprisingly, neither candidate mentioned it.*

The first debate is best remembered, not for anything that was said but instead for its silence. With about eight minutes remaining, the sound system went dead while Carter was in the middle of a response. "The Great Cutoff," as the *Washington Post*'s Haynes Johnson called it, lasted twenty-seven minutes. While technicians tried to figure out what was wrong and fix it, the president and Carter remained standing on the stage. Neither said a word, and neither seemed to want to sit down.

President Ford eventually won the standoff. After about twenty minutes, Carter took his seat. Sound was restored a few minutes later. The first post–Philadelphia Gallup Poll suggested the president had won the debate, too. Carter's 18-point lead (54–36) was reduced to 8 (50–42).

A little more than a month later, with just days left in the campaign, a Harris poll showed the race was a virtual dead heat, with Carter leading Ford by only 1 point, 45–44. The tightness of the race was remarkable considering how far behind we had started, how difficult it was to overcome public concern about the Nixon pardon, and how many new and unexpected troubles came our way during the campaign.

Unbelievably, given President Ford's sterling reputation, one of our first big problems was fighting off an ethics charge. Watergate Special Prosecutor Charles Ruff was appointed by the administration's attorney general, Edward Levi—without prior notice to the president and in the heat of the campaign—to investigate whether, as a congressman, Ford had diverted campaign contributions for personal use. It

---

*Finally questioned about the interview in the third debate on October 22, Carter conceded that it had been a mistake. "If I should ever decide in the future to discuss my deep Christian beliefs . . . I'll use another forum besides *Playboy*." In interviews after he left office, President Carter admitted the interview had cost him a lot of votes.

was a bogus charge from the beginning, and Levi should never have referred it to a special prosecutor. In mid-October, Ruff announced there was no evidence of wrongdoing and closed the case. Nevertheless, the investigation badly hurt our campaign and was, in my opinion, inappropriate and unfair, a perversion of the political process, and a real sign of troubles to come from the post-Watergate independent counsels.

Another ethics question boiled up in the press while Ruff was conducting his investigation. John Dean, President Nixon's White House counsel who pled guilty to obstruction of justice in the Watergate scandal (he admitted paying the Watergate burglars to keep quiet), told reporters that Ford, as a congressman, had—at the behest of the White House—attempted to kill a 1972 House hearing on the Watergate burglary. At his vice presidential confirmation hearing, President Ford testified that he had opposed granting subpoena powers for the investigation but that he had not acted on behalf of the White House. (These events occurred well before the full implications of Watergate were evident.) Both Ford and the White House aide whom Dean cited as his source denied Dean's allegations, and—despite the hair-trigger post-Watergate spirit toward real or imagined impropriety—Ruff did not think the charges were worth investigating. Still, the damage was done. President Ford suffered guilt by association every time reporters wrote another story about Dean's baseless charge.

The Butz affair, another unexpected pothole on the campaign trail, resolved itself with the secretary's resignation, but two days later another key administration official spoke and the result was even more damaging. That official was President Ford himself.

During the second televised debate, the president painted himself into a corner while trying to defend the Helsinki Final Act, which he signed in 1975. It was an extremely important human rights document—among other things—but Jimmy Carter criticized it mercilessly. In defense, President Ford said the Soviets had kept their word and notified us about their military maneuvers. "In both cases where they've done so, there is no Soviet domination of Eastern Europe and there never will be under a Ford administration."

A follow-up question from Max Frankel of the *New York Times* gave the president an opportunity to correct his misstatement. But President Ford responded by citing two communist countries that in some sense had kept the Soviet Union at arm's length—Yugoslavia and Romania—and one other, Poland, that was clearly under the thumb of the Soviets. "I don't believe that the Poles consider themselves dominated by the Soviet Union," he said.

He was, of course, referring to the indomitable spirit of the Poles and other peoples of Eastern Europe—one of the major reasons for the collapse of the Berlin Wall some thirteen years later. And he was also stating a longstanding U.S. policy that refused to accept the legality of the occupation by the Soviets of Eastern and Central Europe after World War II. But it's one thing to have a policy and another to deny the facts on the ground, which is what he appeared to be doing.

At this stage in the campaign, we knew that to win we would have to carry most if not all of the northern and eastern industrial states. That's where the electoral votes were. That's also where the largest blocs of Polish Americans and others of Eastern European descent lived—the population most likely to be affected by the president's remarks.

What to do? Several of us met to discuss damage control. We decided that in the morning Cheney, National Security Adviser Brent Scowcroft, and I would go to the press to explain the president's statement—not an enviable task given the number of Soviet divisions stationed in Eastern Europe.

Interestingly, while both the Ford and Carter campaigns and the press immediately focused on the president's remarks about the Soviets and Eastern Europe, the public did not. Teeter's overnight polling of those who had watched the debate gave the president the win by a comfortable 11 percent margin. Then the newspapers hit the stands, the remark was rebroadcast on television, the pundits weighed in, and the Carter campaign focused on the assertion. Within forty-eight hours, polls revealed that a substantial majority of those who had watched the debate now believed Carter had won.

When you're wounded, you must stop the bleeding immediately. This is a guiding principle of politics. This gaffe had knocked us off message and threatened to keep us there for a long time.

Many of us advised the president to meet the press and clarify his remarks. Unfortunately, Henry Kissinger had called after the debate to tell the president what a wonderful job he had done, which reinforced Ford's view that he didn't need to do that. After all, we didn't officially recognize that the Soviets had any right to dominate Eastern Europe, and neither did the Eastern Europeans—at least in spirit. Only after it became clear to the president that his campaign was being sidetracked—six agonizing days later—did he speak up. "The original mistake was mine," he said. "I did not express myself clearly. I admit it."

That gave us something to work with, and I was soon happily pointing out to reporters that this was the first time in six weeks that the president had had to clarify any remarks, while candidate Carter was constantly revising what he had said. I cited six comparable Carter do-overs, including the famous *Playboy* interview.

Carter gaffes were in part responsible for the statistical dead heat the polls reflected on election eve. So, too, was the fact that voters not only liked Gerald Ford, but also saw him as presidential. The "Joe and Jerry Show" played a big part in reinforcing this perception.

The president and Garagiola had met earlier in the year and hit it off. The plan to team them together in six thirty-minute campaign infomercials was hatched at an October brainstorming session between Bob Teeter and consultant John Deardourff.

In modern baseball parlance, Garagiola pitched the president "cookies"—questions he could easily hit for home runs. I've long since forgotten these confections, but in *Marathon*, Witcover recounts a few of them, including: "Gosh, Mr. President, there sure are a lot of people worried about taxes, and just what are you going to do to help them out?" And, "How many world leaders have you dealt with?" These shows went over extremely well, with viewership well in excess of what we had expected.

By the time the polls opened on November 2, no one could predict the outcome with certainty. As our exit polling data trickled in, however, the picture began to look bleak. At about 5 o'clock in the afternoon, Cheney, Spencer, Teeter, and I presented the numbers to the president. He took the news stoically. As always, he was gracious. Before we left he even offered me a cigar.

"Thank you, but I don't smoke, Mr. President." After smoking cigarettes for years, I had stopped when Mary Stuart got sick, started up after she died, then quit again.

His voice reduced to a whisper by all the campaigning, the president said, "Maybe you might find some use for it."

For a time after the polls closed, it looked as if I might have reason to light it up as a victory cigar. The early results were better than our exit polling had predicted. As the spokesperson for the campaign on election night, I fielded questions from the press, monitored returns from our people in the field, and watched the television coverage from the Ford headquarters in downtown Washington. The president, his family, and several close friends—including Garagiola—watched from the residence in the White House.*

There is a telling photograph of Joe and Jerry, taken at some point during the evening. As the two friends sat together on a couch, the expressive Garagiola has his head buried in his hands. Beside him, the president calmly lights his pipe. Later Joe was reported to have said, "The president took all the news very calmly. I'd seen [Cardinals'

---

*The First Family was a real asset in the campaign. Because the president did not travel extensively until late in the campaign, appearances by Mrs. Ford and the children were very important. "Mrs. Ford is greatly respected because she is independent from the president," said our Vail strategy book. "We should not try to discourage this independence." We didn't, and Betty Ford, a classy woman, won a lot of votes for the president.

teammate] Enos Slaughter get more upset about an umpire saying, 'Strike two,' than Gerald Ford did when he realized he wasn't going to win a presidential election."

That realization didn't come until the early hours of Wednesday morning. In the end a shift of only a few thousand votes in Ohio (25 electoral votes) and Hawaii (4 electoral votes) would have given the victory to the president. Carter-Mondale won the popular vote by about 1.7 million ballots out of almost 82 million cast, 50 to 48 percent. In the Electoral College, where the magic number was 270, Carter-Mondale won 297 to 240. (A renegade elector from Washington gave Reagan one vote.) Not since Woodrow Wilson defeated Charles Evans Hughes by 23 electoral votes in 1916 had a race for president been so close.

As sunrise approached, I thought to myself, *How bizarre. Here you were a Democratic lawyer in Houston seven years ago, and now you've run a campaign for an incumbent Republican president, in what is obviously the closest presidential election you'll ever see in your lifetime.* That assessment held up for all of twenty-four years.

I also lit up the cigar the president had given me. For the next three or four years, until I kicked the habit, I smoked a cigar every night after dinner. Politics can be hazardous to your health.

Because the results were so close in so many states, we talked seriously about asking for one or more recounts. After thinking about it for a day or two, however, President Ford called us all together and said he had decided against it. "I lost the popular vote," he said. "It would be very hard for me to govern if I won the presidency in the Electoral College through a recount." He was right, of course.

Gerald Ford may have been calm about losing, as Garagiola reported, but that reflected the president's character, not indifference to the outcome. He was a strong competitor—all those who aspire to the presidency are—and he was a proud man. Still, he had a sense of perspective. His reputation was secure as the president who had helped our nation pull itself together after Watergate. Against great odds, he ran a strong campaign and almost pulled it off. Now he gracefully accepted the decision of the American people and prepared to move on.

As for me, I took satisfaction in having helped this wonderfully good man win his party's nomination and rally from 33 points down to come within an eyelash of recapturing the presidency. We'd given it a hell of a shot. In the end the Nixon pardon and concerns about the economy were just too much to overcome.

I also took solace from the many letters I received. Tom Brokaw, host of the *Today* show at the time, thanked me for demonstrating "class" in appearing on the program the morning after the election, and added: "I hope that you will take some consolation in knowing that the President Ford Committee conducted a masterful closing campaign. It was an effort of which you can be proud." And George Bush wrote: "Dear Bake: Nobody could have done any better—nobody!! The big thing is that you did it 'first class'—and you emerge with universal respect, your dignity intact. Just know we're awfully proud, Bushie."

ONE DAY during the campaign, I brought Susan and some of the kids over to the White House, and President Ford graciously invited us all into the Oval Office. Our ten-year-old son, Will, looked the place over, then said to the president, "Gee, you have a really pretty office. My daddy's office is really ugly."

The president laughed and said, "Well, son, if we win this election, your daddy will be getting a much prettier office."

Rumor had it the president planned to name me secretary of transportation. After the election, however, the only transportation I had to be concerned about was how to pack up the Baker brood and move it back to Houston. Andrews Kurth had an office waiting for me, and I took it, but resuming the practice of corporate law held little appeal for me. I knew I wouldn't be able to stay out of politics for long. The question wasn't whether I would run for office, but what office I would run for.

FOUR

·———·

"DOESN'T IT PISS YOU OFF?"

RUNNING FOR ATTORNEY GENERAL (AG) in Texas, as I did in 1978, was a far cry from running a presidential campaign. In this, my first (and only) bid for elective office, state dinners in the White House were out; potlucks in Rotary Clubs and barbeques in backyards were in. Over almost a year, I ate every variation of chicken imaginable. (In state politics there's no question about which comes first, the chicken or the ego.)

When I wasn't pressing my case at these gatherings, I was pressing the flesh on street corners and in supermarket parking lots. I had no advance team, and I didn't travel on Air Force One. My entourage, such as it was, usually consisted of two guys—Peter Roussel, a friend from Houston who had worked for George Bush, and Jim Cicconi, a recent University of Texas Law School graduate who had approached me one day on the street in Austin before I had announced and said he wanted to help. (Jim later served with distinction in the White House for George H. W. Bush and, afterward, helped set up the Bush Presidential Library and Museum. More recently, he was vice president and general counsel of AT&T before its merger with SBC.) The press rarely followed me.*

Susan rarely accompanied me. Her job was to stump in the areas I couldn't get to. She covered much of the state in our white Suburban with "Jim Baker for Attorney General" painted on the windows, stopping for coffees and teas organized by family and friends. Karen Jones, a young campaign worker, organized the trips and traveled with her, as did Susan's sister, Klinka Lollar, and other special pals. Much of the time Susan traveled with a portable crib in the back of the Suburban for our daughter, Mary Bonner, the newest Baker, born in Houston in September 1977.†

One hot summer afternoon I found myself in the Texas Panhandle. I saw a small crowd in a shopping center and went over to shake hands and distribute campaign literature.

"Hey, did anyone ever tell you that you look like Jim Baker?" one man said before I could introduce myself.

I was hardly a household name or face, but some people knew "Jim Baker" because I had frequently been on national television as President Ford's campaign chairman. "Yes," I replied with a smile. "Often."

---

*Back at our modest headquarters in Houston, my campaign manager, Frank Donatelli, led a small staff that included his wife, Becki, Carol Townsend, Frank Lavin, Lisa Stoltenberg, and Jan Naylor. (When I was White House chief of staff, Donatelli served as an assistant to President Reagan for political affairs. Today he is a prominent D.C. public affairs consultant. Lavin is under secretary of commerce. Naylor later served as deputy personnel director for Bush 41.) We were also blessed with any number of volunteers, one being my cousin Preston Moore.

†When I learned Susan was pregnant, I said, "Oh my goodness, we're gonna have another boy." "Jimmy, we are going to have a blue-eyed baby girl," she replied. When she went to the delivery room, I stayed behind, true to the old tradition that there are some places men just don't belong.

"Mr. Baker, you have a lovely baby girl," the nurse told me in the waiting room. "That is a really cruel joke," I told her, thinking Susan had put her up to it. But it was true. And the baby had blue eyes. I think it was God's providence that we had this lovely caboose to our train of eight children. She brought the Baker and Winston wings of our family closer together. Mary Bonner took her first steps in a press office in Brownwood, Texas, as Susan was giving an interview.

The guy never batted an eyelash. He looked straight at me and said, "Doesn't it piss you off?"

In those days, it was still hard to be a Texas Republican. In running for attorney general, I was attempting to do what no GOP candidate for statewide office—save Senator John Tower—had done since Reconstruction. Win.

George Bush and others had suggested that I should run for governor, but Dolph Briscoe, the incumbent, was an establishment Democrat, fairly conservative, and I didn't think I could raise enough money to beat him. My likely Democratic opponent for attorney general, former Texas House Speaker Price Daniel, Jr., was liberal enough to give a Republican a chance. It wouldn't cost nearly as much to run for AG, and I knew I was a better lawyer.*

Governor wasn't the only office I had been encouraged to seek. Before leaving Washington for Houston and the Andrews Kurth law firm a few weeks after the '76 election, some Ford supporters on the Republican National Committee (RNC) encouraged me to run for chairman of the RNC. I gave this serious consideration. When a Democrat holds the presidency, as Jimmy Carter would from 1977 to 1981, and Republicans control neither house of Congress, as was the case then, the RNC chair becomes de facto spokesperson for the party and, thus, a player.

I eventually withdrew my name for a couple of reasons. First, several other prominent politicians sought the position, and, as I told the press, I wanted to avoid being involved in "a knock-down, drag-out fight." Second, it's virtually impossible to run the party without being

---

*I eventually raised about $1.5 million. After the race, we had a deficit, but when George Bush received the vice presidential nomination in 1980, he wrote a fund-raising letter on my behalf. More money came in than was needed to pay off the debt, so I refunded the surplus to my contributors on a pro rata basis. Returning unspent campaign contributions is unusual but not unheard of. My father once told me how much he respected a former U.S. senator from Connecticut who had done the same thing in the 1950s—Prescott Bush, the father of my friend George. Even today people tell me, "You're the only politician who ever gave me any money back."

scarred politically. You have to be willing to make hard calls about what campaigns to support with funding and other tough issues. You can never please everyone, and if you're fair, you end up making more people mad than glad. Finally, although the White House privately encouraged me to run, President Ford did not want to endorse one candidate over the others.

As it turned out, not running was one of the best political decisions I ever made. Former Tennessee Senator Bill Brock won the chairmanship on, I believe, the third ballot and did a fine job. When the party reclaimed the presidency in 1981, President Reagan named him U.S. trade representative. Not bad. But Bill never became part of the president's inner circle, even when he served as secretary of labor in Reagan's second term.

When I returned to Houston, Bill Harvin, managing partner at Baker Botts, approached me about becoming a partner at the firm my great-grandfather had helped found. My dad was no longer alive, so the nepotism rule was not a problem. Getting my ticket punched at the family firm, albeit twenty years late, was appealing, but I declined. "I don't think I can do that, Bill," I said. "AK has been very loyal to me. They let me pursue this political agenda. I've got a lot of good friends still practicing there. It just wouldn't be right."

One of those friends was Harry Jones, the man who had taught me so much about practicing law and whom, nineteen years later, I still called "Mr. Jones." "Jim," he asked, "what do you think would have happened if President Ford had won?"

I would probably have been named secretary of transportation, I told him. "Wow," said this man whom I so admired, with genuine awe. "Secretary of transportation." I deeply regret that he did not live to see me serve as secretary of the treasury and secretary of state. He did live to see me run for attorney general, though, and lose.

In the Democratic primary, Mark White, a conservative protégé of Governor Briscoe, beat my opponent of choice, Price Daniel. This was a major upset, as Daniel—"Price, Jr.," in the idiom of Texas politics—

was widely expected to follow in the footsteps of his father, a legendary Texas House speaker, attorney general, governor, senator, and state supreme court justice. Young Daniel—descended on his mother's side from my great-grandfather's old friend Sam Houston—lost, in part because he was reluctant to spend money on TV during the primary. He figured, erroneously, that he would need it more when he faced me in the general election.

Just as George Bush had expected to run as the mainstream alternative to the liberal Ralph Yarborough in the senate race of 1970, I had expected to portray myself as the mainstream alternative to the liberal Daniel. And just as George's unexpected establishment Democrat opponent (Lloyd Bentsen) beat him, my unexpected establishment Democrat opponent (Mark White) beat me, 1,249,846 to 999,431.

Preston Moore recently reminded me that the race would have been a bit closer had I said yes to an offer made by leaders of a community organization that shall go unnamed here. They offered to deliver a large bloc of voters in return for a $5,000 check. "Walking-around money" for local political leaders was standard operating procedure in Texas politics, they said. I told them it wasn't SOP for me.

It was an odd election year. John Hill, a moderate,* upset Dolph Briscoe, a reasonably popular conservative governor, in the Democratic primary. This was an early sign that Texas conservatives were drifting away from their hereditary party. Bill Clements, a gruff Texas oilman, former Democrat with strong ties to John Connally, and former deputy defense secretary in the Nixon and Ford administrations, spent millions of his own money to win the governorship. With Texas Democrats still outnumbering Texas Republicans by a big margin, he almost drilled a very expensive dry hole. In the end, however, he squeaked by Hill, thanks to superb media, good organization, and a lot of crossover

---

*In a footnote to history, my daughter Mary Bonner married John Hill's grandson, Hunter Perrin, in 2005. They now live in Los Angeles, where Mary Bonner is an actress.

votes from conservative Democrats who regarded Hill as too liberal. Clements became the first GOP governor in Texas in 105 years.

Another Texas Republican also made his first bid for office in 1978. George W. Bush, then thirty-two, ran for Congress in a sprawling West Texas district that included Midland. That's where the Bushes lived when they first moved to the state. In the GOP primary, an opponent charged that "Junior" had "Rockefeller-type Republicans such as Karl Rove to help him run his campaign."

Rove "is a twenty-seven-year-old guy who works in my dad's office in Houston," George W. responded. "He has had nothing to do with my campaign. . . . I doubt he even supports Rockefeller." Junior won the primary but lost the general election to Kent Hance, a conservative Democrat.

Everyone knows what became of George W. Bush. Here's what became of Price Daniel, Jr. Devastated by his loss to Mark White, he returned home to Liberty, Texas. In January 1981, his wife shot him to death with a .22-caliber rifle, then beat the rap with Racehorse Haynes as her attorney. This story later showed up in a dreadful made-for-TV movie, a sad testament to a life and career that held such promise.

Another candidate, John Tower, retained his senate seat in '78. We ran into each other on the campaign trail one hot summer day in San Antonio and repaired for drinks to the old Menger Hotel. That's where in 1898 my hero Teddy Roosevelt recruited Texas cowboys of varying degrees of sobriety as Rough Riders to fight in the Spanish-American War. Over vodka martinis, Tower said, "You know something, Baker? This is a squalid business we're in."

"Speak for yourself, Senator," I replied. "I'm new to all this."

After losing my race, I still didn't find the business squalid. I wasn't disillusioned, but I was exhausted. So was Susan, who had attended so many campaign coffees on my behalf that she might have been mistaken for the Folgers Lady. We retreated to Florida for a little R&R.

We hadn't been vacationing for more than a day or two when George called. "Let's get going," he said. I knew what he meant.

George and I had talked many times since 1976 about the possibility of his running for president. I had promised to help if I were in a position to do so. Now he was ready to go.

Early on, George turned to me one day and asked, "Am I crazy to do this?" Even fellow Texans—who tend to admire bold action—were ridiculing him. "George, you don't mean you're gonna run against John Connally?" he was asked more than once.

Connally, a Texan's Texan who looked and sounded like central casting's idea of a president, had been planning a run for as long as George. John and I had crossed paths a few times over the years, but it wasn't until the Ford campaign of 1976 that I really got to know him. One of my duties at the Vail meeting where I was named Ford's campaign chairman was to host this fellow Texan (and fellow former Democrat). Over the next few months, the former Texas governor and U.S. treasury secretary was a great help to our campaign.

When I ran for attorney general, Connally made an appearance on my behalf at a fund-raising event in Fort Worth. Beforehand, he and his wife, Nellie, Susan and I, and Peter Roussel from my campaign staff were visiting in the hotel where the event was to be held. At one point, Connally stood up and in that deep, rich voice of his said, "Jim, if the ladies will excuse us, I'd like to have a word or two." We went into the next room. "Jim, I'm gonna run for president," he said, "and I hope you will help me."

I was never quite sure whether he asked because he was impressed by the job I had done for President Ford or because I was the only guy around who had run a Republican general election campaign for president in the last fifteen years and hadn't done jail time. Either way, I said I couldn't help. My first allegiance was to my friend George, I told him.

While the relationship between George Bush and Connally was always civil, it was never warm. I think George was disappointed when President Nixon appointed Connally as treasury secretary in 1971. It was largely at Nixon's urging that George had given up his safe seat in the House to run for the Senate against Ralph Yarborough. After that, George rightly believed he should have been rewarded with a cabinet position. The Connally family never considered George a real Texan and was, I think, somewhat envious that George, not John, eventually won the presidency.

Most of the business community supported Connally, which gave him credibility and a good source of campaign funds. (John was the only major candidate who turned down federal matching funds in the primaries, which, in theory, permitted him to raise and spend more money than other candidates.) Still, I told George he wasn't crazy to run, and I meant it. In my mind, he was the best-qualified candidate. He had what it took to be a strong campaigner and a fine president. After Nixon resigned in 1974 and the newly sworn-in President Ford was considering whom to nominate as his vice president, I had jotted down my thoughts on why George should be considered. Under the heading "Fit to be Pres.," I wrote: "Look at record in life—a record of success":

> Successful Yale—scholastically (Phi Beta Kappa) and athletically (capt. baseball team); war record—decorated—shot down; successful businessman; Congress—first Repub. from Houston—Ways and Means Committee as freshman; UN Ambassador; RNC—toughest job in country over last eighteen months.

In the four years since I had made those notes, George had added to his résumé, serving as our first liaison to China, then director of the CIA. (George's 1980 campaign slogan would be "A president we won't have to train.") My notes also included several other pluses, including:

> Age, geography (Conn. and Tex.), foreign affairs experience, admired by Repub. Party leaders in all sections of country, respect of those who knew him in Congress (both sides of aisle), reputation for honesty and integrity (above all), outgoing, articulate, intelligent, fair (votes convictions), competitive.

In addition to all this, he had many friends and acquaintances around the country, thanks to his family and business connections and his personal and political travels. George and Barbara's legendary Christmas card list was testimony that they never forgot anyone they had met.

Lest someone tag George as a loser because he had been beaten in two Senate races, I wrote: "Precedent for pres. losing race for Senate—William McKinley." (I later learned that our nation's twenty-fifth president had, indeed, lost two races, but for the House of Representatives in 1882 and 1890, not the Senate.)

Let's be frank about another reason George Bush ran in 1980. He was ambitious. So was I. Despite George's impressive résumé, however, he was a long shot; Ronald Reagan was the clear front-runner for the Republican nomination. But we believed we could win by using a model developed by another long shot, Jimmy Carter, in 1976. And if George made a credible run for the nomination but lost, there was always the possibility that he might be tapped for vice president.

I saw no downside. George was relatively young. He would turn fifty-six in 1980. Even if he lost, he would be only sixty in 1984. Going around the track is very important in presidential politics. The first time out, win or lose, you learn a lot. Besides, you've got to take your shot. Look at Bill Clinton in 1992. Big-name Democrats such as Lloyd Bentsen and Dick Gephardt saw George's 89 percent approval rating after the first Gulf War—the highest in the history of presidential polling—and decided to wait until next time. Clinton jumped in anyway and wound up becoming a two-term president.

After President Ford lost in 1976, George and I talked about taking that shot. On a 1977 trip to China, we quit talking generalities and started talking details. By the end of that year, we had set up a political action committee called the Fund for Limited Government. This was not exactly a campaign vehicle, but it was a legitimate way to raise money to pay for George's travel around the country. On these trips, he spoke about his philosophy of government and strengthened ties with local Republican leaders. By the time he formally declared his candidacy on May 1, 1979, he had already visited forty-two states.

I served as chairman of the fund even before I ran for attorney general. We operated out of a small office on Main Street in what had been the Houston Bank & Trust Company Building. We had a very small staff that included Jennifer Fitzgerald, George's assistant since 1974. Our first two hires were twentysomethings with lots of energy—a young man by the name of Karl Rove and a young woman named Margaret Tutwiler.

No one would ever wonder whatever happened to them. Karl, of course, later became George W. Bush's chief political strategist in runs for the Texas governorship and U.S. presidency. Margaret served as my assistant (her title was deputy assistant to the president for political affairs) when I was President Reagan's White House chief of staff and as assistant secretary for public affairs when I was secretary of the treasury and assistant secretary of state for public affairs when I was secretary of state. In the George W. Bush administration, she served with great distinction as ambassador to Morocco and then as under secretary of state for public diplomacy and public affairs. She is now an executive vice president of the New York Stock Exchange. To this day, I consider her one of my most loyal and capable advisers. She has incredibly sensitive political antennae and an uncanny feel for the way things will play in the press and with the public.

George and I got things going in earnest after my return from Florida. Before the end of 1978, we spooled up the Fund for Limited Government and created an exploratory committee that eventually became the George Bush for President Committee. We also started raising money. And we paid courtesy calls on both Gerald Ford and Ronald Reagan to advise them of George's intentions.

President Ford and George had always gotten along very well, and I still had great respect for the former president. "If you don't run, I would like to help George," I told him. He said he was uncertain of his plans, but he released me to work for my friend. Former Governor

Reagan was very friendly and thanked us for coming out to tell him of George's plans. He was noncommittal about whether he would run, but we believed he would.

This was not my first contact with Ronald Reagan. We first met—very briefly—when he spoke at a 1972 Nixon for President event I organized in Houston. Four years later, we crossed paths in the fight for the nomination during the primary season, and when he helped President Ford in the general election. I fondly remember one exchange we had. I was in my office at the President Ford Committee headquarters when Pete Roussel came running in.

"Bake," he said, "there's a guy on the phone who wants to talk with you. He says he's Governor Reagan."

"He's some kook, just get rid of him," I replied. (Campaigns get a lot of strange calls.)

"He really sounds like the governor," Pete said.

"Well, you don't think he'd be calling me, do you?"

"No, I don't. But it sure sounds like him."

So I picked up the phone. "Hello?"

"Howard?"

It was indeed Reagan, but he was trying to reach a different Baker—the senator from Tennessee, Howard Baker. Over the years, Howard and I became good friends. In the early eighties, my son Jamie worked on his staff when Howard was Senate majority leader. And this wasn't the last time someone confused Howard and me. We refer to each other as "O.B."—Other Baker.

In 1978, Reagan helped me campaign for attorney general. He headlined a fund-raiser in Lubbock at which we auctioned off hunting and fishing equipment.

George Bush spent more than three hundred days on political travel in 1979. Not me. An effective campaign chairman or manager doesn't need to go out on the road very much. Indeed, he shouldn't. His job is to plan the travel, name a good advance team for each visit, help organize the candidate's speeches and public statements, and manage the campaign finances—in short to administer the operation. It's grunt work, but it's necessary grunt work. It frees the candidate to be the candidate. (David Bates, a fine young man from Houston, traveled with George and did a first-class job.)

To better manage the campaign, I moved to the Washington area in January 1980. Susan and little Mary Bonner later joined me in a rented home in Alexandria, Virginia. (The other kids were either away in college or stayed in Houston for the time being.) I didn't immediately take a leave of absence from Andrews Kurth, but I did significantly reduce my partnership share. This resulted in my foregoing much of what I otherwise would have had of the largest payday in the firm's history—a big fee for fighting off ambitious tax collectors, spurious wills, and wannabe heirs to save the Howard Hughes estate for family members in Houston.

Running the primary campaign for a little known, underfinanced long shot would prove to be very different from running the general election campaign for a sitting president. The 1976 Carter model looked nothing like the 1976 Ford model. Still, there are certain characteristics common to all successful campaigns, the most important of which is organization.

The first step was to get the right people in place. George and I recruited his old Houston friend Bob Mosbacher to be finance chairman. Bob, who had served in the same role for President Ford's campaign, gave us instant credibility with Republican insiders and helped immensely as I recruited the rest of our core staff, most from the Ford campaign. Bob Teeter, Ford's pollster, joined us. So, too, did three talented operatives: David Keene, a dyed-in-the-wool conservative who had worked for John Sears; Rich Bond, a young Bush loyalist; and Pete Teeley, a very effective press aide for New York's liberal senator Jacob Javits, who had himself campaigned for President Ford. David served as political director, Rich was field director, and Pete was our press person. Others with the very good team we put together were David Sparks, Bill McInturff, Susan Morrison, Fred Bush, Joe Hagen, Jonathan Miller, Emily Ford, Alixe Glenn, Mary Ashmun, Rob Quartel, Tom Lias, and Betty Green.

It was not surprising that we were able to attract such good people. The American public may not have known or appreciated George Bush at the outset of the campaign, but he was well known and well liked by Republican insiders. They appreciated his service to the party and the nation, and knew that Ford also liked and trusted him.

Most of the other candidates would have been happy to have had these folks. In addition to Reagan and Connally, Senate Minority Leader Howard Baker, Senator Bob Dole, and Representatives John Anderson and Phil Crane joined the race. Although George often noted in his speeches that labels were for cans, not candidates, the consensus was that Reagan, Connally, Dole, and Crane were the conservatives, and Bush and Howard Baker the moderates.

At the beginning, George was an "asterisk in the polls"—a candidate with numbers so microscopic that they did not even show up in the polls. When he later cracked the polls, the campaign staff made some celebratory lapel pins that trumpeted our number, "3%."

As chairman of the RNC, George had inevitably bruised his share of GOP egos, but he also made a lot of friends and established valuable contacts. These friends and contacts helped us raise money and set up organizations in the critical caucus and primary states—particularly the early contests in Iowa and New Hampshire. Our strategy was to do so well in these venues that the cluttered seven-candidate field would quickly be reduced to two—Ronald Reagan and George Bush.

New Hampshire, historic site of the first primary of the season, had long been a make-or-break state. Until 1976, Iowa had not; candidates paid little attention to the state's caucuses, even though they came before New Hampshire's primary.

Jimmy Carter changed that. While opponents Birch Bayh, Fred Harris, Morris Udall, and Sargent Shriver focused on New Hampshire, the lesser-known governor from Georgia worked ceaselessly back and forth across the plains of Iowa. His unexpected victory there gave him momentum in New Hampshire. We knew an Iowa win would have the same effect for Bush.

Looking at the glass as half full instead of half empty—an essential trait for politicians—we believed George's low rank in the early polls was an advantage, not a disadvantage. If he won or even made strong showings early on, he would exceed expectations. In politics—and in governance, too—the name of the game is to do "better than expected." That's why a long shot who scores a strong second can sometimes win more press attention than a better-performing front-runner. In 1968, for instance, President Johnson polled the most votes in New Hampshire's Democratic primary, but his primary opponent, antiwar candidate Senator Eugene McCarthy, won the headlines by doing better than anticipated.

How does a little-known candidate become better known? Some Bush backers thought we should work the major media markets to win face time on television. This is what Connally and Howard Baker did. I disagreed. As I told a reporter early in the campaign, "To cure the name-identification problem . . . you have to win early, the same way Jimmy Carter did, and you can't win those early ones by standing in the lobby of the Waldorf-Astoria in New York."

Ronald Reagan liked to joke that George spent more days in Iowa than he, Reagan, had spent hours. George was a tireless campaigner. With Rich Bond running our operation on the ground, we scheduled appearances from dawn to dusk—on farms, at factories, in homes, and at rallies.

Retail politics takes time. Despite George's intense effort on the campaign trail (and a complementary wholesale effort: television ads that began airing in Iowa in early October), a November 28–December 1, 1979, poll by the *Des Moines Register* showed we trailed Reagan by 36 points—50 percent to 14 percent. The January 21 caucuses were only seven weeks away, and the front-runner looked unbeatable.

By this time, Maine and Florida had each held presidential "beauty contests." These were merely straw polls in advance of state conventions

or primaries, not elections of delegates, but we took them seriously—
and most other candidates did, too—as an important forum for trying
to beat expectations.

Howard Baker was the favorite in Maine, a state in which Reagan
was making no effort. He was also the candidate we had to knock out
early because he and George were fishing from the same pond. We
quietly engaged a young Maine state legislator named Josie Martin to
run an under-the-radar effort. She did a masterful job, and in early
November 1979, George shocked everyone by beating Baker in Maine.
Several days later Reagan won the Florida straw poll convincingly, a
blow to Connally, who had invested heavily there. Howard Baker and
John Connally never recovered from these early knockdowns in straw
polls for which no delegates were at stake.

Each party was to hold a debate in Iowa the first week in January.
The much-anticipated Democratic showdown between President Carter and Teddy Kennedy never materialized. Citing the Iranian hostage
crisis, the president refused to leave the White House. This put the
spotlight on the GOP debate. We, too, had a no-show. On the advice
of campaign manager John Sears, Reagan passed, the only Republican
to do so.

During the final week, we sent out about *one million* pieces of mail
and made thousands of telephone calls. None of our opponents
matched this effort.

One hundred six thousand Republicans attended the caucuses, far
more than ever before. The final preference vote was stunning: Bush
upset Reagan, a candidate who had been running for president since
1968, a man who four years earlier had come close to wresting the
nomination away from a sitting president. The count: Bush 33,530
(31.6 percent), Reagan 31,348 (29.5 percent). "Hell," said Charlie
Black, one of Reagan's political operatives, "I didn't know it was gonna
be a *primary.*"

In the afterglow of victory, an ebullient George Bush announced
that he now had the "Big Mo"—momentum—heading into New

Hampshire. The weekly newsmagazines gave him extensive coverage, and dozens more reporters now clamored to travel on our rented campaign plane, an old nineteen-passenger turboprop Fairchild. (Unlike some other candidates, we never raised enough money to get a state-of-the-art airplane. For a long time George flew coach in commercial aircraft.)

George flew ahead in the polls, too. He had been down 19 points to Reagan in New Hampshire. Suddenly he was 6 points ahead. In the Puerto Rico primary, he whipped Howard Baker by 60 to 37 percent. He also took the lead in Florida (for a time) and built up sizable leads in Massachusetts and Illinois.

Still, as George has since acknowledged, the Big Mo boast was unfortunate because it raised expectations too high. We had every reason to be excited about the win in Iowa, but Reagan had hardly campaigned and we had barely beaten him. One week after the caucuses, *Wall Street Journal* reporter James Perry praised George's "organization and hard work." But, he added, "post-Iowa, Mr. Bush is so confident that he verges on cockiness." Cockiness is bad news for political candidates, and verging on it is nearly as bad as going all the way.

My first big opportunity to lower expectations came at a Sperling Breakfast shortly after Iowa. With the help of Pete Teeley, I jotted down some talking points for this meeting with the Washington press, including these:

> We would like to win New Hampshire and will do everything possible to do so. However, the reality is that N.H. is one of Ronald Reagan's strongest states. Combine that factor with the all-out efforts of Howard Baker and even John Anderson and you realize how difficult it will be. . . .

> After all the work that George Bush put into Iowa . . . his reaction to his victory was one of elation. It is a human quality that all of us have at one time or another. . . . Frankly, that was a week ago. The realities

are that he still remains an underdog, and he and the entire campaign staff realize that.

As we lowered expectations for New Hampshire, we also wanted to raise the public's image of George as a man of substance—the president you wouldn't have to train. In Iowa we had answered the question "George who?" Now, in New Hampshire, we had to answer, "George why?" We also wanted to stress the age difference between Bush (fifty-five at the time) and Reagan (sixty-nine). Our campaign literature featured pictures of George jogging, and he frequently went out for runs with the media in tow.

Teeter's polls showed that George needed to build a substantive base, to give voters a reason to back him other than the fact that he had won in Iowa. Bob, David Keene, and I all told George that he should be more specific on the issues. He wasn't quite as responsive as we hoped. After the campaign, George would tell reporters Jack Germond and Jules Witcover, "There was a feeling, well, now you've got to be more substantive, and I would argue with them: I think I am being substantive, I'm answering questions every day. . . . I just didn't see it. I'll readily concede at this point I may have been wrong. But I didn't feel any great need to do something different."*

The New Hampshire debates offered all seven candidates an opportunity to be substantive. I will wager, however, that few Americans remember the issues discussed at those events. What many do remember, however, is the following exchange between Reagan and moderator Jon Breen in Nashua on Saturday, February 23—three days before the primary. Reagan and Bush had agreed to a one-on-one debate that evening, but when Reagan took the stage, he argued that all candidates should be allowed to participate.

---

*Germond and Witcover's campaign journal, *Blue Smoke and Mirrors,* helped me recall a number of events from the 1980 campaign, as did George Bush's book, *Looking Forward.*

BREEN: Turn Mr. Reagan's microphone off.

REAGAN: I'm paying for this microphone, Mr. Green [*sic*].

Some observers believe this was the turning point in the campaign, that those seven words won the nomination for Reagan. That may be an exaggeration, but there is no question that it created momentum for him that was more real and sustainable than our Big Mo. And while all credit is due to Reagan for seizing the moment, I have to admit that we made our share of mistakes in New Hampshire.

Nashua was the second debate. Three days earlier all candidates had met in Manchester for a forum sponsored by the League of Women Voters. By this time, Reagan had pulled even with George in the polls. Stunned by the Iowa results, he was now campaigning with purpose and energy. Reagan also had the support of William Loeb, influential publisher of the state's largest newspaper, the *Manchester Union Leader*. George, an "oil man from Texas," was a "phony candidate" pushed by "the entire Eastern Establishment, the Rockefellers, and all the other power interests in the East," he thundered. Most viewers thought Reagan did better than George and the other five candidates in the Manchester debate, and by the twenty-third the race was no longer even. According to most polls, Reagan now held a double-digit lead. He was beginning to solidify his base, which was far larger than George's.

Although we were now trailing, we were excited by the prospect of the Nashua debate. This was to be Bush vs. Reagan, *mano a mano*. Our strategy from the beginning had been to engineer a two-candidate race. Still, it had not been our idea to leave the other candidates out. Jerry Carmen, Reagan's New Hampshire chairman, first broached the idea of a two-candidate debate. Hugh Gregg, our state chairman, quickly persuaded the *Nashua Telegraph* to sponsor the event. Why would the Reagan forces want to anoint George as their only serious challenger? Carmen later explained that he believed the debate would cut George down to size.

The other five contenders were not happy to be excluded. Dole complained to the Federal Election Commission (FEC) that the *Telegraph* was, in effect, giving the two invited candidates an illegal campaign contribution. The FEC agreed. When the Reagan camp then suggested that the two candidates split the cost, $1,750 each, Gregg refused, and those of us running the national campaign went along with him. This was a huge mistake.

The Reagan camp, having paid all the costs, then set an ambush, secretly telling the other candidates that if they came to Nashua, they might be included. Everyone showed up except Connally. He was going for broke in South Carolina. When Dole, Baker, Anderson, and Crane filed onto the stage of the Nashua High School auditorium as the debate was to begin, the majority of the 2,500 in the audience applauded. George and the *Telegraph*'s Breen stuck to their guns, however: as previously agreed, this was to be a two-man, not a six-man, forum.

As Reagan began to explain why he wanted to include the other candidates, Breen called for technicians to turn off his microphone. That's when Reagan hit it out of the ballpark.

The debate proceeded without the other challengers. As they left the stage, an angry Bob Dole came up to me and poked me in the chest. "Jim Baker," he said, "you'll regret this." (I worked very closely and effectively with Dole when I was chief of staff and in my cabinet posts. We were, and are, friends.)

Matters didn't get any better later. As Teeley told George a couple of days later, "The bad news is that the media are playing up the confrontation. The good news is that they're ignoring the debate, and you lost that, too."

Reagan had indeed "paid for this microphone," and we paid dearly for getting ourselves in a position where it mattered. His numbers rocketed. On primary day, he took 49.6 percent, Bush got 22.7 percent, and Howard Baker ran third with 12.1 percent. As I said, a candidate and a campaign manager learn a lot by going around the track that first time.

If there was a silver lining to New Hampshire, it was this: Howard Baker, John Anderson, and the others did even worse than we did. A week later, George rebounded to capture the Massachusetts primary. That same evening Reagan won Vermont. Baker, who finished poorly in each of these contests, dropped out. Connally was done four days later when Reagan crushed him in South Carolina.

Anderson held on longer. By finishing second in both Massachusetts and Vermont on March 4, he exceeded expectations and drew press attention away from the victors. His continued presence helped us to a certain degree because it made it more difficult for Reagan to paint George as the candidate of the left. But in the end, it hurt us worse than it hurt Reagan, because Anderson drew moderates who would otherwise have been more likely to vote for George.

Nineteen-eighty marked the first time I led the campaign of a candidate trying to win his party's nomination. When I had assumed the chairmanship of the Ford effort, he was already the party's choice. What does a campaign leader do from headquarters while his candidate is on the road during the primary season?

In addition to running the demanding day-to-day operation, I regularly offered George my counsel. A memo I sent him two days after Massachusetts and Vermont, "Reaction to March 4 Primary Results," is typical.

> You should be careful to stick to your position on Ford's statement that Reagan cannot win in November—i.e., you don't agree with that, but [you do believe] you would be a better candidate with a better chance to win.
>
> You should not refer to Anderson's showings in Massachusetts and Vermont as freakish or aberrations. This makes you look petty. It wouldn't hurt to even congratulate him on a good showing and [say] that it remains to be seen if he can do as well in states where the voting is primarily by Republicans, as it is in the vast majority of states.

I also coordinated George's campaign appearances. He was particularly effective on a series of campaign television broadcasts called "Ask George Bush." An April 8 memo to eleven members of our campaign staff offers a glimpse of the logistics for these events. For the four "Ask George Bush" telecasts in Pennsylvania, I spelled out everyone's duties. The goal was always to leave as little to chance as possible. We wanted a rested and prepared George Bush to meet a candidate-friendly audience that would ask candidate-friendly questions:

John Morgan . . . is responsible for the buying of all required [television] airtime (after checking with me regarding cost).

Red Caveney and Bob Goodwin, working with Dave Sparks, are responsible for securing the four locations . . . and all advance work.

Each lead advance man . . . is responsible for lining up five or six articulate members of the audience to carry the Q&A at his event. Questions will be restricted to non-press members of the audience.

Dave Gergen is responsible for writing the opening and closing remarks for George Bush for each telecast.

Margaret Tutwiler is responsible for seeing that five hours are blocked out prior to each telecast for the following: one hour staff briefing on local issues; one hour jogging; one hour on site with [our television consultant] Bill Carruthers; and two hours off.

After Iowa, we had won only in Puerto Rico, Massachusetts, the District of Columbia, Maine, and Connecticut, but by late April all major candidates except Reagan and Bush had dropped out, and Pennsylvania offered the two-man matchup we had been looking for. We put everything we had into the April 22 primary—that's where the campaign charged that Reagan's plan to stimulate the economy with a tax cut was "voodoo economics"—and came away with a solid victory in the popular vote. Unfortunately, thanks to an odd "blind voting" system in that state, Reagan won more delegates and added to his commanding lead.

The conventional wisdom was that the loss in New Hampshire had put George off his game for a while. Perhaps. Again, this was his first trip around the track. By contrast, Reagan had run for president in both 1968 and 1976.

George is about the most competitive human being I have ever known. He does not like to lose, but as state after state went for Reagan, George never hung his head. Instead, he displayed the same determination he had shown at age eighteen, when instead of heading straight from prep school to Yale, he became a naval aviator in World War II.

Everything came together on May 20 in Michigan. I turned on the television that night expecting George's 57 to 32 percent landslide there to be the lead story, but ABC and CBS had a different take. They proclaimed George the winner in Michigan all right, but the big news, they said, was that by winning Oregon, Reagan had collected more than the 998 delegates needed for the nomination.

Three delegate-rich states—New Jersey, Ohio, and California— would hold primaries in two weeks on June 3. Reagan was way ahead in his home state, but George was strong in the other two. If the arithmetic was right, however—and it seemed to be—even if George won both New Jersey and Ohio, Reagan would still win the nomination. Now what?

We needed to raise about $500,000 to challenge in California. In light of the delegate projections, should we keep fighting? Could we? It would be "goddamn tough" to raise the money in California, I told reporters. At the same time, George told the *Washington Post* that without sufficient funds to contest California, campaigning in Ohio and New Jersey "might be an irrelevancy."

Washington Post staff writers Bill Peterson and David Broder reported that I said we were closing down operations in California. They quoted me as follows: "If you can't do California, then you can't argue to people that you still have a shot [at the nomination] in terms of the numbers. And once you concede that, why do you stay in?"

If I had it to do over again, I would have chosen my words more carefully. I didn't think through all the ways my remarks might be interpreted. It was obviously not my intention to throw in the towel. Only the candidate could do that. Nor was I trying to pressure George himself to call it quits. I was just answering questions honestly and being realistic about our prospects. In New Jersey, however, reporters were telling George, "Baker says you don't have anything going in California. Does this mean you're dropping out?"

George was furious, and I don't blame him. He wanted to know exactly what I had said. I had only talked about not having enough money on hand to compete in California, but I shouldn't have done it, I admitted, because it gave the impression that we had no choice but to pull the plug. The reality, of course, is that George had to decide soon whether to stay or go, but I hadn't done him any favor by talking so openly about our rocky financial position.

George had done a remarkable job in transforming himself from the pollsters' asterisk into the only legitimate challenger left standing. He had won Iowa and seven other contests. "The remarkable thing about Bush's candidacy is not that it failed, but that it kept going as long as it did," the *Post*'s Peterson wrote. I agree. And because it had kept going, George would be the only candidate besides Reagan with a significant number of delegates at the convention. This meant he had a good shot at becoming the party's vice presidential nominee.

Candidates for president should never create the impression that they are really running for vice president or would be happy to end up in second place. We had carefully followed this rule. It wasn't that difficult because George always said privately that he wasn't sure if he was interested in being vice president.

I now told George that it was time to decide and that I thought he would blow any chance of getting on the ticket if he ran a hopeless campaign much longer. Relations between the Bush and Reagan camps were already strained. Each candidate had tried to observe Reagan's Eleventh Commandment, *Thou shalt not speak ill of fellow Republi-*

cans, but opponents in a two-way race invariably rub each other the wrong way.

George decided to return to Houston to think about what to do. He talked at length with family members, close friends, and senior campaign staff. As I remember, senior consultant Vic Gold, Dave Keene, and I argued that he should withdraw. His family resisted. Neither they nor George wanted to disappoint supporters in Ohio and New Jersey. Nick Brady, who was running the operation in New Jersey, believed George could still win his state. Why not try to strengthen George's hand by picking up the delegates there and in Ohio?

For what? I asked. "You're the only person at the convention who's going to have any delegates," I said. "They have to start thinking who they're going to run with, and the longer you hang in if you don't have a mathematical chance of winning, the more you're going to hurt your chances." It went like that all weekend.

On the campaign airplane, Kenny Rogers's song "The Gambler" was sometimes played on the public address system. George and others had often joined the chorus, "You got to know when to hold 'em, know when to fold 'em." It's hard for a campaign manager to tell a candidate to fold 'em, particularly when that candidate is as competitive as George Bush, but I did not back down. On May 26, George announced he would stop campaigning and throw his support to Reagan. "I'm an optimist," he said, "but I also know how to count to 998."

George was a logical pick for vice president, but he was not Reagan's first choice. Nevertheless, he held a good hand. What other candidate had comparable delegate and party support at the convention, or a perfect résumé to balance the ticket?

At the convention, however, the answer switched from George Bush to a most surprising possibility, Gerald Ford. George's future suddenly depended on whether a former president might accept the role of vice president or, as Walter Cronkite suggested on the air, a "copresidency."

My future looked even more uncertain. I had managed two hard-fought battles to deny Ronald Reagan his party's nomination—one successful, the other not. I'm a realist, and realistically there was no room for James A. Baker, III, in the Reagan campaign or a Reagan presidency. It looked like time for me to fold 'em, too.

FIVE

"I WANT TO TALK TO YOU BEFORE YOU GO BACK TO TEXAS"

GEORGE H. W. BUSH is nothing if not likable. Yet it has been reported that when the 1980 primary season ended, Ronald Reagan was not happy with George and did not want to select him as the vice presidential nominee. Let me set the record straight: *This is true.* At that moment, Reagan's preferred candidate for running mate was ABB—Anybody But Bush.

Why? After gracefully withdrawing from the presidential race and throwing his support to Reagan, George seemed the obvious choice. He was a proven vote-getter, the only other candidate who would arrive at the mid-July convention in Detroit with a significant number of delegates. He had a superb record of government service. As a Connecticut Yankee who had relocated to Texas, he balanced the ticket geographically, and he was perceived to be more moderate, politically, than Reagan. Selecting him would give the ticket credibility with undecided voters in the middle. But as Reagan biographer Lou Cannon writes, the governor thought George lacked spunk because he didn't stand up for himself in the school auditorium during the fight over whether to allow the other Republican contenders to debate.* The Bush campaign also lost points when it used the label "voodoo economics" for the policies that would later be known as Reaganomics.

"Lacked spunk"? George joined the Navy straight out of prep school, won his wings at eighteen, and flew fifty-eight combat missions. He parachuted out of a burning aircraft and was rescued by a U.S. submarine. He won the Distinguished Flying Cross. In business, he took the risks of entrepreneurship and started a thriving company. His résumé in politics and public service was replete with tough, high-profile positions. (I've listed his offices often enough in this book and won't do it again here.) Most recently, of course, he had entered the 1980 race as an overwhelming underdog and emerged as Reagan's only serious contender.

But at that time, these facts about the man seemed to matter little. Aware that the party's nominee held him in relatively low regard, both George and I thought he probably didn't stand much chance of winning a spot on the November ballot. We were even less hopeful when we learned that several prominent Republicans and members of the Reagan inner circle were lobbying for themselves or other strong candidates. Nevada Senator Paul Laxalt, one of Reagan's best friends and most ardent supporters, wanted the job. Senator Howard Baker and Congressman Jack Kemp were also apparently in the running. And Henry Kissinger, Alan Greenspan, Bryce Harlow, and others (including, it was rumored, the GOP chairman Bill Brock) pushed their own ABB candidate—the president many of them had once served, Gerald Ford.

Ford? To be sure, Republican polling revealed that a Reagan-Ford ticket in 1980 had the potential to be as appealing and successful as a Ford-Reagan dream ticket might have been in 1976. But the Ford crowd had another motive, the one everyone in politics shares:

---

*Cannon covered the White House for the *Washington Post.* His biographies—Reagan: *His Rise to Power* and *President Reagan: The Role of a Lifetime*—were excellent sources for researching this book.

ambition. If they could return their man to Washington, even in the number-two position, they would enhance their own chances of returning to power and influence.

At first, the odds of seeing Reagan-Ford bumper stickers appeared remote. The contentious battle for the 1976 GOP nomination had left both of these fine men with scars. They were anything but close. Moreover, Gerald Ford had been *president of the United States,* the most powerful man in the world. Traditionally, vice presidents were far removed from real power. The absurdity of having a former president come back as No. 2 became clear when I asked myself how I would address Ford. "Hello, Mr. President–Vice President"? Or was it, "Hello, Mr. Vice President–President"?

On his way to the convention, Gerald Ford stopped over in Omaha. By coincidence, I was there for a corporate board meeting, and he offered me a ride to Detroit. I hadn't heard any talk about his being considered for vice president, and we certainly did not discuss the subject. The flight was too short and the plane too crowded for much more than pleasantries. Even if we had been alone and I had known what was coming, however, I would not have broached the subject. Given my role in George's campaign, that would have been inappropriate.

But now, George's future was very much up in the air, and so was mine. Shortly after George withdrew in late May, I received a call from Reagan press secretary Lyn Nofziger. He asked if I were interested in serving as political director for the Reagan campaign.

As I have noted, titles are important. I did not presume to demand the position I had in 1976—campaign chairman. Governor Reagan had installed his trusted friend Bill Casey in that capacity. But for me to have accepted the title "political director" would have been quite a comedown for someone who had managed the campaign of a sitting president in the last election. I told Lyn I was interested in helping Reagan, but not in that capacity.

My role was still unresolved when I met with Casey in Dallas in late June. He was a Wall Street lawyer and former Securities and Exchange Commission chairman, but he hardly looked the part. Success may have gone to his head, but not to his wardrobe. When he wasn't rumpled, he was disheveled. Still, people paid attention when he spoke. They had to; he was a chronic mumbler. We talked about how to organize Reagan's effort against President Carter and how I might help the campaign.

At that time Jimmy Carter was 10 points behind Ronald Reagan in the polls. The soft economy, foreign policy failures (most notably the Iran hostage crisis), and the president's primary battles with Ted Kennedy were taking their toll. "But if anyone in your organization is wearing rose-colored glasses," I told Casey, "they're making a mistake. You can win this election, but it's going to be close."

I told him he was up against some tough, hard-nosed, capable politicians—accomplished gut-fighters who would do whatever they thought it would take to elect their guy. For all his problems, Carter had one big advantage, incumbency. He also had a campaign team that had been around the track. "They've got their act together," I said.

Governor Reagan had an advantage, too, one the Ford campaign did not have in 1976. As the party out of power, the GOP's convention would come first. "This gives us a head start in organizing and gearing up for the fall," I said.

"But don't expect to get much sleep until the election is over," I told Casey. "You're going to find incredible demands made on you and your time. You won't find enough hours in the day to do all you have to do." This is where I thought I could help. We discussed ways I could make his job easier, including by serving as a deputy chairman. He wasn't ready to make a decision, so we agreed to talk again later.

After we met, I sent him drafts of an organizational structure and budget based on our 1976 campaign, along with more ideas about strategy. He had not solicited this material. I wanted to help, but if the material also happened to remind him of my experience and expertise, so much the better. When the convention began on Monday, July 14, however, my role was still uncertain.

Reagan did not reveal his choice for vice president before arriving in Detroit. If he had, he would have removed all suspense from the proceeding. I'm all for injecting a bit of drama to win votes. That said, I offer this warning to any candidate who waits until the convention to name a running mate: make sure you have thoroughly vetted your choice (and that the press has done so, too) before making the announcement. We did not do that in 1988, the year George beat Michael Dukakis, and it was a mistake.

President Ford and I went our separate ways after we reached Detroit on Saturday, July 12. He stayed at the same hotel where Governor Reagan was headquartered, the Detroit Plaza. I joined George in the block of rooms we had reserved at the Hotel Ponchartrain. The Bush party was relatively small—Barbara and other family members, spokesman Pete Teeley, some other loyal campaign staffers, and a few friends, such as Dean Burch, an old Goldwater hand who had served in the Nixon and Ford administrations. Governors, other elected officials from the primary states where George had done well, and other prominent Bush delegates stopped by from time to time to pay their respects and talk about the one and only topic at conventions, politics.

President Ford's opening-day speech roused the delegates, pleased Governor Reagan, and created momentum for the possibility that Ford might be offered the number-two spot. This set off a series of closed-door meetings that did not conclude, literally, until the eleventh hour Wednesday evening.

Only the insiders know exactly how the Reagan-Ford courtship played out. Later reports said Bill Casey and Ed Meese headed a small group of Reagan loyalists who sat down with a Ford team led by Henry Kissinger and Alan Greenspan. One thing is clear, however: the talks would never have happened without a green light from Reagan.

Meanwhile, back at the Ponchartrain, we were not privy to the private meetings, but rumors were flying. Everyone claimed to have the inside story, so we hesitated to believe anyone. Besides, what could we do? About all George had scheduled during these long hours were a few delegation drop-bys, a duty he shared with other party luminaries, to motivate the troops for the fall campaign. On Tuesday morning, for instance, he met with the California delegation. Then it was back to the hotel to hurry up and wait.

On Wednesday evening, all hell broke loose. In an interview with Walter Cronkite, Ford laid out the general conditions under which he might be willing to take the second spot. He said that he would need "reasonable assurances" that his role would be substantive rather than ceremonial. Cronkite said this sounded like he was proposing a "co-presidency." Ford never used this word, but his failure to correct the anchorman led most viewers to believe that was exactly what he meant. By some later accounts, the former president's team had proposed that he would chair the National Security Council and have veto power over some appointments, which—if not exactly a copresidency—was pretty far down the road in that direction.

"As I watched that interview," Reagan wrote later, "it really hit me that we had some major problems with the idea: *Wait a minute,* I remember thinking, *this is really two presidents he's talking about.*" Still, negotiations continued as Wednesday evening wore on.

While Ford's remarks gave Reagan pause, they brought the floor alive. It now seemed that the dream ticket might soon be a reality. Reagan, the rumor went, would come to the convention center to make the announcement.

Meantime, George *was* on his way to the hall. He had one of the coveted prime-time speaking slots. He delivered a powerful speech, but the Ford story overshadowed his appearance.

Our mood in the Bush suite was not festive. Like those on the convention floor, we awaited the announcement of the once improbable, now seemingly inevitable, Reagan-Ford ticket.

Unbeknownst to us (and the delegates), the deal was not done. Reagan and Ford representatives were still trying to work out the details. Unable to reach agreement on the makeup of Ford's staff and its role, the parties broke off negotiations. Sometime between 10:30 and 11:30 P.M., Ford visited Reagan's suite. It's not going to work, he said. Reagan agreed.

I was not there for that meeting, obviously, but I was present for what happened next. Shortly after the Ford visit to Reagan, the phone rang in George's suite. I answered. Drew Lewis, who had been President Ford's man in Pennsylvania in 1976 and was now working for Reagan, was on the line. "Jim," he said, "Governor Reagan would like to speak to Ambassador Bush."

Was this a courtesy call to tell George that Reagan had selected Ford? Or was it the call we had been hoping for? Nobody was sure, although most in the suite suspected that the news would be bad.

After a brief exchange of pleasantries, George was silent as Reagan spoke. The tension built until George finally turned our way, smiled, and gave us the thumbs-up.

During the conversation, Reagan had asked George two questions, one general and one specific: Can you support my policy positions? And, can you support my position on abortion?

In his campaign literature, George had spelled out his position on that sensitive issue. "I am personally opposed to abortion. I am also opposed to a constitutional amendment that would override the Supreme Court decision, because there is a need to recognize and provide for exceptional cases—rape, incest, or to save the life of a mother. I oppose federal funding of abortion, with the exceptions noted above."

George and Reagan had a fundamental disagreement over whether to overturn *Roe v. Wade* with a constitutional amendment, but they agreed on several points. Both opposed abortion, personally. They also accepted that it was justified to save the life of the mother. (George would add cases of rape or incest.) And they both opposed federal funding for abortions, except in those cases.

Some of Reagan's more zealous backers may have hoped he would select a running mate whose positions on abortion and other social issues were identical to his own. The reality, however, is that just about the only way a presidential nominee and vice presidential nominee who had run against each other in the primaries could be in complete agreement on everything would be through cloning. The best No. 1 can realistically hope for, and unequivocally demand, is that No. 2 supports his policies. If in good conscience George could not have answered Reagan's two questions, "Yes, sir," he should have (and, I'm sure, would have) declined the nomination.

To put an end to the Ford rumors, Governor Reagan then went immediately to the convention hall to introduce his running mate. This broke the tradition that nominees were not supposed to appear on the podium until they were ready to give their acceptance speeches. "The roof almost came off," Reagan wrote later. "As George and I stood there together, it was almost as if we were putting the party back together again."

The next day, not surprisingly, the press honed in on their differences, real and imagined. This was to be expected. The two candidates had offered competing visions in the primaries. Any alliance between former adversaries is bound to raise questions. The goal now was to de-emphasize the issues that divided them and emphasize the ones on which they agreed.

When reporters asked George to state his positions on the Equal Rights Amendment (ERA) and abortion, he answered with language that could not be used to drive a wedge between the running mates or make news: "My view is that the big issues, the major issues in the fall . . . are going to be economic and foreign affairs. I oppose abortion and I'm in favor of equal rights." Note that he didn't say he supported the ERA, which Reagan opposed; he supported equal rights, as did Reagan. Nor did he say that he opposed the constitutional amendment on abortion that Reagan favored; he said, quite honestly, that he opposed abortion.

"I'm not going to get nickeled and dimed to death by detail," he said as the questions continued, adding that he would not "get bogged down in . . . permitting you to accentuate the differences with the governor during the campaign, which have been minimal."

The press also zeroed in on the point that George Bush, not Gerald Ford, was standing beside Ronald Reagan. "Isn't it clear then, Governor, that Mr. Bush was your second choice?"

"I think the situation is unique."

George was also asked if he was the number-two choice for the number-two spot. "It's unique," he echoed. "What difference does it make? It's irrelevant. I'm here."

In 2004, a perhaps even more "unique" situation arose when Democratic presidential nominee John Kerry spoke to Republican Senator John McCain about running as his vice president. After McCain declined, Kerry and the man he did choose, Senator John Edwards, faced questions similar to those faced by Reagan and Bush.

Would a Kerry-McCain ticket have been effective? Perhaps, because McCain appealed to the independents and ticket splitters who most likely made up most of the undecided voters in 2004. But having said that, it's important to remember that in presidential politics, people vote for the *top* of the ticket. Further, party switchers rarely do well. Case in point: John Connally.

In a brief speech accepting his nomination Thursday night, George endorsed the platform, compared Reagan to Eisenhower, encouraged Democrats and independents to vote Republican, and then got off the stage. This was Reagan's night.

Following a film about his life, the nominee walked onto the podium to a thunderous ovation. "Well, the first thrill tonight was to find myself, for the first time in a long time, in a movie in prime time," he joked.

Reagan hammered campaign themes that would take him to the White House and, afterward, provide a blueprint for his administration—repairing what he called "a disintegrating economy" and "a weakened defense."

"We're taxing ourselves into economic exhaustion and stagnation,"

he said, "crushing our ability and incentive to save, invest, and produce." The answer: tax cuts and better control of federal spending.

On defense, "the Carter administration lives in a world of make-
believe," he charged, citing the Soviet invasion of Afghanistan, the
Iranian hostage crisis, increased Soviet military spending, and the general failure of American leadership. His own priority, he said, would
be "in working for peace, to ensure that the safety of our people cannot successfully be threatened by a hostile foreign power." "We know
only too well that war comes not when the forces of freedom are
strong, but when they are weak."

What was even more important than his views on the issues, however, was his soaring rhetoric. "It is impossible to capture in words the
splendor of this vast continent which God has granted as our portion
of His creation," Reagan said. "There are not words to express the
extraordinary strength and character of this breed of people we call
Americans." Language like this was balm to the spirit of a nation
wounded by Vietnam, Watergate, and a fractured economy.

As the convention ended, it was clear what George would be doing
for at least the next three and a half months. My future remained uncertain. Philip Uzielli, a great friend of mine from Princeton who died
in August 2001, once told *Time* magazine, "Jimmy gets depressed
whenever he faces the prospect of having to return to practicing law.
He craves the action." To this charge, I plead guilty.

Reporters on the Reagan plane later fabricated phony book titles
and attributed them to figures in the campaign. Showing that they understood my need to be where the action was, the title they picked for
me was *Third Choice, The Only Campaign in Town,* by Jim Baker, referring
to my serial support for Ford, then Bush, then Reagan. Ouch!

Among the other "books" was *Prospects for Nuclear Disarmament,* by
Amy Carter. When people talk about the debate between Amy's father,
President Jimmy Carter, and Ronald Reagan in 1980, they generally
cite one famous line by each candidate. President Carter's came in response to a question about arms control. "I had a discussion with my

daughter Amy the other day before I came here and asked her what the most important issue was," the president said. "She said she thought nuclear weaponry and control of nuclear arms."

Amy Carter had just turned thirteen. Her father's point, I think, was to suggest in an understated and indirect way that Reagan's views on nuclear disarmament scared children—an echo of the infamous "daisy commercial" Democrats used against Goldwater in 1964. What he did instead was feed a delicious straight line to the press, late-night comedians, and Reagan supporters. Remember the "Ask Amy" posters that popped up at rallies?

Reagan's memorable line had the opposite effect on his campaign. When Carter charged that Reagan had opposed legislation to create Medicare, Governor Reagan looked the president in the eye, sighed, and said, "There you go again."

Point. Set. Match.

I remember a different line from that evening of October 28, one uttered about an hour earlier. Governor Reagan and I were in his holding room at the Cleveland Music Hall, just the two of us. In a few minutes, he would take the stage for his only debate with President Carter—an event that could make or break his quest for the presidency. He was calm, almost serene. "Jim," he said as his stage call came near, "would you excuse me a moment. I want to have a word with the Man Upstairs."

I left the room with a deeper understanding of, and respect for, Ronald Reagan. He was, as I would see again and again, a man of faith who very privately, but very genuinely, drew his strength from a higher power. It was an extraordinary privilege to serve him, that night and for the next eight years.

That term of that service began a month or so after the convention. By then, George and I had agreed that, because of my prior general election experience with President Ford, I should work with Reagan, not Bush, if a suitable role and title could be found. Dean Burch would manage George's run for vice president.

Reagan officials told me they wanted me to work in the campaign, but not as a deputy chairman. Apparently Ed Meese, Reagan's long-time adviser and a deputy chairman himself, did not think the new kid on the block should have such an important title. After further conversations with Casey and others, I finally said, "Why don't you just call me a senior adviser and task me as you need to." This was acceptable to Meese. Soon, I was put in charge of debate negotiations and preparation.

The fictitious bibliography compiled by reporters also included a "book" authored by Casey: *The Man Who Never Was*. There actually is a book by that name about a famous ploy by the British military during World War II. This title, however, was meant to suggest that Casey was a clueless campaign leader.

I had some serious problems with Casey in years to come, but it was not fair to portray him as a cipher as a campaign leader. He had replaced John Sears early in the primary season to provide better organization, not strategy. Until Stu Spencer joined the campaign full-time about six weeks after the convention, however, strategy was the problem.

When Stu jumped to the Ford campaign in 1976, he fell out of favor with the Reagan camp. After Reagan got off to a slow start in August and lost his lead in the polls, several of us, including Mike Deaver, began to lobby for Stu's return. More important, Nancy Reagan wanted him back.

It was a great move. Stu hadn't changed at all since we had worked together on the Ford campaign. He still eschewed memos, still wrote most of his ideas on matchbook covers, and still had great political instincts.

In late August, we came up with a good way to use George's foreign policy experience to help the ticket, by sending him to China, where he had served as the U.S. liaison under Ford. The trip got off to a rocky start, however, when Governor Reagan publicly repeated his commitment to strengthening official relations between the United States and Taiwan. This created confusion about whether the Reagan campaign was supporting or undermining the Carter administration's 1979 joint communique between Washington and Peking that recognized the People's Republic of China and acknowledged that Taiwan was part of China. The Chinese government said Reagan had "insulted one billion Chinese people."

Quite naturally, he became angry at the press for picking apart his remarks on China and other issues. Sensing trouble ahead, I finally decided to offer my two cents' worth. In a letter dated September 4, 1980, I wrote, "Dear Governor Reagan:

> You have not asked for these comments and, having managed two presidential campaigns, I am well aware that the one thing a candidate receives too much of is unsolicited advice. However, it is critical that you be elected president . . . and I would not be discharging my obligations to you unless I gave you my advice when I feel strongly about a matter that could affect the outcome of the election.
>
> A general election for president is, of course, far different than a series of primaries. The attention of the entire country is focused upon the process continuously during September and October. The press scrutiny is intense and many times unfair. Each and every word is scrutinized by hordes of press for the slightest mistake. That simply is a fact, a fundamental rule of the game. And, the campaigns have to play the game by this rule.
>
> You are a tremendous campaigner and the best politician with television that I have ever seen. You are also a person of intense conviction and strong intellectual honesty. I happen to share with you a common political philosophy. . . .
>
> However, if you are to achieve a position to put your beliefs into practice, you will have to, for the next sixty days, be extremely careful about every statement which you make.
>
> Further, you have excellent relations with the press. Most of them like you. They do not like Jimmy Carter. This is a great

advantage. The press should not be blamed for picking your statements apart. They did this to Jimmy Carter in 1976 and, again, it is one of the rules of the game. . . .

Your political instincts are good. Your campaign organization is farther along than we were in 1976 and, in my opinion, you are going to win this election. Just remember that for the next sixty days, every word you say will be picked apart, or rather "nitpicked" apart. All you have to do is be aware of that, accept it, and otherwise be yourself.

This was not an easy letter to write. After signing it, I added a postscript by hand: "I've hesitated about sending this because I know you're inundated with advice. However, I'm confident you'll accept it in the spirit in which it is offered." My confidence was well placed. Ronald Reagan was comfortable enough with himself to listen to advice and even criticism from staff members he trusted. He knew the final decision was always his.

It also didn't hurt that on the same day I sent the letter, Spencer began traveling with the governor. From that point forward, the opportunities for on-the-fly, issues-oriented exchanges between the candidate and the media were kept to a minimum. At the same time, Reagan became less critical of the media.

A *Washington Post* poll on September 14 showed that Reagan had pulled even with Carter at 37 percent. John Anderson, running now as an independent, was at 13 percent.

I wrote my September 4 letter from our headquarters in Arlington, Virginia. I was stationed there with Casey, Meese, Bill Timmons, Clif White, and many others. In addition to Stu, Reagan was accompanied on the road by Lyn Nofziger, Mike Deaver, and Martin Anderson, an issues adviser.

My job as debate negotiator began in earnest after Labor Day. Jody Powell, President Carter's press secretary, who was among those with whom I negotiated, once described the process as "bluff and counterbluff, scheming, conniving, and hard-nosed horse trading." A debate negotiator's client, frankly, is his candidate, not the press and not some abstract ideal of how presidential debates should be conducted. The goal of the negotiator is to try to win a format and rules that play to his candidate's strengths and minimize his weaknesses. Staging can be just as important as format. Just as a movie director doesn't want a vertically challenged actor to appear shorter than his leading lady, for instance, a debate negotiator doesn't want his candidate to appear shorter than the opponent.*

Many Reagan advisers doubted he would do well in a debate. They feared that he might misspeak and sound less than presidential. When I came on board, they told me that unless our candidate fell significantly behind in the polls, we would prefer staying out of any debates.

I disagreed. The Great Communicator would do well, I believed. My well-founded show of faith in the candidate was, I think, an important factor in Reagan's later decision to find a major role for me in his administration.

In 1980, the League of Women Voters lacked the presumptive mandate to sponsor presidential debates that the Commission on Presidential Debates now enjoys. The league had, however, sponsored the 1976 Ford-Carter debates. Without consulting the candidates, the organization proclaimed that it would sponsor three presidential debates in 1980.

And what of John Anderson? The league said that he could participate if he averaged at least 15 percent in the major polls. Anderson was hovering around that figure, so it appeared that he would be eligible for the first debate on September 21.

---

*All three of my candidates—Ford, Reagan, and Bush 41—were taller than their opponents, so we always held a bargaining chip on height. Each time, we let the other side adjust the podium, add a riser, or do something else to compensate, but we always got something good in return. I have a short anecdote about the Dukakis negotiation, but I'll save it until later.

The timing of the league's announcement couldn't have come at a better time for us. It shifted press attention from other issues to President Carter's refusal to participate in a debate that included Anderson. Polls showed that the third-party candidate was drawing more voters from Carter than from Reagan, and the president apparently didn't want to give Anderson any greater stature or to expose himself to a two-on-one attack from opponents with the common goal of removing him from office.

President Carter's decision to boycott the first debate was a magnificent gift to our campaign, because the league went ahead with a two-candidate event. I proposed, not totally in jest, that we place an empty chair on stage to symbolize the chief executive's absence. That didn't happen, of course, but the setup offered Ronald Reagan and John Anderson free airtime to explain why they would be better presidents than the one who hadn't bothered to drive forty-five miles from the White House to the Baltimore Convention Center.

Prior preparation was essential to prevent a poor performance. Republican Senator John Warner and his wife at the time, actress Elizabeth Taylor, graciously loaned Governor Reagan their large country estate in Wexford, Virginia, as a base of operations. We turned the garage into a replica of the stage in Baltimore.

Some critics have portrayed Ronald Reagan as an empty suit whose only skill was reading lines. Nothing could be further from the truth. He was a hard worker and a voracious reader who understood the importance of this first debate and did his homework. I generally presented that homework to him in the form of a briefing book prepared by David Gergen, Martin Anderson, and Richard Allen. Nancy Reagan, fiercely protective of her husband, strongly suggested we avoid giving him overly lengthy memos. He was most adept at digesting material that was already reduced to its essence.

We had agreed with the Anderson campaign on a one-hour debate in which each candidate would have two and a half minutes to respond to a panelist's question, then the other candidate would have one minute and fifteen seconds for rebuttal. We found the perfect stand-in to help our candidate practice—a bright young Republican congressman from Michigan who had previously served on Anderson's staff, David Stockman. He joined us at Wexford and did a terrific job in our mock debates. Among the "journalists" asking questions were John Tower, Alan Greenspan, Jeane Kirkpatrick, and Howard Baker.

Casey, Meese, Deaver, Gergen, TV consultant Bill Carruthers, and Frank Hodsoll, an aide from my days at the Commerce Department, took notes and made suggestions. Stockman later wrote about my role in the mock debates. "Jim Baker looked like the efficient production foreman, with a pencil behind his ear," Stockman said. "He cussed a blue streak and told off-color jokes. . . . He had a way of moving things along, of pointing to the ceiling and spinning his arm around in a 360-degree circle, saying, 'Let's go, let's move it.'"

Reagan made his share of mistakes during these run-throughs, as does every candidate in preparing for presidential debates. These mock debates are always harder than the actual ones because the stand-in candidates and panelists ask the toughest questions they can come up with, and the candidate has to work impromptu. That's why we practiced long hours and filmed the sessions for in-depth post-mortems. When the night of the debate arrived, Ronald Reagan was confident. So was I.

Both candidates acquitted themselves well and, of course, nobody thought the absent president had won. Anderson set the tone with the very first question of the night.

"What politically unpopular measures are you willing to endorse, push, and stay with that might provide real progress in reducing inflation?" asked Carol Loomis of *Fortune* magazine.

"It seems to me that the people who are watching us tonight . . . are truly concerned about the poor rate of performance of the American economy over the last four years," the congressman replied. "Governor Reagan is not responsible for what has happened over the last four years, nor am I. The man who should be here tonight to respond to those charges chose not to attend."

Teddy White, the legendary chronicler of presidential campaigns, said this debate marked the turning point of the election, but I believe the Carter-Reagan debate in Cleveland just one week before the election was more important. Despite Reagan's solid performance against Anderson, the head-to-head debate between President Carter and Reagan almost didn't materialize because some Reagan advisers still didn't trust our candidate.

Reagan had no fear of debating Carter, but he relied on his advisers to determine whether the event would help the campaign. Many at our headquarters, including the well-respected Dick Wirthlin, still opposed a last-minute face-off against the president. Polling suggested that the election was already going our way, they argued. In their view, a debate couldn't help us much, but it might hurt badly if the governor said something akin to former President Ford's remarks about Soviet domination of Eastern Europe. Stu Spencer and I were among the few advisers in the pro-debate camp.

I didn't think we had done a good enough job defining our candidate. He was still seen by many as a mere actor who could not be trusted with our nation's nuclear arsenal. A good debate would reassure people that he had the intelligence and judgment to be president, we argued. He was also more likable than Carter, and after years in television, he understood the medium better than any other political figure at the time.

Stu and I saw one other advantage. Once debates are announced, they tend to freeze the campaign. It's difficult for a candidate who is trailing to pick up ground while prepping for a debate. Carter, who was slightly behind, probably wouldn't see his numbers move until after a debate—and then, of course, only if he won.

Our campaign's greatest fear was an October surprise that could thaw a frozen campaign in a hurry. Just as Democrats in 2004 thought the incumbent administration might apprehend or kill the terrorist leader Osama bin Laden just before the election, Republicans in 1980 thought the incumbent administration might suddenly make a deal to bring home the fifty-two kidnapped American hostages who had been held by Iranian militants since November 4, 1979. An honorable resolution of the hostage crisis would have been welcomed by all Americans, including candidate Reagan, but there's no doubt that it would have given the sitting president a huge boost. Eleventh-hour resolutions of long-running crises may invite widespread cynicism, but they are almost impossible to challenge politically.

Knowing that the release of the hostages would in all likelihood give President Carter a dramatic lift, we wanted the Carter-Reagan debate to take place as close to the election as possible. This would give our candidate one last chance to make his case. If a release came after the debate, we would be out of luck.

On October 16, both candidates spoke at the annual Al Smith Dinner in New York City. Our man came off as warm and charming. The president didn't. This helped move the no-debate faction among Reagan advisers to consider letting the nation see a side-by-side display of the two candidates' personalities. At a meeting the next morning, the brain trust and the candidate discussed the pros and cons of a two-man debate.

We were already leading in enough states to win the electoral vote, but there were still too many undecideds. Our colleagues finally agreed with Stu and me that if the timing could be worked out to our advantage, a debate could help our candidate.

On October 17, the league invited the two candidates to a debate in Cleveland on October 28. Anderson, who had dropped below 10 percent in the polls, was not invited. We accepted the idea of a two-candidate debate, but reserved judgment on the time and place.

On October 20, Dean Burch, Bill Carruthers, and I met in Washington with representatives from the league and the president's campaign (Jody Powell and my fellow Texan, campaign chairman Bob Strauss). We agreed that the league would pick the moderator and panelists, that the debate would run ninety minutes, and that the format would allow for follow-up questions.

We could not, however, agree upon a date. "We really like November third," I told the press later. "About 10 percent of the people make up their minds on election eve; let them make their decision on the basis of the debate." An election-eve debate could become an American tradition, I suggested.

Carter's representatives pushed for the earliest possible date, October 26. They didn't like the election-eve idea because it wouldn't let candidates correct mistakes before the next day's voting. Perhaps, I countered, but it would also give the media less opportunity to influence voters by declaring a winner. (Remember this was before the proliferation of the cable news channels. The instant analysis we take for granted today was not quite so instant twenty-six years ago.)

Truth be told, I was much less interested in establishing an American tradition than I was in getting the best date (meaning the latest possible date) for my candidate. We met again the next day and compromised. The debate would be in Cleveland on the day the league had originally proposed, October 28.

Reagan again prepared at Wexford. Stockman rejoined us, this time impersonating President Carter. There were a few new faces, too, including the conservative columnist George Will. He served as a mock reporter-panelist. In his columns, George had long made it clear that he supported Reagan, but at the time he did not disclose his role in preparing for the October debate. Another Reagan supporter, William Safire of the *New York Times*, turned down our invitation to help at Wexford. Whether it is proper for a political columnist to assist a candidate without revealing it to his readers, is, I suppose, a matter of conscience or editorial policy. Whatever the answer, it wasn't our problem. We were glad to have George's help.

I must wrestle with my own conscience, however, over something else that happened well before the debate with President Carter had been agreed to. At our campaign headquarters in Arlington, Virginia,

Bill Casey handed me a notebook. I looked it over, saw that it contained debate-briefing material for President Carter (as opposed to strategic or tactical matter), and then passed it on to David Gergen and our debate preparation group. Stockman later said the book helped teach him to answer questions as Carter might. He also said Carter's answers during the debate mirrored the material in the book.

Casey did not tell me how he had come into possession of the book and I did not ask. There were only a few possibilities. Someone in the Carter campaign could have provided it. Someone from our campaign could have stolen it. Or someone outside either campaign, but sympathetic to Reagan, could have found it and passed it on to Casey, perhaps after it was misplaced by a Carter staffer. The first possibility seemed most likely. It was no secret that many people in the Carter administration were dissatisfied with the president.

The story of the briefing book did not become public until 1983, when Laurence Barrett of *Time* magazine mentioned it in his book about the early years of the Reagan administration, *Gambling with History*. "Foul play," said many from the Carter campaign. Congress and the FBI initiated inquiries.

President Reagan and all in his administration, including me, cooperated fully with these investigations of what became known as Debategate. I said that Casey had given me the book and that I had no knowledge of how it had come into his possession.

Casey, who was then director of the CIA, told a different story. He said he did not recall seeing the briefing book and claimed he would have remembered if he had given it to me. (Bill Casey died of brain cancer in 1987. It's enough to say now that his memory was not operating at 100 percent of capacity when he gave those answers.)

At one point there was talk of strapping Casey and me up to lie detectors to determine how the book had come into the campaign's possession. That didn't happen; the investigators settled for affidavits. I was glad. I was telling the truth, but I feared that someone who headed the CIA would know how to game a polygraph examination.

After a yearlong investigation, a House subcommittee published its findings in a May 1984 report that found Casey less than credible and corroborated my version after hearing from an aide whom I had told in 1980 about receiving the material from Casey. (In a separate three-page report several months earlier, the Justice Department said it had not uncovered credible evidence of a crime.) In Washington, D.C., a good reputation can quickly become a bad one. Until the report was released, my credibility and reputation for truth-telling were in question, and that disturbed me.

"Baker was fastidious about propriety," Barrett wrote in his book. I was and still am. As an unnamed White House official would tell Lou Cannon during the investigation: "Here's a person who writes his own $700 check when he has a door cut in his White House office and makes a big deal of reporting every gift." And as President Carter's own campaign manager Bob Strauss said, "But I'll tell you, anything Jim Baker says, I would judge to be true. There isn't anyone in American politics whose ethics I place higher than Jim Baker's."

I wasn't responsible for obtaining the briefing book, and I told the truth. But should I have asked Casey where he got the book? Should I have refused to pass the material on to those preparing Reagan? These are legitimate questions. In hindsight, my answer to both questions is yes.

House Speaker Tip O'Neill and President Reagan were good friends who rarely agreed on the issues. One thing they did agree on, however, was that the briefing book did not change the result of the 1980 election.

Going into the debate, Reagan was slightly ahead. He then won the debate, not because of any prepared answers, but because he made no major mistakes, softened his image on defense issues, and came across as the more appealing candidate.

I admire Jimmy Carter for his faith and sincerity. While I do not agree with all he has done, particularly in lobbying other nations not to support a UN resolution to use force to kick Iraq out of Kuwait in

1990, I believe he has handled his post-presidency well and been a force for good in many ways. At the dedication of the Reagan Library in 1991 and at the 1994 groundbreaking for the James A. Baker III Institute for Public Policy in Houston, his remarks about me offered good evidence that he appreciates the fundamental difference between a political adversary and a personal enemy. Considering how hard I worked to defeat him in 1976 and 1980, I'm very grateful for that. In 2005, I had the pleasure of serving as cochair with him on the highly productive Commission on Federal Election Reform, which recommended a number of very useful ways to improve the administration and security of U.S. elections. (I'll say more about that later.)

The first question to Reagan was exactly the one we needed to defuse concerns about our candidate's call for a U.S. military buildup and a less accommodative stance toward the Soviet Union. "You have been criticized," said Marvin Stone of *U.S. News & World Report,* "for being all too quick to advocate the use of lots of muscle—military action—to deal with foreign crises. Specifically, what are the differences between the two of you on the uses of American military power?"

"I believe with all my heart," Reagan replied, "that our first priority must be world peace, and that the use of force is always and only a last resort when everything else has failed. . . . And to maintain that peace requires strength."

Perfect.

After the debate, polls showed a sharp drop in the percentage of Americans who were concerned that Reagan might lead the nation into war.

"There you go again" was not Reagan's only memorable line that night. Another came in his closing statement. "Are you better off than you were four years ago?" he asked. For too many Americans, unfortunately, the answer was no.

Reagan's margin of victory a week later surprised all of us. He won forty-four states and carried the Electoral College 489–44. The popular vote split 50.5 percent for Reagan, 41 percent for Carter, and 6.6

percent for Anderson. America had embraced the California governor and wanted to give his ideas a chance.

On the day after the election, President-elect Reagan called me in my hotel room at the Century Plaza. "I want to talk to you before you go back to Texas," he said. When I relayed this news to Susan, she broke into tears.

SIX

"PRESIDENT REAGAN DOESN'T LIKE YES MEN. WHEN HE SAYS NO, WE ALL SAY NO"

IT WAS TWO DAYS after the 1980 presidential election. I had just walked up to the door of Ronald and Nancy Reagan's home in the Pacific Palisades section of Los Angeles, reluctant to knock. Inside, the next president of the United States was meeting with Bill Casey, Mike Deaver, Ed Meese, and others.

Ronald Reagan had won the election on the strength of his ideas about how to make America a better place. Now he had asked me to serve as his White House chief of staff because he wanted a Washington insider—someone with hands-on experience in our nation's capital—to help him turn those ideas into reality. At this moment, however, I felt much more like an outsider. The other men in the meeting were the president-elect's close friends, two of whom he had relied on for many years. I, on the other hand, was not only a newcomer but also a former adversary who had fought hard, twice, to deny him the presidency. *What are you doing here?* I asked myself as I hesitated at the door.

Ronald Reagan quickly spotted me through the window and rescued me from my momentary paralysis. "What are you doing out there, Jim?" he asked with a smile as bright as the California sunshine. "Come on in."

Some of Ronald Reagan's supporters would have been happier if I had stood outside that door for the next eight years. He was their hero. I was the enemy, as they saw it—someone from the dark side, lacking credentials as a loyalist to the man or his ideas.

They weren't afraid to make their feelings known. Not long after the announcement of my appointment, Pete Teeley sent me a memo about a phone call from Pam Curtis, with whom we had worked in the 1976 Ford campaign. She had bumped into Donald "Buz" Lukens, a Republican state senator from Ohio who had served as a regional political director (RPD) for the Reagan campaign. Teeley reported:

> Curtis said Lukens is bad-mouthing JAB [James A. Baker] in incredible fashion all over town. He is apparently attempting to organize the RPDs to make a stand against what has been happening in terms of building this administration, including the White House staff.
>
> He is furious at JAB ... for the fact that this administration does not reflect the thinking of the New Right, nor is it putting in key positions right thinkers. He went on to call Ed Meese a "dumb shit" and [an] "incompetent" who cannot organize or manage [and] who has sold out to JAB. . . .
>
> When asked by Curtis if he was repeating all this around town, he replied, "I'm telling you and everyone else I run into. JAB is nothing more than a representative of the Eastern liberal establishment, and this is nothing more than a George Bush administration comprised of retreads from the Nixon and Ford administrations. . . ."
>
> Lukens . . . promises to "make life miserable for JAB, Meese, and Bush."

Lukens started out disliking me for ideological reasons, but it quickly turned personal. He wanted to be appointed as the White House congressional liaison, but I passed him over for Max Friedersdorf, who had vastly more experience (he had worked for presidents Nixon and Ford) and was better qualified.

Political loyalty was important, of course, but competence mattered to me, not just whether each job applicant had been with the Gipper from the first step of his long march to Washington. Many Reagan loyalists saw this as a betrayal of their champion and their cause, and they were angry. They were the winners, they thought. Why weren't they getting all the spoils?

Two weeks before the inauguration, I talked to several critics and tried to answer their complaints. It had been my idea, I said, to appoint Lyn Nofziger, a longtime Reaganite, as the White House political director (over opposition from some other longtime Reagan advisers). I also pointed out that I had recommended several RPDs, including Lee Atwater, for important positions in the administration. "I'm a political animal—believe in political loyalty," I wrote in my notes.

What few of the critics could bring themselves to accept was that the crime that so offended their ideological and political sensibilities— placing a prototypical Ford-Bush Republican in a high position in a Reagan administration—had been committed by none other than their beloved leader, Ronald Reagan. Why? For the same reasons he had already accepted me as a campaign adviser: he trusted me to get things done, and he was comfortable enough in his own skin to accept help from any quarter. He didn't need and didn't much like sycophants. "Ronald Reagan doesn't like yes men," we would say, tongues planted deeply in our cheeks. "When he says no, we *all* say no."

Reagan also had enough confidence in his own leadership to know that no one could hijack his presidency. He understood (as did I) that my power would be vicarious, derived entirely from the office of the president. The chief of staff truly holds what is potentially the second most powerful job in Washington, but the rule to remember is that the power comes from the position not the person. The chief of staff is what the title says—*staff.*

Reagan's open-mindedness reflected more than self-confidence.

Contrary to public perception, he was much more a pragmatist than an ideologue. Yes, he had strong convictions and principles, but he was willing to compromise to get the best deal he could. "Jim," he would often tell me as we discussed strategy, "I'd rather get eighty percent of what I want than to go over the cliff with my flag flying."

By contrast, many of his less pragmatic followers hated compromise. To them, it was better to lose everything than to give an inch. They didn't understand how the system works. Pragmatism without principles is cynicism, but principle without pragmatism is often powerless. To turn ideas into policies, a leader must be prepared to fight hard—yes—but also to accept victory on the terms that can be won, even when they are short of perfection. That's the reality of politics. My leader called me to his service because he wanted to change things, not die trying, and he thought I could help.

President Reagan understood what many of his followers did not: that it's more important for the chief of staff to be competent and loyal than to be a so-called true believer (although I had a lot more faith in his ideas than I was given credit for, and that faith grew stronger over the years). He also understood that one of the most important tasks of a White House chief of staff is to look at policy questions through a political prism. After watching me at work in 1976 and 1980, he apparently believed I could do this.

The president-elect offered me the post at a private meeting in the Century Plaza Hotel in Los Angeles on the morning after the election. Almost everyone expected him to tap Ed Meese as chief of staff—including Ed—but I was not surprised. Stu Spencer and Mike Deaver had tipped me off.

Stu and Mike tell slightly different stories about how the offer materialized.* Mike says that over drinks one night about ten days before

---

*My recollection of the events leading to my appointment as chief of staff and my early days in office has been aided by two books by longtime friends—*Behind the Scenes,* by Mike Deaver, and *The Acting President,* by Bob Schieffer and Gary Paul Gates.

the election, he and Reagan were discussing appointments. Reagan said he assumed Meese would be his chief of staff. Ed, a staunch conservative with degrees from Yale (BA) and the University of California, Berkeley (JD), had caught Reagan's eye as a law-and-order deputy district attorney in Alameda County during the Berkeley demonstrations in 1964. After winning the governorship in 1966, Reagan named him legal affairs secretary. Within a few years, Ed was the governor's executive secretary, chief of staff, and chief policy adviser.

Mike says he told Reagan that "Ed would be more valuable in another role." He then suggested me for chief of staff because I knew Washington so well.

"Jim Baker. That's an interesting thought," Reagan responded.

Mike says he later spoke with Reagan confidante Bill Clark about how to head off a problem with Meese if I got the job he had expected. Clark suggested naming Meese chief counsel to the president. Mike passed this idea on to Reagan, who liked it.

In the Spencer version, Stu floated my name a week or two before Mike did, at a dinner in Dallas with Ronald and Nancy Reagan. His reasoning was the same as Mike's: that Washington was not Sacramento and that Reagan would need someone who knew the ropes in Washington. Nancy Reagan agreed.

Mike, Stu, and Nancy had watched Meese over many years and concluded he was better suited for a different position. They saw, as I would later see, that Ed was a wonderful human being, someone whose word you could take to the bank, and a superb policy analyst. He was not, however, a cross-the-t's, dot-the-i's kind of guy—the kind needed in the chief of staff's office. If he had a failing, it was that he took on too many projects and sometimes didn't finish what he started. Even his friends in the administration sometimes referred to his briefcase as the black hole. Once something went in there, it often would never come out again. But he was excellent at synthesizing policy options for Reagan.

Mike and Stu evidently discussed the idea for the first time shortly after the convention. As my stock rose in the Reagan campaign, what had been a wild idea gradually turned into a plausible alternative. Stu approached me first, and Mike joined the discussion later. I told them I would be willing to give it a try if asked, but that I doubted Reagan would want to appoint Ford's delegate hunter and campaign chairman and Bush's campaign chairman as his chief of staff.

Stu and Mike figured that the more the Reagans talked with me, the more they would warm to the idea of naming me to an important position, so they arranged for me to sit with the couple on the campaign plane, to brief them. Mike may even have set up a few Reagan-Baker dinners. Nancy Reagan soon became an ally and lobbied her husband to appoint me.

Susan was proud that I was being considered for chief of staff, but she was not enthusiastic about my taking the job. She feared that I would be so busy that neither she nor the children would ever see me. That's why she cried after that election night phone call from Reagan. She knew, as did I, that the offer was probably coming.

Before going to meet the president-elect, I had breakfast with Meese. We talked about working together under Reagan. Although I said nothing about our titles, I assumed—wrongly, as it turned out—that Reagan had already told him I would be chief of staff.

"I hope you can work with Ed," the president-elect told me when he and I met in his suite a little later. He reminded me that Meese was his friend and had served him well over the years.

I said I was sure that we could get along and suggested that Ed's position carry an impressive title, such as counselor to the president, and that he have cabinet rank. Even though Reagan seemed to like this idea and all the other pieces were falling into place, I asked for a little time to think about the offer. The arrangement would work, I explained, only if both Ed and I understood and accepted the other's powers and duties.

After meeting with me and then breaking the news to Ed that he would be counselor to the president rather than chief of staff, Reagan held a press conference that Susan and I attended. He didn't talk about staff appointments. After the event, however, he did address Susan's concerns about losing me to the job. He pulled her aside, put his hands on her shoulders, looked her in the eye, and said, "Your husband is not going to work fourteen hours a day in my White House. I don't believe in that. I believe in my people spending time with their families. Jim will be home at six o'clock every evening."

My wife is a woman of deep Christian faith. She had been praying for guidance, and this assurance came as an answer. She agreed that I should accept the post. Unfortunately, whatever the president may have believed about his people going home at night, the demands of my office were so intense that it was a very rare evening, indeed, that I got out of the office by six.

Ed was now slated for a major role in the White House, but the boundaries between us were still unclear. My solution was to draft a memorandum to sort out our respective powers and responsibilities. As far as I know, this sort of thing had never been done before, but it was a good, lawyerly way to mark our territory at the beginning. That way, we could spend our time working together for the president, each on his own portfolio, rather than quarreling over who was on first. Ed, also a lawyer, liked this approach, and on November 13 we each initialed the document. (We initialed it again on November 17 after adding handwritten amendments.) A copy appears on the opposite page.

When President-elect Reagan made the staffing announcement on November 14, the *New York Times*'s Hedrick Smith reported that "longtime associates of Mr. Reagan" said his plan was "to do most of his policymaking with an inner circle of his cabinet." This would require "a top-level adviser and cabinet coordinator [Meese] free of the day-to-day management of the large White House operation headed by a chief of staff [Baker]."

One book says I "euchred" Meese into signing the agreement, leaving him with "a nice title and a beautiful office and little else." Yes,

A/e213
6420921
6709161

MEESE	BAKER
Counselor to the President for Policy (with cabinet rank)	Chief of Staff
Member Super Cabinet Executive Committee (in absence of The President preside over meetings) *and V-P*	Member Super Cabinet Executive Committee
Participate as a principal in all meetings of full Cabinet	Coordination and supervision of White House Staff functions
Coordination and supervision of responsibilities of The Secretary to the Cabinet	Hiring and firing authority over all elements of White House Staff
Coordination and supervision of work of the Domestic Policy ~~Council~~ and the National Security Council	With Meese coordination and supervision of work of OMB, CEA, CEQ, Trade Rep and S&T
With Baker coordination and supervision of work of OMB, CEA, CEQ, Trade Rep and S&T	Participation as a principal in all policy group meetings ~~and in full Cabinet~~
Participation as a principal in all policy group meetings	Coordination and control of all in and out paper flow to the President and of presidential schedule and appointments
attend any meeting which Pres. attends - w/ his consent	Preside over meetings of White House Staff
	Operate from office customarily utilized by Chief of Staff

as per published article

11/19/80
OK - JAB III
OK RWR

attend any meeting Pres. attends - w/ his consent.

I wound up controlling the press and legislative operations (among other levers of power), but Ed retained his position as President Reagan's top policy adviser and head of the Domestic Policy Council. In addition, National Security Adviser Dick Allen reported to him. The president and Ed were also longtime friends, and that gave him a degree of access and influence that no memorandum could ever diminish.

The third member—with Ed and me—of what soon came to be known as President Reagan's "troika" was Mike Deaver, assistant to the president and deputy chief of staff. He was a smart and talented guy, a great manager, and a genius at providing rich visuals—whether in the Oval Office or out in the country—to complement the Great Communicator's marvelous speeches. At the same time, by his own admission, he was not terribly interested in the details of policy. Most important, perhaps, he enjoyed the confidence of the Reagans, particularly the First Lady.

Ed was the only one of the troika to have cabinet rank. That didn't bother me or, as far as I know, Mike. For the most part, cabinet meetings are staged show-and-tell events. The real business of the White House is accomplished in small meetings, usually in the Oval Office.

For advice, presidents turn to people they trust, not to bureaucracies. The most heavily relied-upon advisers, generally, are those who have been with the president in the trenches of electoral politics. Traveling together, planning, taking fire and returning it, tending each other's wounds, and finally winning—these shared experiences teach the candidate who can think clearly under pressure, who can get things done, and who can be trusted. When this team comes off the road, the personal bonds are tighter than anything that can be depicted or even hinted at in an organizational chart. The members of the troika—particularly Ed and Mike, due to their years of loyal service—had that bond with their president.

Proximity is also a major determinant of power in the White House. The important business of the executive branch in Washington goes through the Oval Office. When President Reagan would turn and ask, "What do you think?" Ed, Mike, and I were usually there in the room to hazard an answer. The cabinet officers usually were not.

To help President Reagan turn his ideas into realities, I needed control of the staff working with Congress on our legislative agenda, looking after the president's political interests, getting out the message (the press office and speechwriters*), scheduling the president's time, advancing his events, and managing the operation of the White House.

Keeping up with all of this was an administrative challenge of the first order. I hired a young staffer named John Rogers, three years out of college, gave him a great title—assistant to the president of the United States for management and administration of the White House—and crossed my fingers. What a find! He ran the place like he had been doing it all his life, then followed me to Treasury (assistant secretary) and State (under secretary for management). John's flawless stewardship of these agencies gave me the freedom that every executive needs, to focus on the big picture. When I left public service, John helped me with the creation of the James A. Baker III Institute for Public Policy at Rice University. He is now an officer and a member of the management committee at Goldman Sachs.

I took the large office traditionally occupied by the chief of staff, just down the hall and around a corner from the Oval Office in the southwest corner of the West Wing. Meese moved into the office in the northwest corner that had been occupied by President Carter's national security adviser, Zbigniew Brzezinski. Deaver occupied a small dining-room-turned-office closer to the Oval Office. My quarters were not as finely appointed as others, nor was the view as good, but they fulfilled my prime objective: I wanted space where I could host and, therefore, run staff meetings.

President Reagan, by the way, also appreciated that when it comes

---

*In my opinion, the best presidential speechwriter who ever worked in the White House—at least since Lincoln—was Ronald Reagan himself. Until he became president, he wrote all his speeches. Only the constraints of time prevented him doing that in office. Even then, however, he had a fearsome red pencil.

to offices at least, size matters. When he turned seventy on February 6, 1981, the White House staff held a surprise party for him in my office. We were just past two weeks after the inauguration, and the president had not yet been down the hall to see where I worked. "Jim," he said, "this is a *big* office." Then, with the timing of a great actor, he added, "But it's not *round!*"*

Under the Meese-Baker memorandum, I was also responsible for controlling and coordinating "all in-and-out paper flow to the president" and "all presidential schedules and appointments." Except in emergencies, cabinet members were asked to request appointments with the president twenty-four hours ahead of time.

Under our handwritten addendum of November 17, Ed and I could walk into the Oval Office at virtually any time. This meant we were usually present when the president talked with cabinet members and other dignitaries. It also meant that I could walk in when Ed met with the president, and he could walk in when I was in the Oval Office. The president, of course, had the right to keep us out, but I don't think that ever happened. What did happen, however, is that Ed and I sometimes met privately with the president, without the other's knowledge.

A popular myth about the first Reagan administration is that I blocked Ed's efforts to persuade the president to push legislation on school prayer, busing, abortion, and other social issues. That simply wasn't true. Even before taking office, the president had stated clear goals for the first year—to reduce taxes, cut the rate of growth in government spending, and strengthen the U.S. military. We recognized that he would enjoy a brief honeymoon with Congress and the American people. This was the time to push the core Reagan agenda. The Carter

---

*Vice President Bush took former Vice President Mondale's office next door to the chief of staff's office. National Security Adviser Dick Allen, who reported to Meese, got an office in the basement of the West Wing, a remote location that did not bode well for him. In retrospect, layering the national security adviser from the president may have been a mistake. Bill Clark, a closer friend of the president's, assumed a more prominent role in the administration when he replaced Allen. Unlike his predecessor, Clark had Oval Office walk-in rights, just as Meese, Deaver, and I did.

administration had wasted its honeymoon by sending far too much legislation to the Hill. President Clinton would later get his administration off on the wrong foot by raising the issue of gays in the military before he had built a consensus for his legislative program. If President Reagan had immediately introduced legislation on controversial social issues, he would almost certainly have weakened—possibly even destroyed—support for his all-important tax, spending, and defense initiatives. At least that's how he felt, and he was right.

One of my major responsibilities was to protect the president. The chief of staff is, among other things, a catcher of javelins aimed at the president—by political adversaries, by the press, and—surprisingly, perhaps—by members of his own political party. Those last kind come in from close range and are usually unexpected.

I also had to protect the president from traps, and one of the surest signs of one being laid were the apparently innocent words, "Oh, by the way, Mr. President . . ." They usually sounded in the doorway at the end of a cabinet meeting or a meeting with lawmakers. Someone would linger a bit, then pretend to have an afterthought. "Oh, by the way, Mr. President, my brother-in-law Fred would make a great appointee for the Rutabaga Commission." Or "How about supporting my bill to help mass transit in Houston?"

Maybe the petitioner was a friend or political supporter. Maybe he hoped the president was too tired to resist, or that the president would agree to avoid ending a positive meeting on a negative note. Whatever was going on, however, this was obviously not the way decisions should be made. My job was to grab an elbow, say, "We'll be happy to look at Fred's résumé (or your pet legislation) and get back to you," and escort Trapper John out the door.

This preserved the president's freedom. We would consider the appointments in due course, and the president could then decide what to do as part of a coherent plan, not on a first-come, first-served basis. It would also give me time to investigate the political implications of the request.

This is just one form of javelin-catching and trap-dodging. (There are others.) They are necessary, but they win no popularity contests for a chief of staff. That was not my concern, however. I just wanted to help the president succeed.

And the real test of presidential success (and best measure of his power) is whether his policies are enacted into law. We knew from the start that winning passage of the Reagan agenda would be difficult in 1981. Republicans controlled the Senate, where the other Baker— Howard—now served as majority leader, but Democrats ruled the House under a formidable speaker, Boston's Tip O'Neill. Like the president, Tip was a good-natured Irish American with a penchant for salty jokes. The two men genuinely enjoyed sharing drinks and swapping stories, but Tip opposed most of the president's agenda and didn't plan to do him any favors.

Enter the Legislative Strategy Group (LSG), which I formed and chaired. Initially created to implement the policies formulated by Meese's policy councils, the LSG quickly evolved into a policymaking group itself. This was inevitable. For one thing, legislative strategizing inevitably morphs into policymaking, because legislative battles are fought in real time. Success requires flexibility and the ability to make changes on the fly. We could never halt the proceedings to consult every policy guru in the White House. When a key senator needs a couple of tweaks to get a bill through committee, the White House political team needs authority to say yes or no, even if the amendments have significant policy implications. The only policymaker who can be consulted at times like these is the one who counts—the president.

Meese was a member of the LSG. This was one reason it worked so well. The group gave him a way to influence the team's on-the-go work. Other key members were David Stockman, director of the Office of Management and Budget; domestic adviser Martin Anderson; congressional liaison Max Friedersdorf; and my deputy, Dick Darman.

The LSG met in my office virtually every day. The group was the brainchild of Darman, whom I first met at the Commerce Department in early 1976. He arrived there before his mentor at the time, Elliot

Richardson, who was returning from his post as our ambassador to the United Kingdom to replace Rog Morton as secretary of commerce. Dick was an extraordinarily bright and able student of government who could direct traffic through the intersection of policy and politics as well as anyone I ever met. A graduate of Harvard College and Harvard Business School, Dick had worked for Richardson in several departments during the Nixon administration. After serving with me in the White House, he accompanied me to the Department of the Treasury as deputy secretary. He is perhaps best known as head of the Office of Management and Budget from 1989 to 1993 under President George H. W. Bush. Dick is still a good friend.

The best way to succeed in high office in Washington, I believe, is to surround yourself with strong, bright, and hardworking assistants. As chief of staff, I recruited the best I could find. A leader who is afraid of hiring strong people is usually a leader on a glide path to failure. My senior aides were Dick Darman as staff secretary; press secretary Jim Brady and his deputy, Larry Speakes; John Rogers, administration; Elizabeth Dole, public liaison; Fred Fielding, White House counsel; Max Friedersdorf, congressional liaison; David Gergen, communications; Pen James, personnel; Lyn Nofziger, politics; Rich Williamson, intergovernmental affairs; and Margaret Tutwiler, my indispensable executive assistant, who later headed the White House Office of Political Affairs and served as spokesperson at the departments of both Treasury and State. Margaret's grasp of politics and press relations was better than anyone I ever met, and I owe much of whatever success I achieved in public service to her on the political side and Darman on the policy side.

Dick and Margaret aren't shrinking violets, and neither were my other staffers. This resulted in spirited, sometimes contentious, one-on-ones and group meetings with the boss. I wanted straight talk, and these people gave it to me. In the end, this helped us make better decisions.

After the election and the Meese-Baker agreement, I was put in charge of the White House transition team for my area of responsibility.

Meanwhile, we had a team—Gergen, pollster and adviser Dick Wirthlin, and others—working on a strategic plan for the president's first one hundred days in office. That group actually started research before the election on the first terms of Presidents Franklin Roosevelt, Eisenhower, Kennedy, Nixon, and Carter. We wanted to know what had worked and what hadn't.

The group's report began with charts that summarized each president's activities during the first one hundred days in several categories, such as travel, press conferences, and meetings with foreign leaders. Under "Constitutional Responsibilities," for example, we saw that Eisenhower and Kennedy had delivered State of the Union addresses within days of taking office. FDR, Nixon, and Carter had waited a year, and President Reagan decided to do the same.

Under "Domestic Affairs—Meeting with Various Groups," a chart summarized how often the presidents had met with their cabinets, congressional leaders, governors, mayors, and representatives of their political party—even whether they entertained the Supreme Court. FDR, for instance, usually met with his cabinet every Tuesday and Friday. Ike had fourteen cabinet meetings during the first one hundred days. Nixon and Carter usually held weekly meetings. As for JFK: "One [meeting] on 1/26. Preference for individual meetings with cabinet members; on 4/11 says cabinet meetings a waste of time."

Behind the charts were chronologies of each president's first one hundred days. For example, on January 21, the day after his inauguration, President Carter "pardoned everyone who violated military Selective Service Act between 8/4/64 and 4/28/73 (military personnel evading the Vietnam draft); announced nominations of ten people for posts in the State Department . . . ; hosted small inauguration reception for some Democratic National Committee members."

Based on the report and Wirthlin's polling, we developed a day-by-day schedule for the pre-inaugural week and the first three weeks of the Reagan presidency. During the week leading up to the swearing-in, for instance, we planned "emphasis on hard work in preparation for presidency; push story of the Reagan economic inheritance; Iran hostage policy announcement; and ... unannounced visits to Washington memorials, mix with crowds."

During the first week, we planned an "emphasis upon new leadership coming into office; show decisive break with past, fresh hope for future; set brisk but not frantic pace; begin building constituencies support (e.g., blue collar)." We also developed an action agenda for the president to implement these goals. On January 22, for instance, the president would issue "directives to department heads re: fraud and waste and cutting costs."

Like Jimmy Carter in 1976, Ronald Reagan had run as an outsider who criticized the Washington status quo. Unlike Carter, however, we made plans to extend an immediate olive branch to Congress. On January 23, according to our plan, the president would host a breakfast for the GOP leadership and have dinner with Tip O'Neill. On January 25: "Super Bowl—invite in top congressional leaders (including a few Democrats) to watch on big screen, White House family theater."

During the transition period, I tracked down former chiefs of staff and asked for their advice, just as I had asked former delegate hunters and campaign managers for advice before assuming those positions. The counsel I received from my predecessors ranged from the practical to the philosophical to the personal. Notes from my conversation with Dick Cheney filled four legal pages. His suggestions included:

- Restore power and authority to the executive branch.
- Orderly schedules and orderly paper flow [are] way you protect the president. Most valuable asset in D.C. is time of Ronald Reagan.
- Keep a low profile. Talk to press always on background. If you become a major public figure you lose credibility, feathering your own nest rather than serving the president.

Dick also told me to "be an honest broker. Don't use the process to impose your policy views on people." I highlighted that advice, and it served me well during my four years in the White House. I had my own opinions on most important issues—particularly on the politics of doing something about them—and understood, as well, that some issues were not important enough for presidential attention. That said, the president was best served when all sides got a fair hearing in the White House, and that's what I tried to provide.

Dick's predecessor Don Rumsfeld, like a true CEO, presented me with a twelve-page primer that he had written four years earlier, "Rumsfeld's Rules for the Assistant to the President." The first and last notations were the same: "Don't play president." Other advice:

- Assume that everything you say and do will be on the front page of the *Washington Post* the next morning and conduct yourself accordingly.
- Don't take the job or stay in it unless you have, in understanding and fact, the freedom to tell [the president] what you think and feel on any subject with the bark off.
- Obviously, always tell the full truth. If you screw up, tell him and correct it.
- Force responsibility down and out. Find problem areas, arrange them in groups, assign them, and delegate. All the pressure is to do the reverse, to take more and more responsibility yourself.
- Don't get or let the White House or the president get paranoid about the press or Congress or leaks. Relax. Understand the inevitable interaction among institutions.

Rumsfeld also included some valuable personal tips: "Don't be consumed by the job or you will lose your balance. Maintain and tend your mooring lines into the world, your family, friends, neighbors, people out of government. That balance is critically important to your performance. Help your staff, children, and friends to understand that you are still the same person, despite the publicity, good or bad . . . and don't forget it yourself."

As White House chief of staff, I was in a position to help my friend

George Bush stay in the loop more than some past vice presidents. But I was working for Reagan now, not Bush—his principal opponent in the bruising primaries—and my first loyalty would be to the president. Any appearance that my real goal was only to help my old friend would have been inappropriate. I wasn't about to do that. Even the *appearance* that I was more closely aligned with Bush than Reagan would have undermined my effectiveness.

George was present—along with Casey, Meese, and Deaver—at the meeting I attended at the Reagans' home two days after the election. One topic was cabinet selection. We were joined by the president-elect's close friend and confidante Senator Paul Laxalt, and by Pen James, a private-sector headhunter who would run the White House personnel office. Pen had already begun putting together a short list of candidates for each position.

During the transition, James, Meese, Deaver, and I met every day at 5:00 P.M. in my office to go over candidates for key positions such as deputy or assistant secretaries. We would then discuss our recommendations with Reagan, and he would make the final decision.

Reagan tentatively selected General Al Haig as secretary of state. Al had a heck of a résumé. He had just returned from serving as Supreme Allied Commander of NATO. Before that he had combat experience in Vietnam and a stint as an aide to Henry Kissinger. In the last days of the Watergate crisis, he served as White House chief of staff for Richard Nixon.

Before offering the post to Al, the president-elect wanted assurances that he would not use it as a base of operations to run for the presidency, as rumors suggested. In early December, he had told Meese, Laxalt, Allen, and me that he did not want to be president. Furthermore, he said, no one interested in running for president would want to be secretary of state. Too many occupants of that office, he suggested, have been scapegoated by their presidents. That satisfied Reagan, and he soon nominated Haig for the position.

On January 20, 1981, a bit more than a month later, Susan and I sat on the inaugural platform as Ronald Reagan took the oath as our nation's fortieth president. We later watched the parade from the presidential reviewing stand in front of the White House. As bands, dignitaries, and floats crept past, I showed Susan the area under the bare trees in Lafayette Park, just across the street and to the left, where Mary Stuart and I had shivered through the 1953 parade twenty-eight years earlier.

Inauguration day was memorable for other reasons, as well. Moments after President Reagan took office, Iran freed the hostages taken more than fourteen months earlier. While work crews swept Pennsylvania Avenue after the parade, Mike Deaver and I went to Ed Meese's office. We probably talked about the president's response to this momentous event. It's also likely that we lifted a toast to our new administration and the bright possibilities ahead. Suddenly and unexpectedly, Al Haig walked in. He said he had a proposed National Security Decision Directive (NSDD) he wanted the president to sign.

Talk about bad timing. We were still in formal attire. We hadn't even unpacked our briefcases. And here was Al Haig, not yet confirmed by the Senate, with a twenty-page document no one—including the president—had yet seen, proposing to put the secretary of state—that is, Al Haig—in charge of crisis management for the administration. Ed told Haig that we needed comments from Secretary of Defense Weinberger, CIA Director Casey, and National Security Adviser Allen before we could put something this important on the president's desk.

This did not sit well with Al. In his diplomatic memoir, *Caveat: Realism, Reagan, and Foreign Policy,* he suggested that he had an earlier understanding with the president about lines of authority that was now in danger of being reversed. Striking specifically at Meese, Haig wrote: "Surely the President did not want his counselor editing communications from the cabinet, or muddying presidential instructions."*

Instructions? President Reagan had given us none about this document. But as Al Haig and others would soon learn, the president did want communications to his office—including those from cabinet officers—to be vetted, if not edited, by Ed and me. Management 101. This presented a real problem for Al. He thought the president relied far too heavily on the White House staff, whom he later referred to as "a bunch of second-rate hambones."[†]

Just ten weeks after President Reagan took office, tragedy struck. Without warning, senior White House staff, the cabinet, and the vice president were forced to consider a variant of the question Haig had posed: in a crisis, who's in charge here?

---

[*]When I later served as secretary of state for George Bush, 41, the scope of my authority was defined by something considerably more powerful than a National Security Decision Document—the confidence and friendship of the president.

[†]After a thorough review, President Reagan signed NSDD No. 3 on December 14, 1981. It put a "Special Situation Group, chaired by the vice president," in charge of crisis management. In 1988, Al Haig ran unsuccessfully against that same vice president for the Republican presidential nomination.

SEVEN

"SPARED FOR A PURPOSE"

I WAS IN THE White House mess having lunch when Press Secretary Jim Brady dropped by my table and said it was time to leave. It was March 30, and the president was scheduled to speak to 3,500 AFL-CIO members at the Washington Hilton. I had planned to attend.

"I just can't go," I said. "I've got too many things going on today."

Mike Deaver went in my place. After the event, he was at the president's side as the entourage exited the VIP entrance at the lower level of the hotel at 2:25 P.M. to return to the White House. It was a warm and breezy day, the sidewalks were wet from a light drizzle. The president had been in office seventy days.

As the president walked toward his car, "the press started asking their usual questions," Mike recalled later. "I turned and moved [Jim] Brady up because he was the press secretary. I took three steps. Then the first shot went over my shoulder. I knew what it was. I ducked down with the help of a Washington policeman. I smelled the powder. I never saw the gunman."

In less than ten seconds, that unseen gunman, John Hinckley, Jr., twenty-five, fired six hollow-nosed bullets from his .22-caliber re-

volver. It sounded like firecrackers—*pop, pop, pop*—the president said
later. One bullet hit police officer Thomas Delahanty in the neck. Another struck Secret Service agent Tim McCarthy in the stomach as he
rushed between the president and the shooter. A third hit Jim Brady
over the left eye and entered his brain. And although nobody, including Ronald Reagan, realized it at the time, another bullet ricocheted
off the president's limousine, cut into the president's chest, ripped into
his left lung, and embedded itself there, inches from his heart.

Jerry Parr, head of the Secret Service detail, shoved President Reagan into the black Lincoln limousine and told the driver to head for
the White House. Parr radioed ahead. Shots have been fired, he said,
but the president was not hit. About that time, the president began
coughing up blood. Parr immediately ordered the driver to divert to
nearby George Washington University Hospital.

The car arrived there about 2:35. Flanked by Secret Service agents,
the president walked into the emergency room under his own power.
Once inside, however, his legs gave way and he suddenly collapsed.
With the help of agents, a paramedic carried him into a private suite
in the ER and gave him oxygen.

Meanwhile, David Gergen burst into my office with the news that
shots had been fired, but in those first confused moments, neither he
nor anyone else we could find knew exactly what had happened or
whether the president had been injured.

Ed Meese joined me in my office. Now Deaver called. After the
shooting, he had jumped into a limousine and followed the president.
This was the first contact between the hospital and the White House.
Brady and at least one agent had been hit, Mike said, and doctors had
found a small bullet hole in the president's coat. Dr. Daniel Ruge, the
White House physician, was also on the line. He told us the president
had lost an enormous amount of blood. The bad news was getting
worse.

Meese and I agreed that we should get to the hospital ASAP. Before we left, I received a phone call from Secretary of State Al Haig. I told him what I knew and said I was on my way to the hospital. Vice President Bush was in Texas. Haig said he would set up a White House command post with key cabinet members—Secretary of Defense Cap Weinberger, Secretary of the Treasury Don Regan, Attorney General William French Smith, CIA Director Bill Casey, and National Security Adviser Dick Allen. I told Haig he would be my point of contact, and he said he would call the vice president.

Haig arrived at the White House a few minutes after 3:00 P.M. Meese, Speakes, Lyn Nofziger, and I were already on our way to the hospital, about six blocks away—siren wailing, lights flashing.

When we arrived the president winked at us from behind his oxygen mask. "Who's minding the store?" he asked. His greeting to Nancy was just as light: "Honey, I forgot to duck," a line borrowed from Jack Dempsey. But there was nothing funny about the way he looked. He didn't appear to be in danger of dying, but his appearance shocked me. In my two-plus months on the job, I had been impressed with the president's vigor, a testament to his natural good health and active outdoor lifestyle. Now he was ghostly pale. "Doctors believe bleeding to death," Speakes wrote in his notebook. "Can't find a wound. Think we're going to lose him. Touch and go."

The doctors worked fast. They soon found the wound, a small slit in the side of the president's chest under his left arm. Now we knew for certain: Ronald Reagan had been shot. The bullet, flat as a dime, was lodged in his left lung, which had collapsed. At 3:25 P.M., one hour after the shooting, he was wheeled into surgery to try to stop his massive internal bleeding.

As commander in chief, the president is always accompanied by officers and equipment to communicate with the U.S. military. Potential threats to national security don't take time off for weekends, vacations, or—in this case—an attempt to assassinate the president of the United States. A White House team quickly set up a command center at the hospital. Presidential aides Dave Fischer and Helene von Damm staffed it. They were joined by the military aide who always traveled with the president and kept the "football," the black bag containing the codes the president would need in case of a nuclear exchange with the Soviet Union. We would later learn that Hinckley was a disturbed young man, acting alone. In those first minutes, however, it was not clear that something larger and more ominous had not happened.

Under Section 3 of the Twenty-fifth Amendment to the Constitution, the president is empowered to declare his own disability and transfer power to the vice president, as acting president. If the president is in no condition to declare his own disability, Section 4 says the transfer can be effected by a majority vote of cabinet members and the vice president. Congress approved the amendment in 1965 in the aftermath of the Kennedy assassination. The amendment was ratified in 1967, but had never been invoked for presidential succession. (It was invoked twice in the 1970s on vice presidential succession, first to replace the disgraced Spiro Agnew, then to replace Gerald Ford as VP when Nixon resigned as president.)

Meese and I had seen President Reagan at the hospital. With the vice president in Texas, we decided, it would be difficult to transfer power to George Bush during the surgery. More important, we didn't think the transfer was medically required, even though the president would be under anesthesia. Our decision would be second-guessed in the days to come and would rightfully lead to the development of more specific White House guidelines in later years.

When President Reagan was anesthetized for colon cancer surgery in 1985, he did transfer power to the vice president under Section 3. Why didn't we use Section 4 to do so in 1981? In part (and primarily) because doctors told us that the president would be able to make decisions, save for the brief period he was under anesthesia. In part because it was essential to send a clear message to the world: *Despite the assassination attempt, the government is open for business, and the president is in charge.* And in part, frankly, because I was sensitive to the fact (and knew George Bush would be, too) that many Reagan loyalists—mindful that we had campaigned against President Reagan in the primaries—still questioned our allegiance to the president. Unless it was absolutely necessary, they might view the transfer as something just short of a Bush-Baker *coup d'etat*. For these reasons, I think we made the right call at the time. Furthermore, we knew that the transfer could always be made later if, say, complications arose during surgery. By then, Vice President Bush would be back in Washington. There was no harm in waiting.

Back in the situation room in the West Wing basement, Haig, other cabinet members, and White House aides crowded around television screens. They were getting some of their information about the shooting like everyone else in America, from network news reports. They were soon joined by White House counsel Fred Fielding, who had taken it upon himself to prepare documents to transfer power under the Twenty-fifth Amendment if worse came to worst.

Haig later wrote that he thought Fielding's timing was premature and that the preparation of documents was ill advised. Dick Darman's reaction was even stronger. It was out of order to discuss the transfer of power in this manner, he said, taking possession of Fielding's papers. He then called me at the hospital. I agreed with him. The White House counsel reported to me and should not have raised the issue without consulting me. Dick put the documents in his office safe.

At the hospital, the hours passed quickly and are blurred in my memory. I spent most of my time with Meese, Deaver, Nofziger, and other White House staffers. We were all running on adrenaline. For me, it was triggered by three emotional shockwaves—first when I was told of the shooting; then when I saw the president, pale and injured, in the emergency room; and again when I watched him being wheeled away to the operating room. We were all trying to figure out what had happened, what needed to be done, and how to do it. For me, that meant a lot of time on the telephone, primarily with the situation room and my staff back at the White House, but I also fielded several incoming calls from others.

At one point, I remember being in the small hospital chapel with

Mrs. Reagan. We prayed for our country, for the president, for Jim Brady, for the injured officers, and for guidance in responding to this ordeal. I don't remember our exact words, but here's a good summary: "Lord, please help us!"

Meanwhile the press clamored for information. The nation—indeed, the world—wanted to know what had happened and what it all meant. Even before we had the answers ourselves, we needed to share what we knew. In a situation like this, silence fuels anxieties and rumors outrun facts. I briefed Nofziger and Speakes, then sent Speakes to deal with reporters at the White House.

The televised press conference did not go well. Watching from the situation room, Allen and Haig were concerned, understandably, that Speakes, trying too hard to be precise, had left the erroneous impression that the country was not being defended and that no one was running the government. In fact, Weinberger had ordered Strategic Air Command pilots to their bases, and the cabinet and the troika, soon to be joined by the vice president, were quickly coming to grips with the situation.

"This is very bad. We have to do something," Allen said.

Haig agreed. "We've got to get him [Speakes] off."

The secretary of state and national security adviser then bounded up the stairs to the press room. Red-faced, perspiring, and near breathless from the run, Haig briefed reporters on the president's condition and the status of our military. He then offered to take questions. One of his answers would haunt him for a long time.

> *Reporter:* Who is making the decisions for the government right now?
>
> *Haig:* Constitutionally, gentlemen, you have the president, the vice president, and the secretary of state, in that order, and should the president decide he wants to transfer the helm, he will do so. He has not done that. As of now, I am in control here, in the White House, pending return of the vice president and in close touch with him. If something came up, I would check with him, of course.

As Haig himself would later admit, "I am in control here" was an unfortunate choice of words. He also conceded that his physical appearance made him look anything but "in control" and that he should have caught his breath before trying to reassure the nation that all was well. He also famously misstated the line of presidential succession. Under legislation passed in 1947, the speaker of the House and president pro tempore of the Senate follow the vice president. The secretary of state follows them.

In his diplomatic memoir, *Caveat,* Haig sometimes spoke critically of the White House staff. He thought we had too much power, were too protective of the president, and distracted the president from more important foreign policy issues by keeping the focus on a narrow domestic agenda. Early on, for example, he believed that we stymied his efforts to deal aggressively with Central America. (He once suggested solving the Cuba problem by turning the island nation into "a [expletive deleted] parking lot.")*

Before the assassination attempt, the president had decided to accept a crisis management plan that Meese and I had developed. Furious that the vice president rather than the secretary of state was to be put in charge of operations in emergencies, Haig openly criticized us at a congressional hearing.

It's fine to disagree on policy, but it's better to do it privately with the president rather than publicly before Congress. Haig threatened to resign a number of times over the next year. After each such threat, he would eventually cool down, but he never seemed to learn that President Reagan liked team players better than Lone Rangers and did not respond well to management by ultimatum.

Despite the tension between the White House staff and the secretary of state, Meese and I did not fault Haig for his conduct on the day

---

*Haig was at least partly right. In the early months of the administration, we did try to keep Central America on the back burner. We didn't want to distract attention from the president's critical tax and spending reforms.

the president was shot. At a press conference on March 31 and on ABC's *Nightline* on April 1, we were invited to join the Haig-bashing. Instead, we defended the secretary's actions, and I will defend them now: Al Haig served the country well on March 30, 1981; at a very difficult time for our nation, he assured the people—on balance and despite the gaffe—that all was well.

At about 6:15 P.M., I returned to the White House. Vice President Bush was expected to land at Andrews Air Force Base at 6:30. As we waited, I briefed those in the situation room. The surgeons had found the bullet in the president's lung, I reported, but according to the doctors he was in good condition and would make a full recovery.

The vice president arrived at about 7:00 P.M. He had the sensitivity and presence of mind to land his helicopter at the Naval Observatory, the vice president's official residence, and drive to the White House. Setting down on the South Lawn would have sent two negative and inaccurate messages—that the president was no longer in charge and that the vice president was.

As we discussed national security issues and the agenda for the next twenty-four hours, Dr. Dennis O'Leary, dean of clinical affairs at George Washington University Hospital, said in a televised news conference: President Reagan "has a clear head and should be able to make decisions by tomorrow, certainly." And with that, we breathed long-deferred sighs of relief.

The details of what happened next have slipped my memory. I suspect I worked at my desk, conferred with my immediate staff, tried to pick up where I had left off a few hours earlier, returned calls, prepared for the next day, then went home to Susan.

That's how I worked. I would go to my desk every day and cross all the t's and dot all the i's, then I'd go home. I ran presidential campaigns that way and served presidents that way. I never thought too much about history in the abstract sense. In the back of my mind, I knew the things I was involved in were important; that's one reason I enjoyed public life so much. If I had a theory of history, it was: that if we worked hard and worked smart, we could win each day's battles, and that if we won each battle, we would win the war. To the extent I had a larger theory, it was that history is shaped by human actions and re-actions.

I still believe that, by and large, but March 30 taught me how frag-ile it all is, how unanticipated events can change the course of history in an eyeblink. The administration had been in office a bit more than two months. We were still getting our sea legs. Now the voyage had al-most ended before it ever really began. All of President Reagan's great accomplishments lay ahead. What if the president had died on the op-erating table? What if he had been disabled?

And what if the president had never been shot? Looking back, I wonder if this long and emotional day didn't play some role in focus-ing the administration on what was important. I know that it strength-ened my resolve to make every day count. It also reminded me of a lesson of my faith: we are responsible for doing our best here on earth, but at the end of the day, God is in charge, and on March 30, 1981, He spared Ronald Reagan.

The day after the shooting was not a typical day at the office. On a typical day, I arrived at the White House at about 7:00 A.M. A car picked me up at my home about thirty minutes earlier. My driver was Ernie Caldwell of the U.S. Army, a true gentleman and dedicated pub-lic servant, who could always be counted on for efficient services, utter discretion, and a smile that would warm the coldest mornings. After more than twenty-five years, he still drives me when I'm in Washing-ton, now as an employee of Baker Botts.

On my way to the office, I read the White House news summary, prepared overnight by the press office and distributed early each morning to the president, senior White House staff, and cabinet mem-bers. At the office, I caught the top of the morning network news re-ports and read full accounts of what I considered the important stories mentioned in the White House summary. The *New York Times*, the *Washington Post*, the *Wall Street Journal*, the *Washington Times* (after it was founded in 1982), and the *Early Bird* (the Pentagon's sixteen-page news summary) were on my desk when I arrived. I discussed problem stories with Margaret Tutwiler, my executive assistant (who had great instincts about whether to respond, and how), and later with the press secretary, who would handle the response.

My first office project each day was to prepare an agenda for a meeting with Meese and Deaver and (with some sensitive items being deleted) for a general staff meeting afterward. This checklist didn't take long. I always prepared a draft the day before, as I worked. All I had to do in the morning was rewrite and update it. This list and the meetings that followed were examples of the Five Ps in action. (Somewhere, Dad was smiling.)

At 7:30 A.M., Meese and Deaver would gather in my office. Over breakfast, we would go over the agenda I had prepared. Ed and Mike would bring additional items to the table. We generally discussed scheduling, media coverage, and the legislative agenda for the day.

This was an example of the troika at its best. We worked together to serve the president, notwithstanding our differences of opinion and the natural tensions that sometimes developed. This approach to sharing responsibility worked well for President Reagan. It gave him a functional administrative system to keep things moving, plus a useful way to hear competing views on important issues. With the troika, President Reagan had a darn good first term. The second term, without the troika, was in many ways not as successful.

Ed, Mike, and I worked hard to develop a story line for each day. A good economic report, for instance, proved our programs were working, while a bad economic report only showed the need to adopt our programs or stay the course on programs already in place. At one level, this approach may offend logic, but it makes perfect sense under the logic of politics. Ronald Reagan was trying to change the direction of the country. To succeed, it was critical not to lose momentum or be blown off course by events, by politics, or by the press. When the headlines were favorable, we raised our sails; when they were unfavorable, we tacked into them. We believed in what we were doing, and we wanted to succeed.

At 8:00 A.M., Meese, Deaver, and I would go to the Roosevelt Room for a meeting with the president's assistants and deputy assistants, some of whom reported to me, others to Meese (from the policy shops) or Deaver (responsible for the East Wing—the First Lady, scheduling, advance work, and the military office). I chaired the meeting. We talked about most of the same issues the troika had discussed earlier, plus issues from the floor. If senior staff had something useful to say, we wanted to hear it. (One other group I headed, the White House Legislative Strategy Group, did not have regularly scheduled meetings. It was on call to meet when the need arose, sometimes with only an hour's notice.)

We also presented the day's story line to the communications director and the press secretary. To keep everyone in the administration on the same page in telling this story, the press secretary would then hold daily conference calls with spokespersons for the cabinet departments.* We didn't want other agencies out in front of the White House on issues, so at 9:15 A.M., the White House press secretary always held the day's first media briefing. In 1984, we would also coordinate our theme of the day with the president's reelection campaign.

Our initial daily meeting in the Oval Office was always triggered by a call from Kathy Osborne, the president's personal secretary. "The president is in," she would say. This was our cue to gather our papers and head down the hall.

The daily presidential meeting with we three top advisers was my

---

*After Jim Brady was shot, Larry Speakes assumed his duties but, in deference to Jim, not his title. We were intent on making life as good as possible for Jim and his wife, Sarah. Less than three weeks after the shooting I approved continued use of the White House car for Sarah; continuation of the secure military signal phone in Jim's room at the hospital; continuation of his salary (which would otherwise have stopped when he did not return to work after forty-five days); and investigation of the best way to set up a trust fund for the Brady family.

idea, supported by Mike and Ed. When I was named chief of staff, Stu Spencer said, "Listen, Jim, you call the president every day. It's not his style to contact you or to contact others. But he'll want you to call him every day." I went beyond that, gaining the president's approval for these start-of-the-day meetings.

Most days, Ronald Reagan was awakened about 7:00 A.M. While eating breakfast with Nancy, he read the White House news summary and the newspapers. Some newspapers didn't like his policies, but he still wanted to know what they were writing. The president was so genial and had such an uncanny ability to put people at ease that reporters couldn't help but like him personally. This was also true of many of his political opponents and some foreign leaders who didn't agree with his policies.

Out of his deep respect for the institution of the presidency, President Reagan also reversed the 1970s trend toward informality in the White House. It's been reported many times, but bears repeating: he would not remove his suit jacket in the Oval Office. The room where Lincoln, Wilson, FDR, Truman, and other predecessors had confronted the most profound national issues was to him not simply a place to get the day's business done; it was a sacred place, embodying the ideas of freedom and self-government that framed America's history. The only proper attitude, he believed, was one of deep respect, even reverence. Wearing his jacket was a small thing, easy for cynics to mock, but President Reagan was right and the cynics were wrong.

The session in the Oval Office was devoted to matters carried forward from the troika's 7:30 meeting and the larger White House senior staff meeting, except for routine stuff that the president and vice president didn't need to be bothered with. At 9:30, the national security adviser joined us and gave his daily briefing to the president. The vice president, Meese, and I stayed for this unless we had other commitments. At about 10:00 A.M., I would usually return to my office or accompany the president to his next event.

I tried to work at my desk as much as possible, but I would also attend presidential press conferences, accompany the president to events both inside and outside the White House, sit in on important Oval Office meetings (particularly including meetings with the congressional leadership), and participate in cabinet meetings. (Under my bargain with Meese, I sat at the cabinet table, not in the back row with staff.)

The good news for Susan and my family was that the president was true to his word: he didn't force me to work fourteen-hour days. The bad news was that I put in that many hours anyway. As a workaholic with an endless list of things to do, I saw no other way to get the job done. The Five Ps have their price.

I knew from experience and from conversations with previous chiefs of staff how important it was to maintain good relationships with Congress and the press. A simple rule helped me do that. Before going home each night, I returned every phone call from reporters and lawmakers. I wasn't always eager to talk with yet another reporter about yet another hot story or another congressman on the prowl for a quid pro quo that I couldn't provide, but I wanted the overnight call slips to be on their desks, not mine. And I didn't mind leaving a signal that I was still at the office working after they had gone home.

Each evening the president received the next day's schedule. The schedule might include meetings with foreign heads of state, congressional leaders, cabinet secretaries and other administration officials, business and community leaders, old friends, and, of course, the troika. Schedules from a typical month, October 1981, reveal that the president met with—among many, many others—representatives of the National Association of Broadcasters, the prime minister of Mauritania, Governor Pete du Pont of Delaware, Budget Director David Stockman, and eighty-three-year-old character actor Regis Toomey, a pal from Hollywood.

President Reagan also met regularly with a bipartisan group of congressional leaders. Here's a secret: members of Congress generally don't come to the White House to engage the president in deep conversations about policy issues. Those discussions take place with the

president's aides. What lawmakers usually want with the chief executive is simple face time—a handshake, a drink, and a bit of socializing.
That way they can tell the press or the people back home, "I was talking yesterday to the president, and he told me . . ."

Sometimes, of course, congressional leaders might come to the
Oval Office loaded for bear on a particularly contentious issue, such as
foreign policy in Central America. On those occasions, there might be
a good deal of give-and-take, *but in the Reagan White House, the atmosphere
always remained friendly.* Twenty-five years ago, it was still possible to be
political adversaries without becoming personal enemies. You could
disagree agreeably.

Rank partisanship is both undignified and unproductive. It's also
shortsighted. The best way to persuade someone to see things your
way is to start by trying to see things his way. You need to understand
and respect the political imperatives that guide his action, then to deal
with both the person and his politics in a civil and respectful way. I
learned as a corporate lawyer that, more often than not, negotiators
who worked in this way could find a common path that served the
needs of both sides. President Reagan was a master at doing this; he
told me he had cut his teeth as a negotiator when he was president of
the Screen Actors Guild.

Why are things more contentious today? I'm not really sure. I hes-
itate to blame cultural factors because I don't claim to be a cultural
critic. I also don't want to sound like another old geezer who thinks
kids today don't measure up. I will say, however, that President Reagan's and President Bush's upbringing—mine too, for that matter—
put a higher value on courtesy and civility than on unfettered
self-expression. It was the same for Tip O'Neill and many other old-
line traditional Democrats. Maybe that has something to do with it,
and maybe not. Another possible reason for the loss of the old spirit of
comity was the independent counsel law, which created a perverse incentive for politicians to try and win political arguments by getting
their opponents indicted.

Many of the president's Oval Office meetings with visiting dignitaries began with photo opportunities for the press. While photographers and TV cameramen got their pictures and footage, the president and his visitor would joke with each other and banter with the press, usually about light and inconsequential topics. Before his meeting with the president, however, Archbishop Desmond Tutu bulldozed past the president's statement that this was a photo-op with no questions and thoroughly trashed the administration's South Africa policy.

Smelling conflict, a reporter at a different photo-op the next day asked President Reagan: "What about your meeting with Tutu?" The president got a big laugh and totally defused the situation when he looked down at his hands, then slowly replied: "Tutu? So-so." (The first President Bush incorporated the Tutu story into the lovely eulogy he delivered at Ronald Reagan's funeral in 2004. He got a big laugh too.)

President Reagan preferred to have at least one hour each day for personal business. He would take care of paperwork and visit with staff (often regaling us with stories). He also read his briefing material.

I quickly learned how to present briefing material to the president: *briefly*. Ronald Reagan was much more interested in the big picture than in the details, a big-idea man who left the fine points to others. Ironically, however, he was almost too diligent for his own good. If you gave him a long memo or a thick briefing book, he would read every word of it and waste a lot of valuable presidential time on staff-level material. It was better to brief him orally or in short memos.

President Reagan's reputation for having a lack of interest in details led some people to think he was not intelligent. They were wrong and made a big mistake in this underestimation of him. First of all, his radar quickly picked up the signals from friends who patronized him and adversaries who thought they could outsmart him, which put both groups at a disadvantage in dealing with him. Second, lowering expectations about his intelligence gave him an opportunity to exceed those expectations, which he did, time after time.

President Reagan also liked to write letters. He had a private mailbox at the White House, the number of which he could give to anyone. Letters in that box went directly to him, not through the system. He also received hundreds of pieces of mail each week through the correspondence unit of the White House. He could not read or answer all of them, but he believed hearing from ordinary citizens kept him in touch with the mood of the country. He replied to a surprisingly large number of his citizen correspondents, often taking mail with him on the weekend to the presidential retreat at Camp David. A soft touch, he sometimes sent personal checks to individuals with stories of medical or financial hardship.

Unless he had an engagement, the president ate lunch in the Oval Office or the small adjacent study. On Thursdays, he lunched with the vice president. In any administration, it's almost a given that those close to the president, and sometimes the president himself, will view the vice president as a competitor. Often the staffs of the top two officials compete more than they cooperate. Because the vice president had battled the president for the nomination and candidate Reagan originally had doubts about asking his primary opponent to join the ticket, the table was set, so to speak, for a tense relationship—one that could have lasted for four years or more.

It did take the two men a while to get to know each other, but after the first three or four months, Ronald Reagan developed total confidence in George Bush. Without reservation, I can say that George was the perfect vice president. He understood the role. He knew, for example, that it was better to speak privately to the president about differences of opinion than to voice those differences in meetings. Speaking up in groups would inevitably generate leaks to the press about the president and vice president's being at odds over one thing or another.

I helped facilitate this relationship by supporting the idea that they should have as many opportunities as possible to spend time together. The president grew increasingly fond of George and valued his counsel. Although their backgrounds were vastly different, they were both comfortable with themselves and respected each other. Neither had anything to prove to the other. They could let their guard down and talk freely about whatever was on their mind.

When the president was in town, Wednesday afternoons were reserved. He often took this time to go horseback riding at the Marine Corps base in Quantico, Virginia, my old military training ground. He loved horses and kept a sign on his desk that said, "There's nothing better for the inside of a man than the backside of a horse." Knowing that I was a Texan who also liked horses, the president often invited me to join him. Sometimes he would also ride with his close friend Senator Paul Laxalt. We would ride for an hour or more through the lovely Virginia woods, usually at a slow pace. I used a western saddle and rode in blue jeans and cowboy boots, but the president preferred an English saddle, jodhpurs, and polished riding boots. Our conversations on the trails were mostly personal. If I had business to discuss, I would usually save it for the helicopter ride back to the South Lawn.

A riderless horse with boots placed backward in the stirrups is a tradition in presidential funeral processions. For President Reagan's funeral, however, the symbolism was especially powerful. I had seen him wear those boots, or ones just like them, many times.

Remembering Ronald Reagan, the horseman, reminds me of a story. If it's not true, it should be.

The president was visiting Queen Elizabeth II at Windsor Castle. Like him, she was an avid and accomplished rider, so the staffs arranged for a horseback tour of the grounds. After the obligatory photo-op, the monarch and president rode away, the queen in front. A few minutes later, however, Her Highness's poor steed—suffering perhaps from a bad batch of oats—began to expel gas in a remarkably rhythmic way with each step, step, step across the English countryside.

Elizabeth the Second—by the grace of God, queen of the United Kingdom of Great Britain and Northern Ireland and her other realms and territories, head of the commonwealth, and defender of the faith—was suitably mortified. "Oh, dear, Mr. President," she said, "I'm so sorry."

"Quite all right, Your Majesty," the president replied. "I thought it was the horse."

The president often directed his wit at his own alleged frailties in a way that charmed his friends and disarmed all but the most humor-impaired critics. There was lots of talk, for example, about his falling asleep in meetings.* "Someday," the president joked to one Oval Office visitor, "people will say, 'Ronald Reagan slept here.'" After a U.S. fighter plane shot down two Libyan jets one night, controversy erupted because the president had not been awakened. "I've laid down the law, though," he joked later at a dinner for White House correspondents. "From now on . . . no matter what time it is, wake me . . . even if it's in the middle of a cabinet meeting."

At 5:00 P.M. the president would usually leave the office for the residence, a brief, traffic-free commute. He generally took work home with him. He and Nancy would get into their pajamas, eat dinner, and watch the television news. After dinner he would read—he was a voracious reader—and do paperwork. I only occasionally made evening visits to the residence, but I can testify that President Reagan and the First Lady spent their free evenings in pajamas. Why not?

Ronald Reagan's devotion to Nancy was genuine and inspiring. They truly were best friends, and very much in love. He treasured her counsel, which almost always served him well. She had a good political nose and was the one who could get him to make hard political choices, particularly about personnel. I still can't get over the fact that when Don Regan was chief of staff he hung up on her during an argument. This was not only rude, but suicidal. He didn't last much longer.

Nancy Reagan had a fierce desire to protect her husband's health from a stressful schedule and his psyche from critics, be they in the

---

*As far as I could see, the president was always as alert as the rest of us, except for one well-publicized meeting with Pope John Paul II after we'd flown overnight to the Vatican.

press or in politics. She could be a grand ally when we were trying to persuade the president to do something. Mike Deaver, who had her trust, played an indispensable role in these efforts.

As has been reported, the president's close relationship with Nancy did not carry over to all his children, at least while I served him. He was probably not unique among many public figures in this regard. High officials are often too busy or single-minded to spend as much time with their children as they might, and a distance sometimes develops.

It is not for me to psychoanalyze the president I served. I am just happy to know that during his final years, Ronald Reagan reconciled with his children and they with him. At his funeral, the devotion of his surviving children, Michael, Patti, and Ron, was apparent to me and the nation.

While relations between the president and some of his children may at times have been distant, this does not mean he didn't enjoy children. My daughter, Mary Bonner, was three when I became chief of staff. The president took great delight in having her visit the Oval Office or Camp David, even when she once turned to Susan as the adults reached for their dinner forks and loudly announced, "Mommy, we haven't said grace!" The president, laughing, promptly gave a blessing. Another time he taught Mary Bonner how to dive into the pool at Camp David—a lesson that featured beautiful flips, jackknives, and swan dives from the diving board. The president, then past seventy, was showing off his decades-old lifeguard skills to impress a little girl. He also impressed her parents.

AFTER THE assassination attempt, the president, the vice president, senior staff, and cabinet agreed that it was essential to demonstrate that Ronald Reagan was still in command. While he was in the hospital, we couldn't replicate a day at the office. We could, however, demonstrate that the president was conducting business as usual.

On the morning after the shooting, Meese, Deaver, and I met with the president a little after 7:00 A.M. He was sitting up in bed, brushing his teeth. He may have lost half his blood the day before, but he never lost an ounce of his sense of humor. "Hi, fellas," he said smiling. "I knew it would be too much to hope that we could miss a staff meeting."

With the world watching, we couldn't. The president had been scheduled to sign a bill canceling an increase in dairy price-support payments. He did so now, albeit with a shaky hand.*

That afternoon I briefed the press. I gave more details about the shooting; explained that Meese and I had decided it was not necessary to invoke the Twenty-fifth Amendment; played down rumors of tension between Haig and Weinberger in the situation room; supported Haig's conduct during the crisis; and reported that when the president learned that a bullet had entered Jim Brady's brain, tears welled up in his eyes and he said, "Oh, damn! Oh, damn!" Earlier that day, I had also attended a White House cabinet meeting. George Bush presided, but sat in the vice president's chair, not President Reagan's. He wanted to make it very clear that he was not taking over the presidency.

One thing that didn't get much press was the president's postoperative infection. It was very serious, frankly, and we may have come closer to losing him from the infection than from the shooting itself.

Our routine didn't vary too much over the twelve days the president spent in the hospital. Meese, Deaver, and I moved our daily breakfast meeting to the hospital cafeteria, then met with the president afterward. George sat in for him at White House meetings, but deferred all major decisions to the president.

He, in turn, signed legislation, made appointments, and weighed in on pressing matters. He also agreed with my recommendation that we formally review who did what, when, in the White House during the

---

*The president later inscribed a copy of that bill to me. "Dear Jim," he wrote, "having signed this bill lying down the day after [the assassination attempt] ... with your pen, I thought you might like to have it as a memento. Actually it proves there wasn't much of a pause in our operation. Oops! That reads like a pun. Ron."

crisis. I appointed Darman to lead the study and recommend necessary policy changes.

As the president grew stronger, he was eager to return to the White House. When Senate leaders visited him in the hospital, he said he feared that his economic program, still being debated by the Congress, would lose momentum if he stayed in the hospital too long. The symbolic hundred-day mark, April 29, was fast approaching.

He returned home on April 11, wearing a bulletproof vest under his cardigan to be on the safe side. On the advice of doctors and at the insistence of the First Lady, he remained in the residence for the next ten days or so, except for periodic trips to the Rose Garden for sunshine and fresh air. The president also spent a few hours each day working in the Oval Office. We continued to hold our 9:00 A.M. meetings with him, and the national security adviser continued to brief him.

Surviving the attempt on his life had a profound effect on Ronald Reagan. More than once, he told the troika something like this: "Fellas, I feel like I've been spared for a purpose; the rest of my days here on earth belong to Him, with a capital *H*." "Perhaps having come so close to death," he wrote later, "made me feel I should do whatever I could in the years God had given me to reduce the threat of nuclear war; perhaps there was a reason I had been spared."

On April 24, less than two weeks after returning to the White House, the president sent Soviet leader Leonid Brezhnev two letters— one formal, one personal. The formal letter restated the president's well-known public position, that the Soviet Union's arms buildup in recent years exceeded its defensive needs and suggested a desire to achieve military superiority.

The second draft of the president's personal note, in his own handwriting, was given to me by President Reagan. It has been displayed at the James A. Baker III Institute for Public Policy at Rice University and is now at Princeton University with the papers of my public and political service. It reveals the Reagan I knew—a thoughtful and pragmatic student of history, a human being and leader who was secure enough to bare his concerns about the future to a tough geopolitical adversary. No speechwriter, image-maker, handler, or foreign policy expert had anything to do with this draft. Here, as with so many other of Ronald Reagan's communications, he proved again that the best writer on the White House payroll was the president himself. The people of the world "want the dignity of having some control over their individual destiny," he wrote. "They want to work at the craft or trade of their own choosing and to be fairly rewarded. They want to raise their families in peace without harming anyone or suffering harm themselves.... [Mr. Secretary,] should we not be concerned with removing the obstacles that prevent our people from achieving these simple goals?"

I saw the drafts and knew what the president was doing, but he didn't consult me about content, nor did I volunteer any advice. At the time, I was a brand-new White House chief of staff with zero foreign-policy experience.

The president ended the Soviet grain embargo, but unfortunately the unilateral gesture didn't work. Brezhnev did not agree to join in meaningful and constructive dialogue. A summit wasn't in the cards in the near future, he wrote back. He also accused the United States of starting the Cold War and chided President Reagan for telling the Soviet Union how to run its affairs.

Brezhnev was right. President Reagan was lecturing him. The letter was warm and personal, all right, but it was also Reagan 101: a sermon that basically said the Soviets had it wrong on economics, politics, and international relations, and that the United States had it right. It's as if the president thought maybe Brezhnev didn't know this stuff and that if he just heard it, he'd come to his senses.

To foreign policy sophisticates, the president's approach was naive. But history has proven otherwise. Events have validated President Reagan's view of how to deal with the Soviet Union. Only two months earlier, he had charged in a press conference that the Soviets "reserve unto themselves the right to commit any crime, to lie, to cheat, in order to" further their cause. And in his famous 1982 speech to the British Parliament, he would label the Soviets an "evil empire," destined for "the ash heap of history."

What the Brezhnev letter demonstrates is the side of Ronald Reagan that is less well known—his willingness to take a unilateral gamble for peace and his interest in communicating directly and personally with the Soviet leadership. Before Ronald Reagan left office, he would work directly with another Soviet leader, Mikhail Gorbachev, to lay the foundation for an end to the Cold War. The letter to Brezhnev was an important first step in that direction.

The assassination attempt did more than change Ronald Reagan, the man. It changed his presidency. At the time, his ambitious economic plan was stuck in Congress. (His speech to the AFL-CIO union group on March 30 was an attempt to drum up support.) His bravery, dignity, and humor during the crisis, however, were admired by virtually all Americans and gave him enormous political capital. Over the next four months, he used that goodwill and his own enormous skills as a communicator to push the most far-reaching set of tax and spending policy reforms since the New Deal. Would he prevail? And if he did, would his reforms save the economy . . . or wreck it?

EIGHT

"A REFORMED DRUNK"

"JIMMY, DARLING," my ninety-one-year-old mother, Bonner Means Baker, said plaintively, "you didn't really say those things, did you?"

Being honest is the right thing to do and the best way to keep out of trouble, but this time I made an exception to spare my wonderfully Victorian mother the heartache of knowing that her sweet Jimmy sometimes used salty language.

"Of course not," I said.

The truth is that I had said "those things." It was the spring of 1986, and President Reagan's former budget director, David Stockman, had quoted me all too accurately in his new book, *The Triumph of Politics*.*

"A different Jim Baker was now sitting two feet away," he wrote about our meeting of November 12, 1981. "His whole patented opening ritual had been completely dispensed with. No off-color joke. No casual waltz around his big office before he sat down. No jump shot that resulted in the arched flight of a paper wad across the room and

———————

*Stockman's book helped refresh my memory about what happened in 1981.

without fail into the wastebasket. This time it was all business, and his eyes were steely cold."

That was bad enough, but here's what really upset my mother:

> "My friend," he started, "I want you to listen up good. Your ass is in a sling. All of the rest of them want you shit-canned right now. Immediately. This afternoon.
>
> "If it weren't for me," he continued, "you'd be a goner already. But I got you one last chance to save yourself. So you're going to do it precisely and exactly like I tell you. Otherwise you're finished around here."
>
> Baker continued his verbal thrashing without blinking an eye. "You're going to have lunch with the president. The menu is humble pie. You're going to eat every [expletive-deleted] spoonful of it. You're going to be the most contrite sonofabitch this world has ever seen."

Three months before, the president had signed into law the most sweeping overhaul of federal tax and spending policies since the Great Depression. The true author of Reaganomics was Reagan himself, but David Stockman was the numbers man, the technician who had turned the president's ideas into legislative proposals.

What put the young budget director in the hot seat was "The Education of David Stockman" in the December 1981 issue of the *Atlantic Monthly*. At first, none of us saw the trouble it would bring. Not Ed Meese or his deputy Craig Fuller, not Treasury Secretary Don Regan, not my deputy Dick Darman, and not me. If we had, we would never have begun our Legislative Strategy Group (LSG) meeting two days earlier—Stockman's thirty-fifth birthday—by giving him a framed copy of the magazine cover. We even autographed the darn thing.

The laughing stopped, however, when critics began cherry-picking quotes out of the article to cast doubt on the president's economic package. They said it showed that Stockman knew in advance that the tax and budget cuts were based on guesswork and would neither balance the budget nor restore the economy, and that the administration's confidence in supply-side economics was a sham. Democrats had a field day. Stockman was guilty of "one of the most cynical pieces of performance by a public official perhaps since the Vietnam era," said Senator Gary Hart of Colorado.

Stockman quickly labeled the article "wrong and grossly misleading." Later he was even more plainspoken: "I hadn't worked around the clock for seven months to enact the Reagan Revolution because I thought the supply-side tax cut was a scam."

The article was based on taped interviews with William Greider, then an assistant managing editor at the *Washington Post,* now as I write—no surprise—a writer for a hard-left political magazine. Greider was an old friend and intellectual adversary, Stockman would explain. They had begun meeting on Saturday mornings in January so the budget director could test the president's budget and tax plans, and the thinking behind them, against the reporter's skepticism. Stockman later said he had hoped to "convert" Greider and, through him, "the establishment opinion makers" at the *Post.*

In addition to the naïveté of giving no-holds-barred interviews to Greider, Stockman made three mistakes. He didn't set clear ground rules, except that nothing would be written until the legislative battles were over. He had a loose tongue. And he foolishly trusted his friend to report the substance of what was said, not the sloppy language. For instance, Stockman once said low- and middle-bracket tax cuts were a "Trojan horse" for high-bracket tax cuts. Critics took this as a confession that the administration had tricked Congress and the American people. It was really a comment about legislative strategy, and it was factually wrong. From day one, Ronald Reagan insisted on cutting taxes across the board, not as a cynical excuse to help better-off Americans, but because it was the fair thing to do.

Stockman had betrayed the administration, Meese and Deaver told the president at our regular 9:00 A.M. meeting. Furthermore, the story wasn't going away. The networks had hammered us for two straight nights, less about what the article said (in my opinion) than what Democrats said it said. But, no matter. Stockman had to go, they said.

Unfortunately, he didn't have a lot of friends in high places. Like an emergency room doctor, he was often required to deliver bad news. He was also impatient—sometimes a tad arrogant—with anyone who didn't "get it" or who disagreed with him. And it didn't help, frankly, that this former campus radical, divinity school grad student, and Democrat-turned-Republican was barely older than our own kids.

I was the lone holdout. Stockman was smart and articulate. He worked hard and was a super-hawk on balancing the budget. As I wrote in the last chapter, I always believed in surrounding myself— and the president—with the best possible advisers, and Stockman was clearly the best man for this job.

I also knew throwing Stockman overboard would be portrayed as an admission that the administration was guilty as charged. He had made a terrible mistake, I told the president, but it would be better to give him a chance to repent and stay on the team. Invite him to lunch, listen to what he has to say, then make up your mind, I suggested.

When the president agreed, I knew Stockman would probably survive. Ronald Reagan was a soft touch. He was perhaps the only person in Washington who had as hard a time firing someone as I did. Screw up and I'll chew you out, no extra charge for the language that bothered my mother. But I also believe in second chances. Maybe it's because my career in Washington would have ended almost as soon as it started if President Ford or his chief of staff, Dick Cheney, had fired me for predicting that Henry Kissinger would not be in a post-election Ford cabinet.

I had also made mistakes of my own as chief of staff. Three months earlier, for instance, I told a reporter I thought the president would reduce the size of the current proposal for an increase in the defense budget. The next morning, President Reagan and I were having breakfast alone in California when Secretary of Defense Cap

Weinberger called to complain. "Don't do that again," the president lectured me afterward. He was right. I had spoken out of turn. It was a good lesson.

Shortly after I set up Stockman's lunch date, I called him to my office and reminded him the menu was humble pie. "Let me repeat something just in case you didn't get the point. When you go through the Oval Office door, I want to see that sorry ass of yours dragging on the carpet."

The way the press reported it the next day, it was the president, not me, who let Stockman have it. "My visit to the Oval Office for lunch with the president was more in the nature of a visit to the woodshed after supper," Stockman told reporters.

Not so, as it turned out. In his book, Stockman said the president's eyes grew moist. "Dave, how do you explain this?" Stockman said his reply "meandered off into a total digression." But when the unhappy young man offered to resign, the president said no. "I need your help."

The White House then issued a press release saying the president "stated unequivocally that he would not tolerate any attempt to mislead the American people" and "that the policies of this administration were being pursued... in good faith on the basis of the best evidence and judgment possible."

This formally distanced the White House from the most serious charges against Stockman. The next step was to show that the president still supported him. How? "Only on a not-for-attribution basis was an official willing to give Reagan's reason for rejecting Stockman's resignation," the *Washington Post*'s Lee Lascaze wrote later. "He said the president is satisfied Stockman can and will support Reagan's programs; that Stockman is needed and his remarks do not affect the economic program; that Stockman 'is an extraordinarily capable public servant.'"

Sound familiar?

I often spoke to journalists on a not-for-attribution basis. One essential task of the White House chief of staff—as Dick Cheney, Don Rumsfeld, and others told me—is to spend a lot of time explaining the president's policies to reporters. This is called backgrounding and is very different from leaking. Leaking is when you put out unauthorized information to undermine the president's policy or drive the policy debate on an issue the president has not yet settled. Or when you say something for no other purpose than to skewer someone else.

When Don Regan took over as chief of staff, he said he couldn't believe I had spent so much time with the press. All his statements would be on the record, he said. To each his own, I suppose, but he didn't do himself, the president, or the public any favors by refusing to talk privately with journalists. This was another illustration of why individuals who have been principals, such as governors and CEOs (Regan ran Merrill Lynch), generally have a hard time as chief of staff. It's hard for them to think and act in a secondary role. As chief of staff, you hold what is possibly the second most powerful job in Washington, but nobody elected you. You're still staff. All your power is vicarious from the president. Forget that for one minute, and you're in trouble!

Like Don Regan, some media outlets today want everything on the record and say they will limit what they will take on background. So be it. The approach in the Reagan and Bush administrations was simple: if you don't like the rules, don't come. The press is so competitive, particularly with the modern proliferation of news outlets, that I doubt any reporter can really afford to stay away from good sources that other journalists are tapping.

I learned how to get along with the press during presidential campaigns. One ironclad rule: on or off the record, never lie. If I couldn't answer a question, I'd just say I wouldn't comment. Reporters knew I worked for the president and would explain things his way—call it spinning if you wish—but they also knew they could trust, factually, what I told them.

Another thing that worked in my favor was the perception that I was a moderate voice in a conservative administration. I'll leave it to journalists to explain why they are, as a group, more comfortable with public officials on the left and in the middle than with those on the right. Whatever the reasons, this served me well and, through me, the president.

The fact is, I am a Texas Republican. We are a fairly conservative bunch, even among other Republicans. My reputation as a moderate probably stemmed from my pragmatism. I resisted efforts to broaden the administration's agenda to include every item on the Republican wish list, particularly some social issues that would have distracted us from the president's main goals of strengthening the economy and re-building the military. The Carter administration tried to do too many things at once. That was a big mistake, even when the president's party controlled Congress. With the House solidly controlled by Democrats in 1981, we had even less room to chase every good idea that came along. To accomplish anything, we had to pick our fights and put all our energy into winning them.

Some of Ronald Reagan's more ideological supporters thought I kept the president from following his better instincts. "Let Reagan be Reagan!" they proclaimed. All I can say is that they overestimated me and underestimated their president. He was a strong-willed man with clear principles and firmly held views, not a puppet in the hands of staff. Besides, I wasn't the only adviser who wanted to give priority to strengthening the economy and national defense. Meese, Deaver, and Nancy Reagan did, too.

The Reagan-Stockman meeting was big news and, as I had hoped, the focus of the stories shifted. Now it was about what the president said to his budget director, not what the budget director said to a re-porter. The hungry news beast fed on this personality-driven story for a day or two, then moved on, sniffing as always for something new.

WHEN THE HISTORY of the last half of the twentieth century is written, the Stockman flap, justifiably, will be only a footnote. The real story was the revolution in economic policy in that fateful year of 1981.

Ronald Reagan won the presidency because the American economy was broken. He said he knew how to fix it, the voters believed him, and he did what he promised.

In the seventies, an unprecedented combination of high inflation and high unemployment —"stagflation"—put people out of work and hammered living standards. The sum of these two indices was called the "misery index," and when it reached 12 percent in 1976, it helped Jimmy Carter beat President Ford. Now the index was more than 20 percent. The once-mighty U.S. economy actually shrank in 1980. *Newsweek* said President Reagan had inherited "the most dangerous economic crisis since Franklin Roosevelt took office forty-eight years ago." Watergate and Vietnam also cast doubt on our ability to control larger events at home or abroad. By 1980, Iranian militants held American hostages in Tehran and Soviet tanks rumbled across Afghanistan.

The worst part is that no one seemed to know what to do. We tried wage-and-price controls—mandatory under Nixon, "voluntary" under Carter (as long as your company wanted government contracts)—but quickly discovered the old lesson about fixing prices: it creates shortages. Hello, gasoline lines. The famous Keynesian tradeoff between inflation and unemployment also failed, and we got both. Economic pessimists said we needed to accept the "limits of growth" and learn to get along with less. Even President Carter saw "an erosion of confidence in the future that is threatening to destroy the social and political fabric of America."

All during this period, Ronald Reagan—as governor of California, commentator, and presidential candidate—preached economic optimism. The key to prosperity, he believed, was economic freedom. If government would just get out of the way, American workers and investors would do the rest. The elements of what came to be known as Reaganomics were lower taxes, reduced government spending (except for defense), fewer regulations, a sound dollar, and free trade.

Meanwhile, a handful of economists, editorial writers, and politicians (including Stockman) were pushing something called supply-side economics. They said high marginal tax rates created a perverse incentive for American workers and businesses to slow down, work less, and invest in tax shelters, not productive enterprises. Cut the confiscatory rates, they said, and people will work harder and invest more. This was consistent with Ronald Reagan's larger set of ideas, so he and the supply-siders embraced each other as natural allies.

Traditional Republicans believed many of the same things, but put a higher priority on balancing the budget. This set up a primary fight for the soul of the GOP, and if George Bush was anything, he was a traditional Republican. "Voodoo economics" was his campaign's label for the idea that we could dramatically cut taxes and balance the budget at the same time.

The mandate for Ronald Reagan was a mandate for Reaganomics. Now came the hard part, turning the candidate's ideas into law—a job that would consume most of my waking hours in 1981. The outline of the plan was set in the campaign. It would be built around three annual 10 percent tax cuts. We would then have to control spending to put the government on a course toward a balanced budget. (Critics who later said we never intended to balance the budget were dead wrong. We started down that road with genuine confidence and enthusiasm.)

The federal budget process is peculiar. Cuts are not necessarily cuts. They are measured, not against the previous year's spending, but against a baseline of future spending under existing law. If the federal subsidy for widget manufacturers is set to grow by 10 percent, for example, a 5 percent "cut" will still leave the beneficiaries ahead of the game. We tried to cut a few programs below existing levels, but most of our cuts were intended to slow down the runaway train of federal spending, not to throw it into reverse. The federal budget grew during every year of the Reagan presidency.

But Stockman had more ambitious cuts in mind. Early in the game, he identified $40 billion in potential first-year reductions. Much more would be needed to balance the budget, he said, but this was a good start. Cabinet officers went along. At that point, Stockman understood their budgets better than most of them did. They also knew this is what the president wanted. And frankly, cutting the budget is an easy principle to support; what's hard is doing it.

Democrats were in a bind. Existing policies simply weren't working, and the president had carried many of their states and congressional districts. Still, most Democrats were unwilling to undo the programs their party had put in place over the past four decades, and they were far from powerless. They controlled the House by more than 50 votes. If they stuck together, they could obviously block the president's program. There was an opening, however, if we could win the Boll Weevils.

They were the remnant of the once-powerful bloc of conservative Democrats who ruled the Solid South, plus a few like-minded party members from other parts of the nation. As their party moved steadily to the left on economic, defense, and social issues, these forty or so conservative lawmakers occasionally voted with Republicans. We would need them.

Thanks to the president's coattails, Republicans controlled the Senate for the first time in decades. GOP senators supported their president and they could read the election returns, but they also worried about budget deficits, and—like Democrats—were not happy about cutting programs they had backed in the past.

We had a two-part strategy. Ronald Reagan was one of the finest public speakers in presidential history. Using his tremendous skills as a communicator and capitalizing on his popularity, particularly after the assassination attempt, he made repeated televised appeals to Congress and the American people. Every time he spoke, he moved the needle on public and congressional opinion. I've never seen anything like it, and I doubt anyone else has, either.

Meanwhile, the Legislative Strategy Group did the grunt work.

This was a good example of how—contrary to popular belief at the time—Meese and I regularly worked together for the benefit of the president. We settled our differences in LSG meetings, counted our votes, developed strategies, then fanned out to do the necessary cajoling, hand-holding, and trading. Max Friedersdorf headed our very capable Office of Congressional Relations, which included, among others, Ken Duberstein and M. B. Oglesby, but everyone in the administration pitched in. When called on, which was often, even the president would work the phones. It was a helluva team.

President Reagan gave his first televised speech on the economy from the White House on Thursday, February 5, sixteen days after taking the oath of office. Some in our ranks wanted to use campaign-style rhetoric to attack the tax-and-spend Democrats. But the president woke up at 4:00 A.M. and massaged the text to make it more conciliatory. He was, after all, the president now. He would call on both parties to act responsibly and work together to fix the economy.

The speech won rave reviews. So too did a second televised address to a joint session of Congress on February 18. We thought about using this appearance to deliver a full state of the union address, as Eisenhower and Kennedy did early in their administrations, but decided instead to focus exclusively on our number-one issue, the economy.

President Reagan entered the chamber to great applause, then outlined the most revolutionary economic program in at least half a century. He called it "America's New Beginning: A Program for Economic Recovery." Individual income taxes would be cut by 10 percent a year for three years, as promised, and business would get faster depreciation rules. By then, Stockman had worked up about $49 billion in itemized savings for fiscal year 1982, with $44 billion more in "future savings to be proposed." The president ordered cabinet secretaries to postpone the effective dates for hundreds of new federal regulations and put Vice President Bush in charge of a cabinet-level task force on regulatory relief. And he pledged to support the Federal Reserve System in its fight against inflation.

Tax and budget cuts were clearly centerpieces of Reaganomics, but other elements were important, too. Within nine days of being sworn in, for instance, the president had deregulated crude oil prices, shut down a standby wage and price regulatory program, and set up the regulatory oversight process—all by executive order.

A little more than a year later, the president commissioned Peter Grace to lead fellow business executives in an internal management review of federal programs. The Grace Commission recommended more than 2,500 ways to reduce the number of federal employees, eliminate redundant publications, cut travel costs, and otherwise streamline federal agencies and improve their management and financial systems.

President Reagan told the joint session he wanted to balance the budget by 1984. The written version of his plan boldly predicted that economic growth would reach 4 or 5 percent by 1986 and that inflation would fall to less than 5 percent. He challenged Congress to move quickly. "The people are watching and waiting," he said. "They don't demand miracles, but they do expect us to act."

The president was interrupted by applause sixteen times, and he drew an extended ovation when he said, "Let us act together." Stockman went to the Hill the next day to explain the nuts and bolts of the program. The game was on.

But when the Senate Budget Committee started marking up the plan, we immediately had a problem. Chairman Pete Domenici and other GOP senators wanted to protect a lot of existing programs, so they threw out the administration's laundry list of spending cuts and penciled in a one-year freeze on the cost-of-living adjustment for Social Security. Stockman said I went into "red alert" when I heard about this. He was right. I arranged for the president to visit the Hill. By making it a test of loyalty, he talked the GOP senators into taking Social Security off the table.

In early April—the president was then in the hospital—the Senate adopted our budget resolution, pretty much without any changes. A test vote went our way 59–41, with sixteen Democrats, and the resolution was adopted 88–10. For a brief moment it looked all too easy, but our troubles were just starting.

The next problem was Stockman's "future savings to be proposed," a multibillion-dollar item that came to be known as the "magic asterisk." We wanted to show it on the budget documents as a spending cut, out of respect for our plan to announce additional cuts in coming weeks, but Senator Domenici refused. He posted it as a deficit and, predictably, the Senate Budget Committee revolted and voted down the plan 12–8. The senators' appetite for budget cutting wasn't strong to begin with, and the hint of a big deficit gave them a reason to take to the sidelines. The president's plan was in trouble in the Senate.

Over on the House side a furious battle was under way for the hearts and minds of the Boll Weevils. The president invited the Democrats for breakfast in the East Room in early March. I remember it well. The meeting ended with effusive declarations of support for our plan. The only problem was the first priority for many Boll Weevils was deficit reduction, not tax cuts. For us, it was a package deal.

Winning uncommitted or wavering House members is not much different from winning uncommitted delegates. The power of the presidency—certainly one as popular as Reagan's—is hard to resist, so the president regularly invited key Democrats to the Oval Office, to state dinners, even to Camp David. The White House Office of Public Liaison, headed by Elizabeth Dole, effectively organized public-sector support.

The counterattack from Democrats was strong and visceral. The Congressional Black Caucus accused the president of jeopardizing programs that were lifelines for poor people. "Reagan is reverse Robin Hood, robbing the poor and giving to the rich," said a Democratic congressman from Illinois. On May 7, Democratic constituencies—the organized poor, the elderly, farm workers, and people with disabilities—were bused into Washington for a "National Day of Mourning."

Everybody's welcome to his opinion, but the fact of the matter is that we had no intention of touching the big social programs—Social Security, Medicare, and Medicaid. We did propose to cut some smaller programs in education, training, unemployment, and social services, most fairly recent in origin, and mostly by consolidating overlapping programs into block grants and tightening eligibility standards. We also tightened up retirement, disability, and benefit programs for federal workers, railroad employees, coal miners, and veterans—ancient programs that, frankly, were long overdue for a good scrubbing.

A lot of the criticism was not about the merits of our proposals, however; it was personal. Critics said we were out to help the rich at the expense of the poor. Well, I never knew a less class-conscious guy than Ronald Reagan. He himself came from humble beginnings. He loved to correspond with Americans from all stations of life, and he treated them all with unfailing dignity and respect. He honestly believed that the best way to help the poor—and all other Americans— was to strengthen the economy. He also believed that many social welfare programs did more harm than good for their supposed beneficiaries. The success of the 1996 welfare reform bill—post-Reagan Reaganomics, signed by Bill Clinton—proves he was right, in my opinion. President Reagan sympathized with genuine deprivation. "Those who, through no fault of their own, must depend on the rest of us—the poverty stricken, the disabled, the elderly, all those with true need—can rest assured that the social safety net of programs they depend on are exempt from any cuts," he said. And he meant it, as David Stockman learned again and again in his endless search for budget-cutting targets.

Democrats knew the president had a mandate for change, so they set about crafting a Reagan-lite plan with a one-year tax cut and modest spending reductions. Jim Jones, the Oklahoma Democrat who headed the House Budget Committee, worked up the proposal, and it tempted some Boll Weevils. On one Sunday talk show in April, Jones even floated the idea that the president was ready to compromise. Still recovering from the assassination attempt, the president replied the next day: "No compromise!"

The path forward was a substitute bill drafted by Phil Gramm, a second-term Boll Weevil congressman from Texas, and Ohioan Delbert Latta, a senior Republican, both members of the Budget Committee. Except for some sweeteners for key Boll Weevils, it was almost identical to the administration's bill.

On April 28, nine days before the House vote, Ronald Reagan returned to the Hill for his first nationally televised address since the assassination attempt. A thinner president—accompanied by the heroic Jerry Parr, head of his Secret Service detail—entered the chamber to a wild ovation that lasted several minutes. He first thanked the nation for "your messages and flowers and, most of all, your prayers, not only for me but for those others who fell beside me."

Then he said the American people had sent a message in the 1980 election, but now were losing patience. "Six months is long enough. [They] want us to act, and not in half measures." "The old comfortable way is to shave a little here and add a little there," he said, alluding to the Jones bill. "Well, that's not acceptable anymore." Only the bipartisan Gramm-Latta budget resolution would restore the American economy.

Tip O'Neill threw in the towel before the climactic May 7 House vote. "I can read Congress," he said. "They go with the will of the people, and the will of the people is to go along with the president." Sixty-three Democrats joined the GOP to pass Gramm-Latta 253–176. (The tired but happy LSG had expected about forty Democrats to cross over.) A *Washington Post* headline the next day said it all: "Shattered: Democratic Coalition Falls to Pieces on First Test with Reagan." When the Senate approved the budget resolution a few days later, the Reagan revolution appeared to be unstoppable.

Then we shot ourselves in the foot.

The issue was Social Security, the system to provide retirement income for older Americans, plus a cornucopia of other benefits. By 1981, it was financially unsound. Within two or three years, everyone knew, revenues from payroll taxes would not cover the monthly rounds of checks. A major overhaul was needed, and reasonable minds disagreed about how to do it. Unbeknownst to those of us in the West Wing, Stockman had decided to squeeze billions of dollars of "future savings to be proposed" out of the program.

Whoever first called Social Security the third rail of American politics got it exactly right. Every time a policymaker says "Social Security" and "reform" in the same sentence, the Social Security lobby rises up—and damn the consequences for the younger generation, the economy, the budget, and Social Security itself. The reality is that old folks vote, and Congress pays attention to constituents who vote.

Just two days after House passage of Gramm-Latta, the White House received an administration task force report on Social Security. Former Senator Richard Schweiker—the president's 1976 running mate, now secretary of health and human services (HHS)—headed the task force. Stockman was an influential member. The report recommended major reforms, including stiff new penalties for retiring before sixty-five—penalties that would go into effect with little warning on January 1, 1982.

Uh-oh!

At an Oval Office meeting on May 11, Schweiker, Stockman, and domestic policy adviser Martin Anderson pitched the president hard. These experts understood the numbers, but they hadn't adequately considered the political implications. If we appeared to be cutting Social Security benefits to balance the budget, we would face a political disaster. Later, Anderson, Ed Meese, Jack Svahn (the Social Security commissioner), and others quickly led the president through a black binder of recommended options. To my distress, the president agreed with them without taking the matter under advisement as he usually did. Our success on the budget resolution may have encouraged him to shoot for the moon on this issue, which he had talked about for years. The proposal would be released the next day.

Heading off trouble or limiting damage before it occurs is always better than trying to clean up a mess afterward. In a contentious later afternoon meeting with Schweiker and Stockman, I engineered a pre-

emptive damage-control plan to present the new Social Security proposal as an HHS response to a congressional inquiry, not as a White
House initiative. I also recommended that the site for the release be
Baltimore, where the Social Security administration was headquartered. That would put as much distance as possible between the proposal and the president.

Back in my office, Schweiker was very exercised as he told Dick
Darman and me that he had been a U.S. senator! He knew Congress!
He had worked all of this out! All he had to do was take the first step,
and key Democrats would embrace the proposal! "If that's the case,
why not make a bipartisan announcement?" we asked. He said that he
knew what he was doing and that the president was on board.

As I feared, the blowback from the announcement was hot and
heavy. Republicans complained about being blindsided, and Democrats, still smarting from their budget defeat, blistered us. Even though
the plan was never formally put on the table, the Senate preemptively
voted against it 92–0. And that was that. Social Security was off the
front pages, but at significant cost to our legislative momentum.*

Unfortunately, the system still needed repair. Stockman revived
the issue in September. This time, the president said he wanted to address the nation on television. In my view, we were setting ourselves
up for a repeat of the Social Security debacle in May, so I asked the
Republican leaders in the Senate and House—Howard Baker and Bob
Michel—to come to the Oval Office and tell the president what they
had both told me, that we didn't have a prayer of passing a major overhaul of Social Security in either house. The big tax and budget fights
had left Congress with battle fatigue, they said.

The president was not easily convinced, but when Howard sug-

_____

*There was a silver lining to all of this. We used the incident to get the president to agree that
from now on, all significant policy proposals involving Congress had to go through the Legislative Strategy Group before they reached the Oval Office. The effect of this was to better
protect the president, but also to transfer much of the policymaking process from the cabinet council system overseen by Ed to the legislative system overseen by me.

gested appointing a blue-ribbon committee on Social Security, he agreed to think about it. That's an idea we had already been kicking around. Later that year, the president and congressional leaders—all genuinely concerned about the national retirement system—agreed to "take the issue out of politics" by putting it in the hands of a commission appointed by the leaders of both parties.

Was this a case of "not letting Reagan be Reagan"? Not at all. Once the president understood that overhaul wouldn't fly in Congress, he had no hesitation about doing what had to be done to save Social Security. This was the pragmatic "Reagan being Reagan."

In December, the House, the Senate, and the White House each named five members, and the White House appointed Alan Greenspan to head the group. Over the next year, it met secretly in the basement of my D.C. home on Foxhall Road. One of my favorite members was Daniel Patrick Moynihan. The brilliant and personable senator from New York, an academic-turned-politician, was a big man with an even bigger intellect, a man with a thirst for knowledge and a thirst for, well, other things.

One afternoon my son Will Winston, seventeen, answered the doorbell. "Come right in, Senator."

"Thank you, sir. Thank you very much," Moynihan said. "I want to tell you something: you look exactly like your father." (Will was too polite to say I was his stepfather, not his biological father.)

"Is there someplace where a man could get a drink in this house?"

"Yes, sir," Will replied. "We've got coffee, Cokes, ginger ale, iced tea . . ."

"No, son, I mean a *real* drink."

Will had seen adults imbibe before. This was how he learned that for some folks, cocktail hour begins earlier than 6:00 P.M.

But Moynihan was a better public servant with a drink or two under his belt than most others with none. His knowledge of Social Security was exceeded only by his passion for saving it. I treasure my memories of working with him, then sharing laughs and drinks (real ones) with him afterward. When I left public service, he wrote one of the nicest letters I received.

The Greenspan Commission was a great success. It worked out a genuine compromise between those who wanted to increase taxes and those who wanted to reduce benefits.

Because the commission included Republicans and Democrats selected by the White House and the leadership of both houses of Congress, it provided political cover for Congress to make these hard decisions. The 1983 reforms put Social Security on a sound footing for more than three decades (on a cash-flow basis) and about sixty years (with the trust fund).

As I was writing, President George W. Bush proposed new reforms for Social Security. My opinion, for what it's worth, is that the system does not face a crisis today but that the president's proposed personal accounts made sense on their own merits. There's no great risk (and considerable upside) in personal accounts that are designed correctly. An "ownership society"—having assets to pass to heirs—is a good way to give all Americans a stake in our economic system.

At the same time, personal accounts won't cure the future solvency problem. There is no easy way to do that. The best way would be to get the leaders of both parties together privately to work out a solution, as we did in 1983. It'll be hard, and perhaps impossible, to do what needs to be done unless both parties agree not to use the issue as a political battering ram.

Can we do that? I'm not sure. The nation is evenly split today, and relations between the parties are poisonous. It's not like when I first went up in 1975 and throughout the 1980s, when it was still possible— even after Watergate—to "disagree agreeably," where your political adversary was not necessarily your political enemy, and where genuine friendships were forged across party lines.

The reason we put Social Security on the back burner in 1981 was to focus on tax and spending issues. By mid-June, however, it was clear we had a big problem. Gramm-Latta had instructed Congress to come back with $36 billion in spending cuts, but hostile Democratic chairmen produced a budget bill that was "riddled with gimmicks," not real savings, Stockman told the president. So the administration did something unprecedented. We wrote our own budget bill, Gramm-Latta II. This offended congressional Democrats and not a few of our own supporters. They saw this as a challenge to the prerogatives of Congress as an equal branch of government.

A week out, we didn't have the votes. We had lost many budget-balancing Boll Weevils and also faced possible defections from "Gypsy moths"—moderate-to-liberal Republicans, mostly from the Northeast, who often voted with the Democrats. While the LSG horse-traded, the president worked the undecideds by telephone. The key vote came on a June 25 motion to keep Gramm-Latta II off the floor. Thirty-one Democrats sided with us, and we won 217–210. The Senate approved its version of the budget bill in mid-July, and a final bill passed both houses in late July.

All the while, we were fighting on a second front for tax cuts. Dan Rostenkowski, powerful chairman of House Ways and Means, wanted nothing to do with our three annual 10 percent cuts, and what Danny wanted (or didn't want), Danny usually got. More than one pundit declared the president's plan dead. Even supporters lost heart. We'd be lucky to come away with a one-year cut for low- and middle-income taxpayers, commentators said. But, as I mentioned earlier, the president's dramatic April 28 speech changed everything. Suddenly, almost overnight, the momentum began to shift. Stockman says this is when I started playing poker with the tax bill. He's right, but I was playing the hands I was dealt in meetings with Regan, Meese, and other members of the LSG.

The only way to win was to deal. To hold the Boll Weevils, for instance, we reduced the first year's cut to 5 percent and delayed it for nine months. Rostenkowski answered with a 15 percent cut over two years. President Reagan acknowledged, tongue in cheek, that the Democrats' bill might do more for the average guy and gal, *if they planned to live for only two more years.* The principal sponsors of our bipartisan plan were Barber Conable, a respected Republican moderate from New York who later headed the World Bank while I was serving as treasury secretary, and Kent Hance, a Texas Democrat who won his congressional seat in a 1978 race against George W. Bush. The fight between Rostenkowski's bill and Conable-Hance was less a battle of ideas, sadly, than a bidding war over tax breaks, but that was the price for the cuts the president wanted. That's also how we got indexing of federal income tax rates to prevent "bracket creep," the stealth tax hikes that result from inflation, and an immediate reduction of the 70 percent marginal tax rate on investment income to 50 percent, which was more than we had originally hoped for.

As the vote approached, the LSG worked overtime. The showdown in the House would not be on the bill itself, but on a motion to substitute Conable-Hance for the Rostenkowski bill. To hold Republicans, we arranged for each of four soft Gypsy Moths to receive a high-level phone call. We also identified friendly lawmakers to give post-speech statements supporting the president and talked about having some converts step forward after the vote on the motion to create a sense of momentum.

Thanks to our hard work and a final speech by the Great Communicator on July 27, we won the key vote by 238–195. Forty-eight House Democrats supported the president. Jim Jeffords was the only Gypsy Moth who flew away.* Two days later, the Senate passed its version by voice vote. The headline in the *Washington Post* read, "Reagan Triumphant on His 3-Year Tax Cut Bill."

On August 13, the president signed the historic legislation at a morning press conference at his California ranch. The budget bill "represents $130 billion in savings over the next three years" and the tax bill will cut $750 billion over the next five years, he said. Together, "they represent a turnaround of almost a half century of a course this

---

*This is the same Jim Jeffords who left the GOP early in George W. Bush's first term and helped the Democrats regain control, temporarily, of a closely divided Senate.

country's been on and mark an end to excessive growth in government bureaucracy, government spending, [and] government taxing."

W E DIDN'T celebrate long. Ten days before the signing ceremony, in fact, Stockman had called a White House meeting to tote up the numbers. We hadn't won all our proposed budget cuts, many "future savings" still remained "to be proposed," the tax cut was larger than we had estimated, and the nation was slipping into a recession. For these reasons, Stockman said, we were looking at minimum deficits of $60 billion for each of the next four years, maybe even $100 billion. We were stunned. If these numbers held up, the goal of a balanced budget was out the window.

There has been a lot of finger-pointing about who knew what, and when. That's one reason the *Atlantic* article hit us so hard in November. But I didn't have much interest then, and don't now, in the blame game or the excuse game. I also don't believe in going on the battlefield after the fighting is over and shooting the wounded. The fact is that the president could not hope to accomplish the goals of his first administration (not to mention winning a second term) unless he maintained his political viability, and that absolutely required him to win these battles over spending and taxes. We didn't have enough votes—and couldn't get them—for 100 percent of the spending reductions the president wanted, and we were forced into a bidding war over the tax bill. When the dust settled in August we found ourselves staring at a huge deficit. Now we had a problem we needed to try to solve.

Stockman suggested a "September Offensive" to keep up the momentum of budget cutting. We knew it would be tough. More cuts in discretionary spending would be hard for Congress and the public to stomach. Defense had been off limits, but Stockman argued that it needed a second look. I agreed. We made a serious run at the president, but—after having won big increases in the defense budget—he was reluctant to pare them back, and Defense Secretary Weinberger was a masterful bureaucratic infighter. We won modest reductions, nothing substantial. Looking back now at the success of the Reagan-Bush defense policy—"peace through strength"—it's clear that the investment in defense paid big dividends.

Both parties in Congress had simply lost their appetite for major spending cuts. So had a lot of cabinet officers and, in his own way, the president. The September Offensive soon fizzled. We could be proud of the budget cuts of 1981, but we would never again repeat that success.

The recession hit hard in the fall of 1981 and continued for more than a year. The downturn hurt the GOP in the '82 midterm elections. Critics blamed Reaganomics, but the budget and tax plans didn't even go into effect until October 1, 1981, and it would be another year before the first 10 percent tax cut kicked in. The real problem was the Fed's shock therapy to stop inflation. This was something that had to be done, but it happened so quickly that it knocked the wheels off the American economy and messed up our economic assumptions. Still, the president never blinked. Inflation was the cruelest tax of all, he said, and he never leaned on the Fed—as some presidents had—to back off.

Despite the recession, we had to try to do something about the deficits. We had campaigned on cutting taxes by $500 billion over five years, but had actually cut them by $750 billion. In early 1982, Meese, Deaver, Stu Spencer, and I—with the support of Nancy Reagan—tried to persuade the president to raise taxes to recoup some of the cuts beyond the $500 billion campaign target. We could do it without touching the '81 rate cuts, we said, but the president didn't want to do it. "I'd rather be criticized for a deficit than for backing away from our economic program," he wrote in his diary.

After months of wrangling with Congress over the budget and getting nowhere, Meese, Deaver, and I tried one more time in the late spring of 1982. The president listened, then took off his reading glasses and threw them down on the Oval Office desk. "All right, goddammit," he said. "I'm gonna do it, but it's wrong." The resulting

Tax and Fiscal Responsibility Act of 1982 was designed to raise about $98 billion in business and excise taxes over three years. As promised, we didn't touch the '81 rate reductions. The president later said he regretted capitulating.

I SOMETIMES call myself a "reformed drunk" on Reaganomics. Even though I was a traditional conservative, not a supply-sider, when I joined the administration, I worked my butt off to put the president's economic program in place. At the same time, I always worried that Stockman and other pessimists might be right about budget deficits leading to hyper-inflation, intolerable interest rates, and economic decline.

Well, the pessimists turned out to be wrong and Ronald Reagan, economics major at Eureka College, former movie actor, and eternal optimist, turned out to be right. The economy started growing in November 1982 and hasn't stopped yet, except for slowdowns in 1990–1991 and 2001 that were modest by historical standards. When the final tax cuts went into effect in 1984, the economy grew more than 7 percent. That was the best year since 1951, and it hasn't been matched since. Inflation averaged close to 10 percent in the Carter years; under Presidents Reagan and George H. W. Bush, it fell to 3 percent. All told, more than nineteen million new jobs were created during the Reagan-Bush years. And while we never balanced the budget, we dramatically increased tax revenues—despite the tax cuts!— and slowed the rate of growth in federal spending.

What appeared radical in 1981 is now conventional wisdom. No serious politician in the last twenty years—not one—has openly proposed restoring the failed tax policies of the 1970s. The success of Reaganomics and its British counterpart, Thatcherism, also discredited central planning, state ownership, excessive regulation, and heavy taxation worldwide. Today, even China, Russia, and India have liberalized their state economies.

Does this mean that deficits don't matter? Of course not. I still object to running a credit card on the next generation. But the deficits of the eighties, though unfortunate, did less harm than the tax cuts did good. The green-eyeshade crowd said we would have a meltdown. Instead, thanks to Ronald Reagan, our economy boomed.

In the 1990s, Robert Rubin took up the mantle of "fiscal discipline," first as a Clinton adviser, later as treasury secretary. Bob was one of the stars of the Clinton cabinet. I have great respect for him and consider him a friend, but I disagree strongly on this issue. He used "fiscal discipline" as an argument for raising taxes, as Democrats did in 1993. But tax hikes without spending restraint never balance the budget because Congress always spends the new money, and more.

Did President Clinton's "fiscally responsible" 1993 tax bill trigger the prosperity of the 1990s? No. Despite the downturn in 1990–1991, the economy had already been growing smartly for two years before that bill was passed. Let me repeat: you simply cannot deal with deficits with taxes alone, unaccompanied by spending restraint. President Reagan said it best. "Deficits aren't caused by too little taxing, they are caused by too much spending." He was so frustrated at the end that he believed the only way to control the budget was with constitutional amendments to force Congress to balance the budget and give the president a line-item veto.

We never conquered the deficit in the Reagan-Bush years, but our tax cuts triggered what has now turned out to be more than twenty-four years of sustained, noninflationary growth, punctuated only by the two modest slowdowns I mentioned. It's a great legacy, and I'm proud to have had a part in it.

THE WEEKEND AFTER the Stockman–*Atlantic Monthly* incident (Nancy was out of town), the president and I flew to Texas to hunt turkeys on the Winston Ranch near San Antonio, acreage owned by my stepchildren's paternal grandfather—James ("Dear Father")

Winston.* The president, Jerry Parr, and I put on camouflage outfits, then went out with shotguns to wait in the brush for our Thanksgiving dinners to walk by.

Turkeys are smart as hell and have the sharpest eyesight and hearing of any game I've ever hunted. With border patrol officers, Texas highway patrolmen, and Secret Service agents rattling around behind us, we really didn't have much of a chance. Finally, however, a small flock came within range. Unfortunately, they were all hens. (Male turkeys—gobblers—are blacker and larger and have beards.) It fell to me to tell the president it was not legal to shoot them. He was disappointed, but he got his revenge when he signed a photograph of the hunting party. "Jim, see me smile? Of course this was *before* the hunt."

Despite his empty game bag, however, the president clearly enjoyed the outing, probably for the same reasons he enjoyed riding horses and chopping wood. Every now and then, it's good to trade your burdens for a few hours in the sunshine and fresh air. Even when the turkeys don't cooperate, there's nothing quite like a day in the woods to refresh your spirits.

THE FIRST YEAR of the Reagan presidency ended on a somber note, due to the bad economy. We nevertheless had a sense of satisfaction about what we had accomplished. The president "has the best legislative record of any incoming president since Lyndon Johnson," I told reporters at the time. And we were confident, none so much as the president, that better days lay ahead.

My next three years as chief of staff were filled with dramas of

---

*My sons, Bo and Will, had the privilege of cohosting the event with their grandfather. It was quite an experience. The White House staff took control of the house, did the cooking, and served meals on presidential china that had been lugged down from Washington. In addition, the president slept in the master bedroom. "This is the first time I ever felt like a guest in my own house," Dear Father said later. True to their upbringing, both Bo and Will still hunt and fish every chance they get. Bo is now a businessman in the central Texas town of Boerne. Will served in the U.S. Army's Special Forces. He lives in Dallas and works for an oil and gas company.

their own, but nothing that quite matched the excitement and historic importance of that first year. By the end, it was time to move on. At first, I sought another position in the White House. When that didn't work out, I flirted with the possibility of a private-sector job. But as the president's first term drew to a close, I was still unsure what I would do.

Then a member of the cabinet approached me with an unexpected proposition. The president gave it his blessing, and I left the White House for a new job in the administration. Years later, President Reagan would write, with perhaps a bit of understatement, that this move had "created some problems."

NINE

"CATCHING JAVELINS"

ON JULY 12, 2003, the United States Navy commissioned a magnificent nuclear-powered Nimitz-class aircraft carrier, the USS *Ronald Reagan*, at the Norfolk Naval Station in Virginia. Nancy Reagan attended the Saturday ceremony, as did Susan and I and many others who had served and loved the fortieth president. Vice President Cheney delivered the keynote speech, and Mrs. Reagan, as the ship's sponsor, proudly gave the order to "man our ship and bring her to life!"

While we were in Norfolk, Susan and I went to dinner with Mike Deaver and his wife, Carolyn. By chance we were seated near a table that included Ed Meese and his wife, Ursula; former National Security Adviser Bill Clark and his wife, Joan; and former U.S. ambassador to the United Nations Jeane Kirkpatrick. After looking over at that formidable group, Mike smiled at me and said, "Some things never change."

I could only laugh. Ed Meese is a wonderful guy for whom I have genuine affection, notwithstanding differences we may have had during our service to President Reagan. Bill Clark and I weren't as close, but I respect his public service.

Ed, Bill, Mike, and I fought several battles side by side during the first term. In August 1982, for example, we all helped persuade the president to convince Israel's Prime Minister Menachem Begin that the bombing of West Beirut should be stopped. (The air strikes, which targeted six thousand armed PLO members holed up in civilian neighborhoods, had killed and injured many innocent bystanders.) As one might expect of those working in a high-powered environment like the White House, however, we also had our disagreements. That night in Norfolk, Mike was alluding to two well-publicized occasions in 1983 when we were divided as we were in the restaurant—Baker and Deaver on one side, Meese and Clark on the other. Had the second of these two clashes turned out differently, the president might well have avoided the Iran-Contra scandal in his second term.

Clash number one took place on September 14, 1983, and also involved Lebanon. Mike and I were in a car on our way to lunch when he told me that Clark, with Meese's support, had prevailed upon President Reagan to authorize an FBI investigation of a recent leak about U.S. policy in that war-torn Middle Eastern country. A presidential memo, which I believe was inspired by Clark, approved the use of polygraphs on, among others, everyone present at National Security Council meetings on Lebanon three days earlier. Anyone refusing to cooperate was to be subject to immediate dismissal.

Although I was not the leaker, I think Clark considered my side of the White House to be suspect. It was no secret in the White House that I often spoke with reporters, but Clark failed to recognize that I always spoke on background, which, as I have already explained, is important for the chief of staff to do and is far different from leaking. More important, Vice President Bush and Secretary of State George Shultz (who had replaced Al Haig fourteen months earlier) had also attended the meetings. Calling their integrity into question by strapping them to a lie detector would be humiliating to them, demoralizing to others on the Reagan team, and politically disastrous for the president. It would, of course, also be unconstitutional to try to dismiss the vice president, an elected official.

This plan was also inconsistent with a national security directive signed by the president six months earlier. As best I can remember, it gave the White House counsel's office authority to recommend use of polygraphs in investigations of leaks of classified and sensitive information at the White House. And since the counsel's office reported to me, that meant I had the ultimate authority to go to the president on this issue.

I told our driver to turn around.

As we headed back to the White House, I could imagine what had probably happened. Because of his long association with Ronald Reagan, Bill was a more powerful national security adviser than Dick Allen, the man he replaced in January 1982. Dick had reported to Ed Meese, but Bill reported directly to the president. Bill had probably used his Oval Office walk-in privileges to complain, legitimately, about yet another leak that undermined the administration and to persuade the president to take drastic action. Like other presidents, Ronald Reagan hated leaks and was often frustrated that he could not stop them. The president also trusted Bill, his chief of staff as governor of California, particularly so after Ed seconded the idea of using polygraphs. Based on what happened a few hours later, I'm confident I could have headed off this misadventure if I had been there at the time.

Returning to the White House, I was one unhappy chief of staff. I could just see the headlines: "President Orders Bush, Shultz, Others to Take Lie Detector Tests." What credibility would we have with others if it appeared that we didn't even trust one another? Democrats would have a field day. Political cartoonists would fall to their knees and give thanks for an early Christmas present. I stopped in my office and picked up a copy of the directive that gave me authority to recommend White House polygraphs.

The president was having lunch with the vice president and the secretary of state. Ordinarily, I would not have interrupted them, but this was no ordinary situation. "Mr. President," I said, handing him the directive, "here's the paper you signed that says the chief of staff has authority to recommend when we do this in the White House. Do you really mean to strap your vice president and secretary of state to a lie detector?"

The whole thing was a surprise to Bush and Shultz. I don't remember his exact words, but Shultz told the president something to this effect: "If you want me to take a polygraph, you might also want to get yourself a new secretary of state." I suggested that I, too, might leave. The vice president agreed that lie detectors were a bad idea.

As the implications of this decision sank in, the president was obviously troubled. "Bill shouldn't have done this," he said. "Let's get the fellows together and kick it around." He then withdrew the order, pending further discussion.

The "fellows"—the vice president, the attorney general, Clark, and the troika—met a short time later. It was an acrimonious meeting. We kicked the idea around, and we kicked one another. I didn't object to the investigation, I said, just to the mandatory polygraphs. Bill suggested I was afraid of what the lie detector might reveal. Not true! I was worried about the impact on the president's image and on his team's morale. I was also, truth be known, not happy that Clark and Meese had tried to usurp for themselves, without a word to me, authority and responsibility that had been specifically assigned to the chief of staff. After listening to everyone, the president reversed himself. "This is not the thing to do," he said. And that was that. The FBI investigated but never identified the leaker.

This flap led to another barely civil war within the White House. To all appearances, it was just a high-stakes game of musical chairs that bruised a couple of egos (mine included). But it also set in motion the events that produced one of the few stains on the legacy of Ronald Reagan.

Here's what happened. Clark, worn down by the responsibilities of serving as national security adviser, was already contemplating a return to civilian life or another government post. The polygraph incident reinforced his desire to move on.

Enter Jim Watt, secretary of the interior and a member of the "let

Reagan be Reagan" crowd. He was an outspoken proponent of developing our federal lands (responsibly, he believed) and, as a consequence, a lightning rod for most environmentalists. Our polls showed that he would be a liability when the president ran for reelection in 1984, but Ronald Reagan was nothing if not loyal. As the Stockman affair revealed, a Reagan appointee had to go a long way to reach the point of no return.

Watt reached that point on September 21, 1983, when he told a U.S. Chamber of Commerce breakfast that a commission reviewing his department's coal leasing program had "every kind of mix you can have. I have a black, I have a woman, two Jews, and a cripple."

I don't condone what Jim said and we weren't particularly close, but he was a fine and decent man. As he was recruited for the job, he had leveled with the president: "The day may come when you will have to let me go." Now that day had come, and he was quick to offer to leave.

Clark saw Watt's departure as an opening and volunteered to move to the Interior Department. Good idea, said the president. The First Lady, who evidently felt that what Clark had done in the polygraph incident had embarrassed her husband, agreed.

I also liked the idea. Too often the national security adviser was off doing his own thing and encouraging the president to spend time on matters and appearances unrelated to the plan of the day or the plan of the week. These diversions were costly. They made the administration appear unfocused and uncoordinated and made the job of prioritizing our objectives very difficult. This had not been the case with Dick Allen, who reported to Meese rather than to the president.

Clark's penchant for secrecy and his desire to exercise total control over some foreign policy issues also created problems. He once persuaded the president to send Jeane Kirkpatrick, our UN ambassador, on a fact-finding trip to Latin America. Trouble was, neither Bill nor Jeane had cleared the mission with the cabinet officer who ostensibly had the lead on foreign policy, Secretary of State George Shultz. This was an example of a classic problem that has plagued many admin-istrations: the White House national security adviser's bypassing the responsible agency (in this case, State; sometimes Defense) and "go-ing operational" on a sensitive foreign policy or security issue. When I learned that the mission had not been cleared with the secretary of state, I told the president. He was shocked and told Clark to get Shultz's approval.

With the 1984 campaign approaching, Deaver and I wanted to avoid the kind of internal conflicts that inevitably occur when the po-litical side of the White House and the national security side are not singing from the same hymnal. The best way to assure coordination rather than competition is for the national security adviser and chief of staff to work well together. So it occurred to Mike and me (who worked very well together): what if I moved to the national security adviser's office and Mike, who had served as deputy chief of staff for more than two and a half years, took my job?

My status in the White House had long been grist for the rumor mills. For more than a year, newspapers had reported that I was think-ing about leaving the White House. Their "sources" said, variously, that I was tired of the internal strains in the White House, frustrated at my inability to persuade the president to cut the deficit, gripped by "end of the day weariness," and hungry for political advancement—to U.S. attorney general, some office in Texas, or, my all-time favorite, a run for the presidency in 1988. The *Dallas Morning News* floated that one in March 1982, then reported that "Baker responded with an ex-pletive when the prospect of a presidential bid was broached to him." Hell yes I did! I worked for a president who planned to run again and a vice president who was likely to run after that. Whatever ambitions I may have had weren't built around fantasies about one or both of them turning their back on a second term or being defeated.

My principal motivation for wanting to leave the chief of staff's job in October 1983 was "none of the above." Rather I wanted to help Ronald Reagan function more efficiently as a chief executive and get reelected. That said, I won't deny that I thought a change would do me good. Yes, working in foreign policy and national security would be challenging and might prove helpful, though not essential, if I later were offered a shot at a cabinet job. And, yes, I was beginning to wear down.

From the beginning, I knew from talking to former White House chiefs of staff that the job would be brutal. When the president offered the chief of staff position in 1980, I told him it was best done in two-year stints. He agreed. By late 1983, I was already well past my original departure date.

The White House is at the very center of the political process by which our nation governs itself, and the chief of staff is at the very center of operations in the White House. The job is to get things done for the president while catching political javelins that come from all directions. It's important and it's fun, mostly. But to borrow a line from a country song, it surely tires your mind.

One thing that tired my mind was the never-ending chorus from the right about letting Reagan be Reagan. In July 1981, for example, when the president nominated Sandra Day O'Connor to the Supreme Court, Howard Phillips, head of the Conservative Caucus, complained that from the outset, "the administration has been staffed by country-club conservatives who have contempt for social conservatives." M. Stanton Evans, a syndicated columnist, was happy to name names. In the January 29, 1983, issue of the weekly conservative journal *Human Events,* he wrote a piece titled "Time for Jim Baker to Resign." I was a "likable fellow," he said, but "spectacularly ill-fitted to a crucial role in an administration allegedly seeking a conservative revolution in our politics. Baker is about as qualified for such a job as I would be to play left tackle for the Dallas Cowboys."

Evans was considerably gentler than Clymer Wright, a Houston conservative activist who had supported Reagan over Ford in 1976. In a May 1982 letter, he said I was undermining and sabotaging the president's efforts. He attached several news articles to prove his point.

Usually I am thick-skinned about such criticism. What people like

Clymer Wright (who was anything but a likable fellow) failed to realize, however, was that in undermining me, they were really undermining Ronald Reagan. To win votes for the president on the Hill, I needed to approach members of Congress from a position of strength. If they doubted for one minute that I enjoyed the president's full confidence and support—that I spoke for him—they would have no reason to listen to my arguments, trust my promises, or ponder my ever-so-gentle hints about what might happen if they voted the wrong way.

Reagan being Reagan, he promptly replied to Wright. "Yes, there is undermining of my efforts going on, and, yes, there is sabotage of all I'm trying to accomplish," the president wrote. "But it's being done by the people who write these articles and columns, not by any White House staff member and certainly not Jim Baker. . . . Don't join their group, Clymer—you are helping them with their sabotage.

"I'm in charge," the president continued, "and my people are helping to carry out the policies I set. No, we don't get everything we want and, yes, we have to compromise to get 75 percent or 80 percent of our programs. We try to see that the 75 percent or 80 percent is more than worth the compromise we have to accept. So far it has been."

Mike and I knew that Ed Meese, Bill Clark, and others would oppose a job switch that put the two of us in charge of both the National Security Council and the rest of the White House.* So, first things first, we ran the idea by a handful of people whose counsel we trusted and whose support we would need—Vice President Bush, Secretary of State Shultz, Stu Spencer, and, of course, the First Lady. All were in favor. Now it was time to go to the president. He listened to our pitch, looked at who was in our corner, thought it over, and okayed the plan.

---

*Time has clouded my memory of the details of what the *New York Times*'s Hedrick Smith called "the staff coup that failed." Revisiting Smith's book *The Power Game*, and Lou Cannon's *President Reagan: The Role of a Lifetime* helped me reconstruct the events. I trust their accuracy on this episode because both interviewed me about the "coup" way back when.

D-Day was Friday, October 14, the day after the president had announced that Clark would be leaving the National Security Council to replace Watt at the Interior Department. Mike and I thought we had orchestrated the schedule so that nothing could go wrong. After lunching with Shultz, the president would go to the situation room for a one o'clock meeting of the National Security Planning Group (NSPG)—the highest-ranking members of the NSC, chaired by the national security adviser. Participants generally included the vice president, secretary of state, secretary of defense, CIA director, chairman of the joint chiefs of staff, and the troika (although on this day Mike and I decided it would be prudent not to attend).

Under our plan, the president would announce to the NSPG that he was appointing me to succeed Clark, and Deaver to succeed me. We would then give the press office a release about the switch. At four o'clock, the president would make an appearance in the briefing room and announce the personnel changes to the press. He would then head off to Camp David for the weekend.

Timing is everything, and our timing failed us. Instead of being in the situation room at one o'clock, as scheduled, the president was in Mike's office going over his NSPG remarks. This was to be Clark's last meeting, and when the president failed to show, Bill came upstairs to fetch him. We should have accompanied them. On the way to the situation room, the president told Clark about the planned changes. From what I understand, Clark betrayed no emotion, but did ask the president to postpone the announcement until the two of them could talk. The president obliged him.

Notes get passed at White House meetings all the time. Some are frivolous, distractions from the tedium of meetings that won't end. When my pal George H. W. Bush was president and I was secretary of state, he would pass notes asking if I might be available for an all-too-rare game of golf or tennis. Once he even asked if I thought a visiting head of state was responsible for the unpleasant odor in the room. (Was George telling the truth, I always wondered, or only trying to cover his own backside?)

Other notes are more substantive. In the situation room on this day, Clark sent Meese, Casey, and Weinberger notes asking them to stick around and meet with him and the president. They all are reported to have argued vigorously against the changes, with Jeane Kirkpatrick loudly joining the chorus. Apparently Clark also volunteered to stay at the NSC and suggested that I take his job at Interior. The president said this wouldn't work because I owned oil and gas interests back home. He knew this because I always declined to participate in White House decisions on energy issues.

Mike and I didn't know the president was meeting with the four horsemen of our apocalypse. When he failed to return upstairs on schedule, however, Mike tracked him down. At this point, to mix a couple of metaphors, we could see the handwriting on the wall, which said: your goose is in the oven and the thermostat is set on high.

When he came back, the president told us that there was opposition to the plan and that he wanted to think about it over the weekend. "Mr. President," I said, "I don't want to be a problem for you. If there's that much opposition, let's forget it." Mike took it much more personally. He thought the president's hesitancy reflected, in part at least, a lack of confidence in him as a potential chief of staff.

The president did review the decision over the weekend. Some say his thinking was aided by calls ("Don't do it!") from critics recruited by Clark, et al. On Monday morning he told us he had decided against the switch. He later said he did it to avoid friction among the cabinet and White House staff. By the end of the day, he had named a new national security adviser—Bud McFarlane, who had served on the staff of the Senate Armed Forces Committee under Senator John Tower, as counselor in the Haig State Department, and as the president's special representative in the Middle East.* Bud was clearly a compromise choice. Casey had lobbied strenuously for Jeane Kirkpatrick. The less hawkish Shultz, however, strongly opposed her, and the president

---

*Things later went south for Bud, but I always liked him and worked well with him. On Iran-Contra he just took a wrong turn trying to do what he thought was the right thing.

didn't want "bad chemistry" (as he wrote later) between these two high-ranking officials.

Disappointed as I was, I decided to stay put as chief of staff for the time being, but to keep my eyes open for opportunities outside the administration. Why? The rodent-related expletive I used earlier to describe a certain form of political infighting again comes to mind. Sometimes it's not much fun. It wasn't fun for the president, either. "Jim took it pretty well," he wrote in his diary, "but Mike was pretty upset. . . . It was an unhappy day all around."

Seven years later, former President Reagan reflected in his autobiography on the impact of that hassle: "My decision not to appoint Jim Baker as national security adviser, I suppose, was a turning point for my administration, although I had no idea at the time how significant it would prove to be."

How so? One hyphenated word: Iran-Contra. The president was suggesting that if I had been his national security adviser—rather than Bud McFarlane and Bud's successor, John Poindexter, a retired admiral—the scandal that rocked the administration during its second term might never have happened.

That trouble began on Bud's watch in 1985, when Iran secretly made a request to buy weapons from our government. An embargo against such a sale was in place, but Bud asked the president for authority to talk to the Iranians. His reasoning: the sale would lead to better relations with Iran and, quite possibly Lebanon, where Iranian-backed terrorists were holding seven U.S. hostages. The president had long made it clear that he would not deal with terrorists, but he was, as I've already stated, a very sentimental man.

That same sentimentality led him, I believe, to approve the arms-for-hostages gambit. He also sincerely believed that dealing with Iranian moderates—the administration never dealt directly with terrorists—might influence the direction Iran would take after the death of Ayatollah Khomeini. Casey also favored the deal, but the president probably should have known it was a bad idea from the fact that Shultz and Weinberger, who rarely agreed on anything, both gave it a thumbs-down. In the end, however, sentiment trumped good sense, and McFarlane was authorized to make overtures to the Iranians.

In time, talk turned to action. Israel sold several million dollars' worth of U.S. weapons to Iran, and the U.S. sold replacement weapons to Israel. Then under Poindexter, millions of dollars from the arms sales were diverted to the anti-communist Contras in Nicaragua, who were attempting to oust the Russian- and Cuban-backed Sandinista government from power. This diversion, it was argued at the time, violated the Boland Amendment, a congressional mandate that restricted U.S. involvement in Nicaragua. Regardless of whether it did or did not violate that legislation, however, the White House was running an off-budget foreign policy project outside the agencies, outside the system of congressional oversight, and in conflict with both congressional and stated White House policies.

From beginning to end, Iran-Contra was wrong, a textbook example of what can happen when the White House "goes operational." The White House isn't always right, State and Defense aren't always right, and Congress isn't always right. But policies developed through the rough-and-tumble of politics—within the administration, between the administration and Congress, and in a continuing dialogue with the American people—are more often right than wrong. Bypassing these institutions and processes put dangerous weapons in the hands of known terrorist sponsors, drove up the market price for hostages, and weakened rather than strengthened the case for helping the Contras. Iran-Contra crippled the administration and it hurt our nation, at home and abroad.

One of the worst injuries, ironically, was the commissioning of Independent Counsel Lawrence Walsh to investigate. He spent millions of dollars proving the obvious, then cynically influenced the 1992 elections. (I'll have more to say about that later.) McFarlane, Poindexter, and Oliver North (an NSC staffer)—the architects of Iran-Contra—were convicted of crimes, along with several other lower-level players. But

Walsh also went after Weinberger and, through innuendo, President George H. W. Bush, neither of whom was ever credibly alleged to have had anything to do with the operation itself. George was right to pardon Weinberger, McFarlane, and four other Iran-Contra figures in December 1992. And the nation was right, finally, to let the independent counsel law expire in 1999 after it became apparent, even to Democrats, that on balance, independent prosecutors and the "gotcha" politics associated with trying to get them appointed did more harm than good.

As George said in 1992, the Walsh prosecution reflected "a profoundly troubling development in the political and legal climate of our country: the criminalization of policy differences. These differences should have been addressed in the political arena without the Damocles sword of criminality hanging over the heads of some combatants. The proper target is the president, not his subordinates; the proper forum is the voting booth, not the courtroom."

Amen.

President Reagan approved the arms deals with Iran, but insisted he had no knowledge of the diversion of funds until Ed Meese, then attorney general, uncovered an Oliver North memorandum about the scheme. Subordinates who knew of his ardent support for the Contras took it into their own hands to arm them, the president said. Had he been asked to approve such action, he wrote later, he would have refused. I believe that. I also admire what he did when he found out. "There are reasons why it happened," he said, "but no excuses. It was a mistake." And he ordered his administration to cooperate in the investigation.

Would Iran-Contra have happened on my watch as national security adviser? It's easy and potentially self-serving, I suppose, to say I don't think so. Hindsight is always perfect. I also have sympathy for the folks who tried in good faith to do what they thought was right, then had it blow up in their face. But the fact is, they messed up. Iran-Contra was wrong and it wasn't likely to work. The fantasy upon which all the other fantasies were constructed was that no one would ever know. But, as Secretary Shultz warned at the time, you can't do something on this scale in Washington, D.C., and keep it secret. From the start, Iran-Contra had the potential—no, the near certainty—of blowing up and damaging the reputations of, among others, the president of the United States. And that's exactly what happened.

Unfortunately, I never got a chance to weigh in. As secretary of the treasury during this period, I still sat on the National Security Council, but as I would later learn, Poindexter made it a point to exclude me from meetings at which the arms-for-hostages deal was being discussed. He said he knew I would object, perhaps because at a June 1984 NSPG meeting I was quoted by Shultz and Casey as saying that the United States government may raise and spend funds only through an appropriation of Congress. Poindexter later apologized for having kept me in the dark. "John," I said, "that was the biggest favor you could have done for me." But not for President Reagan.

What I *might have done* about Nicaragua as national security adviser can perhaps be measured against what I *actually did* when I took office as secretary of state in January 1989. The Sandinistas were still in power, the Contras were still fighting, and Congress was still locked in a fierce struggle over U.S. policy. I knew we would never solve this foreign policy problem until we removed it from the domestic political debate. So we negotiated a bipartisan accord on Central America, an agreement between congressional Democrats and Republicans,* calling for an election that both sides in Nicaragua would pledge to respect. When the Sandinistas were voted out of power— much to their surprise— they honored the election results, thanks in large part to the efforts of former president Jimmy Carter, with whom the administration worked closely and effectively.

---

*I've often said that my first major negotiation as secretary of state was not with a foreign power but with the Congress of the United States.

. . .

DURING THE AUTUMN of 1983, I was presented with an intriguing job possibility outside the administration: commissioner of Major League Baseball. Bowie Kuhn was about to retire, and Bud Selig, major shareholder of the Milwaukee Brewers and head of the search committee to find a new commissioner, approached me about the position. We talked in my home on Foxhall Road, then sat down with legendary trial lawyer and political insider Edward Bennett Williams, co-owner of the Baltimore Orioles and Washington Redskins. Despite his evident interest in seeing me take the job, Williams doubted I would accept. "Jim, you're not going to do this," he said, "because President Reagan is going to put you in his cabinet." It was a prophetic remark, although I had no reason to think so at the time. Anyway, it soon became clear to me that the baseball owners did not want to vest their commissioner with real authority on labor contracts, TV rights, and other big issues, so I withdrew my name. I wasn't looking for a ceremonial job. *Washington Post* columnist George Will, a big baseball fan, said I should have taken the job if I ever wanted to run for president because more people would know my name as baseball commissioner than as a cabinet officer.

When the story got out, Jack Ohman, political cartoonist for *The Oregonian,* created a three-panel masterpiece. It was prefaced by the words: "White House chief of staff James A. Baker III may become the new major league baseball commissioner. His experience?"

Panel One read, "Takes abuse well," and showed a pitcher from the "New Right" firing a baseball off my noggin. "BONK."

Panel Two read, "Has practical experience dealing with prima donnas and egomaniacs, as he will likely encounter in the form of players and team owners," and showed me talking with four men in baseball uniforms: Clark, Meese, Bush, and Shultz.

The final panel read, "Has both fielding and hitting experience." Here I was shown fielding reporters' questions with a "No comment" and hitting Bill Casey over the head with a bat. "THOK."

. . .

SOME WROTE at the time that I was driven from the White House by pressure from the family residence. The First Lady blamed me, so the story goes, for President Reagan's poor performance in the first 1984 presidential debate against Walter Mondale. I was reported to have been demoralized by her alleged tongue-lashing, to have seen this as another example of how the Reagans failed to appreciate me, and to have decided then and there, enough is enough. Like so many Washington stories, however, this makes for good gossip but bad history.

If you look at the results of Reagan vs. Mondale, it's hard to believe that the president's team could have been too worried. Running on a strong record with an improving economy against an opponent who admitted he would raise taxes, the well-liked president was reelected with 58.8 percent of the popular vote and won a staggering forty-nine out of fifty states and 525 out of 538 electoral votes. Yet it *is* true that after the first presidential debate in Louisville, we were somewhat worried* ... and that some of the blame was laid on my doorstep.

Let's go back to early October 1984. As chief of staff, I was effectively in charge of the reelection effort and of the debate negotiations and preparation. Darman was my principal deputy. For the most part, we followed the successful script of 1980. Again, we gave the president briefing books, and again, David Stockman played the role of his opponent in full-scale ninety-minute rehearsals.

Unfortunately, the president was off his game at the first debate in Louisville. In his own words, he began okay but "flattened out." This was evident in his closing statement. Instead of reminding voters of our campaign theme—"Morning in America"—with his usual eloquent paean to our nation and his vision of an even better tomorrow,

---

*One reason we were concerned is that the GOP had lost twenty-six House seats in the November '82 midterm elections. That was the political price we paid for an economy that had then not yet turned around. By coincidence, the Reagan boom began that very same month, which set up the big victory for the president in 1984.

he got bogged down in minutiae. Morale was not high in our camp after the debate, but I was honest with reporters. This was not one of the Great Communicator's better efforts, I said.

We knew what was coming: that nasty three-letter word, *age.* Newspapers asked if the president was too old to serve another four-year term. Worse, the television network news trotted out footage of the president falling asleep in the Vatican in June 1982 after an all-night flight from Washington to Rome.*

But it wasn't age that did in the president in Louisville. Uncharacteristically, he had not done his homework, the only time I ever witnessed such a failure. It's really important in a presidential debate to open strong and close strong. Candidates generally memorize their closing statements. If you review the tape of that debate, however, you'll see that the president didn't do that, and after a confusing back-and-forth exchange with the moderator about how much time he had, he lost his train of thought.

Nancy Reagan didn't see it that way, and who can blame her? She loved her husband dearly and was accustomed to seeing him perform smoothly. After the debate, she expressed her concerns to Deaver, Stu Spencer, and Paul Laxalt, a close friend of the Reagans and general chairman of the campaign. Paul said he had reservations about the way the president had been prepared, or, in his eyes, over-prepared. "He was brutalized by a briefing process that didn't make any sense," Paul said publicly. "It filled his head with so many facts and figures that he lost his spontaneity and his visionary concepts."

That put the blame squarely on the staff, with Darman (whom Laxalt disliked) being nominated as the scapegoat. Deaver and

---

*He deserved a nap. On that same trip, the president and Pope John Paul II met for almost an hour in the Vatican library and set in motion what *Time* magazine later called "a clandestine campaign to hasten the dissolution of the communist empire." Their short-term goal was to help protect the Solidarity movement from a military crackdown, but their ultimate aim was nothing less than the liberation of Eastern Europe. The deaths of President Reagan in 2004 and Pope John Paul II in 2005 reminded us of how much we owe these two great men.

Spencer suggested that I should fire him, but I refused. "Look," I said, "if he's the problem, I'm sure I'll hear about it from the president himself. If he orders me to fire anyone, I'll do it." Of course, I was fairly certain that wouldn't happen. I am aware that the president later said he was "overtrained," but in interviews at the time, he refused to blame staff. And in his conversations with me at the time, the president took personal responsibility for his poor performance.

In the days that followed, both the staff and friends outside the campaign worked to restore the president's confidence. It seemed to work. For good measure, just before he took the stage for the second debate in Kansas City on October 28, I handed the president a note that called to mind his successful debate against Jimmy Carter four years earlier. "Chuckle again and have fun out there," I wrote.

He had fun with at least one question. The *Baltimore Sun*'s Henry Trewhitt reminded the president that John F. Kennedy had gone with little sleep for several days during the Cuban missile crisis, then asked, "Is there any doubt in your mind that you would be able to function in such circumstances?"

"Not at all, Mr. Trewhitt," the president replied, "and I want you to know that also I will not make age an issue of this campaign. I am not going to exploit for political purposes my opponent's youth and inexperience."

Everyone laughed, including the fifty-six-year-old Walter Mondale. From that point on, our campaign never looked back.

Did I resent the criticism directed at Darman and me? Yes. Was it the final straw that caused me to leave the chief of staff position? No. In my mind, I was already out the West Wing door. I just didn't know what new door I would be entering. In serving four years as chief of staff, I had caught about as many javelins as I could, and Susan wanted me to find a job that would allow me to come home at a regular hour.

SHORTLY AFTER I got into the office on November 16, 1984, just ten days after the election, Treasury Secretary Don Regan chewed my ear off in an expletive-filled telephone call. He was furious about a *Washington Post* article detailing some of his remarks at the previous day's cabinet meeting and assumed that someone on the White House staff had been the source. After he hung up, he sent a letter of resignation to the president. I told the president about the letter, which I knew he would not want to accept, and said I would sit down with Don and straighten things out. I then went over to Treasury to make nice with the former Merrill Lynch chairman, who was one of the president's favorite cabinet members.

We quickly and calmly resolved the matter—ex-Marine to ex-Marine—then Don asked me to stay for lunch. As we visited, he sensed that I was one tired guy. "You're right," I said. He later wrote that he surprised himself with his response. He certainly surprised me. "We should swap jobs," he said.

I had already given some thought to serving in the cabinet, if President Reagan should ask, but the "no vacancy" sign was up at what would have been my top four choices—State, Treasury, Defense, and Justice. I'd had no reason to believe Regan was interested in leaving the second-ranking cabinet department. But now . . .

"Do you really mean that?" I asked.

"I guess I do."

"Well, watch out. I may just take you up on it."

"When you're ready to talk, I'll be here," he said.

I wasn't ready to talk until I had consulted my own troika—Susan Baker, Dick Darman, and Margaret Tutwiler. Dick, as he so often did on issues of policy and personnel, boiled everything down to a sharp one-page analysis of the upside and downside of the proposed move. In a way, he provided the same service to me that I had provided to others, first as a business lawyer, then as a political and policy adviser. He helped sort out the issues, offered an independent perspective, and gave good advice. Margaret, in turn, helped me analyze the prospective benefits and costs. I relied heavily on her political instincts—using "political" in the broadest sense—and good judgment. Finally, Susan's common sense and grounding in faith and family helped me keep things in perspective.

All three liked the idea of moving to Treasury, and after I weighed their advice, I did too. As soon as I made the decision to move (if the president approved), I felt an excitement that I hadn't felt since the day I was asked to serve as chief of staff. I was ready for a new challenge.

On November 30, 1984, Don Regan and I lunched at Treasury. The biggest item on his plate was tax reform, and I had a lot of questions. Near the end of the lunch, I told him I was ready to switch, if he was serious and if the president liked the idea. He asked for a few days to think it over.

"We need to get Deaver involved," I said before I left. "We could never do this without telling Mike." Why? First of all, as a courtesy. Mike had wanted to be chief of staff. He was now about to leave the administration to work as a lobbyist, but he still deserved to be told. And second, because Mike was the best person to talk to the First Lady about the switch.

Darman and I put together a plan to win Deaver's support. "It's time for a change," our memo said, because both Regan and Baker "are tired of their current jobs and have spent a fair amount of political capital in them [and] both would be reinvigorated by the shift, as would the administration." The plan would put me, "our top legislative negotiator," in charge of "the difficult tax simplification fight," we wrote. And it would put Regan, "our top economic policy maker," in charge of "the difficult job" of reducing the budget deficit. In addition, we argued, the succession "would be respected by most internal and external factions, senior cabinet officials, financial markets and the international community, and . . . would be enjoyed by the president."

I mentioned the idea to Deaver, and Darman followed up with him. Deaver then talked to the president. Because the president knew both Regan and me so well, we hoped he would say yes rather quickly. "Leaks could stimulate conflict, which could destroy one of the main benefits: infusion of momentum," we cautioned. After checking, Mike told us the president liked the idea and Nancy was on board, too.

On January 7, 1985, Deaver, Regan, and I met with the president in the Oval Office. "I've brought you someone your own age to play with," Mike said, smiling. The president truly enjoyed Regan's company. They were close in age, they were both Irish Americans, and they both loved a good joke. I also reminded the president about our discussion four years ago about how it would be best if I served just two years as chief of staff. He laughed and gave the switch his blessing. The announcement was made the next day.

LOOKING BACK on my time in the White House, a few dos and don'ts come to mind. The most important, as I've already mentioned, is to remember that all your power as chief of staff is vicarious through the president. Nobody elected you; you're staff. Powerful, yes, but staff nonetheless.

Understand what the president wants, then help him get it. If you think he's wrong, tell him, but always respect and carry out his decisions. On contentious issues, be an honest broker so he hears all sides (and all sides know they have been heard). Make the trains run on time so he doesn't have to worry about the small stuff. Husband the president's power, and your own, by using it wisely. Don't start more fights than you can win, and win the ones you start. Success builds on success.

Surround yourself with the best people you can find. You can't do this job without help. Give loyalty and demand loyalty. Delegate. Expect performance. When you get it, show appreciation.

Politics ain't beanbag, but there's no reason to be uncivil. Disagree agreeably. Listen respectfully. Treat everyone, allies and adversaries alike, with dignity. Return telephone calls. Count the votes. When you're ahead, call the question. When you're behind, work harder. If you can't get everything you want, get what you can. When you can't win, fall back and fight another day.

Respect the press and get to know reporters. Talk to them, on background most of the time, but on the record when necessary. Help them understand the administration's position. And never lie to them.

. . .

I WILL ALWAYS treasure my memories of those times and my good fortune in being able to work at the right hand of Ronald Reagan. He was a wonderful man, a lovely human being, and without doubt one of our greatest presidents. He refreshed the nation's spirit, rebuilt our economy, and—more than any other president before him —hastened the collapse of communism. The vast majority of the American people loved him. Even the media, which disliked so many of his policies, could not dislike him as a person. It's good to see that history is beginning to treat him with the respect and honor he so richly deserves.

For me, however, four years in the White House were enough. It was time to do some prior preparation to prevent poor performance at Treasury.

"JIMMY, YOU'RE MASSAGING ME"

MEASURED BY my new responsibilities, the move from the White House to Treasury was a long journey. Measured by the tape measure, however, it was only a few hundred feet. The Treasury building faces the East Wing of the White House, across East Executive Avenue. The Greek Revival building with its thirty great stone columns is one of the most majestic in Washington, befitting Treasury's role as the second-oldest executive department (after State) established by Congress in 1789.

You can see a picture of the building on the back of a ten-dollar bill. On the front is Alexander Hamilton, the first treasury secretary and one of the most brilliant of the Founders. Against great opposition, he had the good sense to pay off the nation's Revolutionary War debts dollar for dollar, not at a steep discount as his critics urged. With this one act, the new American government secured its financial reputation. To do this, Hamilton had to make a deal with Southern lawmakers to build the new federal capital in the South. That's how the District of Columbia came to be located between Virginia and Maryland.

I took my official oath of office as Hamilton's successor, the sixty-seventh secretary of the treasury, from a White House notary public in the basement of my D.C. home on Foxhall Road just after noon on Sunday, February 3, 1985. Susan was in Houston, so Mary Bonner, then seven, held the Bible.* Longtime friends from Houston, Will and Fran Lummis, served as witnesses. Five days later, I had a ceremonial swearing-in by Attorney General William French Smith in the Oval Office with Susan holding the Bible and my family, Barbara Bush, and President Reagan as witnesses.

At the time, of course, the pundits wrote less about "Team Baker Goes to Treasury" than about "Regan and Baker Switch Jobs." A political cartoon by Pulitzer Prize winner Tony Auth showed the "Gipper" addressing a huddle of football players, including one labeled "Secretary of the Treasury" and another "Chief of Staff." "OK guys. It's halftime," the president says. "I want you all to exchange jerseys."

The jersey exchange was also a source of interest, possibly even concern, on Capitol Hill. At my two-and-a-half-hour confirmation hearing before the Senate Finance Committee eleven days before my official swearing-in, Senator Russell Long asked if the relationship of the treasury secretary, chief of staff, and president was "going to be the same." This was important because President Reagan wanted to streamline our federal income tax system, and Long—ranking Democrat on the Senate committee that would oversee that project—was curious about how the job switch would affect the working relationship between the White House, Treasury, and Congress. I assured him

---

*As chief of staff, I would often take Mary Bonner with me to the White House, particularly when I worked on weekends. She added a delightful irreverence to the proceedings, as in the fall of 1981 when the president and I prepared to depart by helicopter one day from the South Lawn. Three-year-old Mary Bonner was kicking the leaves outside the diplomatic entrance. As he passed, the president bent down to say hello. "Hi there," she replied, still kicking the leaves, "you old silly." This grandfatherly relationship between our nation's oldest president and one of his youngest admirers grew warmer each time she visited him in the Oval Office or at Camp David. When we told her four years later that I would serve as secretary of the treasury, she burst into tears. "You're leaving the White House, and I won't get to see the president again!"

that Don and I had worked closely for four years and would continue to do so. Moreover, I would still be a member of the Legislative Strategy Group.

A very detailed tax reform plan was already in play. Three weeks after President Reagan won reelection in November, Treasury had laid out a plan to simplify and restructure the federal income tax system. Don was a major architect of the plan, and had I remained chief of staff, I would have been the major architect of the strategy to get the bill passed. Now the two architects were changing places.

"We must, on a bipartisan basis, bring greater fairness to the American tax system and make it simpler," I told the senators. Malcolm Wallop, the Republican senator from Wyoming, was not impressed.

"Jim, let me add my words of admiration and affection for you in wishing you well as you go forward," he said.

I enjoy "words of admiration and affection" as much as the next guy, but when you appear before congressional committees—which you do often as a cabinet officer—kind words are often a warning signal. Having unburdened himself of the obligatory niceties, Senator Wallop set about his real work, which was to torch my opening statement.

"I am particularly glad that you are still chief of staff of the White House and not coming to us green from Wall Street," he said, "because I would assume then that you had written, and not somebody in Treasury, the opening statement which you gave, which I really would have to define as a sort of tapioca, which is an indefinable thick fluid surrounding equally sweet squishy lumps, and when you have finished it, you have found it totally unsatisfying."

When the laughter subsided, Malcolm continued. My opening statement, he said, was "just full of platitudes and devoid of definition. You know, like 'bringing greater fairness to the American tax system.'"

I don't recall if I wrote those platitudes myself, but I certainly approved them. I never delivered a speech that I hadn't written myself or thoroughly vetted. And, yes, my remarks were short on definition and long on motherhood, apple pie, and, if you wish, tapioca. Better to serve that menu at breakfast than to eat crow for lunch.

Confirmation hearings are not the proper forum for detailed policy agendas. The more specific you are, the greater the chance that your words will come back to haunt you. Some political opponent or reporter will dig up the transcript or videotape of the hearing and point out that you said one thing last year and another thing last week, never mind that circumstances may have changed. People start calling you a flip-flopper, and you spend all your time explaining the past, not getting things done in the here and now. Cabinet nominees should say enough to show that they support the president's agenda and understand the issues, then—when questioned about details—promise to "get back to you on that, Senator."

And get back we did. The November tax plan had been written by technicians with a tin ear for politics. When I got to Treasury, we worked with Congress and the White House, and in May 1986 the president offered a new plan with plenty of details—no tapioca here— to reform the system. Our goals were to simplify the tax code, broaden the tax base, and reduce rates while maintaining "revenue neutrality"— neither increasing nor decreasing the overall tax revenues of the U.S. Treasury.

But it wouldn't be easy. Every time the federal government tinkers with tax policy, you can count on interest groups showing up to influence the tinkerers. The corridor outside the Senate Finance Committee room was known as Gucci Gulch, in honor of the fashionable wardrobes and fancy footwear of the lobbyists gathered there. We had a fight on our hands.

And what a fight it was! From the day Don Regan laid out the first tax reform proposal until President Reagan signed the bipartisan Tax Reform Act of 1986 took almost two years. This turned out to be the greatest domestic achievement of the president's second term. One knowledgeable reporter later called it "the most extensive overhaul of the federal tax system since the income tax was created in 1913." The

story of how, against great odds, that remarkable legislation was enacted shows how Washington works—or can work—when a president
provides leadership on an issue that is ripe for change. It also offers a
glimpse into the styles of President Reagan, Speaker of the House
Tip O'Neill, House Ways and Means committee chairman Danny
Rostenkowski, Don Regan, and other players.*

Some background first. Tax reform was not a new idea. A thicket of
tax preferences had swallowed our tax code. It's easy to criticize those
preferences now, but they were put there, one by one, over the decades
to protect Americans, first one group then another, from the punishing
rates in our tax code, once higher than 90 percent for some unfortunate taxpayers, believe it or not.

In the language of journalism and retail politics, we needed to
"close loopholes" that favored "special interest groups." President
Reagan would talk that way, and sometimes I would, too. But I rarely
used those terms with members of Congress. They tend not to react
well when you call their favorite tax preference a "loophole" and their
political friends "special interests."

President Reagan first called for tax reform in his 1984 state of the
union speech. "I am asking Secretary Don Regan for a plan for action
to simplify the entire tax code, so all taxpayers, big and small, are
treated more fairly," he said. "I've asked that specific recommendations . . . be presented to me by December 1984."

We would use the election year to build public support for the
principle of reforming the tax system. There would be plenty of time in
the second term to deal with the messy details. It's the same approach
that worked for tax cuts in 1980 and 1981—offer a big idea in the campaign, win a mandate in the election, then push the legislation through
Congress.

---

*I am indebted to *Showdown at Gucci Gulch: Lawmakers, Lobbyists, and the Unlikely Triumph of
Tax Reform,* by Jeffrey Birnbaum and Alan Murray, *Wall Street Journal* reporters, for re-
freshing my memory of these events. It should be clear to anyone reading their book that
I was one of their behind-the-scene sources.

The wild card was how Walter Mondale, the Democratic nominee in 1984, might respond. Two Democratic lawmakers, Senator Bill Bradley and Representative Dick Gephardt, had pushed a serious tax reform bill in 1982. What if Mondale campaigned on tax simplification, took the issue away from us, and trumped our December '84 target date? Fortunately for us, however, he preferred to fight a rearguard action against the highly popular Reagan tax cuts. "Mr. Reagan will raise taxes," Mondale predicted (erroneously), "and so will I. He won't tell you. I just did." So much for the wild card.

The tax reform plan offered by Don Regan's Treasury had a lot to recommend it. For instance, it would have cut the fourteen different individual tax brackets (the highest being 50 percent) to just three. But the proposal would also have raised business taxes by about $150 billion over five years to help pay for individual rate reductions. For a president who viscerally opposed high corporate taxation, this was too much. The business lobby was not amused, and neither were GOP lawmakers. The only endorsements we got were from liberals like George McGovern and Ralph Nader. The plan was DOA. Don acknowledged as much when he said as he introduced it, "This thing is written on a word processor. It can be changed."

Bad choice of words. Tax reform is so tough that everyone knows it will be subject to a lot of give-and-take in the legislative process. But the only way to win is by laying out a plan you are willing to defend, then defending it as you work for principled compromises. Saying "it can be changed" on the same day you introduce a plan is like throwing blood in a shark tank.

When the plan was announced, I was in a peculiar position. Eleven days earlier, Don and I had first discussed the possibility of switching jobs, but we hadn't made a final decision. If we did decide to swap and the president approved, I would be selling reform, not as chief of staff but as secretary of the treasury.

Looking at the Treasury proposal solely as chief of staff, responsible for getting the president's proposals through Congress and for looking out for his political well-being, however, I didn't like what I saw. So I arranged for the proposal to be unveiled by Don at Treasury, not by the president at the White House. The White House then issued a terse statement saying President Reagan would withhold judgment until he had studied the plan. Translation: it's a good thing it was written on a word processor.

But President Reagan didn't abandon his tax reform vision. "We have cut tax rates by almost 25 percent," he said in his 1985 state of the union address, "yet the tax system remains unfair and limits our potential for growth. Low-income families face steep tax barriers that make hard lives even harder." He praised the Treasury plan ("excellent"), but instead of calling for its passage, he said only that its "principles will guide the final proposal we will ask you to enact. . . . I am instructing Treasury Secretary James Baker—I have to get used to saying that—to begin working with congressional authors and committees for bipartisan legislation conforming to these principles."

Back to the drawing board.

By then, my staff was in place, starting with a core group that migrated across the street with me from the White House. Dick Darman served as deputy secretary. Margaret Tutwiler was assistant secretary for public affairs. And John Rogers, the president's assistant for management and administration, came over as assistant secretary for management.

We also recruited an impressive group of others: George Gould (a founder of Donaldson, Lufkin & Jenrette) as under secretary for domestic finance; David Mulford (a Regan Treasury holdover) as assistant secretary for international affairs; and Bob Kimmitt (a West Pointer who had served in Vietnam and on the National Security Council staff in President Reagan's first term) as general counsel. Bob followed me to State and served with distinction as the No. 3 official in the department. He now serves as deputy secretary of the treasury in George W. Bush's administration. Don Chapoton, a tax lawyer with Baker Botts, served as assistant secretary for tax policy and helped immeasurably with the nuts and bolts of reform.

Darman also hired a bright young Harvard law grad named Bob Zoellick to serve as a staff aide. A friend of mine later described Bob, who was famous for his yellow legal pads with neat hand-lettered points lists, as "the best prepared guy in the room." He and I quickly hit it off. Bob worked his way up through a series of posts at Treasury, including executive secretary to the department, deputy assistant secretary for financial institutions policy, and counselor to the secretary. Like Darman and Tutwiler, he later followed me to George H. W. Bush's presidential campaign in August 1988, and after that to the State Department. In President George W. Bush's first term, he served as U.S. trade representative. He is now deputy secretary of state for Secretary of State Condoleezza Rice.

Finally, I also had the good sense to take Caron Jackson to Treasury as my executive assistant. She is an administrative wizard. In the White House, at Treasury, and at State—and afterward, working for me in the private sector—she always made sure that everything that needed doing got done, and done right.

One thing that took some getting used to in my new job was that I no longer had the daily, even hourly, contact with President Reagan that I had enjoyed as chief of staff. Generally speaking, cabinet officers need appointments to see the president, so my walk-in privileges were gone. Still, anytime I needed face time, I could expect to get it, thanks to my years in the trenches with President Reagan in the 1980 and 1984 elections and as chief of staff. But that was a privilege I was careful not to abuse. I also understood that the president's White House advisers—Don Regan and others—would have the last word after I left the room. Proximity is power. The dynamics had changed and I would have to change with them. At the same time, I got along quite well with Congress, the press, and the interest groups. Treasury was an important portfolio, and most folks understood that I had a special relationship with the president and enjoyed his confidence.

Before I went to the president on tax reform, however, I would need a plan that stood a fighting chance in Congress. Cleaning up the tax code is one of those good-government ideas that almost everybody supports in principle. The problem is translating principle into policy. To lower rates substantially in a revenue-neutral way, for instance, requires that a lot of tax preferences be eliminated to offset the rate reductions. If you think that's easy, look at your own tax return. Consider giving up your standard deduction or personal exemption. Or your itemized deductions for mortgage interest, state and local taxes, or charitable contributions. Which ones would you send to the chopping block? The usual answer, to repeat a very old joke, is: "Don't tax me; don't tax thee; tax that fellow behind the tree."

To make the math of tax reform work, and the politics, the "guy behind the tree" in 1985 and 1986 would turn out to be American business. To get individual rates down substantially, we would need to go after business preferences. The first Treasury proposal would have done this, of course, but it overshot the mark. The trick now would be to work with both parties in Congress to figure out what was doable.

The key to bipartisan consensus was Danny Rostenkowski, the veteran Chicago Democrat who chaired Ways and Means. The GOP-controlled Senate would later present its own challenges, but nothing would ever even get to the Senate that had not already been blessed by Danny in the House. He supported tax reform, but he was also a cautious realist who had no interest in joining a doomed crusade. "Danny," I would tell him, "we can do this." To which he would reply, "Jimmy, you're massaging me."

It was possibly Danny's concern with being massaged that led him to stay away from the private meetings Dick Darman and I organized in February to craft a bipartisan bill. This was the same strategy the administration had used for Social Security in 1983—convening a small number of leaders from both parties with agency experts to write a bill everyone could live with. Our group included Bradley and Gephardt, sponsors of the 1982 Democratic tax reform proposal; Senator Bob Kasten and Representative Jack Kemp, sponsors of a GOP counterproposal in 1984; Senate Finance chairman Bob Packwood and the committee's ranking Democrat, Russell Long; and John Duncan, the ranking Republican on House Ways and Means. If these key players could reach a compromise, maybe we could get tax reform through the gulch before the lobbyists had slipped on their Guccis. Unfortunately, however, this approach failed. Without Danny's participation and endorsement a compromise bill stood no chance, and Danny was neither participating nor endorsing.

So what to do? We quickly convened another group, the tax policy experts at Treasury, to craft a bill. In *Gucci Gulch*, reporters Jeff Birnbaum and Alan Murray accurately captured the flavor of these gatherings, which "set a very different tone" from the way my predecessor had operated.

> The meetings were frequently held on Saturdays, a practice that Regan nearly always avoided. Baker would show up in casual corduroys and pick a seat on the side of the table (unlike Regan, he seldom sat at the head). He propped his cowboy boots on the table, crammed a wad of Red Man chewing tobacco in his mouth, and placed a large plastic cup in front of him.... Where Regan avoided all talk of politics, Baker talked about little else. He had scant patience for the theoretical presentations of [Treasury tax experts Ron] Pearlman and [Charles] McClure. He would lean back and spit in his cup or scratch his nose and then demand, "What are we hearing on that one?" or "Who's working against it?"

Pearlman, assistant secretary for tax policy, and McClure, his deputy, were brilliant guys who knew the tax code inside and out. They were also the same guys who had put together the original doomed proposal. I was happy to stir a pinch of political realism into their idealistic recipes.

One day a member of our Treasury team, Manley Johnson, complained that another team member was slow to get him the numbers he needed to make some important projections.

"Manley," I said, "this reminds me of the Easter back in the sixties when my four Baker boys got four fluffy little yellow ducklings that you couldn't tell apart. That night we put the ducks in a big cardboard box in the kitchen, with a light bulb to keep them warm. Before the sun came up, unfortunately, one went to duck heaven. When the boys ran into the kitchen the next morning, Jamie, the oldest, said, 'Poor Dougie. His duck died.' Doug—at six, the youngest—tearfully bought the story. 'Yeah,' he said, 'my duck died.'

"I'll bet you feel like Dougie did," I said to Manley.

He laughed and nodded.

"Well, you're not gonna have to wait for those numbers anymore," I said. And he didn't, after I had a considerably saltier talk with the offender about not ducking his number-crunching responsibilities.

I got a few talking-tos myself. Business executives, association leaders, and heads of charities lined up at my doorstep. They were all in favor of fairness and simplicity for taxpayers, they said. They just wanted to make sure that our package didn't hurt *their* interests. I knew we were in trouble when some of the president's, and my, friends in the oil and gas industry launched a campaign to send back the Eagle pins they had been awarded for making big contributions to the '84 campaign.

We didn't hear nearly as much, frankly, from the great majority of Americans who would benefit from lower individual rates. You see the same thing in fights over free trade. Open markets help most everyone by increasing overall economic growth. But "everyone" doesn't have a lobby in Washington. Instead, the political heat—and it's intense—comes from industry and labor groups that will be hurt. That's when politicians become statesmen, by doing the right thing anyway. And we were trying to do the right thing on tax reform.

I presented our plan to the president toward the end of May. He tweaked it, then offered it to the nation in a twenty-minute televised address on May 28. "We call it America's tax plan because it will reduce tax burdens on the working people of this country, close loopholes that benefit a privileged few, [and] simplify a code so complex even Albert Einstein reportedly needed help on his 1040 form . . ."

A family taking the standard deduction would pay no taxes on the first $12,000, he said. Above that, individual income would be taxed in just three brackets—15 percent, 25 percent, and 35 percent. The top corporate rate would be cut to 33 percent from 48 percent. To make up for lost revenues—that is, to maintain "revenue neutrality"—we would limit or do away with scores of tax preferences, including deductions for business meals (the famous "three-martini lunch"), state and local tax deductions, the investment tax credit, the oil depletion allowance (except on marginal wells), and so on.

Rostenkowski delivered the Democrats' response to the president's address. Nowadays, such replies from the opposition party (whether Democrat or Republican) are all too predictable. They begin with lip service about working with the president, but quickly devolve into a criticism of virtually everything he has just said.

Danny's response was different—"a strong, if qualified endorsement," as the *Washington Post* characterized it the next day. "Every year politicians promise to make the tax code fair and simple, but every year we seem to slip further behind. . . . But this year there's a difference. . . . It's a Republican president who's bucking his party's tradition as protectors of big business and the wealthy. . . . If we work together with good faith and determination, this time the people may win."

It wasn't all sweetness and light, however. Danny later groused to reporters that we had worked up the president's plan without consulting him. And he and his staffers were less than thrilled the next day when they saw the details of the proposal.

Okay, we said, draft your bill, then we'll work on a compromise. We hoped the Democrats would have something ready before Congress recessed in August. To our dismay, however, Danny insisted on running his hearings well into the fall. He was serious, I believe, about wanting to give everyone a say, but it was frustrating nonetheless. Too often, congressional hearings are held to score political points and win thirty-second sound bites back home. But then, that's our system. Call it "just politics," if you wish, but politics is the basis of our democracy. At their best, congressional hearings can also highlight important public policy issues and help educate the public.

BY LATE NOVEMBER, Danny was finally ready to schedule a committee vote on his markup of the president's bill. Dick Darman and I went over to the White House on Friday the twenty-second to brief the president and get our marching orders. We thought it was a routine visit, but it turned out to be the start of a near-death experience for tax reform. And congressional Democrats weren't to blame. It was the White House, itself.

The president, who had returned the day before from a meeting with Mikhail Gorbachev in Geneva, was very tired but listened carefully. Others present that day were Don Regan and Dennis Thomas, who was to Don as Darman was to me. We weren't in love with the bill, but—though far from perfect—it would broaden the tax base and bring down rates. Furthermore, we told the president, Danny's markup was also written on a word processor. Keep the process moving, we counseled, and encourage Republican House members to support the bill. Our party controls the Senate. We can fix it there.

The president, always a pragmatist, agreed and promised to do two things before the day was out. He would call Congressman Duncan, the ranking Republican on Ways and Means, to urge him to support the bill. He would also write letters of support to the other Republicans on the committee.

Neither step was taken. No phone call. No letters. Why? Dennis Thomas had not objected to the plan at the meeting with President Reagan. But afterward, we learned, he told Don Regan that the bill had little support from leading Republicans in the House. That was true. Regan and Thomas then apparently persuaded the president to remain neutral, at least for the time being. Proximity is power, and tax reform had just been proximitied into the ditch.

When I learned of this Friday evening, I was furious. This might very well mean the end of tax reform. Wavering Republicans had no reason to support the Democrats' markup if the president himself was unwilling to go public with an endorsement.

There's a protocol to handling these problems. First, Darman called Thomas. No satisfaction there. Then I got on the line and tried to get Regan. Again, no satisfaction. Tired, like the president, from the Geneva trip, he was home resting.

By then, it was about ten o'clock. The only way to get this straightened out, I thought, is to go to the top. I reached for the telephone to call the president in his private quarters. I would wake him up and tell him what his chief of staff had done and how tax reform was dead without the president's support . . . and . . . and . . .

Then I had second thoughts and put the receiver down. As I later explained to the authors of *Gucci Gulch,* life was too short. I'd try to fix this some other way.

Instead of calling the president, I paid a late-evening call on Rostenkowski on Capitol Hill. I told him President Reagan thought the new version was a positive beginning. "He will call on House Republicans to support it in its present form," I said. We had problems with certain provisions, I added, but hoped our concerns would be addressed in the Senate. In a late-night session of Ways and Means, the Democrats made the bill somewhat worse, particularly the deductions for state and local taxes. Rosty then called a surprise voice vote. Republicans on the committee were upset, but the administration—represented by Dick Darman—did not object. If we did not get a bill out of committe, tax reform was dead. The bill was voted out of committee about 1:00 A.M. It was ugly, but we had what we needed, which was a live bill. Now we had to get it through the full House, then on to the Senate to be fixed.

Fresh from a good night's sleep, President Reagan, we trusted, would give his support to the tax bill, warts and all, in his weekly Saturday morning radio address to the nation. That didn't happen. Okay, a statement on Monday would do. Then Thomas told Darman that Tuesday was a better bet. But there was nothing on Tuesday, either.

We kept pressing the White House for action, and the White House kept putting us off. Danny tried to telephone the president, but his call was not returned. The president appeared willing to let tax reform die, some newspapers reported. And, as feared, the White House's silent treatment gave cover to House Republicans who didn't like the bill. The White House was signaling, in effect: "The president doesn't care, so you don't have to, either."

I'll never know exactly why this happened, but the president later blamed some of his second-term troubles on his isolation in the Oval Office and on Don's "oversized ego," mistreatment of staff, and appetite for power. "Don thought of himself as a kind of 'deputy president' empowered to make important decisions involving the administration," the president wrote in his memoir. "Although I only found out about it later, he resisted having others see me alone and wouldn't forward letters or documents to me unless he saw them first. In short, he wanted to be the *only* conduit to the Oval Office, in effect making the presidential isolation . . . more complete."

Perhaps Don put up the roadblock because he was unhappy about having had his Treasury's tax plan pushed aside and the Baker Treasury's plan advanced in its place. I'll never know for sure. What I do know is that Don was hearing from a lot of people—business groups and Republican lawmakers—that we were going too far, too fast with tax reform. If Don agreed, this was odd, to say the least, because the first Treasury plan had gone further and faster than the version in Ways and Means. Whatever the reason, by late November 1985, the White House was inexplicably withholding public support for even the principle of tax reform.

On December 4, the White House finally issued a statement. The president thinks the legislative process should go forward, it said. Talk about damning with faint praise. This all but invited a GOP revolt.

By this time, Republicans on Ways and Means had fashioned their own bill. It was more business friendly. It also didn't have a chance in hell of passing the Democrat-controlled House. In response, the

White House sent another bad signal: the president would not choose between Danny's proposal and that of the Republicans.

Two days later, however, President Reagan got back on board. Frankly, I can't remember what caused the turnaround. *Time* magazine said I was able to convince Nancy Reagan of the growing threat to her husband's top domestic priority of his second term. I'm also almost certain I talked to the president and told him directly that White House indecision and neutrality were about to kill tax reform. At any rate, that's how I normally would have operated. In his Saturday morning radio address of December 7, President Reagan finally settled the question. He called on the House to pass the bill and let the Senate have a go at it. He then sent every House member a letter supporting the bill.

By then, unfortunately, the momentum had gone too far in the wrong direction. Trent Lott, then a Mississippi congressman, rallied GOP opposition and won a test vote 223–202. Only fourteen Republicans supported their own president. GOP congressmen had "voted to humiliate the man who had led them to victory," Tip O'Neill told the press.

The president *was* humiliated, and angry. The White House hadn't seen the rebellion coming, nor had I. We both *should* have, however, in light of the White House's bizarre actions—or inaction—of the previous three weeks, but what was done was done. We now had to play catch-up.

Prodded by Danny, the speaker agreed to schedule another vote, but on one very big condition: President Reagan had to promise him personally that at least fifty Republicans would vote for the package. We had until 8:00 P.M. on December 16 to round up the votes, he said. I left his office with a sick feeling. The game might very well be over.

Although we didn't think so at the time, Tip probably did us a favor by setting the tight deadline. He forced the administration to act quickly and, more important, to focus. And at this point, the only person who could save President Reagan's tax reform was President Reagan himself. He wanted to, and he did.

For a multitude of reasons, presidents rarely travel from the White House to Capitol Hill to meet lawmakers on their own turf, but Ronald Reagan—who had already come to Congress once to save the 1981 tax bill—came again. On the afternoon of December 16, about six hours before Tip's deadline, he sat down on the Hill with House Republicans. (My best memory is that I accompanied him.) By our count, he started with somewhere between thirty-five and forty supporters.

Earlier that day, the president had attended a memorial service at Fort Campbell, Kentucky, for 248 servicemen who had died when their plane crashed in Newfoundland. He began the meeting by asking the congressmen to join him in a silent prayer. "This took the sting out of our bite," Trent Lott later told Birnbaum and Murray.

But not entirely. After the president asked for their support, several House members unloaded. Their opposition was based on a combination of principle (they thought it was bad legislation) and pocketbook politics (why had the president thrown in his lot with that rascal Rostenkowski to take down our friends' tax breaks?).

The president listened patiently, then assured the critics that he would veto any bill that didn't include the major items on their wish list. But there wouldn't be a chance to fight, he pointed out, if the bill didn't make it to the GOP-controlled Senate.

The president's remarks struck a chord with one of the more prominent holdouts, Henry Hyde, an influential conservative congressman from Illinois. When he came over to our side, a handful of colleagues followed. A secret ballot at the end of the meeting showed that we had forty-eight votes.

Could we count on these forty-eight to go public? Could we find at least two more? We assembled a team in the office of my old friend, House Minority Leader Bob Michel, and started working the phones. It took a lot of calls and a lot of horse-trading. I even agreed to come stump for one representative. A breakthrough came when we persuaded Bob and another influential Republican, Jack Kemp, to sign up.

At six o'clock, I phoned Regan to tell him we'd reached our goal and that the president should call the speaker with the news. O'Neill was not immediately available. The 8:00 P.M. deadline came and went with no word from him. Four frustrating hours passed before the men talked. Why so long? I suspect the speaker just wanted to play us a bit before he closed the deal.

Trent Lott and his allies did not go gently into the night. They kept working their votes, so I set up a boiler-room operation on the Hill to hold ours. Henry Hyde helped man the phones, as did Guy Vander Jagt, my buddy from the Gerald Ford campaign, now an influential minority member of Ways and Means.

Was it unusual for a cabinet member to play politics like I did here, at least so publicly? The answer is yes. I rolled up my sleeves and got involved in the grunt work because of the importance of the issue, because of what it meant politically to the president, and because I knew how to do it. I had spent four years as chief of staff shepherding legislation through Congress on behalf of Ronald Reagan. And let's face it: I also knew that if we lost, my reputation and effectiveness would have taken a big hit.

Shortly before the vote, Tip O'Neill gave an excellent speech in support of the bill. Seventy Republicans—far more than we had counted on twelve hours earlier—joined 188 Democrats on a second test vote. We were on our way. Later that evening, the bill itself passed the House on a voice vote.

There would be several more bumps in the road over the next ten months. In April, for example, Senate Finance Chairman Bob Packwood of Oregon personally saved tax reform in the Senate. He had asked senators what it would take to win their votes. They answered with a shopping list of tax breaks they wanted to protect. The resulting business-as-usual approach was a disaster. Bob saw what was happening, scrapped the bill, and started from scratch. The White House supported his new version, and in June the Senate approved it 97–3. Pat Moynihan reportedly called it "the most ethical event I've ever seen in this place." The conference committee took two agonizing months. By late September, however, each house was ready to vote on a final bill.

On September 23, I delivered public remarks about tax reform at the White House. First I read aloud from old headlines about the president's package being "in trouble" or "in limbo" or "a loser" or "moribund" or "down for the count." Then I recited a little ditty called the "Tax Reform Shuffle."*

> *They said tax reform was dead. Now it's alive.*
> *Here's its story. It began in '85.*
> *We drew up a plan, and sent it out in May,*
> *But the special interests said, "Ain't no way!"*
> *Rosty started hearings before the fall;*
> *They were Gucci-to-Gucci in the hall.*
> *December came, reform was off the track,*
> *So to the Hill rode the Gipper to bring it back.*
> *Chorus: All along it's been a big tussle,*
> *But we keep doing the Tax Reform Shuffle.*

Both houses approved the final bill on September 27. Unbelievably, we had pared the brackets from fourteen to two—15 percent and 28 percent. We won the $2,000 personal exemption and increased the standard deduction for married couples to $5,000, both indexed for inflation (as were the brackets). These provisions, together with the earned income tax credit, meant that a family of four would pay no taxes on the first $15,380 of income. We limited some deductions and eliminated many others, including deductions for many work-related expenses and for interest on most personal loans. (Mortgage interest on the principal residence was still deductible.) Business lost the investment tax credit, full deductions for business meals and entertainment, and other tax breaks. In return the top corporate rate was reduced to 34 percent, from 48 percent.

---

*I had no luck finding out who wrote this piece. It was obviously someone with a keen eye and a wonderful sense of humor.

On October 22, President Reagan signed the legislation on the South Lawn. I was on the podium, along with Danny Rostenkowski and other key players. "When I sign this bill into law," the president said, "America will have the lowest marginal tax rates and the most modern tax code among the major industrialized nations." He thanked everyone who had helped pass the bill, including "my two incomparable secretaries of the treasury, Don Regan and Jim Baker. I feel like we just played the World Series of tax reform," the president said, "and the American people won." As I watched the ceremony—even now as I look back—I was amazed that we had pulled it off. It was something of a miracle, frankly.

My pride about the Tax Reform Act of 1986 is tinged with sadness. The code today is as complex as ever, perhaps worse. We wiped the blackboard fairly clean in 1986, but this only encouraged Congress to come up with a new generation of preferences. As it became harder and harder to pass spending bills, Congress turned to "tax expenditures" and used the IRS to reward favored constituencies by reducing their taxes. That's a bad idea for a lot of reasons, not the least of which are that it junks up the code and forces Congress to tax the majority of taxpayers more heavily to finance benefits for the few.

Marginal rates were pushed back up to 31 percent under President George H. W. Bush (who famously traded the tax hike for congressional spending cuts), then to almost 40 percent under Bill Clinton (who liked to use the tax code for social engineering on savings, education, and other issues). President George W. Bush has gotten the top rate back down to 35 percent, which helped our economy recover from the 2001 recession and from 9/11, but with all the new preferences in the tax code, it'll be hard to cut the rates any lower.

Like President Reagan, President Bush 43 has also announced a second-term goal of reforming the tax code. He has one big advantage, GOP control of both houses of Congress, but for many reasons—including his decision to give his unsuccessful effort to reform Social Security a higher priority—it will be a tougher fight now than it was back in 1986, and it was plenty tough back then. I wish him well. A more sensible tax code would do a lot to help our economy.

The tax-reform fight—and particularly the White House's weeks of indecision in late 1985—revived talk that President Reagan was a puppet of his staff. As troubled as I was by what happened, I still don't believe that. Every president has eighteen thousand things coming at him. It is the staff's job to prioritize his time. For instance, it would be very rare for a president to telephone the ranking member of Ways and Means unless his staff recommended it as part of a White House legislative game plan, then set up the call. Any president who goes down in the weeds to handle that kind of detail himself will lose control of his presidency. In that sense, every president is to some extent hostage to his staff, and President Reagan was no different. The White House staff certainly let him down on the tax-reform fight, but it was more likely the result of political indecision or confusion, in my opinion, than of cynical manipulation. Once the president understood what was going on, he stepped up and personally saved tax reform.

There has also been talk that the president exhibited symptoms of early stage Alzheimer's disease in his second term, based, for instance, on his responses to Iran-Contra and his stumbling over some facts in a 1985 interview with the *Wall Street Journal.* Well, I wasn't at his side every day, as before, but every time I was in his presence or talked to him by telephone during the second term, he was alert, capable, and vibrant. When the president announced in 1994 that he suffered from Alzheimer's and had begun "the journey that will lead me into the sunset of my life," I was deeply saddened and genuinely shocked.

AS RONALD REAGAN'S second term drew near its end, I was again approached about suiting up in a different jersey (albeit one I had worn before), this time by George H. W. Bush. I agreed, and we went to the president. One might have expected the outgoing president to give his immediate blessing to this request by his vice president and treasury secretary. To our great surprise, however, he resisted.

ELEVEN

"IF THAT'S WHAT YOU WANT, GEORGE, THAT'S WHAT WE'LL DO"

IN APRIL 2005, I celebrated my seventy-fifth birthday in Houston with family and friends, more than six hundred in all. The size of the event was a subject of intense diplomatic negotiations with Susan and others. I reluctantly agreed to a large party on three conditions: first, that the occasion be used to raise money for the James A. Baker III Institute for Public Policy at Rice University (more about the institute later); second, that it be casual; and third, that all speeches be short.

The birthday celebration, held under a huge tent on the Rice campus, raised almost $4.5 million for the institute. The theme was western. I wore a beige cowboy-style shirt with button-down pockets, brown pants, a big silver belt buckle with two eagles on it, well-worn but highly polished cordovan cowboy boots, and a narrow-brim felt Stetson in a style favored by Texas ranchers and businessmen.

Country-western star Clay Walker, a Texas native, sang "Happy Birthday," then provided music for an evening of dancing. I'm a big fan of country music. I don't collect recordings or keep up with the latest releases from Nashville (or anyplace else), and when I was courting age, I danced to big band swing and listened to Frank Sinatra and Tony

Bennett. These days, however, I usually tune my satellite radio to George Jones, Conway Twitty, Tammy Wynette, Loretta Lynn, Merle Haggard, and the others, particularly as I drive south from Houston on hunting trips. I like the human-interest stories in country music ("D-I-V-O-R-C-E," "Hello, Darlin'," "Don't Come Home A-Drinkin' with Lovin' on Your Mind"); the humor ("I Miss You Only on Days That End in Y"); and the themes ("When they're runnin' down our country, hoss, they're walkin' on the fightin' side of me"). I'm just *comfortable* with that kind of music. For one thing, I haven't met a country singer yet who is ashamed to sing about friends, family, country, and faith. Even the cheatin' and drinkin' songs usually have a moral.

The Baker family knows something about other kinds of lyrics. In 1985, Susan encouraged Tipper Gore to join her, Pam Howar, and Sally Nevius in forming the Parents Music Resource Center (PMRC). The goal of their group was to educate parents about the sick lyrics in popular music, primarily rock and rap, that glorified violence, drug use, suicide, murder, and other criminal behavior. The group did not set out to censor recordings, as some charged. Instead it urged the record industry to put warning labels on records with "explicit lyrics or content" so consumers, young and old, would at least know what they were buying.

In response to the PMRC, a U.S. Senate committee began investigating rock music in September 1985. Within two months, the Recording Industry Association of America had agreed to label explicit albums. This is similar to the motion picture industry's rating system and the one adopted by the cable television industry.

Tipper and Susan became good friends during this mission and remain so today. Both testified before the committee. So did several recording artists, most notably Frank Zappa of the long-defunct rock band Mothers of Invention. The PMRC was a "group of bored Washington housewives," he said, who wanted to "housebreak all composers and performers because of the lyrics of a few." He even mocked Susan's Texas accent. This was mild, however, compared to *Hustler* magazine, which awarded Susan and Tipper their coveted Assholes of the Month Award.

Zappa needn't have been so concerned. The rating system didn't silence anybody. If you think it did, just scan your radio dial today and listen to some of the outrageous music that debases women, promotes drug use, and glorifies violence. Thank goodness only a few stations play it.

Truth is, Susan was never out to housebreak composers, and she was anything but a bored Washington housewife. When she wasn't running the ever-lively Baker household—try organizing life for eight children—and advising me daily on the hard decisions I brought home from work, she always lived out her Christianity by giving food, clothes, and other material comfort to "the least of these." She was involved with food banking in Washington and Houston, then in 1983 cofounded the National Alliance to End Homelessness, which she serves today as cochair.

Public service is not all glamour and fun. It's tough, but it is toughest on spouses and children because the public servant generally works very long hours and is totally absorbed in the job and the important issues of the day. Legislators spend many days away from home to campaign in the home state or district. Long hours at work make it difficult to help the spouse with family problems. The spotlight of public scrutiny falls not just on the public figure but also, and sometimes unfairly, on the family. If your child gets caught speeding, it's a family problem. If an officeholder's child does the same thing, it can be a national story. A lot of families crack under the strain of public service. Susan is a strong woman. I was blessed, and our children were blessed, to have her in charge of our home.

The speeches at my birthday party were, thank goodness, brief. Even if he had wanted to, George Bush 41 couldn't have spoken for long. He had a bad case of laryngitis, but I will always treasure his scratchy remarks that evening. He characterized me as "a man to whom friendship means everything." True. He also said that I was "a man without whom I would not have become president of the United States." Maybe.

IF TWO other presidents—Nixon and Reagan—had had their way, I might not have been able to help George make his run for the presidency against the Democrats' Michael Dukakis in 1988. A history refresher first.

George's path to the White House started with the '88 Republican primaries. Although he was a two-term vice president and the clear front-runner, seven candidates lined up against him—Bob Dole, Jack Kemp, Pat Robertson, Howard Baker, Al Haig, Don Rumsfeld, and Pierre "Pete" du Pont. The race did not begin well. George finished third in the Iowa caucuses. No surprise that Dole won. He was from neighboring Kansas and, as Senate majority leader, was good at delivering for Midwest farmers. But few expected televangelist Pat Robertson to take second place. He did a good job of getting his supporters to the Iowa caucuses.

The flight from Iowa to New Hampshire, the first primary state, was glum, but George kept his composure, campaigned hard, and regained momentum by winning there, just as Ronald Reagan had done eight years earlier. George then won sixteen out of sixteen primaries on Super Tuesday, March 8. That sewed it up.

Former New Jersey senator Nick Brady chaired the Bush effort. Lee Atwater was campaign manager. George's chief of staff, Craig Fuller, pollster Bob Teeter, finance chairman Bob Mosbacher, and media expert Roger Ailes were also members of the brain trust. Within the campaign, they were called the "Gang of Six," or "G-6." I watched it all from the sidelines at Treasury. Every once in a while I was asked to contribute my two cents' worth to the campaign. Generally, however, I tended to my knitting at Treasury and George and the G-6 tended to the campaign.

Because of my long friendship with George and my experience in running presidential campaigns (including his in 1979–1980), conventional wisdom was that I would resign from Treasury before the party convention in mid-August to run the fall general election campaign. But Richard Nixon thought that was a bad idea. On May 15, the former president said in a letter to George that it "would be a serious mistake" for Baker to "take a leave of absence" and join the campaign. "The antis in the media would take it as a lack of confidence in your ability to win and too much deference to Reagan," Nixon advised George.

Interesting. Having entered the Reagan administration with the reputation of being the vice president's man, I was now seen, at least by the politically savvy Nixon, as the president's guy.

George had obviously asked Nixon for his opinion about my taking on the fall campaign. Nixon's reference in his letter to a "leave of absence" reflected perhaps how much things had changed after Watergate. By 1988, no cabinet official could just take a leave, as opposed to resigning from government, to run the presidential campaign of another cabinet or constitutional officer. Even if a way could have been found to do it legally, a leave of absence would have given the Democrats a political club.*

Nixon's counsel notwithstanding, George approached me to run his fall campaign. The G-6 had not functioned as well as he had hoped. Without one acknowledged leader who spoke with authority and credibility for the candidate, differences of opinion were difficult to settle. I was happy where I was, frankly, and the prospect of resigning my cabinet post left me with mixed emotions. Don't get me wrong, however. There was never really any doubt about whether I would do it. This wasn't just a campaign; it was my friend's campaign.

I believed in George. He had one of the best résumés in the history

---

*If I had left government when I resigned as secretary of state to lead George's campaign against Bill Clinton in 1992, new ethics-in-government laws would have prohibited my even talking to those with whom I had served in the cabinet. That's why I stayed in government and became White House chief of staff and senior counselor to the president.

of presidential politics—great education, military hero, successful businessman, respected congressman, party chairman, UN ambassador, head of the CIA, envoy to China, and the most active and engaged vice president in American history in one of the most successful administrations in American history. Even more impressive was the flesh-and-blood George Bush that I knew so well, a man who embodied honor and decency. They say that integrity is doing the right thing when nobody knows. It's also doing the right thing when the only person who knows is your friend. And in our countless hours of playing tennis or golf, shooting quail and dove, downing Otto's barbeque, visiting each other's families, and doing both politics and public service together, I never saw him cut a corner or do anything disreputable. He always went by the book.

I also owed George, personally and professionally. He and Barbara stood by me and the boys when Mary Stuart died. They were the last outside the family to visit her in the hospital. Afterward, they welcomed Susan and her children into our circle of friendship. He led me into politics and public service, then helped me by example and with advice to do my jobs at Commerce, the White House, and Treasury.

And yes, I also knew that if George won, there would probably be something in it for me. But we never discussed it. We were both conscious—very conscious—of the fact that it was illegal to promise anyone a job in exchange for campaign help.

Of course I would help George. We wanted to do it the right way, however, and that meant we needed President Reagan's blessing. But when I approached the boss about resigning from Treasury and moving to the campaign, he politely said no. "You can be more valuable by staying here and keeping the economy on course," he said.

"It doesn't look to me like this is gonna fly unless *you* talk to the president," I told George, who promptly did so and, I believe, got the same response. Sensing George's disappointment, however, the president suggested that we talk it over one more time. Shortly thereafter, President Reagan, Nancy, George, and I gathered in the living quarters on the second floor of the White House. The president listened to

George's pitch, then said, "If that's what you want, George, that's what we'll do. It just occurred to me that Jim might be more valuable as secretary of the treasury."

Over the past seven and a half years, I had walked in and out of the Reagan White House countless times, always as a member of the team. As I departed that day, however, I had a real sense of separation, of moving on. I would be back a few more times for the goodbyes, of course, but if I returned in January, it would be to a Bush White House—an old and familiar setting for an exciting new act in the great drama of American history. Imagine walking into the Oval Office and seeing your best friend behind the desk! At the same time, I could not deny a quiet sadness as I shook hands with President Reagan that day and walked away, symbolically transferring my loyalty from one great president to the friend who could, and would, be another.

George and I had a lot of work ahead of us, but first I needed to wrap things up at Treasury. On August 5, I submitted my letter of resignation, effective August 17, the day before George would formally accept the party's nomination at the convention in New Orleans.

I thanked the president for giving me the opportunity to serve and for entrusting me with such great responsibilities. "In seeking to advance your vice president's candidacy, I [can] best help insure the survival of your legacy and assure that your remarkable contributions are extended on toward the twenty-first century," I wrote. I wanted him to know that we would be running *on* his legacy, not *against* it.

The letter in which the president accepted my resignation "with mixed feelings" is among the most important keepsakes from my life in government. In part, it's typical end-of-service boilerplate about a departing officer's "solid record of accomplishment and extraordinary service to the American people." But, as usual, the president knew how to touch the heart.

> I was somewhat surprised to learn of your grandfather's admonition to "work hard, study, and keep out of politics." His view represented a healthy strain of American skepticism about the potential pitfalls of

involvement with politics. But in your career you have set an important example: You have clearly demonstrated that the best of the political arts can be combined with first-class professionalism in the effective pursuit of America's interests.

After the markets closed on August 5, President Reagan and I appeared in the White House press room to announce my resignation and the nomination of Nick Brady, then cochairman of the investment firm Dillon, Read & Company, to succeed me. "You've been a secret of our success," the always-gracious president said to me in front of the assembled reporters. "Now, Jim, go do it for George."

Federal Reserve Board Chairman Alan Greenspan issued a statement calling me "one of the most effective secretaries of the Treasury in the nation's history" and "a tough act to follow." At that point Alan had been in office less than a year. The summer before, he had replaced the highly respected Paul Volcker. Alan is one of the great legacies of the Reagan years and was reappointed again and again by presidents of both parties. As I write, he has just retired after almost nineteen years in office. (I will interject here to ask: what has America done to be so fortunate as to have two such outstanding men as Paul Volcker and Alan Greenspan to lead our central bank? Both deserve enormous credit for our nation's prosperity over the past quarter century.)*

Besides looking back at my time at Treasury, the press looked ahead to my role as campaign chairman. In a front-page story, the *Washington Post*'s David Hoffman wrote that I was assuming "command

---

*Hobart Rowen, veteran reporter on economic matters for the *Washington Post,* summed up my legacy in a column on August 11. "Baker has been a dominant international presence, perhaps the most influential U.S. Treasury Secretary of modern times.... Baker's arrival at the Treasury had a positive effect on the global economy."

In the appendix to this book, readers may read about our successful efforts to stabilize international currency exchange rates and negotiate the Canada-U.S. Free Trade Agreement, and also about "Black Monday," the day in October 1987 that the Dow Jones Industrial Average dropped 22 percent.

of the deeply troubled presidential quest . . . at the outset of a critical two-week period in which Bush hopes to climb out of a distant second place in the polls and use his national convention to more clearly define his goals and identity. . . . Many Republicans have also concluded that Bush needed a strong manager to replace the diffuse organization running his campaign. With Baker's arrival, campaign sources said the so-called 'G-6' . . . would now lapse."

A presidential campaign needs strong organization and a way to make decisions quickly. The best way to do that is with a leader who can get things done *now,* not with a committee that can get things done *after* a meeting that takes two hours to organize and two more to conduct. Still, "lapse" was too strong a word to describe what happened to the G-6. On the same day I announced my resignation, George and I met with about thirty top people in the campaign. He told them I would be in charge, but I assured them that I had no intention of reinventing the wheel. Atwater, Ailes, Teeter, Fuller, Mosbacher, and the others had done good work and would continue to play important roles through November, I said.

I already had some ideas about strategy. The slow start in the polls didn't alarm me. (Early polls tell you what you need to know to win a campaign, not whether you will win it.) Nor did the critical stories about the campaign operation. (That could be fixed.) The biggest problem, in my view, was structural. It may sound trite, but it's true that "change is the only constant in politics." If you can't portray your candidate as an agent of change, he will have a tough time winning.

That's one reason it's hard for any political party to win the presidency a third time after having held power for eight years. Since the Twenty-second Amendment (limiting chief executives to two elected terms) was ratified in 1951, no party had held the Oval Office more than two successive terms. In peacetime, at least, voters usually want a change.

As the perfect vice president, George had served the Reagan presidency superbly, but at significant cost to his image as a man with his own ideas. One thing in Nixon's May 15 letter to George was correct. From now on, he needed to be seen as his own man, not just as President Reagan's vice president. He could not expect to win by totally piggybacking on the prior administration, even one as successful as the Reagan presidency. He needed to say how he would change things for the better. This had to be done carefully, however, because new ideas could sound like implied criticism of the old order, prompting questions about why he didn't do something about the issue when he had a chance.

Al Gore would later have the same problem. President Clinton's reputation was tainted by personal scandal, so Al had a particularly tough call to make—whether to enlist a great campaigner who was still popular with the party's base or to cut the cord. Al separated himself from his president, in part by refusing Clinton's help on the stump and in part by embracing a more aggressively liberal agenda. I think he made a mistake on both counts. Bill Clinton wouldn't have helped much in the reddest states or hurt much in the bluest ones, but in a race as close as the one in 2000, he could have made the difference in the states that were the closest.

The GOP convention in New Orleans promised to be a big snore. George had bagged the nomination months earlier. His acceptance speech would be covered, but to restless reporters, it was already old news before it happened. Political conventions once featured brutal floor fights over the nomination. Now, however, primaries were the true battlefields of presidential politics, with conventions serving only to formally tie up the loose ends. They had become media events, useful for rolling out the candidate, stirring the party faithful, and—most important—reaching through the television to give voters a chance to get to know the candidate.

Unfortunately, we had little to offer the media, other than President Reagan's political valedictory on the first night of the convention and George's speech on the last night. If we didn't gin up more excitement, George would be presented to the nation through the jaundiced filter of journalistic boredom. The one big mystery we had left, of course, was selection of a vice presidential nominee. As the convention began, George still hadn't picked his running mate. If we played it right, that would add some drama, or so we thought.

Well, we didn't play it right, but we got the drama anyway. The star was James Danforth Quayle and the plot was about whether his wealthy family had or had not pulled strings to get him in the Indiana National Guard during Vietnam.

Before I tell the story, however, let me get one piece of old baggage out of the way. Despite it all, Dan Quayle was a good choice in 1988. The Bush-Quayle ticket went on to win every state but ten. What more could any vice presidential candidate have delivered? Dan worked hard in the campaign and, more important, served effectively and honorably as vice president, just as he had as a senator from Indiana. How we messed up was in not announcing the selection until we got to the convention.

Vice President Bush publicly introduced Dan Quayle as his choice on the second day of the convention, Tuesday, August 16, after taking a cruise on the Mississippi in the paddle wheeler *Natchez*. Minutes earlier the ever-playful presidential son, George W., had boarded the boat with a sign reading, "Dad, you can tell me!"

For perspective, remember that no matter how much noise the parties make at their summer conventions about the running mate, voters almost uniformly ignore vice presidential nominees in deciding how to vote in November. The office is of the utmost importance constitutionally, but often of little consequence in swaying voters.

Before the convention, George had narrowed his choices to five men and one woman. Alan Simpson (Wyoming) and Pete Domenici (New Mexico) brought strong credentials from the Senate, but Simpson was pro-choice—a position that was anathema to most Republican delegates—and Domenici took himself out of consideration a few days before the convention. That left four possibles. Bob Dole and Jack Kemp had opposed George in the primaries. Picking either of them would have echoed what Ronald Reagan did in 1980, which was to select a worthy adversary from the primaries. Elizabeth Dole, Bob's wife, had served most recently as transportation secretary. Dan, the junior senator from Indiana and less well known than the others, was good-looking, conservative, and, at forty-one, a generation younger than the sixty-four-year-old presidential nominee—a real advantage, some of us thought.

As the convention approached, most pundits predicted a Bush-Dole (Bob, that is) ticket, despite the pair's sometimes contentious relationship during the primaries. Bob made no secret about wanting the nod. He told reporters he had left a two-word message on his answering machine: "I accept." He still had his pride, however. A few weeks before the convention he told me he would do whatever George wished, even pull out of contention, but he would not "grovel" for the nomination. I couldn't understand why Bob thought George would want his running mate to grovel, but I promised to pass it along.

George may have made the vice presidential decision alone, but he asked friends and family members for advice. I was still at Treasury at the time, but he apparently met with his other top advisers on August 6 and August 12. The only time I remember weighing in was on a Wyoming camping trip with George in mid-July. In our shared tent in the wilds of the Shoshone National Forest, he went through the list one night, and I gave him my thoughts. I don't recall the details, but I remember that I thought Bob Dole and Dan Quayle were the most logical choices.

Dole was a proven leader, a man with experience and the gravitas to serve as vice president or president. On the other hand, he had shown a tendency in the 1976 presidential election and the 1988 primaries to make controversial statements. It has been reported that I expressed reservations about his ability to run a well-coordinated campaign and to serve as an effective number-two man. I don't recall ever doing so. In fact, I have always admired Bob and his service to our country. He and I worked well and closely together when I was at the White House, the Treasury, and State.

I remember being impressed by Quayle's positives, and he had strong backing in Ailes, Teeter, and Brady. He was young, handsome, and conservative, and he came from the heartland. But I also thought he was a little green, politically. For the record, I don't believe any of us knew about the National Guard issue.

George had one more source of information, a most important one—background checks by Bob Kimmitt, an old hand from the Ford administration, the Reagan White House (national security staff), and the Baker Treasury (general counsel). I had recommended him. He was a good man for a tough job, supercompetent and absolutely trustworthy.

Background checks are a necessary evil of modern political life. They are intended to keep unqualified or corrupt candidates out of high federal offices, but their most important role, if we're honest, is to prevent embarrassment for the person making the nomination. You may be better qualified than any other person on earth for the job for which you've been nominated, but if you've ever consulted a psychiatrist, hired a gardener from Tijuana, failed to withhold from your nanny's paycheck, or worked for (or invested in) an unpopular company, you're probably toast. A lot of well-qualified candidates simply won't submit to the process. It's intrusive and time-consuming; it tears down hard-won reputations on account of youthful indiscretions; it makes journalistic mountains out of ethical molehills; and it fuels partisanship. Who needs the grief? A lot of good people still endure it, thank goodness, but the process can give opportunists an advantage over better-qualified candidates with rough edges.

I wonder how many of our nation's Founders would have failed federal background checks. "Mr. Hamilton, when you started paying the old continental debt, didn't a lot of the money go to your rich friends at the Bank of New York, which you helped organize?"

George told the press that no one other than Kimmitt would see the results of the background checks. He kept his word. I never saw them, and I don't know of anybody else (other than George and Bob) who did. I admire George's concern for the privacy of the people under consideration and Bob's absolute sense of discretion about the sensitive information he handled. By keeping the information away from his political advisers, however, George might have missed an opportunity to head off the trouble that lay ahead. That's not to say that any of us would have spotted it. Who knows? But more review might have increased the chances that at least one person would have seen what was coming. (Of course, it could also have resulted in damaging leaks.)

The best way to avoid this sort of thing, however, is not through background checks; it is to select nominees who have already had a run at national politics, high-profile senate or gubernatorial races in states such as New York, California, Florida, or Texas, or federal appointments requiring Senate confirmation. You can be sure that the backgrounds of these kinds of candidates have been vetted by the toughest possible investigators—their opponents and the press. Bad news usually outs. Candidates who can deal with it survive. Those who can't are swept away, as Democratic front-runner Gary Hart was in mid-1987. Donna Rice and the *Monkey Business* ruined his chances, not only for the White House, but also for being considered as Dukakis's running mate. Another benefit of this approach is that it can give the candidate a laboratory for appraising the hopefuls' talents for winning votes or for serving in public office. The downside of limiting the universe of possible vice presidential nominees to experienced pols or appointees, obviously, is that it eliminates a lot of very good people from consideration.

The way to handle a proposed vice presidential nominee who has not been tested in national or big-state politics or high appointive office—and I have the obvious benefit of hindsight—is to float the name a few weeks before the convention and let the games begin. By opening gavel, the candidate will have run the gauntlet of press scrutiny or opposition research, or have dropped out. This approach wouldn't necessarily work in a contested convention and, unfortunately, it eliminates the drama of dropping the name at the convention. But it would pretty well guarantee that the news from the convention would not be dominated by questions about the vice presidential selection. If you do it the other way (as we did) in, say, New Orleans, be prepared to spend your time in the press room knocking down stories rather than at Galatoire's knocking down oysters.

If George had limited his consideration of potential candidates in this way, however, Dan would not have been selected. And if George had floated the Indiana senator's name a few weeks earlier, the National Guard question would probably have come up earlier and allowed the campaign to deal with the issue beforehand. Either way, the selection wouldn't have blown up the way it did on the second day of the convention.

Why did George make the decision alone, then hold the choice so close to the vest? Well, he had been vice president for eight long years. The office is hard on its occupants. "Cactus Jack" Garner, FDR's first vice president (a Texan), said the position wasn't worth a pitcher of warm spit. George would sometimes repeat an old Mark Twain joke about two brothers. "One went to sea and the other became vice president. Neither was heard from again." I think he wanted to use the selection of his running mate to step out of the shadows and assert his authority as leader of the party.

On our Tuesday flight to New Orleans aboard Air Force Two, George told Teeter, Fuller, and me that he'd made up his mind, but he didn't tell us which candidate he had picked. He also told us he wanted to make the announcement that day, not later in the convention as planned.

The first person (other than Barbara) to learn of the decision was President Reagan. He had given his emotional political farewell the night before. As usual, the speech was a masterpiece. He reminded the misty-eyed delegates of all he and they had accomplished together on their "national crusade to make America great again." "While our triumph is not yet complete, the road has been glorious indeed."

He reminded Americans how much their lives had improved since 1980, with sixty-seven months of economic growth and years of foreign-policy successes. Responding to the theme of the recent Democratic convention—"time for a change"—he answered, "Well, ladies and gentlemen . . . we are the change."

Then he handed off the baton to candidate Bush with skill and grace.

"Go out and win one for the Gipper!" he concluded.

The delegates answered with a thunderous demonstration for the man they would always love and revere.

Great start.

The next day, President Reagan departed, and George arrived to stake his claim to the nomination. A well-publicized handshake at Belle Chase Naval Air Station marked the passing of political command. During their photo-op on the tarmac, George leaned over and shared his secret with the man he would succeed.

As soon as we got back to the hotel, George told me his choice. George first telephoned all the unsuccessful candidates, then told me to get Senator Quayle on the phone. George then told Dan that he was his first and only choice.

Our schedule that day called for us to take the *Natchez* down the Mississippi to the Spanish Plaza in downtown New Orleans. Quayle was instructed to meet us at the dock. The announcement didn't go off well. Veteran reporters Jack Germond and Jules Witcover described the scene this way:

> Quayle was absolutely giddy with happiness, grabbing his benefactor by the shoulder and repeatedly hugging his arm, gamboling around the platform like the jackpot winner on a television game show. The bizarre scene was reminiscent of the memorable moment at the 1972 Republican national convention in Miami when entertainer Sammy Davis, Jr., came up behind President Richard Nixon and gave him a full-blown bear hug. . . . Bush himself looked on a bit thunderstruck at the display of juvenile enthusiasm he had unleashed.

I was standing in the audience. I was surprised by, but only mildly concerned about, Dan's excess exuberance.

Would that Quayle's enthusiasm had been our only problem. Until now the national press had had little reason to scrutinize his personal story or public record. But two negative stories quickly surfaced. One was about a 1980 golfing vacation. Dan and two congressmen had briefly shared a cottage with Paula Parkinson, a blond lobbyist who would later display her wares in *Playboy*. That one faded quickly. The other, about the National Guard, had more legs. Within hours, it was attracting all the ink and TV time we had counted on for George's official rollout as nominee.

There's a phenomenon, pack journalism, where reporters compete to outdo one another on a story, and that happened here. It's not always fair, because information that is inconsistent with the storyline sometimes gets short shrift. Still, the reporters were doing their jobs and we had to do ours.

The connection between military service and the American presidency is strong. Our first president was a general. So were Andrew Jackson, Ulysses S. Grant, Dwight Eisenhower, and several others. Every president from Harry Truman to Ronald Reagan served as a military officer, and George H. W. Bush, if he won, would extend that list. The U.S. president is commander in chief of the most powerful military force on earth, and voters seem to prefer candidates with command experience. In addition, millions of Americans have served in the military. They identify with candidates who, like them, have sacrificed and, in some cases, risked their lives for our nation.

That's why I think the military records of recent presidential and vice presidential candidates have become such important issues. In 1992, questions were asked whether candidate Bill Clinton had dodged the draft. More recently, similar questions have been raised about President George W. Bush's Air National Guard service and the legitimacy of Senator John Kerry's combat medals in Vietnam. These subjects arouse passion and are capable of moving elections.

That's why in 1988 we clearly had to answer the questions about Dan's service. He had served honorably in the Indiana National Guard, but the real question was whether he signed up in 1969 to avoid serving in Vietnam and, more to the point, whether his prominent family had used its influence to move him up the waiting list.

At a Wednesday morning press conference, a reporter asked Quayle why he had opted for the Guard. After explaining his desire to get married and go to law school, Quayle added, "I did not know in 1969 that I would be in this room today."

Uh-oh. Our candidate had just provided a new definition of "selective service."

By now, it was clear that we'd be hammered in the Thursday morning papers. There was nothing we could do about that. Our goal was to get ahead of the story (or put it to bed) before George gave his acceptance speech that night.* That's when he would step out from the shadow of the great president to whom he had been so loyal and reveal his own vision for the country. We wanted Friday's headlines to be about our candidate for president, not our candidate for vice president.

We needed to do three things. The first was dig up the facts. The second was to disclose them. (The worst thing with a negative story is for it to dribble out in installments.) And the third was make it clear that, despite it all, George was standing by his selection.

While the delegates at New Orleans's Superdome were nominating George, I met with my gang of strategists and operatives, including Dick Darman, Margaret Tutwiler, Lee Atwater, Bob Teeter, Craig Fuller, Stu Spencer (who would manage Dan's campaign), Jim Lake (our communications director, who would also work with Quayle), Bob Kimmitt, and political specialists Paul Manafort and Charlie Black.

First, we needed to know what Kimmitt had uncovered in his

---

*A good place to read more about how the campaign responded to the National Guard issue is *Whose Broad Stripes and Bright Stars*, by Jack Germond and Jules Witcover, which helped me remember who did what, and when, during those hectic days in August.

background checks. My focus was not, however, on assessing whether anything went wrong with the vetting process and, if so, who was to blame. There wasn't time for that. Besides, as I've already said, the blame game serves little purpose. The real issue is always what to do about a problem, not what you can dig out of the ashes of the past about who knew what, and when.

After our meeting, I called Dan and told him we needed better answers to the questions the media were asking. I then sent Darman and Kimmitt to his suite to get those answers. They reported back that he truthfully didn't know or remember the relevant particulars. Not good enough. We made several calls over the next few hours to National Guard officials and politicians from Indiana. We even woke up Dan's father to ask what he remembered.

As dawn approached, we still didn't have all the answers, but it appeared that Dan's father had, indeed, made a call or two to help his son get in the Guard. Three hours later, I got out of bed to make the talk shows. At each interview, the message was that we would have more to say about Dan's military record later in the day and that George Bush had complete confidence in his running mate.

As the day wore on, we considered several scenarios short of dropping Dan from the ticket, which was never in the cards. He could hold a press conference. (Bad idea.) He could deliver a speech to explain his Guard service. (Slightly better.) Or we could do the talking for him. (Even better.)

On Thursday evening, shortly before George was to deliver his acceptance speech, Fuller, Teeter, and I each appeared on a different television network to lay out what we had discovered. "There's nothing to hide," I said, disclosing what we knew so far—that Dan's father had made telephone calls to help his son get in the Guard but that Dan hadn't received preferential treatment.

Quayle's brief acceptance speech was also orchestrated. We added a few sentences, including this one: "I served six years in the National Guard and like millions of Americans who have served in the Guard and serve today, I'm proud of it." We also gave the press pool a few minutes with Dan before the speech.

George and Dan spent the day after the convention in Dan's hometown, Huntington, Indiana. When reporters asked about Dan's military record, he answered with the information we had pieced together. Yes, he'd asked for his father's help. And, yes, a family friend—a retired Indiana National Guard officer who worked for one of his family's newspapers—had made a few calls. There was nothing wrong with that, he said.

Questions about Dan's military record didn't seriously sidetrack the campaign. One reason is that the head of the ticket was a certified World War II hero. Another is that on the last night of the convention, George single-handedly changed the direction of the campaign.

TWELVE

"IF YOU'RE SO SMART, JIMMY, HOW COME I'M VICE PRESIDENT AND YOU'RE NOT?"

GEORGE REGAINED THE SPOTLIGHT with his acceptance speech—the speech of his life. It is now best remembered for the phrases it added to our lexicon: "kinder, gentler nation," "one thousand points of light," and, darn it, "Read my lips: no new taxes." But it was much more than that—substantively, politically, and personally. It revealed to the nation the George Bush whom I knew and respected, a modest man with the experience to serve as president, with deeply held values, and with a clear and inspiring vision of the role of government in the lives of Americans and the role of Americans in the world.

At their mid-July convention in Atlanta, the Democrats had tried to define George as a wimp, and worse. Actually, "define" is too polite a word. They ridiculed him, both as a public figure and as a human being. If that's how they wanted to play their hand, more power to 'em. The irony, however, is that many of the same people who jumped from their seats to cheer these mean-spirited attacks would later whine about George's campaign being too negative. For what it's worth, I think the sharp anti-Bush rhetoric at their convention hurt the Democrats with undecided voters.

Ted Kennedy, whose party had rejected his presidential hopes in 1980, taunted the vice president. The senator read a laundry list of what he deemed shortcomings of the Reagan years. After each one, he asked: "Where was George?" Soon the delegates joined the refrain. "Where was George? Where was George?"*

Keynoter Ann Richards, the Texas treasurer—who would win her state's governorship in 1990, then lose it four years later to a young baseball executive named George W. Bush—was even more acerbic. "For eight straight years, George Bush hasn't displayed the slightest interest in anything we care about," she said. "And now that he's after a job he can't get appointed to, he's like Christopher Columbus discovering America. . . . Poor George. He can't help it. He was born with a silver foot in his mouth."

California congressman Tony Coelho, the House majority whip, told the audience George was blue blood, not blue collar. Noting that the vice president was then on a fishing trip with me in Wyoming, he quipped that I had accompanied him "in case George is too squeamish to bait his own hook."

Coelho got one thing right. We were in Wyoming. I had made plans to go trout fishing with my pal, congressman Dick Cheney. When Dick had heart-bypass surgery, I suggested to George that he and I go. He trailed Dukakis by as much as 17 percent in some polls and was down in the dumps. I figured the trip would invigorate us both for the coming campaign and would also spare my friend from having to endure the Democratic convention. (When we returned George joked to reporters that the beauty of the wilderness is that "you don't have to listen to Teddy Kennedy.")

Accompanied by Steve Mealey of the U.S. Forest Service, director of the Shoshone National Forest and a friend of mine from prior fly-

---

*In 2003, the Bush Library Foundation honored Ted Kennedy with the George Bush Award for Excellence in Public Service in a ceremony at the Bush Library. George himself handed the award to the senator. This generosity toward an old political foe speaks volumes about the man George Bush.

fishing trips with Cheney, we packed into the wilderness by horseback along the North Fork of the Shoshone River in northwest Wyoming. The Shoshone National Forest borders Yellowstone National Park. The trip did wonders for both George and me. We talked a little business, but not much, and we enjoyed the unhurried rhythm of riding our horses, fishing, eating our catch, sleeping, then doing it all again the next day. The sight, sound, and smell of the mountains, the woods, and the streams invigorated our spirits. And as a bonus, we avoided the ear pollution of the other party's convention. When we returned, we were refreshed and ready to roll!

In his convention speech, George hit all the marks. To connect with the audience in the Superdome and around the nation, George cast himself as the underdog and used self-deprecating humor ("I'll try to hold my charisma in check").

Much of the speech was a triumphal account of what the Reagan-Bush administration had accomplished, and George firmly embraced the Reagan legacy. "For seven and a half years I have helped the president conduct the most difficult job on earth," he said. "The most important work of my life is to complete the mission we started in 1980."

George made it clear, however, that he brought his own ideas and his own sensibility to the table. That's where "kinder, gentler" came from. "Let's be frank," he said. "Things aren't perfect in this country. There are people who haven't tasted the fruits of the expansion.... And, you know, it doesn't do any good to debate endlessly which policy mistake of the seventies is responsible. They're there and we have to help them."

After eight years in the shadows, George also set out to define himself, to answer—in an indirect and gentlemanly way—the ad hominem attacks from the Democratic convention. George explained his philosophy this way:

> At the bright center is the individual. And radiating out from him or
> her is the family, the essential unit of closeness and of love....

From the individual to the family to the community, and then on out to the town, the church, and the school, and, still echoing out, to the county, the state, and the nation—each doing only what it does well, and no more. . . .

I am guided by certain traditions. One is that there is a God and He is good, and His love, while free, has a self-imposed cost: we must be good to one another. . . .

Does government have a place? Yes. Government is part of the nation of communities—not the whole, just a part. And I do not hate government. A government that remembers that the people are its master is a good and needed thing.

George also spotlighted his differences, philosophically and politically, with the Democratic candidate, Michael Dukakis—a bright, hardworking, and, by all accounts, personable man who served as governor of Massachusetts. Dukakis had a great résumé and one that played well against George's. Son of Greek immigrants. Swarthmore undergraduate. Harvard Law School. Military experience in Korea. A long, successful career in state politics with some interesting policy initiatives such as no-fault auto insurance. All capped by a well-earned victory in the Democratic primaries over Gary Hart, Richard Gephardt, Al Gore, and civil-rights leader Jesse Jackson.

And yet the fact of the matter is that when the Democrats nominated Michael Dukakis, they all but elected George Bush. No matter how many reporters and editorial boards referred to him as a moderate—and no matter that he presented himself as a nonideological centrist—he was in fact a classic Democratic liberal in the mold of George McGovern and Walter Mondale. Pick any topic—defense, the death penalty, tax policy, you name it—he was off to the left. The more the American people knew about him and his core beliefs, the less likely they would be to vote for him for the simple reason (which even in 2004 still seemed to baffle some Democrats) that the great majority of Americans don't agree with those policies. Eight years of Republican peace and prosperity made it even harder to pitch the liberal agenda.

What would make Dukakis even easier to beat, however, was that his campaign apparently didn't understand the importance of *symbolism* in American life and American politics. He had vetoed a bill in the 1970s that would have required teachers in the Massachusetts public schools to lead students in reciting the Pledge of Allegiance. I'm confident the governor loved his country, but this act gave voters reason to doubt. His campaign also demonstrated a severe lack of political imagination about how to deal with the issue. Every time we served the issue, he volleyed it straight back into the net.

The Dukakis pitch was that he was "competent," not ideological. The problem with that approach, however, is that the American people weren't looking—and they never have looked—for a technocrat-in-chief. They were looking for someone who could also lead and inspire them, as President Reagan did. In his speech, George blew Dukakis away on this point. "Competence is a narrow ideal," he said in New Orleans. "Competence makes the trains run on time but doesn't know where they're going. . . . The truth is . . . this election is about the beliefs we share, the values we honor, and the principles we hold dear."

"I . . . may not be the most eloquent," George said, "but I learned . . . early that eloquence won't draw oil from the ground. I may sometimes be a little awkward, but there's nothing self-conscious in my love of country." Then he ended the speech by leading the convention in reciting these words: "I pledge allegiance . . ."

Thanks to George's great speech, we got our convention bump and more. Immediately after New Orleans, polls showed Dukakis 49–Bush 46. We were still behind, but we were headed in the right direction.

THE 1988 CONVENTION is memorable to the Baker family for another reason wholly unrelated to politics. At the end of our stay in New Orleans, former PepsiCo CEO Don Kendall, a loyal and generous Republican, told me he was off to his ranch in Wyoming.

"I'm a jealous wreck," I told him. I had fallen in love with Wyoming in 1944 when my father took me there as a fourteen-year-old to hunt elk. For some time Susan and I had wanted a place in the Mountain West, and we had begun actively looking after I moved to Treasury in 1985. The fishing trip with George in July had only reinforced my hunger for blue skies, big mountains, sagebrush, and trout streams.

I had a great helpmate in Susan. She was reared on a ranch, loves the outdoors as much as I do, and welcomed the notion of having a retreat away from Washington and Texas. Whenever we had free time—which we occasionally did at Treasury, unlike at the White House—we'd go looking for a place in Idaho, Montana, or Wyoming. We even made a bid on a place near Tom and Meredith Brokaw's ranch in Montana. I'm not sure why, however. It was remote and beautiful, but had no river or creek, although there were some streams nearby that I might have been able to fish. What I really wanted was a ranch that was remote and offered both hunting and fishing.

Kendall told me he'd keep his eyes open and let me know if he heard of anything. Two weeks later he called me at campaign head-quarters. "I think I've found a place that you might like," he said. It was a 1,600-acre ranch an hour and a half south of Jackson Hole in the Wind River Mountains and about twelve miles from the metropolis of Boulder, Wyoming, population seventy-five. It had had only three own-ers since it was homesteaded in the early 1900s. "But," said Kendall, "it's not gonna last long. You better get out here if you're interested."

What timing! "I can't go," I said. "We're just starting a presidential campaign. But I'll send Susan."

She flew out and back in one day. To help me visualize the place, she climbed a big rock formation left by the glacier that had scoured out the valley that covered about one-third of the ranch. From that vantage, she took enough photographs to provide a panoramic view. I loved what I saw—a beautiful place nestled in the western foothills of the Wind River range, surrounded on three sides by wilderness, with a wonderful mountain-fed trout stream. It was also home to an abun-dance of game.

We quickly bought it, sight unseen by me, which was very much out of character with my usual cautious approach to a matter like this. Then we learned the eternal truth about what happens when a man and woman fall in love with a piece of land that is still just like God made it. They don't own it; it owns them. We are in the truest sense stewards, privileged to hold it for a while, obligated to protect it.

I swear by prior preparation, but this was one time when it was better to be lucky than good. Susan and I love Silver Creek Ranch. The fishing is great. We catch and release four kinds of trout from the stream, but eat the rainbows and cutthroats that we have stocked in some small spring-fed ponds that we built on the place. We hunt elk, antelope, and deer, but don't allow any hunting of the moose, black bear, and mountain lions that roam the ranch and surrounding wilderness.

I was also luckier than good when I bought a South Texas ranch in the late 1960s. My dad loved hunting and fishing, but as the frugal descendant of Scottish ancestors, he never considered paying good money to buy land of his own. "I've seen too many of my land-poor friends ruined by the Depression," he would say to me when I would plead with him to get a place where we could hunt together. "The last thing I need is a pile of rocks somewhere!"

After Dad became ill, I managed his affairs under a power of attorney. He had some U.S. government bonds that paid only 1.5 percent. When they matured in 1969, I used the proceeds—with my mother's approval—to buy 1,350 acres of prime hunting land near Pearsall, Texas. In time, I would inherit the acreage. I named it "Rock Pile Ranch," its name to this day.

Mary Stuart died shortly after I bought it. Following her death, that piece of South Texas brush land became a source of great comfort and joy for me and our four sons.* In addition, there have been at

---

*In his spare time, my third son, John, runs the ranch for the family. He developed his street smarts and common sense by running his own oilfield service company for several years, then he joined Hollywood Marine, a Houston-based company that operated tanker barges. It was later acquired by Kirby Corporation, for which John now works.

least four oil and gas plays on the property. Lease bonuses and royalties have paid for the ranch many times over. That money also helped offset the significant loss of income I suffered when I quit practicing law and went into politics and public service. Silver Creek Ranch has also appreciated in value. As I said, it's better to be lucky than good!

Why are the outdoors so important to me? Part of it is nostalgia. When I was six, my dad started taking me hunting. I still feel his presence when I am in a duck blind or tracking an elk. I hope Silver Creek and Rock Pile have planted the same kind of memories in the hearts and minds of my own children and grandchildren.

Part of it is just the need to escape. The more complicated my life got, the more I needed simplicity. Anytime I could slip away from the State Department to Silver Creek Ranch for a day or so to stand in that cold mountain stream with a fly rod in my hand, I'd get well in a hurry.

For me, it is spiritually refreshing to go into nature and see the glorious evidence of God's handiwork. The sun rising over the mountains through the east window of our cabin, then setting across the rolling sagebrush plains to the west. A bull moose suddenly appearing behind me on the grassy bank of the creek where I am fishing, then scaring me to death as I hear it jump loudly into the water and cross the creek. A bunny feeding among the wildflowers Susan planted in the front yard, ready to fly under the cabin in an instant if our English cocker spaniel, Josh, picks up its scent. Noisy hummingbirds fighting for space at the feeders. A majestic herd of elk cresting a ridge, eyeing the human interlopers below, then galloping away. Pronghorn antelope running effortlessly through the sage. A lumbering black bear, the "ghost of the forest," suddenly and noiselessly materializing at last light as I photograph it from my ground blind twenty yards away. Millions of stars wheeling overhead in the vastness of the universe, undimmed by artificial light.

SOMETIMES there is a lull after the party-in-power's convention in mid-August and before Labor Day, the customary date for kicking off presidential general-election campaigns. Candidates catch their breath, and their staffs retreat to organize and set strategy for the big two-month push. Trailing so badly in the polls going into New Orleans, however, we knew we could not afford the luxury of taking ten days or two weeks off. After George's terrific acceptance speech, we had what George once referred to as the Big Mo, and we weren't about to let it dissipate. We planned to run hard until November 8, and that's what we did.

I spent most of my time at our D.C. headquarters on Fifteenth Street. Our goals were to be prepared for everything that might come our way and to leave nothing to chance. For instance, we kept up with the Dukakis ad buys in major markets, so we would always know where his campaign was fighting and where it had surrendered. In addition, we had to provide leadership and resources to the small army of national, regional, state, and local volunteers who wanted George to be president and who, before the campaign was over, would contact millions of voters by telephone and mail.

Craig Fuller, George's vice presidential chief of staff, traveled with the candidate. Two or three times each day, he would touch base with me by telephone. George and I also talked fairly often. Headquarters had to stay in close touch with the candidate and his road team to coordinate events, pass along information (we had wire-service tickers in the office), and receive intelligence from the field. Stu Spencer traveled with Quayle, but that didn't work out as well as we had hoped. Dan thought he was being overmanaged.

In *Whose Broad Stripes and Bright Stars*, their book on the 1988 election, political reporters Jack Germond and Jules Witcover wrote: "The Republican campaign was quintessentially shallow but dramatically effective." Yes, it was effective. George won 53.9 percent of the popular vote, forty states, and 426 electoral votes. It doesn't get much more effective than that. But to say it was shallow was just as wrong as these two normally accurate political reporters were when they said in 1979 that George's campaign for president peaked on the day he announced. To say that our campaign was shallow presumes that the American people could be fooled by campaign smoke and mirrors, and that's not true. They knew exactly what they were doing when they elected George. They were extending the Reagan revolution for one more term and giving George a chance to move it in new directions. They also knew that George was better qualified to serve as president and better reflected their principles and values.

Some have characterized the general election in roughly the following manner: George H. W. Bush, a decent man, wanted to win the presidency so badly that he allowed himself to be manipulated by his managers. Instead of running a positive campaign based on the candidate's obvious credentials and vision, these critics say, Bush's handlers ran one of the most negative campaigns in history. Rather than putting forth a clear picture of his presidency, they add, Bush spent most of his time posing for pictures and attacking Dukakis. Moreover, the issues he did choose to talk about had little relevance to the lives of most voters. Two examples: the Pledge of Allegiance and Massachusetts's prison-furlough program.

My response to this is that the analysts couldn't delegitimize the numbers on the scoreboard, so they tried to take the victory away on style points. "Well, he may have won, but wasn't it just awful! No mandate for George, not after the way his campaign behaved!"

Let's set the record straight, first on the question of manipulation. This came to a head when *Time* magazine's October 3 edition ran a cover featuring me and John Sasso, Dukakis's manager. "It's the Year of the Handlers," read the headline. The article described me as a "backstage puppeteer" who controlled Bush just as I had controlled Reagan. I was miffed and George was, too.

As I've already pointed out, President Reagan was his own man. So, too, was George H. W. Bush. Did he rely on me and others for advice and counsel? Of course. That was my job. He may have placed more confidence in me than most other candidates did in their campaign managers. So what? It made sense. We had been friends for more than thirty years and we understood and trusted each other, but this hardly made me a puppeteer. Look at one of the most important appointments George made. He named John Sununu, the former governor of New Hampshire, as his chief of staff, despite my lobbying for Craig Fuller. I could fill this chapter with other examples of George's overruling me and his other advisers.

Having the world think that you are a candidate or president's alter ego actually has certain advantages. As I've previously written, proximity is power. But there are disadvantages, too. In '88, it seemed as if every time campaign advisers couldn't persuade George to do something, they begged me to work on him. Once Roger Ailes and others on the staff asked me to urge George to go after Dukakis more aggressively. I exploded. "Do it yourselves," I said. "You're not the ones who have to go in, deliver the message, then listen to him say, 'If you're so smart, Jimmy, how come I'm vice president and you're not?'"

As I wrote earlier, Michael Dukakis was a bright, honorable man. He evidently represented the values of the people who had elected him, but he was running now for president of the United States, not president of Massachusetts. And it was George Bush, not Michael Dukakis, who better reflected the values of the majority of Americans. The goal of the Bush-Quayle campaign was to drive home that point. George did so by explaining his positions on issues ranging from defense to disabled rights, from the environment to energy, and, yes, from prison furloughs to the Pledge of Allegiance. Those who insist that he was short on specifics should review the many detailed issues papers we released.

But there's also a place in politics for going after the other guy. It is, after all, a contact sport, and has been since at least John Adams and Thomas Jefferson. And going after your opponent is also an appropriate part of politics in a free society. Think about it: what better way is there to explain how your candidate is right than to show how the opponent is wrong? I make no apologies for going after Dukakis on prison furloughs, the Pledge, or anything else. He led with his chin on a lot of these issues, and we used them to take him out.

As for the idea that these issues had "little relevance to the lives of most voters," that's baloney. In our nation, the flag and our other symbols serve to unite us, despite our many differences (including our political differences). The vast majority of Americans love this country, and they want their children to love it. The Pledge is a useful ceremony for planting love of country—patriotism—in the hearts of our children.

One thing that disturbed our critics was that the Pledge had never before come up as an issue in presidential politics. That's true, as far as I know, but the reason is simple: Dukakis was the first major candidate for president who thought it was important to veto a bill on reciting the Pledge.

Some describe what we did as "going negative." A better term would be to say that we were showing the "contrasts" between the candidates, a fair tactic as long as the ads were factual, and ours were. Did those "contrasts" reflect negatively on our opponent? Yes, they did. Factual contrast ads are used all the time in political campaigns today, and there is no reason they should not be.

How do you get your own message across and drive home the differences between your candidate and his opponent? In 1988 and for some time before and since, the answer has been relatively simple: use the airwaves. Most voters form their opinions of presidential candidates from what they see on television. As campaign manager, it's not your task to worry about whether that's a good thing or a bad thing; your job is to deal with that reality.

Nowadays, television viewers can follow candidates twenty-four hours a day on cable networks and the Internet. Speeches, rallies, town hall forums, and other appearances are covered, many times live and in their entirety. Cable pundits pontificate hourly. In 1988, our job was somewhat simpler. Most Americans relied then on the evening news broadcasts by the three major networks. We devoted ourselves to trying to get positive coverage every night on ABC, CBS, and NBC—preferably at the beginning of the broadcasts when the most people were watching.

With few exceptions, the top network reporters and anchors (who often double as the editor responsible for selecting stories) are bright, savvy men and women who know when they are being spun. But they also know that they only have a minute or two to tell most stories and that television is a medium that depends on pictures. A presidential campaign is an eight-hundred-pound gorilla; it can't easily be ignored, and neither can the visuals and sound bites it generates.

When I was Ronald Reagan's White House chief of staff, we tried to steer coverage toward our story of the day. Mike Deaver brilliantly choreographed those events, scheduling the president to appear before the perfect backdrops for appealing visuals that the networks could hardly ignore. In the Bush campaign of '88, the troika of Roger Ailes, Bob Teeter, and Lee Atwater planned the visuals, which were executed by an experienced team of advance men and communications specialists.

It is not a stretch to say that we probably would not have won that year without any one of these three named individuals. Each one brought different skills to the campaign. Media consultant Roger Ailes, who has gone on to an extraordinarily successful career as chairman, CEO, and president of Fox News, was indispensable in planning and implementing our advertising strategy. He also helped prepare the candidate for the presidential debates.

Bob Teeter was recognized as one of the nation's foremost political pollsters. He practically invented the tracking poll, which is to old-fashioned spot polls as movies are to photographs. With Lee Atwater, he was also one of our principal political strategists, a reprise of his role in the 1976 Ford campaign. In later years, his polls would appear on *NBC News* and in the *Wall Street Journal*. Sadly, he died from cancer in June 2004. He was a wonderful friend, and I miss him.

Lee Atwater, who died from a brain tumor at age forty in 1991, was our able campaign manager.* He received, and deserved, much of the

---

*My daughter Elizabeth Winston Jones worked for Lee in the '84 campaign and did a terrific job. She later earned a law degree. Today her energy and talents are being put to good use as a wife, mother, and active volunteer in Houston.

credit for our win. I first met him in 1980 when Senator Strom Thurmond called me at the office of the Reagan transition team to recommend him for the White House staff. I hired him for the political office, where he did an excellent job. In 1984, he was our White House liaison with the campaign in the Reagan reelection landslide. After the 1988 election, he served until his death as chairman of the Republican National Committee. When he became ill, he underwent a spiritual conversion. "My illness helped me see what was missing in society was what was missing in me: a little heart, a lot of brotherhood," he wrote shortly before he died. He lived not far from me in D.C., and as his disease progressed, I visited him both in his home and at the hospital.

These men were artists whose job was to listen to what the voters were saying (through the polls), then to try to craft messages that would work on television and help influence the public's perception of their candidate. Does this mean that image trumps substance in evening news stories? I think most campaigns, and most broadcasters, hope that image *complements* substance.

Consider how we rolled out George's position on the environment. On August 31, he raised the issue in a photo-op in up-for-grabs Michigan. (Again, anyone—voter or reporter alike—who wanted more details was always welcome to read candidate Bush's position papers.) The next day he went to Dukakis's home state and took the media on a boat tour of Boston Harbor. Pointing to the floating garbage, he questioned the governor's "competence" in dealing with the pollution. All three networks gave the tour extensive airtime. One network described the event as "floating political theater."

Exactly.

By comparison, some of Dukakis's photo-ops were poorly conceived. The most damaging came on August 13. To provide visuals for a foreign policy speech he had given early that day, he traveled to a General Dynamics plant in Michigan and donned an oversized combat helmet with built-in earphones and "Mike Dukakis" stenciled across the front. Then he rode around in the open hatch of a sixty-eight-ton

Abrams M1A1 battle tank,* smiling and waving to reporters like a kid on a carnival ride.

There's no kind or gentle way to say this: Dukakis looked goofy. The photo of that event has to be one of the most damaging in political history. Watching this, I remembered one of the "don'ts" in the campaign manual we gave President Ford: don't ever put on a hat that makes you look silly.

In case anyone missed the incident on the evening news, we put the footage into a television ad. "Michael Dukakis has opposed virtually every defense system we developed," the announcer said, mentioning seven instances from new aircraft carriers to the stealth bomber. All the while, the on-screen candidate bounced around, incongruously, in the giant tank. "Now he wants to be our commander in chief. America can't afford that risk."

We were charged with distorting Dukakis's position. My answer is that we did nothing more than take an image his campaign had created and put it on the air with factual commentary about how he had opposed or criticized most of the new weapon systems and defense initiatives of the Reagan administration.

We were also criticized for a commercial about the Massachusetts program that granted unsupervised weekend furloughs to convicts. The program started under Dukakis's Republican predecessor, but the governor wholeheartedly supported it and during his first term proudly vetoed a bill to keep first-degree murderers locked up. In 1987 a furloughed murderer named Willie Horton stabbed and tortured a Maryland couple, then raped the young woman. The outraged people of Massachusetts collected seventy thousand signatures for a referendum to end the program. When the legislature passed a fur-

---

*Three years later in Kuwait, Abrams tanks got their first real combat test against Saddam Hussein's much-vaunted tank corps. The Abrams has night vision, can fire while moving over rough ground, and can find targets over the horizon. Iraqi tanks were being killed by a foe they could not even see.

lough ban by a veto-proof majority, Dukakis signed the bill, but reluctantly. Meanwhile, Horton was put away for two life sentences by a Maryland judge who made a point of criticizing Massachusetts for letting him loose.

We developed a thirty-second commercial to nail Dukakis for his support of furloughs for convicted murderers. It showed a long file of men in prison garb (every one of them white) exiting and entering prison through a revolving door. The narrator said Governor Dukakis's "revolving-door prison policy gave weekend furloughs to first-degree murderers not eligible for parole. While out, many committed other crimes, like kidnapping and rape." This text was superimposed over the images: "286 escaped ... and many are still at large." "Now Michael Dukakis says he wants to do for America what he's done for Massachusetts. America can't afford that risk." This ad, too, was factual and effective.

Unfortunately, a second prison furlough commercial came out about the same time. It differed from our spot in two big ways. First, it included a photo of Willie Horton, who was not pictured or mentioned in our ad. Horton was an African American, and the commercial immediately drew criticism for what some considered a not-so-subtle attempt to play on racial fears. I found the commercial offensive and said publicly that the Bush campaign deplored it and wanted it off the air. Second, the Bush-Quayle campaign did not produce this commercial; the National Security Political Action Committee did, and it was wholly independent of our organization.

Skeptics accused the Bush team of coordinating with a not-so-independent political action group to produce the inflammatory ad, so we could then repudiate it and enjoy the best of two worlds. In other words, we were accused of using a two-track system to get an outside group to do our dirty work for us.

I have three responses. First, as far as I know—and I was campaign chairman—we had nothing to do with that ad. Second, given the uproar that followed, I'm fairly sure it did us more harm than good.

Third, I truly deplored the Horton ad. I condemned it then and I condemn it now.

As in the two Reagan campaigns, I was responsible for negotiating the debates on behalf of our campaign. Across the table was Paul Brountas, a respected Boston lawyer who was my counterpart as Dukakis's national campaign chair. I started with the better hand. George was now ahead in the polls, and Dukakis, a skilled speaker, needed the debates more than George, who by his own admission was not the world's most eloquent guy. (At New Orleans, he joked that he was prone to turn "make my day" into "make my twenty-four-hour time period.")

At the beginning, Brountas came on strong. He wanted three presidential debates, one devoted exclusively to foreign affairs and one to domestic policy, plus one for the vice presidential candidates. He also wanted the candidates to be able to direct questions to each other. And he wanted the debates to begin as soon as possible.

I thought we couldn't get away without debating, but that's not exactly the way I played it. The American people expect and deserve televised face-to-face meetings of the candidates. Refusing to debate gives your opponent a wonderful political issue, as President Carter found out in 1980. But I told Brountas we were willing to do only what had been done in the previous two elections. In '80 and '84, there were just two presidential debates, and the candidates did not ask questions of each other. I also turned down his timetable. We wanted the debates to come later in the campaign, between September 25 and October 15. Why? Because debate preparation freezes the campaign. I hinted that if they held fast to their position, I might stop negotiating altogether and blame the Dukakis camp for being unreasonable. End result: two presidential debates within our timetable.

Had I been bluffing when I suggested I might stop negotiating? As I later told Michael Kramer of *Time* magazine, "Let's just say that whatever edge they thought they had, they convinced themselves they didn't have it."

We did agree to Paul's demand that the debates be ninety minutes instead of one hour. We also agreed that Dukakis, who was considerably shorter than Bush, could stand on an unseen riser behind his podium, but we had a lot of fun before giving in. "This race is for the presidency of the United States! Do you mean to tell us that if your man wins and has to go face-to-face with the leader of the Soviet Union, he's going to ask for a riser to stand on?" we asked.

We prepared for the debates as in previous elections. After George studied his briefing books, we held mock debates at the vice president's residence. The sessions were not without their light moments. Darman, our Dukakis stand-in, came to one wearing a tank-crew helmet.*

You can prepare a candidate all you want for a debate. When he stays up too late the night before the big event, however, all bets are off. That's what happened before the first debate at Wake Forest University on September 25. PBS's Jim Lehrer moderated, and both sides got in their licks. All in all, nothing unexpected or particularly memorable came of the debate, but most observers scored it for Dukakis.

George didn't get a good night's sleep. By one account, the vice president had been up searching for Spikey, his granddaughter's missing stuffed animal. Whatever the reason, George left the stage disappointed in himself, but confident he would do much better in the second debate.

The vice presidential debate was sandwiched in between the two

---

*Among the others who helped prepare George were Roger Ailes, Margaret Tutwiler, Bob Goodwin, Jim Pinkerton, Debbie Steelman, Lee Atwater, Craig Fuller, Bob Teeter, Vic Gold, Sheila Tate, and Dennis Ross, the campaign's foreign policy adviser who would later serve under me at the State Department.

In the Dukakis camp, D.C. attorney Bob Barnett played the role of Bush. He later helped both Clinton and Gore prepare for their presidential debates by standing in for their GOP adversaries. He also served as my lawyer and literary agent for *The Politics of Diplomacy* and this book. Small world.

presidential debates. On October 5, Dan Quayle and Dukakis's running mate, Texas senator Lloyd Bentsen, met in Omaha. Dan was asked several questions about his qualifications to be president. "I have as much experience in Congress as Jack Kennedy did when he sought the presidency," Dan replied.

Quayle had used this line on the campaign trail, but his team warned him against invoking Kennedy's name in the debate. Comparing yourself to one of the other team's icons is inherently risky. Bentsen responded with one of the most memorable and devastating lines in debate history, obviously scripted beforehand. "Senator, I served with Jack Kennedy. I knew Jack Kennedy. Jack Kennedy was a friend of mine. Senator, you're no Jack Kennedy."

To this day, I'm still not sure that Lloyd truly was a friend of Kennedy's. Four years later, Tom Brokaw reported that a search of the Kennedy Library failed to turn up "much evidence Lloyd Bentsen knew John Kennedy very well." Friend or not, the audience ate up Bentsen's riposte. So did the media. It dominated coverage of the debate and, for that matter, coverage of the vice presidential candidates for some time. Lloyd's verbal comeback was such a success, politically, that it's almost bad form to point out that the same folks who thought our campaigning was too rough didn't seem to mind this cheap shot.

Lloyd's insult wasn't fair to Dan, but I don't hold any grudges. Politics is politics. Furthermore, I knew Lloyd Bentsen. I served with Lloyd Bentsen. Lloyd Bentsen was a friend of mine. The reason he was even in the Senate is that he had beaten George for the seat in 1970. Like George, Lloyd was a decorated combat veteran of World War II (he flew B-24s out of Italy), a former three-term congressman, and a successful Houston businessman. He turned out to be a fine senator, well respected on both sides of the aisle, a moderate Democrat of the sort that, while not extinct, is far too rare in today's politics. Two months after the bitter 1988 race ended, Lloyd graciously introduced me to the Senate Foreign Relations Committee for my confirmation hearing as secretary of state. This was a perfect example of the old way of doing things—fighting like hell in the campaign, then working together across party lines to do the public's business. Lloyd later served ably as President Clinton's first secretary of the treasury.*

The second presidential debate on October 13 in Los Angeles produced an equally memorable moment. Moderator Bernard Shaw, a CNN anchor, began by asking Dukakis a shocker: "Governor, if Kitty Dukakis were raped and murdered, would you favor an irrevocable death penalty for the killer?" Dukakis replied without an ounce of passion, as if he were discussing the weather.

> No, I don't, Bernard. And I think you know that I've opposed the death penalty during all of my life. I don't see any evidence that it's a deterrent, and I think there are better and more effective ways to deal with violent crime. We've done so in my own state. And it's one of the reasons why we have had the biggest drop in crime of any industrial state in America, why we have the lowest murder rate of any industrial state in America. But we have work to do in this nation.

He then went on to pledge more international cooperation to combat drugs and more attention to early childhood education on the dangers of drugs.

It's too much to say that I knew right then that the race was over, but it would be hard to lose to someone who couldn't manage to get visibly angry about the rape and murder of his wife. The American public identifies with crime victims. In a way that is difficult to explain but easy to understand, his lack of passion and his overintellectualizing a simple, human question essentially proved everything we had said about his being soft on crime.

In his rebuttal, George seized the moment. His syntax may have meandered, but his core beliefs didn't.

---

*Sadly, Lloyd suffered a stroke in 1998 and was in a wheelchair for the last eight years of his life. He died in 2006. I was honored to be a pallbearer at his funeral.

Well, a lot of what this campaign is about, it seems to me, Bernie, goes to the question of values. And here I do have, on this particular question, a big difference with my opponent. You see, I do believe that some crimes are so heinous, so brutal, so outrageous, and I'd say particularly those that result in the death of a police officer, for those real brutal crimes, I do believe in the death penalty, and I think it is a deterrent, and I believe we need it.

George's clear win in that debate was a sign of what was to come, despite a strong push by Dukakis in the final days of the campaign. Still, I never stopped worrying, even as we piled onto airplanes late Monday, November 7, to fly to Houston. One of my rules is never to claim victory until the votes have been counted. Polls can be wrong. It's better to assume the worst and try to do something about it than to assume the best and get blindsided.

Susan and I voted, then I spent most of the day on the telephone. When nothing more could be done, we went out for a Mexican food dinner, then drove over to the home of Charles and Sally Neblett to join the Bush clan in waiting out the election returns. Before George and Barbara moved to Washington in 1980, they had lived next door to the Nebletts. Charles, a neurosurgeon, was an old college pal of Susan's. In the 1990s, he would operate on both Susan and me (twice) to cure spinal disk problems.

By election day all polls, ours and the media's, pointed to a solid Bush-Quayle victory, but I never stopped worrying, first about one state, then another. Other people who were there that night remind me that I was the last to accept that George would win, much less by a landslide. "We need to wait on Michigan," I recall saying. As the others began to celebrate, they joked about my caution. "NBC, ABC, and CBS have called it, but Baker's still out."

The numbers kept getting better and better, of course, and finally, tired but elated, I accepted the outcome. George Bush—war hero, successful businessman, dedicated public servant, my friend—would, indeed, be the forty-first chief executive of the United States, the first sitting vice president since 1836 to be elected to the Oval Office. As events over the next four years would richly demonstrate, our nation had just elected the right man for the right job at the right time.

"Congratulations, Mr. President," I said at last.

George won because he offered the three most important things American voters look for in a president—someone who shares their vision of America, someone with whom they are comfortable, and someone who can lead. These provide the structure on which every successful presidential campaign is built. Everything else, including questions about the issues, important though they are, must hang on that framework.

All too often, I think, the other side sees voters as a collection of discrete interest groups to be picked off, one by one, with government programs—teachers with this, trial lawyers with that, farmers with something else. From this perspective, the first real measure of a candidate is found in the scope and generosity of his programs. When that approach fails, as it did in 1988, the instinct of the losers is to blame the political adversary for tricking the American people. The fact is, however, that people have passions for things greater than themselves and greater, certainly, than government programs.

Late Tuesday night, George, Barbara, and the rest of us motorcaded to Houston's cavernous George R. Brown Convention Center to share the moment with thousands of happy supporters and, through television, with the American people. Country singer Crystal Gayle had warmed up the crowd. Many were hometown friends who had worked for George in every campaign since his first race for Congress back in the 1960s. His appearance at the podium, decorated with a giant replica of the facade of the White House, set off wild applause and cheers. When it subsided, George spoke.

"I have just received a telephone call from Governor Dukakis," he said, "and I want you to know that he was most gracious."

The crowd already knew its man had won, but news of the concession sparked another round of celebration. Susan and I joined with joyous applause and countless handshakes and hugs with the Bush family and others on the large stage.

"We can now speak the most majestic words that democracy has to offer," George continued—"'the people have spoken.' Now we will move again for an America that is strong and resolute in the world, strong and big-hearted at home."

It was an intoxicating moment, doubly so for me because of what George had said to me immediately after his election was assured. "I want your appointment as secretary of state to be the first appointment I announce," he said, "and I want to do it at tomorrow's press conference."

My responsibilities for the campaign were over.* Now I had to get ready for what would be the most exciting and demanding four years of my professional life. But prior preparation for that new challenge would have to wait a few days. Susan and I had a new (and, for me, yet unseen) ranch in Wyoming we needed to visit.

---

*When the campaigns ended—in 1980, 1984, and now 1988—my focus would always shift from electoral politics to public service. In 1999, I attended a conference at Lake Como, Italy, with Democratic political operative Bob Shrum. He had just helped Ehud Barak win election as prime minister of Israel. When Bob was asked what Barak might do about the peace process, he said, "You ought to ask Jim Baker that question, because I just do campaigns. He does campaigns and governing." That's true, and I've always thought it was important, if possible, to have had political experience with the president you serve. It secures your political bona fides within the administration and, more important, gives you a political perspective on public policy issues, which is always helpful in getting things done in government.

THIRTEEN

"FROM 'FENCING MASTER' TO 'FOXTAIL'"

AT THREE MINUTES past noon on January 20, 1989, a left-handed George Herbert Walker Bush raised his right hand and took the oath of office as the forty-first president of the United States. As this solemn act of constitutional succession unfolded, Susan and I stood not far behind George and his family. Patriotic red-white-and-blue bunting snapped in the brisk northeasterly wind. The moment was rich in symbolism, linking our nation's past and future in a simple and elegant ritual. I reflected on the responsibilities ahead and the path that had led me to this place.

Twenty years earlier, James Addison Baker, III, was a thirty-eight-year-old Houston lawyer, a little restless perhaps, but otherwise content to carry on the family tradition of providing legal advice for banks, oil companies, and other business clients. Then, all too quickly, my wife Mary Stuart died, followed three years later by my father. I was left with a broken heart, four confused and distraught young boys, and new questions about what to do with my life. Since then, providentially, Susan and her children had come along to form a new family, and George* had talked me into trying my hand at politics and public service. Now my friend was president. I was days away from becoming his secretary of state, the sixty-first in a line of succession that began with Thomas Jefferson in 1790.

After the inauguration ceremony, George and Barbara escorted Ronald and Nancy Reagan through the majestic space of the Rotunda and out the east side of the building. After the usual hugs and handshakes, the former commander in chief—ever the showman and model president—drew himself erect, saluted his successor, military style, then climbed aboard the waiting Marine helicopter. It lifted, circled to give its passengers a last look at the White House, their home for the last eight years, then disappeared over the trees en route to Andrews Air Force Base. This was a graceful end to a great presidency, but for all of us who had worked alongside this wonderful man for so many years, unavoidably sad. I could not hold back my tears.

President Reagan left behind what George called in his inaugural address "a moment rich with promise." Paradoxically, much of that promise rested on the troubles of the world's other nuclear superpower, the Soviet Union, which suffered from a failed ideology, a moribund economy, and a dispirited people. With his new policies of perestroika (economic reform) and glasnost (openness), Mikhail Gorbachev had signaled that change was needed and would come, but what specific type of change? "Our most powerful foe, the Soviet Union, so aggressive a decade ago, is undergoing an ideological soul-searching of historic proportions," I said in my confirmation hearing. Managing the decline of Soviet power would be our biggest challenge. If we succeeded, the prospects were indeed rich with promise—for

---

*To maintain the flow of the narrative of this book, I refer to my friend as "George." After he won the Oval Office, however, I always called him "Mr. President," just as I did Presidents Ford, Reagan, Carter, and Clinton, and just as I do President George W. Bush. The office deserves that respect, even from the occupant's close friends. I still call him "Mr. President" when others are present, but when we're by ourselves or with close friends, I call him "*Jefe*," which is Spanish for "boss" or "chief."

democracy, economic freedom, and personal liberty. If we failed, the Cold War might well end with a bang rather than a whimper.

I sounded the same theme at my swearing-in ceremony seven days after the inauguration. "We are entering a new era of international relations, one that's filled with more than its share of promise, but perhaps more than its share of perils as well," I said. As the new president looked on, Susan held the Bible and Chief Justice Rehnquist administered the oath in the East Room of the White House. Our eight children were there, along with many members of our extended family. At ninety-four, my mother was unable to travel to Washington for the ceremony, but I called her right afterward to tell her about it.

"This is a very special occasion for me," George said, "because as you all know, Jim and I have been friends a long time, going back perhaps more years than either of us would care to admit." He concluded with some of the kindest words I have ever received: "Those of you who are here today—Jim Baker's family, closest friends—know something that many other people will soon learn for themselves: Jim Baker will be a great secretary of state."

"I hope that in foreign policy, we're going to make a better team than we oftentimes did on the tennis courts in Texas," I replied.*

The forty-three months I would serve as secretary of state were, indeed, marked with promise and peril. The world as we had known it for all our adult lives changed entirely. No administration since the post-war 1940s had faced any more consequential issues. It was a time of fundamental change. I have already told this story in *The Politics of Diplomacy*, published in 1995. It is a 672-page account, sometimes hour by hour, of my time as secretary of state. I cannot repeat that full story here. Instead, I will tell how the Cold War ended and Eastern Europe and Central Asia were liberated, then how our administration led an

---

*One price of public service at this level is that during his presidency, George and I rarely played tennis or golf, or got away on hunting and fishing trips. When we did take time to relax together, we found ourselves talking business. The pressures of the Oval Office are omnipresent. A president clocks in on Inauguration Day and clocks out four or eight years later. In between, there's almost no escaping the weight of presidential responsibility.

international coalition to victory in the first Gulf War and, afterward, advanced the prospects for peace in the Middle East. I will also explain why the Bush foreign policy and defense team was so successful and offer some thoughts on a few of today's foreign policy issues.

My first task upon taking office was not to deal with the Soviet Union, the Middle East, or any other international hot spot, however; it was to work out a modus vivendi with the department I would head. State was established in 1789 as the Department of Foreign Affairs, the nation's first government agency. Two centuries later, befitting our nation's leadership role in world affairs, it was large and powerful, with posts in more than two hundred locations around the world and in every time zone on earth.

In shorthand, it was called simply the "Building." That term refers literally, of course, to the eight-floor behemoth, covering two and a half city blocks in the Foggy Bottom section of the District of Columbia, that houses the State Department. Metaphorically, however, it refers to the elite foreign service officers and career staff members who so effectively administer our nation's foreign policy, year in and year out, as administrations come and go. Our nation is fortunate to have the services of these talented and hardworking men and women, and I am grateful for the support they provided me.

But George Bush had won the presidency and with it the right and responsibility to make foreign policy. No doubt, he was prepared for the task, thanks to his years of service in the United Nations, the Central Intelligence Agency, China, and the vice presidency. In addition, he had surrounded himself with a foreign policy and national security team of individuals who had worked together for years, who actually liked one another (and, thus, got along well), and who brought an impressive array of skills to the table—Dick Cheney (President Ford's former chief of staff) at Defense, Brent Scowcroft as national security adviser (a post he also held in the Ford administration), Colin Powell (national security adviser in President Reagan's second term) as head of the Joint Chiefs of Staff, and me at State.

Behind closed doors, this group would bump heads plenty of

times. We were all strong-willed men, dealing with terrifically important issues. With the rarest of exceptions, however, we sang from the same hymnal in dealing with foreign leaders, Congress, the agencies, and the press. We also didn't leak. George demanded a tight ship, and, of course, he was right to do so. Disunity signals confusion and lack of resolve; unity signals clarity and strength of purpose. These are important assets in politics, diplomacy, and—if worse comes to worst—in a military conflict. As sorry as I am to say it, the scrimmages between State and Defense in the first four years of the George W. Bush administration hurt the president and made it more difficult for him to win public, congressional, and international support for U.S. foreign and security policy, particularly for U.S. operations in Iraq.

The knock on me was that I lacked foreign policy experience. That was not quite true. I had had some terrific mentors-by-example (Ronald Reagan and George Bush) and unparalleled on-the-job training. Serving as White House chief of staff gave me daily exposure to foreign and security policy issues. As treasury secretary, I worked closely with foreign finance ministers and central bankers on international economic issues. All eight years, I attended National Security Council meetings. And in the ten weeks before the inauguration, I gave myself a crash course in international relations, once again following my father's adage that "prior preparation prevents poor performance." As things turned out, however, not having held an office with primary responsibility for foreign or security policy may have helped more than it hurt. With no vested interest in old policies, or the battles to formulate them, I had greater flexibility in dealing with the revolutionary changes of 1989–1992.

I brought other assets to the job, including a strong relationship with Congress and the press. I also understood the inextricable linkage of politics (in its broader sense) and policy, not just domestically, but also internationally. Political constraints inevitably shape the outcome of any negotiation by defining what is possible and what is not. With a nod to Clausewitz, diplomacy is the continuation of politics. This un-

derstanding came from my years in electoral politics and public service, but it was also grounded, I think, in my experiences negotiating
deals and working out disputes as a business lawyer.

My biggest asset, however, was simply this: I was George's friend
and he was mine. We had a degree of trust and loyalty that tran-
scended anything that could be represented by the lines and boxes of
an organizational chart. He also made clear that mine was the first
chair on international affairs. "As secretary of state, he will be my
principal foreign policy adviser," George said. That, and the fact that I
had been his political campaign manager, meant that no one in the administration was going to come between the president and his secretary of state. When foreign officials talked with me, they knew I was
speaking for the president. I also had the freedom, as a friend, to tell
George exactly what was on my mind without worrying about offending the boss. By setting up his cabinet this way, then backing me when
the going got rough, George avoided the destructive turf battles that
characterized the Nixon, Carter, Reagan, Clinton, and George W. Bush
administrations. We were the exception to a very unfortunate rule.

I told interviewers in January that I intended to be the president's
man at the State Department, not State's man at the White House, a
statement that certainly got the Building's attention. And I staffed the
seventh-floor executive offices with a formidable and close-knit team
of Baker loyalists, most of whom had followed me over from Treasury
or the campaign. One was Robert Zoellick, the brilliant policy analyst
one journalist called my "second brain." (Ever since, I've accused Bob
of telephoning the reporter and yelling, "Second! Second!") He would
serve as department counselor and gatekeeper for my in-box. Another
was Dennis Ross, a specialist on the Middle East and the Soviet Union,
who would serve as director of the policy planning staff. He was an
idea man with good common sense, and he was very laid-back. I didn't
hold it against him that he had at one time been a liberal Democrat
(and maybe still was!). He later served as special envoy to the Middle East in President Clinton's administration. Margaret Tutwiler—

Nixon once told me she was "tough and smarter than a shithouse rat," excellent qualities for a political adviser and spokesperson—would be assistant secretary for public affairs and spokesperson for the department.

The second-ranking position in the department, deputy secretary, went to Lawrence Eagleburger. I had not worked with him before, but for more than thirty years, he had served the nation with distinction as a foreign service officer, assistant to Henry Kissinger, ambassador to Yugoslavia, and high-level appointee in the Reagan State Department. Robert Kimmitt, who had served in the Reagan White House and with me at Treasury, was the third-ranking official as under secretary for political affairs, and Janet Mullins (whom I had met in the campaign) served very ably as assistant secretary for congressional affairs. I could always count on this group to run the shop and manage problems while I traveled or worked on special initiatives, and to help with those initiatives. Collectively, they and the regional assistant secretaries (most of them, career diplomats) would serve as my brain trust.

Of course, I also had the help of my invaluable executive assistant, Caron Jackson—always at the office when I arrived, always there when I left. My extensive travels (more than 750,000 miles to more than ninety countries) were successful because of the organizational skills and formidable protective presence of Karen Groomes, as well as Lynn Dent and Pat Kennedy. Kim Hoggard ably assisted Margaret Tutwiler with press, and John Rogers joined us later as under secretary for management.

On a typical day, my security detail* would pick me up about 7:00 A.M. I would review my schedule in the ten-minute ride between home and the Building. Over breakfast, I would read intelligence reports, press clips, and the *White House News Summary*. At least twice a week, I

---

*With the move from Treasury to State, my Secret Service code name changed from "Fencing Master" to "Foxtail." Susan was "Featherweight," and Mary Bonner, our only child still living at home, was "Footnote."

would go over to the White House for freewheeling talks with the president. I had walk-in rights to the Oval Office, and I would also go to the White House whenever the president met with a foreign leader. On a good day, I would get home about 7:30 or 8:00 P.M., but good days (in that sense) were rare. Formal dinners and other social events for visiting dignitaries claimed many evenings. As secretary of state, I usually had to attend, but I sometimes slipped away early. I needed my sleep.

On international trips, my old Boeing 707 had a private stateroom that allowed me to rest in flight. I occasionally used the sleep aid Halcion to help me rest. When that plane hit the ground in a foreign capital, it was the United States of America calling. Even a hint of fatigue or jet lag might reflect badly on my country, interfere with my concentration, and diminish the sense of authority—what the military calls "command presence"—that is an important, though generally unacknowledged, part of diplomacy. From the moment I stepped off the plane until the moment I stepped back on, I represented the United States of America, and I wanted to embody our nation's strength and spirit in my own dress, demeanor, and vitality.

My family paid a heavy price for my public service, particularly when I traveled. One of the hardest moments came in April 1991. While I was on a diplomatic mission, my mother died in Houston, just short of her ninety-seventh birthday. Susan reached me with the news in the office of Yitzhak Shamir, the Israeli prime minister. I still regret being away from her so often in her last years. In 1995, I co-dedicated *The Politics of Diplomacy* to "my wonderful mother, whose love and support gave me wings to fly."

The twin tyrants of any executive are the in-box and the calendar. Secretaries of state are particularly susceptible to schedule overload. Almost every foreign dignitary who visits Washington wants face time. If you are too generous with your availability, you will become a ceremonial figure, not an effective one. If you are too restrictive, however, you may offend someone who doesn't need offending. You also miss opportunities to develop personal relationships with heads of government and their ministers, which is an important part of the job.

Sometimes events overruled the calendar. That happened spectacularly on November 9, 1989, as I hosted an eighth-floor luncheon for Philippine President Corazon Aquino. Toward the dessert course, an assistant passed me a note saying East Germany's communist party chief, Günter Schabowski, had just announced that the border points between East and West Germany were being opened.

It took a moment for this news to sink in. For twenty-eight years, totalitarian East Germany, a Soviet satellite state, had locked its people behind the concrete and barbed wire of the Berlin Wall and a separate fence along the main border between East and West Germany. Guards in watchtowers, the dreaded *Grenzschutzpolizei* (Grepos), had orders to fire on anyone who ventured into the death strips—two hundred yards wide in some places, lighted with floodlights, cut in places by deep ditches, armed with mines and trip wires, sometimes patrolled by vicious dogs. Now, suddenly, the gates were open! The Berlin Wall was falling! With some emotion, I read the note aloud, then we toasted the moment—the symbolic beginning of the end of the Cold War. As I write, I can see a segment of that wall, a monument that today sits outside the window of my office at the Baker Institute on the campus of Rice University.

My entire adult life had been defined by that conflict, which began immediately after the German surrender in World War II. The Soviet Union, our ally of convenience, refused to liberate Poland, Hungary, Czechoslovakia, the eastern sector of Germany, and the other countries it had occupied. Instead, Moscow installed puppet governments backed by secret police and the Red Army. Worse, the Soviets began trying to expand their reach into Greece, Turkey, and elsewhere.

In 1946 Winston Churchill warned that an "Iron Curtain" had descended across Europe. The next year, the U.S. ambassador in Moscow, George F. Kennan, famously recommended a policy of "long-term, patient but firm and vigilant containment of Russian expansionist tendencies." The outcome, he predicted forty-two years before the event, would be "either the break-up or the gradual mellowing of Soviet power." In 1949, policy became program when the United States and its Western allies established the North Atlantic Treaty Organization (NATO) to guard against Soviet expansion into Europe. The Cold War was officially under way.

As this happened, I was a teenager focused more on making grades, playing tennis and rugby, and chasing girls—not necessarily in that order—than on U.S. foreign policy. In 1950, however, the East-West conflict ceased to be an abstraction for me and other draft-eligible young men. Between my sophomore and junior years at Princeton, North Korea invaded South Korea. The Cold War had suddenly turned hot. That is how I wound up serving from 1952 to 1954 as a young Marine officer, much of the time with the Sixth Fleet in the Mediterranean. I was a bit player in a very large world drama.

In time, the fighting stopped in Korea, but the East-West conflict continued. President Reagan posed the central question to the British Parliament in 1982. "Must civilization perish in a hail of fiery atoms?" he asked. "Must freedom wither in a quiet, deadening accommodation with totalitarian evil?" The answer, he said, is that if we stayed the course, the Soviet Union would simply fail. It was destined, he predicted, for the "ash heap of history." This was a stunning thing for any president to say, much less one sometimes derided as a former movie actor, but events would prove that he had a better understanding of the realities of the Cold War than many of his critics.

President Reagan believed passionately in "peace through strength," which is why he put defense off limits during the budget-cutting wars of 1981. His policy might be called "containment-plus." He wanted to roll back Soviet beachheads in Afghanistan, Nicaragua, and elsewhere and push for victory—peaceful victory—in the Cold War. In June 1987, he laid down this historic challenge at Berlin's Brandenburg Gate: "General Secretary Gorbachev, if you seek peace, if you seek prosperity for the Soviet Union and Eastern Europe, if you seek liberalization, come here to this gate. Mr. Gorbachev, open this gate! Mr. Gorbachev, tear down this wall!"

Immediately after the Bush administration came into office, we initiated a top-to-bottom review of policy toward the Soviet Union. From the start, we understood that we would have two historic responsibilities. The first was to exercise leadership to see that the Cold War ended peacefully. The other, equally important, was to set a new course for the post–Cold War era.

Until then, the U.S. had hedged its bets on whether glasnost and perestroika represented genuine change or merely a fresh coat of paint on a rotten structure. Against the advice of some who mistrusted Gorbachev and preferred to wait and see (with an emphasis on *wait*), George decided on an activist policy. We would take the Soviets at their word (but test their rhetoric), while engaging them and trying to move them in directions that advanced our national interests.

In April, George announced trade and financial aid in support of Poland, where a Solidarity-inspired liberalization program was already under way. This was a crucial signal that, despite Moscow's disapproval, we would support communist countries that took steps to move toward political, economic, and personal freedom. In mid-May, George spoke of going "beyond containment," toward a policy of integrating the Soviet Union into the community of nations. At the same time, he said our response would be determined by the actions of Moscow, not by its promises; by reality, not by rhetoric. And in late May, he made clear what one of those actions had to be. "Nowhere is the division between East and West seen more clearly than in Berlin," he said. "And there this brutal wall stands as a monument to the failure of communism. It must come down!"

My job as our nation's chief diplomat was to communicate with Soviet leaders about our desire for warmer relations and, at the same time, to push for concrete steps toward liberation of the captive nations of Eastern Europe. I made my first personal contact in March 1989, shortly after the administration and Congress reached a bipartisan accord on policy toward Nicaragua. If the Soviets would stop sending arms and other support to the Sandinistas and would back free and fair elections, I told Soviet Foreign Minister Eduard Shevardnadze, the United States would honor the results. He agreed. With this step, Central America ceased to be an issue in both our domestic politics and geopolitically, and the Shevardnadze-Baker understanding on Nicaragua set a pattern for U.S.-Soviet cooperation on a host of larger issues.*

I had met Shevardnadze near the end of the Reagan administration. He was an old-school politician from Soviet Georgia, a year older than I was and distinguished by his long white hair, sharp eyes, and gentle manner. George Shultz, my predecessor at State, told me this was someone I could do business with, and he was right. Over the months, Eduard and I would meet again and again.

A climax of sorts came in late September 1989. With domestic turmoil mounting in the Soviet Union, I invited Shevardnadze for one-on-one talks in Jackson Hole, Wyoming—the first time an official of the Soviet Union was allowed anywhere in the United States other than Washington and New York. Over three days and nine formal meetings at a lodge in the shadow of the Tetons, we made good progress on chemical weapons, arms control, and other East-West issues. Between sessions, we would speak informally about the growing strains inside the Soviet Union and other sensitive issues. At the end, I gave him a pair of cowboy boots (symbolic of the venue) to commemorate the talks, and he gave me an enamel picture of Jesus Christ. "You see, even we communists are changing our worldview," he said.

It was in this pristine and glorious setting that Eduard and I developed a personal friendship—a friendship that would prove invaluable in the tumultuous days ahead. His candor made it clear to me that the Soviets were feeling their way, gingerly, toward economic and political

---

*Fortunately, the Sandinista's Daniel Ortega lost the election to Violeta Chamorro. Former President Jimmy Carter persuaded the Marxist leader to leave office peacefully.

liberalization, but I was also struck by how little they appeared to understand the difficulties of achieving either. On Eastern Europe, particularly, the Soviets were being driven by events they did not fully comprehend and could not fully control. On the flight to Jackson Hole on my military aircraft, Shevardnadze said something about East Germany that may have foreshadowed what was to come: "It is not up to us to solve this problem; it is up to them. If I were in their shoes, I'd let everyone who wants to go, leave."

Only seven weeks later, Shevardnadze's wistful musing became reality. The Berlin Wall fell and East Germans left by the thousands. (Others, knowing they *could* leave, decided to stay.) After my lunch with President Aquino that day, I rushed to the White House. All afternoon and into the night, George and I watched live broadcasts of young Berliners dancing atop the hated barrier and chipping pieces away as souvenirs.

The fall of the Wall was a triumph for the U.S.-led Western alliance—a vindication of a policy put in place by the Truman administration, of four decades of bipartisan support for our nation's Cold War policies through nine administrations, of "peace through strength," and of George's decision to engage the Soviet Union and promote the liberation of Eastern Europe. It was also a delicate moment, particularly for Gorbachev and Shevardnadze. In rejecting the use of force to keep the Soviet empire together, they were on the side of the angels. But would hard-line elements in their government and military accept this public humiliation or try to do something about it? The Soviets had sent tanks to crush revolts in East Germany in 1953, Hungary in 1956, and Czechoslovakia in 1968. Now Gorbachev worried aloud that a "chaotic situation may emerge with unforeseeable consequences." This was not a threat, in our judgment; it was a warning. The stability of both the Soviet Union and the region were at risk.

George decided to respond in a deliberate and low-key manner. We must not overreact, he said. That is why we did not dance, rhetorically, on the ruins of the Berlin Wall. Our cool response that day and afterward puzzled many observers and was criticized by some in the D.C. press corps, but it created trust and goodwill in Moscow and helped with the difficult negotiations to follow.

Would East and West Germany now unite as one country? If so, on what terms? Would the Soviets permit a unified German state to remain in NATO, the military alliance that protected the West against Soviet aggression? Six parties participated in the negotiations under a "Two-Plus-Four" structure designed by my close advisers in the State Department. The "Two" were East and West Germany. They would settle "internal" issues. The "Four" were the occupying powers after World War II—the Soviet Union, the United States, France, and Great Britain. They would have a voice on "external" issues.

Beginning in January, I flew to Europe repeatedly, first to push the Two-Plus-Four concept, then to participate in the negotiations. We faced deep concerns and, indeed, initial resistance—not only from the Soviet Union but also from France and Britain—about the implications for Europe and the world of reconstituting the state responsible for two of the bloodiest wars of the century.

Despite this, and the fact that we had only a very narrow window of opportunity to get it done, the outcome was an almost-unqualified success. On October 3, 1990, West Germany annexed the East, and the new enlarged state continued as a member of both the European Community and NATO.* This would never have occurred without U.S. leadership. We framed the talks, kept them on course with endless telephone calls from the Oval Office and State, flew again and again to Europe for meetings, and helped settle disagreements on borders and other issues in sensible ways. As the president would later write, we

---

*After unification, prosperous West Germany embraced the poverty-stricken East with unparalleled generosity. Unfortunately, the East's legacy of communist rule—a decrepit infrastructure, widespread environmental pollution, a dysfunctional economy, and a people whose spirits had been deadened by life in a police state—has proved very difficult to overcome. These difficulties contribute even today to Germany's economic and political troubles.

accomplished "the most profound change in European politics and security for many years, without confrontation, without a shot being fired, and with all Europe on the best and most peaceful terms."

Germany was just one story. Within weeks after the Berlin Wall fell, all Soviet satellite states in Europe were free. Within twenty-six months, the Soviet Union itself would implode, releasing the former republics of the Soviet Union in Eastern Europe and Central Asia to go their own way. Except in North Korea, Cuba, and China (in an at- tenuated form), communism simply melted away, ending the deadly illusion of the twentieth century that took the lives of uncounted mil- lions and impoverished those who survived, both materially and spiri- tually. Communism as a governing philosophy is as dead as the divine right of kings.

None of this happened spontaneously, however. As with German unification, I logged tens of thousand of miles on the 707 that served as my second office (and home), landing in capital after capital and ne- gotiating, first with one leader then another, to push events in the right direction. One ten-day trip in early 1992 took me from Germany to Moldova to Armenia to Azerbaijan to Turkmenistan to Tajikistan to Russia to Uzbekistan. I could have been an explorer for *National Geo- graphic*, except that I was not out to see mountains, rivers, and wildlife. Much to our surprise and the surprise of many, the Soviet Union was gone forever, and I was trying to influence the newly independent states of Central Asia to deal responsibly with the Soviet nuclear weaponry on their soil, to adopt political and economic reforms, and to engage in a positive way with the United States.

At every stop, I was greeted like royalty, showered with gifts, feted with the best national food and drink. After years of forced isolation, these fledgling nations were starved for contact with America and ea- ger to establish good relations. The most dramatic moments came in Albania, then the poorest country in Europe, which had been misruled for decades by Enver Hoxha, a hardcore Stalinist. Men, women, and children lined the streets in Tirana, eager to touch, even kiss, my car.

People hung from every window and lined every roof. Between a quarter and a half million people—more than the whole population of the city—packed the square. "USA! USA! USA!" they chanted. "Bushie! Bushie! Bushie!"

"On behalf of President Bush and the American people," I said when I could finally speak, "I come here today to say to you: *freedom works!*" The Albanians went berserk.

That was a better crowd reaction than the polite applause George had received for the same two-word phrase in his inaugural address. But that is because after more than two hundred years, Americans treated political, economic, and personal freedom as part of the natural order of things. Albanians knew better: freedom is precious, and they owed theirs to the American people. Why? Because the American people—by their political choices and through their taxes and their military service—had accepted the same burden after World War II that the "greatest generation" had borne during the war, which was to risk all to protect others.

Something that put it all in perspective occurred on the very day the Wall fell. About 5:00 P.M. in Washington— six hours later in Bonn— German Foreign Minister Hans-Dietrich Genscher telephoned me. Before he came on the line, however, his secretary, speaking in a thick German accent, said this:

"God bless America! Thank you for everything, sir!"

"DON'T WORRY. Nothing's going to happen."

That was Shevardnadze's reply on August 2, 1990, to my concern about whether the Iraq army would invade its tiny neighbor, Kuwait. He and I were meeting in Irkutsk near Lake Baikal in Siberia, the largest body of fresh water in the world. He was reciprocating for my invitation to Jackson Hole nearly a year before. Our agenda included arms control, conventional forces reduction in Europe, and conflicts in Afghanistan and Cambodia—the sorts of things two superpowers talk about as they move to stand down from long years of conflict. We also planned to do some fishing.

What was really on my mind that day, however, were reports of Iraqi troops massing on the Kuwaiti border. Even though Shevardnadze seemed certain nothing would happen, I suggested that he check with Soviet intelligence. Iraq was a client state of the USSR. Surely the Arabists back in Moscow would know what was going on.

If they did, they did not tell their foreign minister. "Saddam would not be so foolish," Shevardnadze assured me after lunch, referring to Saddam Hussein, the Iraqi dictator. Later that day, however, Iraq's army poured across the border. The invasion and occupation of Kuwait, virtually defenseless, proved notable for their gratuitous brutality—torture, mutilation, and rape.

Before learning of the invasion, I had already flown from Siberia to Mongolia, the latest stop on the Baker freedom-and-democracy tour. When the news reached me, I cut the visit short and immediately headed for Moscow. Once again, events had overwhelmed the calendar.

The fall of the Berlin Wall was richly symbolic, but in my opinion the Cold War actually ended nine months later. With me standing by his side in a Moscow airport on August 3, 1990, Shevardnadze announced that the Soviet Union would join the United States to condemn the invasion and impose an arms embargo on Iraq. "This aggression is inconsistent with the principles of new political thinking and, in fact, with the civilized relations between nations," he said. It was a remarkable moment. In the past, the United States and USSR would have faced off across the geopolitical chessboard. Now we were together on the same side.

It is difficult to know quite why Saddam Hussein invaded Kuwait. An eight-year war with Iran had wrecked Iraq's economy. Perhaps that is what tempted him to try to plunder the oil wealth of Kuwait. He might also have imagined that the end of the superpower rivalry had created a power vacuum in which a weakened Soviet Union would not stop him, nor would an irresolute United States. In any event, he was wrong, at least about America. "This will not stand, this aggression against Kuwait," George Bush said on August 5. The only issue from then on was whether Iraq would go peacefully or would be forced out at gunpoint.

Under international law, the United States did not need the permission of the United Nations to liberate Kuwait. Chapter 51 of the UN charter gave the Kuwaitis an inherent right of self-defense against territorial aggression, and the UN's core doctrine of voluntary collective security meant the United States could answer the call of the Kuwaiti government-in-exile for help. George had once served as U.S. representative to the United Nations, however, and he knew that if we could win a Security Council resolution authorizing the use of force to eject Iraq from Kuwait, our task would be easier. It would then be the "international community" versus Iraq, not just the United States and a few other countries. He also appreciated that we might use a UN resolution to leverage or embarrass a hostile U.S. Congress into supporting the effort. And he understood that it would be useful in winning political support, domestically and internationally, for whatever had to be done.

We started on the day of the invasion with a unanimous Security Council resolution—even Cuba voted yes—that condemned Iraq's action, demanded withdrawal, and imposed economic sanctions. This was the beginning of a program of coercive diplomacy designed to isolate Iraq from the world community and cause enough pain, diplomatically and economically, to force withdrawal. In coming weeks, the UN resolutions would grow stronger and stronger, with the Soviet Union providing crucial support at each stage.

In November we asked the Security Council to approve the use of force, albeit delicately, through the euphemism of "all necessary means." I met personally with all my Security Council counterparts, at one point traveling to twelve countries in eighteen days, in an intricate process of cajoling, extracting, threatening, and occasionally buying votes. I celebrated Thanksgiving Day in Sanaa, Yemen. The administration also began banging the tin cup to win international financial support for the posting of U.S. military forces to the region and, if necessary, for war. And win it we did, to the tune of about $50 billion. This pretty much wiped out congressional objections to the cost of the effort.

One of the oddest moments in my diplomatic career came when I authorized Lieutenant General Howard Graves* to explain our war plans against Iraq, a Soviet client state, to Shevardnadze. The combined air and ground campaigns would take no more than three months, the general said. Privately, however, we believed three or four weeks would do it, largely because Iraq's Soviet-built tanks and other armaments were so thoroughly inferior to U.S. weaponry. Shevardnadze, a realist, soon agreed that a military solution might be necessary, but Gorbachev initially resisted and later agreed only reluctantly. To the end, he kept alive the hope that Saddam could be talked into pulling out of Kuwait.†

The United States chaired the Security Council meeting of November 29, 1990, so I wielded the gavel. To add weight to the proceeding, we had persuaded most of the other fourteen members to send their foreign ministers, not their UN representatives. I started by reminding the ministers how the League of Nations had responded halfheartedly and ineffectually to Haile Selassie's desperate plea for help when Italy invaded Ethiopia in 1935. That failure doomed the

---

*General Graves, a fellow Texan, represented the Joint Chiefs of Staff on my trips. He was an extraordinarily fine man who later served five years as superintendent of West Point and four years as chancellor of Texas A&M University System, then—sadly—succumbed to cancer in 2003.

†Diplomacy had its lighter moments. In a September meeting, I showed Gorbachev a small package I had been given with Saddam Hussein's picture on the outside and a condom on the inside. The legend said, "For big pricks who don't know when to withdraw." Gorbachev and Shevardnadze roared when they heard the translation, and Gorbachev promptly pocketed the trophy. The story to this point was in *The Politics of Diplomacy,* but not Gorbachev's reply. "Making love with a condom is like licking sugar through a glass," he said.

League and set the table for further aggression by Germany, Italy, and Japan. "History has now given us a second chance," I said. "With the Cold War now behind us, we have the chance to build the world envisioned by the founders of the United Nations. We have the chance to make this Security Council and this United Nations true instruments for peace and justice ..."

The Security Council vote for Resolution 678 was twelve for, two against (Cuba and Yemen), with China abstaining. It gave Iraq until midnight, January 15, 1991, to withdraw unconditionally. After that, member states would be authorized "to use all necessary means ... to restore international peace and security in the area."

This was only the second time the United Nations had ever authorized the use of force to protect a member state from aggression. The first was the Korean Conflict, and the only reason the United Nations could act in 1950 was because the Soviets walked out and did not use their veto. In 1990, by contrast, the Soviets voted with the United States.

Even after the Security Council acted, however, Congress was still reluctant to support the use of force. Many lawmakers wanted to give economic sanctions more time. The administration was convinced, however, that the only way to make sanctions work was to set a firm deadline for withdrawal, backed with a mailed fist. "We did not stand united for forty years and bring the Cold War to a peaceful end in order to make the world safe for the likes of Saddam Hussein," I told one committee. On January 12, 1991—just three days before the withdrawal deadline set by the Security Council—the Democrat-controlled Congress grudgingly gave the president authority to wage war under the UN resolution. A shift of just three votes in the Senate, which voted 52–47, would have meant defeat.

Before pulling the trigger, we made one last attempt to avoid war—a head-to-head meeting in Geneva on January 9 between me and Tariq Aziz, the foreign minister of Iraq. "Our objective is for you to leave Kuwait," I told him. "That's the only solution we'll accept." If it came to war, I said, the Iraqis would face "devastatingly superior firepower." I also warned him of severe reprisals for using chemical or biological weapons. "This is not a threat," I said, "it's a promise."

Aziz obviously had no authority, except to try to talk us into delaying the inevitable. He spoke with forced bravura ("war doesn't frighten or intimidate Iraq") and striking fatalism ("I hope you won't miscalculate our capability to endure the costs of war"). Iraq was a victim, he argued, and the Arab world would rise up against U.S. aggression. More than six hours after we began, we shook hands and parted, each certain that war was inevitable.

On January 16, the U.S.-led coalition launched air attacks on Iraq. In mid-February, the Iraqis—sensing now that they would never enjoy their plunder—set the rich Kuwaiti oil fields afire, an ecological and financial disaster of unimaginable proportions. After weeks of allied air strikes, military ground operations began on February 24. One hundred hours later the war was over. The Iraqis never had a chance. Secretary of Defense Dick Cheney, JSC Chairman Colin Powell, and General Norman Schwarzkopf, the field commander of Operation Desert Storm, designed a brilliant campaign, and the men and women of the coalition forces, most of them American, implemented it almost without a hitch.

For years, the question I was most often asked about Desert Storm is why we did not remove Saddam Hussein from power. There were many reasons, as I wrote in 1995 in *The Politics of Diplomacy*. A coalition war to liberate Kuwait could then have been portrayed as a U.S. war of conquest. Furthermore, even if Saddam were captured and his regime toppled, American forces would still have been confronted with the specter of a military occupation of indefinite duration to pacify a country and sustain a new government in power. The ensuing urban warfare would surely have resulted in more casualties to American GIs than the war itself, thus creating a political firestorm at home. And as much as Saddam's neighbors wanted to see him gone, they feared Iraq would fragment in unpredictable ways that would play into the hands of the mullahs in Iran, who could export their brand of Islamic fundamentalism with the help of Iraq's Shiites and quickly transform themselves into a dominant regional power. Finally, the Security Council resolution under which we were operating authorized us to use force only to kick Iraq out of Kuwait, nothing more. As events have amply demonstrated, these concerns were valid. I am no longer asked why we did not remove Saddam in 1991!

Am I implicitly criticizing President George W. Bush for having done twelve years later what his father's administration declined to do in 1991? No, I am not. Iraq's continued violation of UN resolutions and its expulsion of weapons inspectors in 1998 prompted the Clinton administration to adopt regime change in Iraq as U.S. policy—a policy President George W. Bush also followed. After the 9/11 terrorist attacks, U.S. patience with Saddam Hussein finally ran out. By 2003, the Iraqi dictator had thumbed his nose at UN resolutions for twelve years, turned the UN's oil-for-food program into a cesspool of corruption (what one critic called an "oil-for-palaces" program), and continued to abuse his own people. Every intelligence service in the world, including those in Russia and France, also believed—erroneously, it now appears—that Iraq still possessed weapons of mass destruction. I do not doubt that President George W. Bush in acting militarily against Iraq weighed the concerns we considered in 1991. He simply decided that the costs I had described in 1995, though real, were justified in 2003. That's why the buck stops in the Oval Office.

In an August 2002 op-ed column in the *New York Times* seven months before hostilities began, I argued that "the only realistic way to effect regime change in Iraq is through the application of military force, including sufficient ground troops to occupy the country (including Baghdad), depose the current leadership and install a successor government." But "it cannot be done on the cheap," I counseled. The right way to proceed, both politically and substantively, I said, was to seek a Security Council resolution requiring Iraq to "submit to intrusive inspections anytime, anywhere, with no exceptions, and authorizing all necessary means to enforce it." If Saddam employed his usual "cheat-and-retreat" tactics (as he subsequently did), I argued, we should then act to remove him from power.

I also warned that winning the peace would be difficult and potentially costly—"politically, economically and in terms of casualties." "We will face the problem of how long to occupy and administer a big, fractious country and what type of government or administration should follow." "Unless we do it the right way," I wrote, "there will be costs to other American foreign policy interests, including our relations with practically all other Arab countries (and even many of our customary allies in Europe and elsewhere) and perhaps even to our top foreign policy priority, the war on terrorism." The costs could be reduced, I said, "if the president brings together an international coalition behind the effort. Doing so would also help in achieving the continuing support of the American people, a necessary prerequisite for any successful foreign policy."

In January 2003, the James A. Baker III Institute for Public Policy and the Council on Foreign Relations published a joint study entitled *Guiding Principles for U.S. Post-Conflict Policy in Iraq.* "There should be no illusions that the reconstruction of Iraq will be anything but difficult, confusing, and dangerous for everyone involved," the report said, warning that a long-term U.S. occupation "will neither advance U.S. interests nor garner outside support." The working group recommended that the Iraqi army be preserved, not disbanded, to serve as a guarantor of peace and stability, and declared that it was "wishful thinking" to suggest that Iraqi oil revenues would be sufficient to pay for post-conflict reconstruction.

President George W. Bush did, in fact, win a unanimous Security Council resolution in November 2002, demanding that Iraq comply or face serious consequences. To help its most steadfast ally, Tony Blair, prime minister of the United Kingdom, the administration later sought a second resolution that would have defined "serious consequences" to mean the use of force. The Security Council, led primarily by France, balked. In retrospect, it was a mistake to have sought the resolution without first knowing that we could get the votes to pass it. Better to have just put our own interpretation on "serious consequences" and gone ahead without trying and failing to get a second resolution. I wrote in February 2003 that the United States could not permit itself to be held hostage by the lowest common denominator of opinion on the Security Council. Acting in reliance on the first UN resolution and congressional authority, the United States led a coalition of the willing into battle against Saddam Hussein's army in March 2003, winning quickly, decisively, and predictably.

Unfortunately, the formulation and implementation of policy in the lead-up to, and aftermath of, the war were negatively affected by substantial and continuing turf battles between the State Department and the CIA on one side, and the Defense Department and the vice president's office, on the other.

The Defense Department made a number of costly mistakes, including disbanding the Iraqi army, pursuing de Baathification too extensively (and thereby prohibiting many qualified Iraqis from serving in a successor Iraqi government), failing to secure weapons depots, and perhaps never having committed enough troops to successfully pacify the country. One thing is for sure: the difficulty of winning the peace was severely underestimated.

Despite the troubles that have followed, however, the Iraqi people are better off now than under their murderous dictator. In polling released while I was writing, seven in ten Iraqis said their lives were going well and two-thirds expected things to improve in the year ahead. Once again, sacrifice by America and its allies has brought down a totalitarian government and delivered a degree of hope for political, economic, and personal freedom to an oppressed people. But the costs to our nation—primarily in terms of sacrifice by brave young Americans and their families, but also the economic, diplomatic, political, and military costs—are very real and canot be ignored.

Those costs will have been worth paying, however, if we can promote progress toward representative government and individual freedom for many countries and people of the Middle East. The jury is still out on whether we will succeed, although Iraq has held democratic elections, as have the Palestinians, notwithstanding that the results in each may prove unfavorable to U.S. interests. In addition, the "Cedar Revolution" has ended the twenty-nine-year Syrian occupation of Lebanon, and Libya has given up its weapons-of-mass-destruction programs.

Regardless of one's views about the wisdom of going to war in Iraq, what is important today to our country's international political, diplomatic, and military credibility is that we find a way to manage the end-game effectively and successfully. The "Lebanonization" of Iraq through a descent into sectarian fragmentation and violence, or an Iraq that erupts into full-blown civil war, or an Iraq with a government hostile to America—each would be an extraordinarily undesirable result for the United States, the region, and the world. Unfortunately, the jury also remains out on whether these outcomes can be avoided.

At the urging of members of Congress, a bipartisan group (the Iraq Study Group) was formed on March 15, 2006, to make a forward-looking and fresh assessment of the situation in Iraq and to provide Congress and the administration with insights and advice. I was named cochair of the group, along with Lee Hamilton, former Democratic chairman of the House Foreign Affairs Committee. The administration welcomed the effort. As I write, the Iraq Study Group has just begun its work.

IN THE GULF WAR, Israel and some of Iraq's Arab neighbors, including Syria, found themselves on the same side for once, however uncomfortably. The administration wanted to capitalize on the momentum created by this first-ever experience with regional cooperation in the Middle East and on the goodwill generated by the unselfish leadership of the United States in dealing with Saddam Hussein.

"We must now begin to look beyond victory and war," the president said on the day the fighting stopped. "We must meet the challenge of securing the peace." This was more than post-conflict happy talk. We wanted to stabilize the balance of power in the region, prevent a resurgence of Iraqi power, reduce U.S. reliance on oil from the Middle East, and revive the Arab-Israeli peace process. In short order, most of our proposals—for example, a Mideast development bank—died for lack of support, but we refused to give up on efforts to promote peace between Arabs and Israelis.

We wanted the leaders of Israel and its Arab neighbors—Syria, Jordan, and Lebanon—plus representatives of the Palestinian people (but not the Palestinian Liberation Organization) to sit down across the table and start a conversation about peace. Whatever the outcome, this would break the Arab states' taboo of that time against talking peace with Israel because to do so would recognize, at least implicitly, Israel's right to exist. Almost everywhere, I was met with delays, refusals, evasions, unreasonable demands, broken commitments, and endless lectures about the untrustworthiness of the other side, not to mention policy initiatives such as aggressive Israeli settlement activity in the Occupied Territories that almost seemed designed to scuttle the project. Syrian president Hafez al-Assad, for instance, demanded that the United Nations sponsor the event. Reasonable? Not really. It was a way of trying to torpedo the conference. He knew very well that Israel would never participate in anything sponsored by the international body that famously resolved in 1975 that "Zionism is racism."*

In all, I made eight trips to the Middle East before all parties agreed to the conference. Each diplomatic mission was marked by its own frustrations, but the payoff was sweet. On October 30, 1991, Presidents Bush and Gorbachev hosted the opening ceremonies in Madrid's splendid Royal Palace. The meetings that followed were stiff

---

*With administration leadership, that resolution was revoked in December 1991. "To equate Zionism with the intolerable sin of racism is to forget history and forget the terrible plight of the Jews in World War II and indeed throughout history," President Bush said at the time.

and formal. The principals offered neither handshakes nor eye contact, and their public statements were canned and predictable. Nevertheless, Madrid was a success. Its enduring legacy is simply that it happened at all. After forty-three years of bloody conflict, the ancient taboo against Arabs talking with Israelis was dramatically broken. Like the walls of Jericho, the psychological barriers of half a century came tumbling down. Within two years, Israel had signed a treaty with Jordan and the Oslo Accords with Palestinians. It was a period of great hope, and I take a measure of pride in having contributed to the prospects for peace in that troubled region.

Sadly, that period of hope ended in November 1995 when Yitzhak Rabin, prime minister of Israel, was assassinated by a hardcore right-wing Israeli who opposed Rabin's peace efforts. Yitzhak and his wife, Leah—both deceased now—hosted Susan and me as guests of the government of Israel after I left office as secretary of state.* We still miss these dear friends. To honor them in the most appropriate way possible, we have established the Yitzhak Rabin Fellowship in Middle East Peace and Security at the Baker Institute. In November 2005, at President George W. Bush's request, I led the American delegation to the ceremonies marking the tenth anniversary of Yitzhak's death.

ON TUESDAY, September 11, 2001, I was in my office at Baker Botts in Washington, D.C. Later that morning, I was scheduled to speak at a Carlyle Group investors conference. Word that an airplane had hit the north tower of the World Trade Center in New York probably reached me around 8:50 A.M.

Early reports were confused. A light plane had struck the tower. Or maybe it was an airliner. It was surely an accident. Or was it? No one was certain. At 9:37 A.M., however, we watched the television in horror

---

*The U.S. ambassador to Israel at the time was Edward Djerejian, who soon would be the founding director of the James A. Baker III Institute for Public Policy.

as a large commercial airliner flew directly into the south tower. Not long afterward, both towers collapsed and, with them, any doubt about whether the strikes were intentional.

About this time, my daughter Mary Bonner called. "Are you and Mom all right?" she asked. "Don't worry, darling. We're fine," I said. But as we talked, I saw a big plume of black smoke rise in the distance, from across the Potomac. We would later learn that a third hijacked airliner had hit the Pentagon. To add to the confusion, the air was quickly filled with wailing sirens, the *thump-thump-thump* of helicopter rotors, and sonic booms as fighter planes scrambled to defend against whatever else might come.

My speaking event was scheduled for 10:45 A.M., and—not sure whether it would be canceled—I arrived early and chatted with John Major, the former British prime minister. We were on the same program. Our topic: "World Affairs Overview."

The conference was soon canceled, however, and I returned to my office and the continuing television coverage. That afternoon, I gave telephone interviews to Peter Jennings, Tom Brokaw, CNN, Fox, and many others. It was now clear that the United States had been struck by terrorists.

American interests had been hit before. The Marine barracks in Lebanon in 1983, the Khobar Towers in Saudi Arabia in 1996, and the USS *Cole* in Yemen in 2000 all come to mind. But 9/11 was different. It brought death to our own soil, it targeted innocent civilians, the scale was larger than anything that had gone before, and it was an unambiguous act of war against our nation. Like Pearl Harbor and the fall of the Berlin Wall, 9/11 marked with finality the end of one era of history and with awful clarity the beginning of another. Events in Madrid, London, Moscow, Bali, Casablanca, Riyadh, and elsewhere would later confirm that terrorism was a global threat that demanded a global response. By virtue of its military power, economic strength, and international preeminence, only the United States could lead that effort—in direct military action, joint law enforcement, and intensified sharing of intelligence. The new administration, not yet in office for a full year, was called to action and would forever be defined by its decisive leadership, at home and abroad, in the months and years that followed.

Terrorism is best defined, I think, as the intentional killing of civilians to achieve a political end. It is a tempting weapon for stateless radical groups that lack the resources to fight conventional wars. But it is doubly dangerous when those groups seize control of a state, as the Taliban and al Qaeda did in Afghanistan before the 2001 attacks on America. Except when terrorists come to ground, as in Afghanistan, conventional military tools are of little use. You cannot target a cruise missile on a meeting of terrorists in a Hamburg apartment complex. What is needed instead is good intelligence, international cooperation, national confidence, strong leadership, and realism about the possibility that, despite it all, dedicated terrorists will succeed now and again in killing the innocent. Most of all, there must be a determination not to let acts of terrorism weaken our resolve.

As I write more than five years later, America has not been attacked again inside its own borders. By that measure, the administration's 9/11 policies have succeeded. Realists, however, should understand that the costs of our defense are high and the terrorists, though weakened, have not yet been defeated.

In time, America and its allies will prevail, just as we prevailed in the Cold War and in World War II. We have firefighters, police officers, and medical personnel who will rush into burning buildings and sacrifice their lives to save others. We have air passengers like those on United Flight 93 who will rise from their seats and fight hijackers with their bare hands. We have troops who will go where asked and do what is needed with skill and professionalism unmatched in military history. And we have a people whose generosity in helping others around the world is wondrous to behold. No nation so blessed will be defeated by a small band of hate-filled killers of innocent men, women, and children.

. . .

ANOTHER ISSUE that emerged after George and I left office was the dilemma of failed states—territories where governments cease to function, the rule of law breaks down, and competing warlords and their private armies of thugs seize power. This is what happened in Somalia, for instance, and later in Liberia, the Congo, and elsewhere. The proper response of the developed world to these political, economic, and human train wrecks is yet to be settled. George H. W. Bush probably had the right idea in sending soldiers on a limited mission to deliver humanitarian aid in Somalia. When President Clinton later escalated the mission to nation-building, however, the cost of going up against the warlords—Black Hawk down!—proved to be higher than he or the American people would easily tolerate.

One other feature of our post–Cold War foreign policy, sadly, is a deterioration in our nation's relationships with many other countries. At the end of the first Bush administration, America was the most admired nation on the face of the earth. That began to erode in the late 1990s, interrupted briefly by the outpouring of world sympathy after 9/11. Today, it is probably safe to say that majorities in most countries oppose our policies and distrust our motives. Some of this loss of confidence from the highs of the end of the Cold War and the first Gulf War was inevitable. As the world's sole remaining superpower, we occupy a uniquely preeminent place in world affairs. This sets up natural anxieties, resentments, and jealousies, and makes it all the more important that we exercise our power in as understated and collaborative a way as our national interests permit. It will take many years to repair the international loss of trust in our motives, but we must do our best to do so, and as I write, that effort is under way.

SO MANY THINGS happened during my tenure as secretary of state that I can barely mention them, much less do them justice. Besides the end of the Cold War, victory in the Gulf War, and efforts to promote Arab-Israeli peace, we dealt with Tiananmen Square, Panama, the end of apartheid in South Africa, ethnic warfare in the Balkans, and many other challenges. A second Bush administration would have brought more, and I have no doubt that George would have handled them as well as those he faced in the first term, which is to say, very well indeed. My hope and expectation, frankly, was to remain in office as secretary of state and continue to help him. In July 1992, however, he asked me to run his reelection campaign, and I could not say no to my friend. My resignation as secretary of state was effective August 23, 1992, and my farewell was the most emotional speech I have ever given. After all we had accomplished, it was hard to leave the best job I'd ever had. Once again, however, I felt a duty to leave the world of public service and return to the world of electoral politics.

FOURTEEN

"THE ONE CONSTANT IN POLITICS IS CHANGE"

AS AFTERNOON TURNED to evening at the Gerald R. Ford Museum in Grand Rapids, George Bush took the microphone to fight for his presidency. In five days, American voters would go to the polls. Michigan was in play, and he could not win reelection without it. "The choice before the American people," he said, "is a vast difference on experience, philosophy, and, yes, character."

The president was not a naturally gifted stump speaker (he admits as much), but as I listened that day in October 1992, he was on his game—buoyant, smiling, assertive. I was running the campaign, a reprise of my role in 1988, but this was the first time I had traveled with him in 1992.

Despite having served with distinction as president, George was the underdog. With the Cold War over and the world largely at peace, foreign policy leadership, his biggest political asset, was yesterday's news. As often happens after a period of conflict, America was turning inward. A mild nine-month recession in 1990–1991 had created an opening for Bill Clinton, the politically gifted governor of Arkansas. He exploited it skillfully, especially here in the Industrial Belt. For weeks George had trailed by double digits. In the last week or ten days, however, he had closed to within one or two points in some major polls. We were still behind, but for the first time in the campaign, we were moving.

Clinton had exaggerated our nation's economic troubles for political purposes, George told the Grand Rapids audience. His voice betrayed few signs of long days on the road and a gathering cold. "The only way they can win is to convince America we're in a recession," he said, but the economy had actually grown for the past eighteen months—at a rate of 2.7 percent in the third quarter alone.

"Four more years! Four more years! Four more years!" the crowd chanted.

George was absolutely right. The recession was over. The economy was growing. So successful was the Democratic mantra, echoed by a sympathetic press, however, that many people erroneously believed that America was in a deep recession on election day. On this issue, perception had not caught up to reality, and it still hasn't.

Clinton's track record in Arkansas did not inspire confidence, George said. The state was "fiftieth in environmental quality ... fiftieth in per capita spending on criminal justice ... forty-sixth on teacher salaries, and forty-fifth in overall well-being of children." "And in the debate the other night he says, 'I want to do for America what I've done for Arkansas.' No way! No way!"

Then came the delicate character issue. George Bush—war hero, family man, successful businessman, veteran public servant—had a hard-won reputation as an honorable man, even among most Democrats. By contrast, polls showed that many voters were still uneasy about Clinton. (The complaint that character should be off-limits in a campaign for the American presidency is both absurd and not historical. What could be more important?)

"I do not believe you can be president of the United States and try to be all things to all people," George said.

In the Gulf War, for instance, "we had to mobilize world opinion and then make a very difficult decision to send someone else's son or daughter into combat. And what did Bill Clinton say? He said, 'Well, I agree with the minority [the Democrats in Congress who voted *against* giving the president authority to use force], but I guess I would have voted with the majority.'"

"The thing that bothers me is there is a pattern of deception. . . . You cannot lead by misleading."

"Bush! Bush! Bush!"

The president had been worked over pretty good in the campaign, not only by the Clinton campaign, but also by H. Ross Perot, the on-again, off-again third-party candidate. Seeing George counterpunch was fun. As he spoke, I chatted with Ann Compton of ABC News about George's surge in the polls. Ann could sense my optimism. I don't remember her exact comment, but it was something like this: "You all seem to be upbeat now, but in a day or two you're not going to be so happy."

She would not elaborate, so I filed her strange remark away and moved on. George had an interview that night, then we were on to Missouri, excited by the possibility of pulling off the biggest late-surge upset since Truman beat Dewey.

I HAD KEPT out of sight for much of the campaign. For one thing, running a campaign requires spending most of the time taking care of business in the office, not lighting up the television screen. But early on, I also got boxed in and had to keep somewhat of a low profile to avoid hurting my candidate.

How did that happen? Well, let's begin at the beginning.

In mid-July of 1992, President Bush and his son Jeb—later a two-term governor of Florida—joined me, Susan, and my son Jamie for a few days of fishing at our Wyoming ranch. As in 1988, George wanted to get away from the Beltway during the Democratic convention. Better to refresh himself for the battle ahead than listen to four days of Bush-bashing. George trailed Clinton by serious double digits, and we knew that gap would get worse with Clinton's inevitable convention bounce.

Perot, a controversial Texas billionaire, was also a worry. His backers had already gathered enough signatures to put him on the ballot as a third-party candidate in twenty-five states, and that number was sure to rise. Starting with a *Larry King Live* appearance in February, he had parlayed a series of folksy talk-show appearances into an antiestablishment movement. As late as June 2, he led both major-party candidates in some polls and, unfortunately for us, was drawing far, far more voters from Bush than from Clinton.

Perot probably decided to run for president for a number of reasons. Only he really knows what they were. In my view, however, one of them was that he disliked George Herbert Walker Bush. The trouble started when Perot decided that live American prisoners of war were still being held in Vietnam. He wanted to go over there, look for them, and bring them home. The war had ended about a decade earlier and there was no evidence the Vietnamese still held any of our troops (and none have shown up since), but Perot was adamant. I think he had a meeting with President Reagan about this. The president then ordered a complete review of the situation by our defense, intelligence, and security apparatus, which reported that there was no basis to believe the Vietnamese still held any American POWs. It would be a mistake for Perot to go over there, President Reagan decided.

George and I met with the president in the Oval Office to discuss how to break the news. "I'm willing to tell Perot," the president said, "but I don't really know him. Maybe you Texans can tell him." As chief of staff, it was usually my job to deliver bad news, but I also barely knew the man. The vice president stepped up. "I know him very well," George said. "He's supported me in the past. I'll be glad to tell him."

When George called, however, the hot-tempered Perot apparently blamed the messenger for the message. From that day on, it seemed that he hated George. Sometimes it got ugly . . . and bizarre. During the campaign, for instance, he accused the Bush camp of planning to sabotage a daughter's wedding—a ludicrous charge, notable both for the number of times Perot repeated it to nodding TV interviewers and for the total absence of any credible evidence that it ever occurred.

At Perot's request, he and I once met privately at my D.C. home. All I remember is that he was full of conspiracy theories, including the wedding story. Two days later, details of the supposedly secret meeting appeared in the press. He also came by to see me at the site of the first presidential debate that fall, shortly before the three-way event was to begin. I still don't know why!

But Ross Perot was the last thing on my mind when I went to the ranch in July. All I wanted was a little R&R. A few weeks earlier, I had worked long hours with the Russians in Lisbon, London, and Washington to finish the START II agreement. Finally, on June 16, President Bush and Russian President Boris Yeltsin announced an accord to reduce the number of nuclear warheads on both sides to the lowest levels in more than twenty years and to eliminate all land-based missiles with multiple warheads. It was a landmark achievement in both nuclear arms control and normalization of relations with the new Russian Federation. (The formal treaty was signed in January 1993.) I would soon head to the Middle East to try to restart peace talks after a change of government in Israel. All I wanted to do in Wyoming, however, was wade out into Silver Creek, plant my feet on the rough gravel bed, and drop a fly line over the big brown trout that lurked in the eddies of its cold mountain waters.

George had other ideas. One morning he asked Jamie and Jeb to leave us alone in the cabin. He told me his campaign was not going the way he wanted it to and asked me to leave State and try to put it back on track.

I have said it before, and I will say it again here: I did not want to leave the State Department and run another presidential campaign, but I immediately said yes. George was my president and my friend. He had made me secretary of state. We had accomplished a lot together and, given the chance, I believed, we would accomplish more. I also thought I could help him against his tag-team opponents. The only real issue was when to start. George and I agreed that I would close up shop at State and officially take over the campaign on August 23, immediately after the GOP convention in Houston.

IT IS TRUE, as popular history reminds us, that the president came out of the 1991 Persian Gulf War with an 89 percent approval rating. Those kinds of numbers never hold up, however, and by 1992 he was flying into heavy headwinds.

One big problem was that Republicans had occupied the White House for almost twelve years. This was four years beyond the normal expiration date for party control. For fourteen election cycles over fifty-six years—Eisenhower to George W. Bush—the natural order has been two terms for Republicans, two for Democrats, two more for Republicans, and so on. There have been only two exceptions to this powerful trend—Carter (four years, because things were not going well) and Reagan and Bush (twelve, because they were). To win, we would have to extend twelve years to sixteen.

Then there were the media. I respect the press, acknowledge its important role, and get along well with journalists. It's an open secret, however, that the great majority of political reporters and editors vote—and think—Democratic. In 1992 they were clearly ready for a change.

This is not to minimize Bill Clinton's achievement. He came from a family of modest means, but parlayed a good mind into an undergraduate degree from Georgetown, a law degree from Yale, and a Rhodes scholarship at Oxford. Then he returned home to Arkansas and worked his way up to the governor's mansion. In 1992, he had the courage to run against George when more prominent Democrats demurred, and he ran a good race. Only in America.

Over the years, I've had the opportunity to spend a fair amount of time with him. He's brilliant, charming, engaging, and politically savvy. Even when you're in a crowded hall with him, Susan and I have noticed, he has that rare ability to make you feel as if you are the only other person in the room.

Still, George Bush was the right man for the job in 1992, just as he was in 1988. The world had changed dramatically between 1988 and 1992. It would continue to change from 1992 to 1996. America's post–Cold War foreign policy was necessarily a work in progress. We still needed a chief executive like George, who understood these issues so well, had a successful security and foreign policy team in place, and enjoyed good relations with world leaders, old and new. The Arkansas governor, by contrast, had no serious experience in international affairs. He finessed this point in the campaign by simply agreeing with George on most foreign policy issues, or differing only modestly.

He did speak up on one foreign policy issue with domestic overtones—the North American Free Trade Agreement then under negotiation with Canada and Mexico. To his everlasting credit, he supported free trade against the wishes of some important constituencies of his own party. Perot, on the other hand, bitterly charged that Mexico would siphon jobs from the United States with a "giant sucking sound." He was wrong, but he convinced many voters that their jobs were at risk. Clinton split the difference. He promised to support NAFTA, but only after it was amended to protect jobs and the environment. By putting a little paint on George's policy, he could claim it as his own. This was a good example, by the way, of how Perot and Clinton sometimes delivered one-two punches against their common adversary.

GEORGE'S REQUEST THAT I run his campaign against Bill Clinton and Ross Perot was not a huge surprise. What happened next was. As the Democratic Convention drew to a close, Perot dramatically dropped out of the race. (In October, of course, he would dramatically drop back in.) "Now that the Democratic Party has revitalized itself," he said, "I have concluded that we cannot win in November." His theory was that no candidate in the three-way race would get a majority of the electoral votes, leaving the race to be decided by rank-and-file Democrats and Republicans in the House who would never support him.

Out in Wyoming, we weren't buying that reason. Neither were many of Perot's people. Some disappointed supporters said their man didn't like the intense personal scrutiny attendant to a run for the presidency and had buckled under the pressure. "I thought he had more guts," said Dick Peters, vice chairman of the Arizona Perot campaign.

Whatever the reason, Perot's withdrawal set off a political tug-of-war. "Big Voter Block Is Cut Adrift; Bush and Clinton Rush to Court the Disaffected," read a front-page headline in the *Washington Post*. Clinton was in a better position to make his pitch. Only hours after Perot's announcement, he would have a nationwide audience for his acceptance speech. George, on the other hand, was virtually incommunicado at the ranch.

George was fishing when the news broke. I rushed down to the creek and said, "You need to call him right now. Tell him you share his principles and values, and hope he will support you." I handed George a satellite telephone and he placed the call from the middle of the Wyoming sagebrush.

George then phoned a statement to the White House press corps, stationed about seventy-five miles away in Jackson Hole. That did not work too well. The audio quality was too noisy for use on the air. Even if the sound quality had been good, however, there were no pictures, and if you've read this far, you know that television needs pictures.

With time running out, we bused the press two hours out to the ranch. Reporters shot video of George's statement in front of the foothills of the Wind River Range and quickly relayed it to satellite uplinks for the evening news. This worked. George's remarks were picked up on all three networks, with pictures. "I have a message for anyone who supported Ross Perot and anyone who identified with the frustration that brought them together," George said: "I heard you."

. . .

IF I WERE in the business of writing political fortune cookies, I would put this message in a lot of them: "The one constant in politics is change." The electorate wants to know that a candidate, even an incumbent, is an agent of change, someone who will make things better. This was a particularly salient point in 1992. George understood this: "You want action and you want change, and to anyone who wants to block change, I say, 'Get out of our way and let America move forward once again.'"

There was one obvious way for George to demonstrate that he was a change agent: by replacing his running mate. Dan Quayle was not a problem in 1988. Despite the distraction caused by his nomination, the ticket won forty states. By 1992, however, Dan had become a liability in George's uphill fight for reelection.

A second fortune cookie might read: "Politics is perception." Dan suffered—unfairly in many ways, but to a degree that could not be ignored—from a negative image among voters at large. He still had the strong support of many in the party, but Bob Teeter's polls showed that the verdict with too many voters was "no sale."

Teeter said George would fare much better with undecided voters if he replaced Quayle with Colin Powell, Dick Cheney, me, or any number of other prominent Republicans. (For the record, I would never have been a serious option. The Constitution says a state's presidential electors may not cast their votes for both a presidential and vice presidential candidate from the same state as themselves.)

There were some private meetings within the campaign's inner circle to consider whether an effort should be made to encourage the vice president to leave the ticket. One thing was clear, we decided: Dan could not be removed against his will. That would be bad politics, suggesting panic and disarray, and would be seen, wrongly in my opinion, as an admission that it had been a mistake to pick Dan in the first place. It would also give critics an opening to criticize George. "Don't you

318 ♣ JAMES A. BAKER, III

understand? Quayle is not the problem. You're the problem." What
was needed was to persuade the vice president to remove himself from
the ticket and exit gracefully, stage right.

Easier said than done. It was no secret that Quayle wanted to run
for president in 1996. He had worked hard and honorably to advance
the goals of the administration. No scandal had touched him. Why
should he allow himself to be pushed out?

I won't speak for George, but I think it's fair to say he would have
accepted Dan's decision if the vice president, on his own, had concluded that the best way for George to be seen as an agent of change
(and thereby give us a chance to win) was to take himself out. At one
point, it was even suggested that Barbara Bush give Dan a nudge. No
way, George replied. Looking back, he was right. She would have been
seen as a courier for the president. Ditto for George W. In the end,
George would neither send a signal to Dan nor authorize anyone else
to do so.

When rumors of the "Dump Quayle" movement surfaced, Dan did
not take the hint. "If I thought I was hurting the ticket, I'd be gone," he
said in one interview. "I want George Bush reelected." At the same
time, he insisted he was not a drag on the ticket. "I've been tested," he
said. In late July, George cut off speculation by telling reporters that
Dan's spot on the ticket was "certain." And that was that. Afterward,
Dan campaigned hard and did a great job against Al Gore in the vice
presidential debate. Still, the biggest favor he could have done for the
president—and the country, in my opinion—would have been to graciously take himself off the ticket.*

----

*Something Marilyn Quayle said when Dan threw his hat into the ring for the 2000 GOP
presidential nomination still disturbs me. She called George W. Bush "a party frat-boy
type," "a guy that never accomplished anything; everything he got Daddy took care of."
These remarks were offensive enough in their own right, but doubly so from the wife of a
man who was himself the object of equally inaccurate personal criticisms, and who was
plucked from relative political obscurity by the father of the man she was criticizing. I
know for a fact that these remarks did not endear her to the Bush family.

. . .

ON AUGUST 13, 1992, I gave one of the most difficult speeches of my life. "I have decided to resign as secretary of state, effective August 23, to work with the president to help develop a second-term agenda that builds on what has been achieved and that fully integrates our domestic, economic, and foreign policies," I told the foreign service officers, career civil servants, and political appointees gathered in the Dean Acheson Auditorium at Foggy Bottom. For one rare time in my public life, I struggled to maintain my composure. But looking out at all the dedicated men and women who had served and would continue to serve their country so capably and so loyally and reflecting on what we had done together, I became quite emotional.

I was less emotional when I addressed the American people in the same speech. Here, my first goal was to make the point that there were "contrasting philosophies" and "sharp differences" in the approaches of George Bush and Bill Clinton. My second goal was to enunciate the president's philosophy, as simply as possible. "We should build on the fundamentals of lower tax rates, limits on government spending, greater competition, less economic regulation, and more open trade that can unleash tremendous private initiative and growth," I said. "But I think that in the nineties government can add to this growth program by building opportunity and hope for individuals, families, and communities."

The analysis began almost instantly. The *Washington Post*'s David Broder had some nice things to say about me . . . and a few questions.

> Years ago, when he was President Reagan's chief of staff, Baker was described in this column as "the most capable unelected official Washington has seen in years." Nothing in his later service in the Treasury and State departments would cause me to revise that judgment. There is no one in either party I'd rather see working for the U.S. government than Jim Baker.

His return to the White House will improve morale in the administration and the Republican Party. His masterful speech at the State Department yesterday was the most coherent and persuasive case for Bush's presidency that anyone—including the president—has offered.

Still, there are reasons to wonder—from the country's point of view—about the costs and benefits of this shift. It takes Baker away from day-to-day diplomacy at a time when his personal efforts, particularly in the Middle East, seem on the verge of bearing fruit. That is clearly a loss.

One can also question whether Baker brings to the task an understanding of how much America has changed in the past four years and why the voters are so sour on Bush. Baker is as much an Establishment man as the president, a polished Princetonian, a wealthy lawyer whose skill lies in dealing with other power brokers, domestic and foreign.

Although he referred in his speech to the "anxiety and anger" in the American people, he has not heard the voices of the jobless engineers and construction workers or the complaints of taxpayers who see all too clearly the costs of paralysis in Washington. He can read the polls, but I wonder if he can feel the fear and frustration that Bush so far has failed to address.

I won't address the question of the costs and benefits to the nation of my move back to the White House, except to say that my successor as secretary of state, Larry Eagleburger, was a consummate professional who kept the department on course and moving ahead. As to whether I could understand the "anxiety and angst" of the unemployed and feel the "fear and frustration" of the voters, there's really no answer I can give that would satisfy critics. But I'll point out a few things Broder overlooked.

Yes, George and I were brought up in accomplished (and loving) families, we both had good educations, and we both succeeded in our careers. So what? Each generation of mothers and fathers wants its children to have better opportunities than the last generation, and George and I were the beneficiaries of the hard work, discipline, and frugality of our ancestors. Because of our advantages, we were also taught that we had special responsibilities to others. Furthermore, our faith instructed us that all men and women were created in the image of God and were equal before God and man, clothed in dignity and deserving of respect. It is also worth remembering that many of America's great leaders, starting with George Washington, were Establishment men.

THE BIGGEST MISTAKE our administration made in 1992 was not following up "Desert Storm," the successful war to eject Iraq from Kuwait, with "Domestic Storm," an economic revitalization program that we could have built a reelection campaign around. George could have capitalized on his strong approval ratings from the first Persian Gulf War to engage Congress in a political battle over fundamental economic policy.

Why didn't that happen? My understanding is that Dick Darman, head of the Office of Management and Budget, suggested the idea, but that other advisers assured the president that the economy was turning around, that no dramatic federal action was needed, and that voters would soon see that things were better. And things were, in fact, better, although this did not become fully apparent until after the election.

The recession began shortly before Iraq invaded Kuwait in August 1990 and ended shortly after the U.S.-led coalition ejected Iraq from Kuwait in February 1991. It was part of a worldwide downturn that was nastier than anything we experienced here.

When the recession ended in early 1991, growth resumed. Unfortunately, voters accustomed to the glory years of the 1980s were disappointed by the more routine growth of 1991–1992. Worse, the Rust Belt and some other hard-hit regions stayed down while the rest of the country moved ahead. All of this created an opening for Clinton and Perot—one warm, the other brusque, both claiming they could fix a broken economy. Just by talking about the issue, they scored points with voters, even though their answers (big tax increases and in Perot's case, magic-wand budget cuts) were wrong and simplistic.

The federal debt was a legitimate issue, however. President Reagan had sharply increased federal revenues, but Congress spent the money faster than it came in. While Clinton and Perot talked about deficit control, George had actually tried to do something about it. In 1990, he agreed to higher taxes as part of a complex budget deal. This would have been controversial enough, but it was double trouble for George because it broke his 1988 pledge—"Read my lips: no new taxes."

I was at State at the time, but I remember thinking George's agreement to higher taxes, even conditioned on spending cuts, might present a political problem. And it did, with our Republican base, which accounted for some of George's weakness in the early primaries. By the summer of 1992, however, the question was not what we coulda or shoulda done about Domestic Storm or the deficit issue, but what we would do now.

WHEN PRESIDENT BUSH announced that I would return to the White House as chief of staff and senior counselor, he said that I would be in charge of integrating foreign, economic, and domestic policy and formulating the plans for how such policies would be implemented in a second Bush term. Rumors circulated that instead of going back to State if the president were reelected, I would be given a "super-cabinet" post. This led to silly-season editorials and columns in several newspapers, including one in Peoria: "If Baker is as good as the president thinks, maybe he should be chief of the country, not just chief of staff."

These comments did not sit well with me or anyone else in the Bush camp. One aide referred to speculation about my role as "the copresidency problem." The notion was preposterous, but puffing up my role was an indirect way for critics to imply that voters should be concerned about George. Perceptions were what counted, and the best way to manage them, he and I decided, was for me not to keep too high a profile—a decision for which I was later criticized by some.

The mid-August GOP convention was in Houston. To stay out of the spotlight and gather myself for the campaign, I hung out the "Gone Fishin'" sign and repaired to Wyoming for a couple of days. I came back for the final two days of the convention and helped a little with George's acceptance speech, but limited my public appearances to a prayer breakfast and the closing session.

When I officially took over as chief of staff on August 23, I was accompanied from State to the White House by what some referred to as my "plug-in unit." Margaret Tutwiler became communications director. Bob Zoellick assumed the role of deputy chief of staff. Dennis Ross became a top foreign policy adviser to the president. And Janet Mullins became assistant to the president for political affairs. All reported to me.

It has been written that these folks were unenthusiastic about making the move. Maybe, but such feelings did not affect their commitment to the president or their performance in their new roles. We hit the ground running and had little time to catch our breath until the election.

Back in the West Wing, I occupied the same office that I had as President Reagan's chief of staff. Each day at 7:30 A.M., I met with Margaret, Bob, Dennis, and Janet. Darman, press secretary Marlin Fitzwater, and national security adviser Brent Scowcroft regularly joined us, as did campaign officials Bob Teeter and Fred Malek. Oftentimes, Mary Matalin, Charlie Black, and others with the campaign would join us.

A top priority was creating a message of the day or issue of the day, and making sure that both the White House and the campaign got that message across. One goal was to set up "quick-turnaround" systems so the president could move from place to place and issue to issue effectively and swiftly. We also spent time on major policy initiatives and speeches for the days ahead.

Whether in the daily message or a major address, we encouraged George to make several points. First, he needed to show that he truly cared for people and felt their pain. (He did, of course, but he was not a hugger, physically or rhetorically, and Clinton was.) Second, for the reasons I have already discussed, he needed to be seen as an agent of change. Clinton and Perot said they would shake things up. For George, it was a bit trickier. Granted, the economic reforms he was proposing were not as radical as those of his opponents, but that was good. Our proposed remedies were tried and true. As mentioned, we also tried to make Clinton's character an issue. Looking back, we were unsuccessful.

One successful thing I did was call George's and my old friend Robert Mosbacher of Houston, to help with fund-raising. Bob had served as national finance chairman for the 1976 Ford campaign, then for George in 1988. In between, he served for a period as chairman of the Republican National Committee. As George's secretary of commerce, he saw that the 1990–1991 recession had left the nation in a sour mood and that many voters thought George was out of touch with that mood. Bob lobbied hard, but fruitlessly, for the administration to follow up Desert Storm with a domestic economic program that would demonstrate the president's concern about, and intention to address, the problem. He was right but unsuccessful. By the time I took over the campaign, Bob was back in private life. He initially resisted my plea to help with fund-raising. "Listen, buddy," I said, "if I can resign from State for George, you can come out of retirement for one more campaign." He did, of course, and with great results.

We believed the presidential debates would offer our best opportunity to overtake Clinton. (Underdogs always need the debates more than front-runners, and we were the underdogs this time.) But we knew the Arkansas governor would be a formidable adversary. He was almost congenitally articulate (although he sometimes tended to ramble—and ramble and ramble) and he was also trained to think on his feet. George (as he acknowledges) is a better do-er than debater. Still, he worked hard in our mock debates, and we had reason to hope he might hit a home run.

It didn't help that Ross Perot had reentered the fray in early October and would get equal time with the two major-party candidates. As a talker, he was no Bill Clinton, and he lacked George's substance, but he could be counted on for comic relief. In 1980, candidate Reagan had been very happy to team up with independent John Anderson to hammer the incumbent president Jimmy Carter. This time George would face that same two-on-one dynamic.

Under these conditions, George performed admirably in the first debate at Washington University in St. Louis on October 11. He stressed his experience in foreign affairs and outlined his program for economic renewal. By most accounts, the debate was a draw. We didn't hit a home run, but there would be two more chances.

Unfortunately, one line that George delivered in St. Louis that night thrust me back into the spotlight. "What I'm going to do," he declared, "is say to Jim Baker when this campaign is over: 'All right, let's sit down now. You do in domestic affairs what you've done in foreign affairs, be kind of the economic coordinator of all the domestic side of the House, and that includes all the economic side, all the training side, and bring this program together.'"

This was a total surprise to me. He never hinted to me that he intended to do this. When asked in the post-debate spin session about the president's plans for me, I said he had not "defined what it was specifically" that my responsibilities would be. Over the next couple of days, the press and the opposition paid more attention to me and less to the president than either one of us liked. Clinton spokesman George Stephanopoulos, grinning, asked publicly whether *I* planned to announce a role for *Bush* in a second term.

In mid-October, we tentatively planned for me to give a speech in Detroit on our economic program and, secondarily, to fill in the blanks about what the president had in mind for me in a second Bush administration. But the more he and I thought about it, the more we were convinced that I should not give the speech. The attention needed to be on the president, and on September 10, he used Detroit as a forum to outline the "Agenda for American Renewal," his detailed economic plan.

In the third debate, October 19 at Michigan State University in East Lansing, Bill Clinton won laughter and applause when he made an issue of my role.

> In the first debate, Mr. Bush made some news. He'd [previously] said Jim Baker was going to be secretary of state, and in the first debate he said, no, now he's gonna be responsible for domestic economic policy. Well . . . I'll make some news in the third debate. The person responsible for domestic economic policy in my administration will be Bill Clinton. I'm gonna make those decisions . . .

"Well, that's what worries me," George replied, earning a well-deserved round of laughter of his own.

I SAID EARLIER that George had been worked over pretty good in the campaign. Al Gore was the attack dog on one issue, the so-called "Iraq-gate" scandal. Hardly anyone remembers it now, but it was a big deal that October, a twofer designed to knock George down a peg or two on foreign policy and to sully his reputation. It was based on two things. First, federal agents discovered in 1989 that the Atlanta branch of an Italian bank had partially financed Saddam Hussein's arms buildup. Second, early in our administration we tried to improve our relations with Iraq (a country we had helped in its long war with Iran) with trade credits, primarily agricultural. Unfortunately, the policy had failed, as policies sometimes do. "The objective was to try to include Iraq in the family of nations," I said when my name was linked to pushing agricultural loan guarantees for Iraq through the bureaucracy. "That's what we did. You can argue in hindsight, but that was the policy."

Critics conflated the two events—the genuine bank scandal and the unsuccessful policy of trying to engage Iraq—to create an imaginary political scandal. Al Gore's job was to keep it in the news that October, and he handled his assignment with what appeared to be genuine enthusiasm.

Iraqgate "involves the biggest bank fraud, it involves $2 billion of the American taxpayers' money that we're stuck with," Al said. "It involves the decision by George Bush to arm Saddam Hussein and to lead him to miscalculate and launch a war that never should have taken place and would not have except for the poor judgment and bad foreign policy of George Bush, and he ought to be held accountable for it."

This was not the first time the Baker and Gore names had been linked (and it would not be the last). In 1985, Susan Baker and Tipper Gore helped found the Parents Music Resource Center to fight for the labeling of violent and obscene music. They have been friends ever since. If you were to visit the room in our home that serves as Susan's office today, you would see a silver-framed picture of Al Gore, Susan, and me watching Mary Bonner and Kristen Gore in a lacrosse game at National Cathedral School. It is inscribed: "I will always cherish our friendship. With love, Tipper."

I got to know Al about the same time our wives became friends. When I was secretary of the treasury, I joined a Christian prayer group on Capitol Hill. Al, who was then in his first term as a senator, was also a member. Among the others were senators Mark Hatfield, Sam Nunn, Lawton Chiles, Paul Tribble, and Pete Domenici. Our group was totally bipartisan. It included Democrats and Republicans, liberals and conservatives.

We would meet once a week, usually in Pete's office, for forty-five minutes or so. First we would read a short Scripture. Business and politics were off limits, but we would then talk about whatever else was on our minds or troubling us. At the end, we would have a short prayer and go about our business. These meetings comforted us, created a circle of friendship, and reminded us of something that everyone— high-ranking public officials included—needs to remember: we are all subject to a higher power. One important rule was that nothing said in the room was ever to leave the room, and it did not.

This was part of a worldwide small-group movement coordinated by a remarkable man named Doug Coe. His organization also sponsors the nondenominational Prayer Breakfast in Washington each February. The small-group meetings were designed to help create a "family of friends" organized around the teachings of Jesus. I continued to attend as secretary of state, both in Washington and abroad, and even helped establish groups in Germany and Japan.

I've been around long enough to know that politics ain't bean-bag, but I was extremely disappointed that Al would accuse President Bush (and me, indirectly) of what appeared to be criminal behavior. "George Bush is presiding over a coverup significantly larger than Watergate," he said again and again.

That always stuck in my craw. There are certain rules in politics, and one of them is that you never accuse anyone, much less the president of the United States, of breaking the law unless you can back it up with something more than innuendo.

After the campaign ended, Iraqgate more or less evaporated. Writing in *Atlantic Monthly,* the highly respected *National Journal* columnist Stuart Taylor, Jr., delivered this postmortem:

> One staple of Washington life is the phony scandal: a conflagration of bogus accusations and intimations of criminality and sleaze, fanned to an inferno by the media and partisan enemies of the accused, only to finally fade away for lack of evidence.
>
> It's a bipartisan phenomenon. The classic of the genre was "Iraqgate," aka the Banca Nazionale del Lavoro (BNL) scandal. Not to be confused with Iran-Contra (a real scandal), Iraqgate was whipped up in 1992 by Democratic congressional investigators, sloppy journalists,

and a partisan federal judge. It erupted into thousands of newspaper articles and a gaggle of network television specials, turning President Bush's greatest triumph—his victory over Saddam Hussein in the 1991 Persian Gulf War—into a political liability. . . .

These charges were false. All of them.

One other controversy boiled up in 1992. Over the summer there were rumors that Bill Clinton had renounced his citizenship to avoid the draft while he studied in England. Newspapers filed freedom-of-information requests to see his passport files. Our campaign group heard about the requests and talked about them in mid-September, but did nothing. On September 30, the State Department, acting on the freedom-of-information requests, checked its files and found no such renunciation. Unfortunately, staffers there tried to call some individuals then working at the White House.

The State Department's inspector general, Sherman Funk, investigated and recommended that an independent counsel be appointed. That was ridiculous, but Attorney General William Barr—who had done the right thing in refusing to ask for an independent counsel on Iraqgate—seemed to cave in to demands from the media (principally the *Washington Post*) and didn't have the guts to say no this time. As a result, an independent counsel was named on December 14, one day before expiration of the law authorizing such appointments. Three years and millions of dollars later, the independent counsel, Joseph diGenova, issued a final report that found no criminal wrongdoing. His staff's report on Sherman Funk's investigation was "one of the most chilling accounts of government incompetence I have ever read in my life," diGenova said. His conclusion: no independent counsel should ever have been appointed, and the government owed an apology to the White House aides who were the subjects of the investigation. In fact, he apologized by name to the White House and State Department staffers targeted by the investigation, and some of them later won financial settlements from the government.

. . .

PRESIDENT BUSH'S appearance in Grand Rapids on Thursday, October 29, was perhaps the high point of the campaign. Despite everything, he had closed the gap to a point or two and was in position to pull a major upset. He was smiling as he campaigned, and by some accounts, Bill Clinton was not.

Then came October 30. After six years of investigations, Lawrence Walsh, the independent counsel in the Iran-Contra investigation, picked the Friday before Tuesday's presidential election to indict Caspar Weinberger, President Reagan's secretary of defense, for allegedly lying to Congress. It was a legal missile with a political warhead, fired straight into the heart of the presidential election and clearly timed to try to destroy President Bush.

What was wrong with the indictment? Let me count the ways. First, it was a rehash of an earlier charge that had already been thrown out of court. Second, this flimsy new indictment was, itself, thrown out exactly six weeks to the day after it was filed. Why? Because the statute of limitations had run on the alleged crime, a point that a serious prosecutor might well have considered beforehand. Third, the indictment did not charge Cap with *participating* in Iran-Contra. Every scrap of evidence in the investigation showed that Caspar Weinberger *vigorously opposed* that misguided adventure from beginning to end. Walsh knew this. Instead, he indicted one of the most honorable men who ever served in our government for allegedly lying to Congress, a charge that the respected cochairmen of the Iran-Contra committee, one a Democrat, one a Republican, said was inconceivable. Fourth, the Weinberger indictment was handled by James Brosnahan, a major contributor to Democratic campaigns, including the Clinton campaign.

Fifth, and most egregiously, the indictment quoted from Cap's diary to suggest that George Bush himself had favored the proposed arms-for-hostages deal with Iran at a January 1986 White House meeting.

This bit of text, a few words fished out of thousands of pages of evidence, was pasted into the document for one reason and one reason only, which was to smear the president. It had *nothing whatever* to do with the indictment of Weinberger. (Walsh later conceded—with his typical lack of grace—that he had no evidence that George had ever violated any criminal statute.) The purpose was to cast doubt, not on George's sworn testimony about Iran-Contra, but on his *public* statements. In other words, the purpose was obviously political and, it seemed to me, a clear abuse of prosecutorial discretion and simple decency.*

The indictment was a godsend for the Democrats. An extraordinarily detailed three-page rapid response from the "war room" of Clinton's Little Rock headquarters—released almost immediately, but dated one day before the indictment was even filed (an "error," his office later said)—called it "the smoking gun showing that George Bush lied to the American people about his role in the arms-for-hostages affair." Suddenly the issue that had helped move the polls our way, concerns about the opponent's character, lost traction. The press spent the entire weekend asking George what he knew and when he knew it. And that was that. Ann Compton turned out to be right. One day after George's strong performance in Michigan, we were "not so happy."

George fought back, but vainly. "Being attacked on character by Governor Clinton is like being called ugly by a frog," he said at one point.† Nothing in the indictment contradicted his deposition testimony "under oath, under oath," he protested again and again, a point that would be confirmed in Walsh's final report. But it was too late. We never caught up with the story.

---

*A federal appeals court would later chastise the prosecutor for smearing others. His final report "repeatedly accuses named individuals of crimes, although in many instances the individual was never indicted, if indicted was never convicted, or if convicted the conviction was reversed," the judges said.

†George later received a complaint about this statement from the Worldwide Fair Play for Frogs Committee. He apologized . . . to the frogs.

. . .

WOULD WE HAVE won if Lawrence Walsh had not tossed his stink bomb into the American political process? Who knows? Even as the polls tightened the week before the election, we were always behind. All I know is that on Thursday before the election we had a chance and on Friday we didn't.

There were three big reasons that we lost, however, and I have already mentioned two. One was that Republicans had held the White House for twelve years, and both voters and the press were tired and ready for change. The other was the administration's failure to follow Desert Storm with Domestic Storm, an economic revitalization program.

The third was Henry Ross Perot. On his best day, he had no chance to win the presidency, but he succeeded spectacularly as a spoiler. His 18.9 percent of the popular vote was the best showing by a third-party candidate since Teddy Roosevelt's 1912 Bull Moose candidacy split the Republican majority and allowed a politically weaker Democrat to win the White House. Back then, it was Woodrow Wilson. This time, it was Bill Clinton.

The Democrats won 43 percent of the popular vote and Bush-Quayle took 37.4 percent. The electoral vote was 370–168 for the Democrats. I believe about two-thirds of Perot's supporters were natural Republican voters who would have supported George in a head-to-head race. If I'm right and if Perot had never entered the race, George might have won more than 50 percent of the popular vote and— applying the same two-thirds/one-third split on a state-by-state basis— he might have won the Electoral College, too.

"WHEN YOU WIN, your errors are obscured; when you lose, your errors are magnified," George said in a radio address five days after the election. "But as for what has passed, I can only say that it was my administration, my campaign, I captained the team, and I take full responsibility for the loss. No one else is responsible. I am responsible."

That was George Bush at his best—a general, wounded himself, thinking only of his troops. That's what character looks and sounds like.

In truth, of course, all in the campaign shared responsibility for the loss, and in view of my position in the campaign, my share was greatest. There are no mulligans in campaigns, but I've sometimes wished for a "do-over" on some of our decisions. Still, we did our best as we understood it at the time. We just lost, and losing is not easy.

In the aftermath, emotions were raw. Some critical words indirectly came my way, primarily over whether I should have done more talk shows and interviews. By one account I was "the invisible man." Maybe I should have been more public and out front. All I can say is that at the time, as I've written above, the president and I discussed the issue more than once and we both believed that it would be better for me to say less and him to say more.

Fortunately, time helps heal the pain of losing. George and I and our families are bound by a lifetime of deep friendship. These days, he, Barbara, Susan, and I enjoy time together on the golf course, hunting quail, or just remembering old times. As I write, Susan and I have just returned from visiting them in Kennebunkport.

ON JANUARY 20, 1993, William Jefferson Clinton was inaugurated as our nation's forty-second president. That morning, Susan and I joined George, Barbara, the Quayles, and a few others for one last time in the Blue Room. I had already cleaned out my White House office. Bill and Hillary Clinton and the Gores soon dropped in for the traditional pre-inaugural coffee. Hillary assured me that the new administration was determined to work with Republicans. We then rode in a motorcade to the Capitol for the peaceful transition of power that is the hallmark of our great democracy. After the ceremony, Susan and I joined George, Barbara, and other Bush friends and staffers on Air

Force One for the flight back to Texas and a welcome-home rally at the airport.

We were all sad and weary. The initial pain of seeing my friend lose the presidency—like being hit in the stomach with a baseball bat—had now dulled a bit. Between election day and inauguration day, we had all adjusted to the new reality. What might have been was not to be.

For me, the excitement and responsibility of public service began to slip away shortly after the election. I still attended to my duties, but fatigue settled deep into my bones. I'm sure George went through the same experience on some levels. Truth be told, I also felt an enormous sense of relief. After running for attorney general of Texas, leading five presidential campaigns, serving four years-plus as White House chief of staff, and serving almost four years each as secretary of the treasury and secretary of state, I was simply worn out.

Soon after the election, Vernon Jordan came by my home to discuss the transition. Twelve years later, he and I would negotiate the terms of the 2004 presidential debates between President George W. Bush and Senator John Kerry. Warren Christopher headed the Clinton transition team, and I worked with him to achieve a smooth handoff. In a twist of history, Chris would soon be appointed secretary of state, then of course we would meet again in Florida in November 2000.

Unlike many of my colleagues in the Reagan administration, I never got Potomac fever. My view is, when it's over, it's over, and the best place to go is back home. D.C. is a wonderful place to live when you're in power, but it's a one-industry town and, for me at least, not a particularly good place to live when you're out of power. Susan and I remained in Washington until Mary Bonner graduated from National Cathedral School, but there was never any doubt that we would come home for good after she got her diploma.

Still, what a grand experience it all was! The only thing I miss is not having had another four years as secretary of state. I think we could have accomplished a lot that did not get accomplished. For one thing, my good friend Yitzhak Rabin was elected prime minister of Israel in June 1992. I would like to have worked with him to promote peace between Arabs and Israelis.

Sadness and weariness were natural as our time in office came to an end, but George was not one to mope, and neither was I. We were going home to Texas, to families and friends, to new opportunities and responsibilities. George would soon turn to the important work of setting up his presidential library, writing about some aspects of his public life, and pursuing a long-deferred dream—skydiving.

As for me, I had a few plans of my own.

FIFTEEN

"I DON'T MISS WASHINGTON"

BY THE CALENDAR, presidential transitions occur in the fall and winter. For the triumphant administrations-in-waiting, however, it always feels like springtime. The air is sweet with enthusiasm and ideas. Profiles of top executive branch nominees bloom like flowers on fertile newsprint. Rivers of wisdom flow from the high peaks of the big talk shows.

Almost unnoticed in all the excitement, at least when the White House changes hands from one party to the other, is the operation of an iron law of politics: for each high-spirited newcomer, one weary officeholder from the outgoing administration is packing files and memories in cardboard boxes, saying goodbye to colleagues and power, and looking for a new job. In late 1992, one of those weary officeholders was me.

I would soon be sixty-three, and my first project would be to repair the family finances. I had spent my prime years, so far at least, on a government payroll. Susan and I were certainly well-off when we came to Washington in 1981, but not, contrary to popular belief, extremely wealthy. Over twelve years, we had seriously tapped our family savings to pay living expenses and educate children. To top it off, Mary Bonner was still at home working on her SATs and college applications.

Finances were not the only consideration. I also had an obligation to history, I thought, to write a diplomatic memoir. In addition, Rice University had a proposal that deserved serious consideration. At a personal level, my wonderful family needed attention. Our children had grown up and moved away while, too often, I was not at home. Now I had grandchildren to spoil, with more to come. In my closets were golf clubs, hunting paraphernalia, and fishing equipment to dust off and put to their natural and intended uses. And lurking in the back reaches of my mind was the idea that maybe, just maybe, I had one more presidential campaign in me, this one for myself.

But first I needed to find work. Offers came almost immediately. They always do for high public officials who leave office. Multinational banks, major law firms, and Fortune 500 companies today operate in global markets, subject to the laws, regulations, and taxes of many nations, and vulnerable to disruptions—some swift, others slow-moving—in their economic and geopolitical environments. Cabinet officers and other top officials generally have useful experience in steering through these heavy currents.

Some prospective employers wanted me to stay in Washington and lobby our government. This was definitely out. The decision to return to Houston was unshakable, and I long ago had decided I would never lobby on policy, personnel, or anything else. A former high-ranking Republican senator had showed up in my office at Treasury one day with a client in tow who wanted permission for his company to do business with Libya at a time when that was a definite no-no. It was not a happy experience. I respect the decisions of others to take offices on K Street, but it was not for me.

When the right opportunity finally knocked, fortunately, I found Bill Barnett of Houston on the other side of the door. We had met at the University of Texas School of Law in the mid-fifties. Thanks to

the alphabetic seating chart, he and I were near neighbors in the class-
room. Together, we sweated out the dreaded calls to recite cases.* Bill
and I became friends and later worked together on the law review.

Now, more than thirty-five years later, Bill was one of the first visitors to my White House office after the November election. Thanks to
his talent, hard work, and integrity, he was one of the most highly respected attorneys in Houston. More to the point, he was also managing
partner of the law firm, today known as Baker Botts, that my great-
grandfather James Addison Baker had helped build more than a century earlier. That's where the "Baker" in the firm name came from. Both
my grandfather (Captain James Addison Baker) and father (James Addison Baker, Jr.) had worked there, and my son, Jamie (James Addison
Baker, IV), was now a partner. After law school, I would have joined the
firm myself, but fortunately, as I've written, the firm's nepotism policy
blocked my path back then.

Bill proposed that I enter the firm all these years later as senior
partner. Even though Jamie was there, nepotism was no longer a problem. Either Baker Botts had decided that the policy ran downhill, not
uphill or—more likely, perhaps—determined that it did not apply to
former secretaries of state. I had other offers, of course. Al Ebert and
John Cabaniss, two old friends, invited me to return to Andrews Kurth,
the respected Houston firm I joined immediately after law school. In
1976, I had refused an earlier job offer m Baker Botts because Andrews Kurth had been so good to me and because a lot of my contemporaries still practiced there. By 1992, however, most of them had
moved on. Other major firms from New York, Washington, and Houston also came to see me. But Bill offered something none of the others
could ever match—an opportunity to have my ticket punched at the
one law firm that carried my family's DNA.

---

*"And now, Mr. Baker, Mr. James ... Addison ... Baker ... the ... Third, please recite the
facts of *Ghen v. Rich*, the issue presented, and the holding." I had been in the Marine Corps,
but when my property law professor, Corwin Johnson, a former FBI agent, called my
name, I felt more like a mouse tied to a cat by a very short string.

For decades, Baker Botts had been a strong regional law firm, primarily serving local banks, railroads, and energy companies. In recent years it had gone national, with offices in New York, Washington, and elsewhere. The firm was now building a strong international presence. In part, this was to serve the energy companies in Houston as they fanned around the globe to search for oil and gas, but Baker Botts was also finding new clients overseas. The liberalization and integration of the world economy created a demand for American lawyers, and the firm had positioned itself to compete for the work.

I told Bill I would not lobby, draft legal documents, handle routine business negotiations, or serve on the management committee. "I have managed everything I ever want to manage," I said.

No problem, Bill replied. My role would be that of a graybeard, a special resource, an adviser to the firm and its clients on big or unique problems. As I write, for instance, I am overseeing an investigation— called for by a federal agency—into safety issues at a large energy company in the refining business. I have also corresponded occasionally with foreign governments to sort out controversies involving Baker Botts clients in those countries. Sometimes my letters help; sometimes they don't. (My no-lobbying rule does not apply to foreign governments.) I do advise the firm's lawyers and clients on strategies for dealing with Washington but I never lobby our federal government on their behalf. In some ways, I have served much the same function at the firm that my great-grandfather, the first James Addison Baker, did late in his career. Even after he withdrew from active practice, it was later written, "his judgment was relied on." One more point: when Baker Botts recruited me, it did not go unnoticed, obviously, that my presence at the firm might help attract new clients.

There is also a tradition among big law firms of supplying candidates as directors for important clients, and I agreed to serve on the boards of two public companies. Why so few? Because being a director of a public corporation today is time-consuming work and carries weighty responsibilities. Too many former public figures overload themselves with board appointments, and I did not want to make that mistake. I no longer serve on the two boards I accepted, but to this day I am still fending off a lawsuit in which I am a defendant just by virtue of once having been a board member. This is something that, unfortunately, goes with the territory in today's litigious society.

Baker Botts gave me two offices, one in Washington and one in Houston, each staffed with two assistants. Until Mary Bonner graduated from National Cathedral School in 1994, Susan and I kept a home in Washington, and I worked primarily at the D.C. office, where I was assisted by Bridget Montagne, who had worked for George H. W. Bush when he was president, and Caron Jackson. In recent years, however, I have spent most of my time in Houston.

My able executive assistant in the Houston office today is Charlotte Cheadle. The two sides of her personality are symbolized by her size (small) and her dog (a rottweiler). Ninety-nine-point-nine percent of my callers, correspondents, and office visitors—the polite and reasonable ones—deal with Ms. Petite, a modern Texas woman. When I hear that unmistakable low growl from the direction of her desk, however, I know she is talking to the other one tenth of one percent. I'm happy to report, though, that she hasn't bitten anyone yet.

Now let me do a little growling myself. The practice of law today is very different from when I started. Computers, instant communications, and overnight deliveries changed everything, generally for the better. I remember going to the office with my dad in the forties and fifties, and watching his secretaries—first Mollie Jones, then Virginia Cooper—bang out long real estate contracts on a manual typewriter, with carbon paper for the copies. In my early years of practice, we had electric typewriters, but everything else was about the same.

Not all the changes since then are so welcome, however. The practice of law today has to a large extent ceased to be a true profession and become a business. It has to be that way, I suppose, when firms are so big and far-flung that the partners in New York, say, may not even know those in Hong Kong.

But firm size is not the only factor in the decline of professionalism. I blame greed, advertising, and the almost-total breakdown of respect, even in the courts, for lawyer-client confidentiality. Attorneys have special responsibilities to their profession that should always transcend the contract, case, or controversy at hand—responsibilities such as truthfulness, loyalty to clients, respect for law, and a common code of ethics. One of the great pleasures of my time at Baker Botts has been to work with lawyers, young and old, who still think the way I do.

One more rule I laid down before joining Baker Botts was that I would never keep or report hours, even though for most attorneys that is probably a necessary evil of practicing law. When I showed up for work on my first day, however, Jamie escorted me to my office, and there on my pristine desk was one equally pristine copy of the red, hardbound timekeeping diary the firm issues to new lawyers.

I opened it to March 12 and made two entries: "9:00 A.M., arrived for first day at Baker Botts, found time book on desk; 9:12 A.M., resigned from Baker Botts." Then I sent it to Jamie.

The book was a joke, of course, and so was my resignation. My years at Baker Botts have been satisfying beyond measure, personally and professionally. I hope and believe I have repaid the favor of being invited into the firm.

ANOTHER FINANCIAL opportunity was the Carlyle Group, now one of the world's largest private equity firms. Back in 1992, however, the five-year-old D.C.-based outfit was much smaller. In fact, when David Rubenstein, Bill Conway, and Steve Norris came to see me after the election, their goal was to create a fund of $100 million. They thought I might be able to help. Today the firm manages more than $30 billion and operates out of offices on three continents.

I had never met the Carlyle executives before, but two friends of mine who had worked with David Rubenstein in the Carter White

House said they were good guys. One endorsement came from Bernie Aronson, a former speechwriter for President Carter, later assistant secretary of state for inter-American affairs while I was secretary of state. Another was from Bob Strauss, a longtime eminence in the Democratic Party, but also a good friend of mine and the president's, who had served in the Bush administration as ambassador in Moscow.

Carlyle raises money from what it calls "high net worth individuals" (in plainer English, very wealthy people) and from private institutional investors, including large pension funds. The firm then invests that money in going concerns, start-up ventures, real estate, and the like. In most cases, it acquires a majority interest in the target companies. Carlyle is private, so it does not publish its results, which vary from investment to investment. Overall, however, the firm has been extraordinarily successful in generating good returns for its investors.

I agreed to become senior counselor to Carlyle, a post I held until my retirement in April 2005 at age seventy-five. As with Baker Botts, I set boundaries, particularly about lobbying, and I refused to solicit funds directly from potential investors. Typically I would be asked to speak to groups invited by Carlyle—usually at an overseas conference, sometimes in the United States—about economic, political, or geopolitical issues. Later, Carlyle representatives would pitch the invitees on investment opportunities at the firm. I also advised Carlyle on international business and political issues and, in some cases, introduced the firm to key figures in the countries where it wished to do business.

Carlyle promised it would never do anything to embarrass me, and it never did, except once. When I was serving as President George W. Bush's special envoy on debt relief for Iraq, a Carlyle representative—unbeknownst to me—was apparently talking to the Kuwaitis about engaging a consortium of Carlyle and other firms to help collect and manage the reparations owed to Kuwait by Iraq. That was improper. When I first heard about it, I called David Rubenstein, and the proposal was dropped almost before the sun went down.

The best evidence of my continuing respect for Carlyle is that, even though I am probably still dollars short of most of the other high-net-worth individuals who invest with the firm, I still commit investment dollars there when I can.

About the same time, I also signed up with the Washington Speakers Bureau to handle my public appearances. Like me, most folks on the circuit are "formers"—former public officials, former business executives, formers from the worlds of sports and entertainment. But personalities from the news media often hit the road while they still have day jobs on television or in print. I figured speaking was something that should be done soon, because name recognition usually decays rapidly for public figures who are not regularly in the news. Susan said I needn't worry about that, however, because my experience enabled me to speak on numerous topics—politics, foreign policy, economic policy, and public service.

In a way, we were each partly right. More than thirteen years after I left full-time public service, I still get quite a few speaking invitations, though fewer than in years past. The honoraria are still generous, and welcome, and speaking to interested people about interesting topics is not a hard way to earn a living. Still, I am not sure I would go as far as Jack Kemp, the 1996 GOP vice presidential candidate, who once nicknamed it "white collar crime."

Another opportunity came eight years after I left Washington. Despite my general reluctance to serve on corporate boards, I made an exception in 2001 for the privately held King Ranch, a Texas legend.

At first I declined. "I don't do boards," I said when Julia Jitkoff first approached me. Julia is a longtime friend, a talented painter and sculptor, a descendant of the ranch's founder, Captain Richard King, and—as I soon learned—a gifted recruiter.

"Would it make any difference if I told you that directors have the same rights to hunt on the ranch that family members do?" she replied.

Asking a hunter if he would enjoy access to the King Ranch is like asking an art lover if he wants a key to the Metropolitan Museum. At almost 900,000 acres, the ranch is larger than Rhode Island. The experience of hunting there is as close as possible to what Spanish and Anglo pioneers might have enjoyed centuries ago, and Native Americans before that.

"Where do I sign up?" I asked.

I also agreed over the years to serve on a number of nonprofit boards. Both Princeton University, my alma mater, and Rice University invited me to serve as trustee. (I would be the second James A. Baker on the Rice board, after my grandfather, Captain Baker.) I have also served on boards or held honorary positions at Howard Hughes Medical Institute in Chevy Chase, Maryland, and St. Luke's Hospital and the M.D. Anderson Cancer Center in Houston.

Early on, I also signed up—briefly—with Enron, but not as a board member. It was the hottest energy company in town, perhaps in the country, when I returned to Houston, and Ken Lay recruited Bob Mosbacher and me as consultants. Susan thought it was a really bad idea, but after thirteen and one-half full years and three part-time years in politics and public service, we needed to make some money, so I accepted anyway. I helped write a few reports and occasionally met with company officers about international projects they were trying to win.

It was an underwhelming experience. I remember telling both Susan and Mosbacher after about six months, "I just don't understand how this company works." What threw me was seeing the present value of a long-term power contract posted as current earnings when the contract was signed and before either party had even begun to perform. "It doesn't seem to me there's any way to grow the company except to keep putting these kinds of deals on the books," I said. Another problem was that corporate executives won big bonuses by signing these contracts, regardless of whether the transactions were good or bad for the company. My misgivings never crystalized into a clear understanding of the troubles that lay ahead, much less their magnitude. Still, I was not unhappy when my relationship with Enron ended by mutual agreement after two years, in February 1995.

. . .

IN MY SPARE TIME, I wrote a book.

President Bush's and my primary responsibility in office was to see that the Cold War ended without bloodshed and left behind a world that was peaceful, prosperous, stable, and congenial to U.S. interests. We succeeded. My obligation out of office, I believed, was to create a detailed and accurate record of what happened, for the benefit of historians, public officials, journalists, and other interested readers.

I started my research on *The Politics of Diplomacy* shortly after I left government, and the book was published in the early fall of 1995. It was hard work. I've done my share of writing over the years—in school, in law, in politics and public service, in columns and speeches, and for a while after leaving office as a columnist for the *Los Angeles Times* Syndicate—but long-form composition was more demanding than anything I had ever done before. It gave me a new respect for those who scribble, scribble, scribble for a living.

I wanted to put down in black and white exactly what happened during my tenure as secretary of state, as gleaned from contemporaneous records. Writing everything, immediately and in detail, would head off later revisionism, I thought. My first priority was to create a historical record; my second, to sell books—an approach that undoubtedly caused heartburn for my publisher. I had a lot of help with the project, of course, from many individuals, all of whom are credited in the book.

The Politics of Diplomacy was reasonably well received by academics and the foreign policy establishment, but was not—I am sorry to say—wildly popular with general readers. In my desire to create a complete record of those tumultuous years, the book grew and grew, to 672 pages. That may be why one hardback printing satisfied the demand for the book, which can be found today in most full-service libraries. Previously owned copies, to borrow a euphemism from the used-car business, are also available in specialty bookstores and on the Internet.

I'm sorry *The Politics of Diplomacy* was not a best seller, but I'm very proud of it, nonetheless. It testifies to the vindication of American leadership under both Democrats and Republicans, beginning after World War II with Dean Acheson's generation and climaxing four decades later with mine. It tells how to effectively organize the foreign and security policy apparatus of the United States government. And of the liberation of hundreds of millions of men, women, and children in Eastern Europe and Central Asia; of the triumph of democracy, free markets, and the rule of law; of the dramatic and peaceful end of the superpower nuclear threat; and of freedom for Kuwait and new hopes for peace in the Middle East. And at a personal level, *The Politics of Diplomacy* is also one man's testimony to the privilege of having served as our nation's secretary of state in a time of war, revolution, and peace.

ANOTHER PROJECT, an unexpected one, also presented itself as I prepared to leave office. Charles Duncan, then chairman of the Rice University board of governors, and George Rupp, president of the university, asked to see me. This was November 1992, about the same time that Bill Barnett was talking to me about joining Baker Botts. "We are thinking about setting up a public policy institute bearing your name at Rice University," they said. "Would you have any problem with that?" Political science professor Ric Stoll had come up with the idea, they said, and the board and president liked it.

So did I. What an honor! After all, my grandfather, Captain James A. Baker, had been instrumental in founding Rice University. He drafted the school's charter, then famously proved that a devious butler and crooked lawyer had murdered William Marsh Rice in hopes of taking his estate under a forged will. Rice's money was used as an endowment to set up what was then called the Rice Institute. For the first fifty years, Captain Baker was chairman of the board at Rice, and one of the university's residential colleges is named for him. Now the Baker legacy at Rice would be extended in a new and unexpected direction, and today many Rice faculty are engaged in the institute's public policy research and programs.

I had no problem with the idea, but I did have two conditions. One was that I not be asked to raise the money. (In time I expected to be asked to help with fund-raising, and I was. I just did not want to be obligated to say yes.) The other was that the institute not grant degrees. This was Dick Darman's suggestion. By offering a master's degree in public policy, say, the institute could soon be expected to get crossways with other elements of the university over money, professors, courses, space, and prestige. By standing outside the formal academic process, however, the institute could work cooperatively, not competitively, with the Rice faculty and university administration. And that is exactly how things have worked out, I am happy to say. We are seen to be an integral part of Rice University.

In a speech on March 31, 1993, I laid out my vision for the institute—to "draw together statesmen, scholars, and students" and to "build a bridge between the world of ideas and the world of action." (Those words would later be inscribed on the north face of the building that today houses the James A. Baker III Institute for Public Policy.)

Charles Duncan made an extraordinarily generous cornerstone gift, and thanks to the support of friends of Rice University (and mine) around the nation and the world, we soon had enough money for a building, a staff, and our first research fellows. Our original goal was $30 million, and to date we have raised more than $75 million. Space does not permit me to list our donors, but their names are written on my heart.

We broke ground for the building in October 1994. All four former U.S. presidents participated in the ceremony—Gerald Ford and George H. W. Bush (in person), Jimmy Carter (by teleconference hookup), and Ronald Reagan (by taped message). As far as I know, this was the last time President Reagan ever spoke in public.

James A. Baker III Hall was dedicated in 1997. I am biased, of course, but to me it is far and away the most beautiful building on a very beautiful campus. The style echoes the Italian Renaissance, with Byzantine elements and other features from the eastern Mediterranean. Administrative and academic offices are arranged around a central commons that extends upward three stories to a skylighted roof. The commons seats about four hundred for speeches and conferences. Our international conference center seats another 130 and offers state-of-the-art communications equipment for simultaneous translations and broadcasts over the Web or by television.

The institute will continue to thrive after I pass from the scene, I believe, because of the quality of its work, its nonpartisan spirit, its strong base of financial support, and—most of all—its association with a world-class university. We now have fifteen endowed fellowships, most from the world of action, others from academia. Our fellows have included the former head of Israeli military intelligence and the former head of NASA. Most important, however, our scholarship and recommendations on domestic and foreign policy are widely respected.

Founding Director Edward P. Djerejian deserves enormous credit for our success. Before being recruited by our search committee, he served thirty-three years in the foreign service, including stints as assistant secretary of state for the Near East and ambassador to Syria, both while I was secretary of state, and ambassador to Israel under President Clinton. Besides his leadership of the institute and its first-class staff, he is an authority in his own right on Mideast policy, and particularly on Arab-Israeli relations and our nation's public diplomacy in the region.

Ed's wife, Françoise Djerejian, has drawn on her longtime experience as the spouse of a career diplomat in making many essential contributions to the institute's success, including serving as its de facto curator. And she has done it all with her usual quiet elegance.

IN THE FIRST YEARS after leaving public service, I was obviously very busy working at Baker Botts and Carlyle, writing the book, starting the Baker Institute, and handling the other projects I have mentioned. Because of this activity and the fact that I was pretty well worn out by my thirteen years in politics and government service, I did not find the transition from public figure to private citizen to be all that difficult. Coming home was, in fact, quite enjoyable. I did what I wanted to do, when I wanted to do it, and I no longer had to open the papers first thing every morning to see what nasty things were being said about me or my president.

I never regretted being out of the political centrifuge, which continued to spin quite nicely, I noticed, without any help from me. My only real regret is about what was *not* accomplished—some things, particularly in foreign policy, we might have gotten done with another term. I treasure my opportunities to serve this wonderful country of ours, but I don't miss Washington, and I don't miss being in government.

FOR TWO OR THREE YEARS, my name popped up regularly on talk shows and in newspaper stories and columns about the 1996 presidential race. And the fact of the matter is, I thought very seriously about running.

There is a certain audacity in imagining yourself in the Oval Office, but audacity, if we're honest, is one of the job requirements. There were a lot of entries on the positive side of the ledger. I had the résumé. I knew how our government worked. And I knew the job of the presidency about as well as it can be known without ever having held the office. I also had gotten along well with representatives, senators, foreign heads of state and government, and many in the media.

Having led five presidential campaigns, I also knew politics firsthand. My name identification was way up in the eighties, and my approval/ disapproval numbers were strong. I am pretty sure I could have raised the money. I had many friends around the country, thanks to my work with the five campaigns and my service to three presidents. The 1996 GOP primaries were certain to be contested, but I enjoy competition.

But there were a lot of negatives, too. I was still dog tired. As my strength and spirits returned, I invested them heavily in the projects I have mentioned, and I was happy. Day by day, the idea of exposing myself to the rigors of a campaign for president became more and more unattractive.

Serious candidates in an open race for the nomination must start work at least two years ahead of election year. For me, that would have meant beginning in January 1994, just one year after having left office. Hello, Iowa and New Hampshire. Hello, living out of suitcases on the road. Hello, rubber-chicken dinners and nonstop events. I just wasn't ready for that.

Then, too, I would be sixty-six in 1996. Presidents Reagan (sixty-nine when he took office) and Bush (sixty-four) showed that senior citizens can run and win, but they had both run before (Reagan more than once), and George was a two-term vice president. Presidential politics is really more of a young man's game (and someday soon, I'm sure, a young woman's). President George W. Bush was sworn in at fifty-four, Clinton at forty-six, Carter at fifty-two. You've got to really want it, to have that legendary "fire in the belly." I didn't. As a rule, running for president is just not something a person does for the first time when he's already eligible for Social Security.

The best thing to say about any presidential ambition on my part is this: for two years, I did not rule out the possibility, but I also never really pushed the start button. Campaigning for the White House was something to think about, not a plan and certainly not an obsession. Even when I was out campaigning for GOP candidates in the fall of 1994, the buzz from those who would have supported me was I probably wouldn't run myself. Susan and I talked about it often, and I discussed it with a number of other friends and advisers. In the end, we just concluded it was not something we wanted to do.

Could I have won? Who knows? If I had run, I would have run hard, but I'm not sure I could have defeated Senator Bob Dole in the primaries. And even if I had captured the Republican nomination,

President Clinton would have been hard to beat. A corollary of the rule I mentioned earlier—about how rare it is for one party to maintain control of the White House longer than eight years—is that history shows that it is equally difficult to unseat a sitting president after only four years.

While the GOP sweep of the 1994 midterm elections exposed President Clinton's vulnerabilities, the nation in 1996 was prosperous and largely at peace. The federal deficit was also declining, thanks to the post–Cold War peace dividend, congressional budget discipline (which, sadly, has since evaporated), and the continuation of the economic boom that began in November 1982 and was fueled in the 1990s by the liberalization of the world economy. President Clinton's personal troubles still lay ahead, and he was, as I've said, a gifted politician. He easily won reelection against Bob Dole.

Let me say here that my relationship with President Clinton has always been cordial and respectful. In his first term, he invited me to speak in the East Room with him, President Carter, and Secretary Kissinger, in the final push to win congressional support for the North American Free Trade Agreement. I also helped his administration win ratification of the Chemical Weapons Convention, which our administration had negotiated. In 1995, President Clinton invited me to be a member of the official American delegation to the funeral of Yitzhak Rabin, but I had just had back surgery and could not fly. Later, however, I flew with President Clinton on Air Force One to attend the funeral of King Hassan II of Morocco. For some time, the former chief executive has had a standing invitation to speak at the Baker Institute.

I am not given to regrets about things political, and today I have no regrets about not having run for president. Susan and I just decided against doing that at our age and stage in life. I did try to help Bob Dole's campaign, first by giving a political foreign policy speech with a little red meat in it at the 1996 GOP National Convention in San Diego, and later by consulting with Bob and his running mate, Jack Kemp, about debate strategy.

My decision not to run for president liberated me. I would never again return to full-time government service, but if the telephone were to ring with other opportunities for public service, I would now be more available to listen.

And, indeed, the telephone did ring.

KOFI ANNAN, secretary-general of the United Nations, called in 1997. "Would you be willing to help us with the conflict over Western Sahara?" he asked.

Western Sahara is the last decolonization issue on the UN docket. When Europe carved up Africa in the nineteenth century, Spain claimed this territory on the northwest coast of the continent, which became known as Spanish Sahara. It is a desert, about the size of Wyoming, and originally peopled by the Sahrawis—once-nomadic Arabs and Berbers.

After decades of conflict and pressure by the UN, Spain withdrew in 1975. Neighboring Morocco from the north and Mauritania from the south quickly claimed the territory. The International Court of Justice, while it recognized that both protagonists had claims that did not affect the decolonization of the territory or the principle of self-determination, failed to settle the issue of sovereignty. Mauritania pulled out under pressure in 1979, leaving Morocco in possession, but in a running battle with a Sahrawi group and government-in-exile known as Frente Polisario.

The UN brokered a cease-fire in September 1991 under a settlement plan designed to lead to a referendum of self-determination that would allow the people of Western Sahara to choose between integration with Morocco or independence. The cease-fire, however, left thousands of Sahrawis in Algerian refugee camps, both sides holding prisoners of war, and the Polisario awaiting the promised referendum. For six years, little progress had been made, Kofi said, but the parties might finally be ready for some kind of resolution. What was needed, he said, was an experienced mediator to help them. As U.S. secretary of state, I had helped resolve international disputes, and I felt an obligation to try to use that experience in this conflict.

I signed on as an unpaid volunteer. Kofi named me as his personal envoy, won the support of the Security Council, and backed the project with all necessary resources, including the help of the under-secretary-generals in charge of political affairs and peacekeeping, and of Anna Theofilopoulou, a UN senior political officer with expertise in this issue. For the next seven years, we worked to find a political solution to give the people of Western Sahara a shot at self-determination.

I first met privately with the government of Morocco, the Polisario, and two other interested parties, Algeria and Mauritania, then arranged a number of meetings of those four parties, the first in June 1997. In all, we met fourteen times on three continents.

I also toured the region several times and developed a real sympathy for the humanitarian costs of this frozen-in-time conflict. Despite the harsh conditions in which they lived, the Sahrawi people had exercised a degree of democracy, maintained a high literacy rate, and never resorted to terrorism. At the same time, my relations with Morocco had always been good, going all the way back to the 1980s when, as treasury secretary, I assisted King Hassan in obtaining satellite photography to help in building a huge sand wall, or berm, as part of Morocco's military efforts against the Polisario.

As the years passed, however, my frustration grew. There were small victories—persuading the parties to talk face-to-face; winning the release of some prisoners of war; resuming efforts to develop a voter list; and maintaining the UN-monitored cease-fire—but never any real progress on the big issues. The animosity and mistrust were too great, and both parties had a winner-take-all mentality that ruled out compromise. More often than not, my requests for new proposals or comments from the parties were met with silence, reiteration of their hardened positions, or harsh rhetoric. As long as I saw any hope, however, I stuck with it, working through one failed approach after another.

Toward the end, the Security Council voted 15–0 to support a "Peace Plan for Self-Determination for the People of Western Sahara" that I had crafted in response to the Council's earlier request that I make one last effort to develop a political solution that provided for self-determination. It called for a transitional period of limited autonomy for Western Sahara. Morocco would retain military authority and control of foreign policy, and its flag would still fly over Western Sahara. After an appropriate number of years, the United Nations would conduct a referendum, with the electorate being all bona fide residents of Western Sahara, not just those covered by the ancient Spanish census (the proposed electorate under the 1991 settlement plan) or the voter list developed by the UN. This would have given a voice to all Moroccans who had moved into Western Sahara during the occupation.

Surprisingly, even that plan was not acceptable to Morocco. It had won the war, occupied the territory, and suffered few if any negative consequences for having done so. Why should it agree to anything? The answer, which Morocco continues to reject, is that unless it finds some way to resolve the issue, it will never receive the imprimatur of international legitimacy for its occupation of Western Sahara. Fortunately for Morocco, however, and unfortunately for many Sahrawis, this conflict involves a remote and barren land, and a small group of very poor people. As a result, the dispute has never really engaged the attention of a busy world, and very few countries are willing to use up any political chits to help settle it.

"The UN will never solve the problem of Western Sahara without requiring that one, or the other, or both of the parties do something they do not wish to voluntarily agree to do," I told the Security Council more than once. Despite the continuing impasse, however, the Security Council was never willing to move beyond calling for settlement to be based on a never-yet-achieved consensus of the parties.

I kept at it until 2004, then resigned. I had given it my best shot and it now was time to give someone else a chance. I still think often of the people in the camps—victims of forces beyond their control, never returning home, largely forgotten—and of many others living unhappily under occupation in Western Sahara itself.

IN 1998, George W. Bush won a landslide second term as governor of Texas. I had known him since he was maybe twelve or thirteen years old, when his family moved to Houston and I began to play tennis with his father. I always liked him, but I wouldn't have taken a bet in the late fifties or early sixties that he might ever be a governor, much less a candidate for president. (Heck, I wouldn't have taken a bet at that time that his father would ever be president.) Almost four decades later, however, it made perfect sense.

In the old days, the Bush and Baker families often got together after Thanksgiving lunch. The two dads, George's four boys (George W., Jeb, Marvin, and Neil) and my four (Jamie, Mike, John, and Doug) would repair to a vacant lot at the end of Greentree Road in Houston to play what we called the Turkey Bowl. It was touch football, but the touching sometimes looked a lot like tackling.

It's no secret by now that George W. was the cutup in the Bush family. His younger brother Jeb was always more serious. Many of us thought that maybe, just maybe, Jeb would be the one to carry on the Bush family tradition in politics.

In 1978, George W. and I both decided to run for public office: I for attorney general of Texas, he for Congress from a large West Texas district that included his childhood home, Midland. We both lost, of course, but the experience would later prove useful for both of us.

George W. ran that year against Kent Hance, a conservative Democrat, who would later become one of the congressional Boll Weevils who supported President Reagan's 1981 tax and spending cuts. Hance won by painting George as an Eastern establishment kind of guy, someone who had actually attended—gasp!—Yale University. It's hard to explain Whiffenpoofs and Skull and Bones to Texas rednecks.

George W. took this as a lesson about maintaining his roots, and he would never again be out-Texaned. Although he was born in New Haven while his father attended college there after World War II, young George spent his childhood in Midland, a wild and woolly oil town, and absorbed the spirit of his home state in his bones.

In the 1980s, George W. took a more active interest in his father's campaigns and became a sort of enforcer. He got to be good friends with Lee Atwater, his father's campaign manager in the 1988 primaries. When the vice president asked me to come over to run the general election campaign, Lee was distraught. He took it as a demotion, a downgrading of his role. George W. helped me persuade him that it was for the best—that my friendship and prior experiences with the candidate would help the campaign and that I would respect Lee's position in the campaign. And I did. Lee came to all my morning meetings and played a very important role. George W. was not directly involved in the day-to-day decisions or the overall strategy. It later became clear to me, however, that he was keeping up, absorbing what was going on, and developing a political acumen of his own.

At some point during this period, George W. had turned his life around. By then, he had a wonderful wife, Laura, and two beautiful daughters. He quit drinking, started attending Bible classes, and became much more serious about his family, business, politics, and life in general. I sensed that something was different, but I was not around him much and might have been slow to recognize the full implications. I don't recall discussing this development with his father or mother.

Others may be cynical, but to me, George W. Bush is living testimony of the power of faith to change lives. He went on to serve as managing partner for an investor group that bought the Texas Rangers baseball team and did a good job building a new stadium and upgrading the team (although I'm sure he'll always regret trading Sammy Sosa).

In 1994, George W. ran for governor against Ann Richards, the salty Democrat who made the famous crack at the Democratic Convention in 1988 about father George's being born "with a silver foot in his mouth." Even though Texas was known to be trending Republican, few commentators thought George W. stood much of a chance against a reasonably popular sitting governor.

We had a big fund-raiser for him in Houston. I had just gotten out of public service myself, and people were still talking about me as a possible presidential candidate, so I was a pretty good draw. We raised a lot of money. George W. went on to beat Governor Richards, 53–46 percent, in an extremely well-run campaign.

His big three advisers were Karl Rove, the campaign strategist; Karen Hughes, his communications director; and Joe Allbaugh, his campaign manager. I didn't know Karen or Joe at the time, but Karl and Margaret Tutwiler were the first two people I hired for the political action committee I set up in 1979 as a vehicle for George H. W. Bush's pre-campaign activities. Karl left to work for the Republican Party about the time we folded that committee into the 1980 presidential primary campaign, and I had little contact with him again until 1994. By then, he had mastered Texas politics and become the go-to Republican political consultant in the state.

George W. did a great job as governor, especially on taxes (he cut them), crime (more money to fight drugs), welfare (work requirements), and education (more testing). Democrats still controlled the Texas legislature, and he developed a genuine friendship with legislative leaders from that party, Bob Bullock and Pete Laney. In 1998, he won reelection with 69 percent of the vote against a McGovern-style liberal.

When George W. started preparing for his possible presidential run, a steady stream of policy advisers, political consultants, and GOP heavyweights began flowing into Austin to test his intentions and offer advice and help. I was not among them, and that was okay with me.

"The reason you didn't see him in my campaign was not because of a family feud or anything," George W. said later. "It was more that we were trying to give the indication that we were moving forward in a way, away from my father's generation and into my own."

That's exactly what happened and exactly what should have happened. If he really wanted to be president, Governor Bush should not be seen as a clone of his father. That ruled me out for any public role, much less running the campaign or being seen as part of an administration-in-waiting. It was important that George W. be perceived as his own man, not as a stalking horse for a restoration of Bush I. We had had our turn. Now it was his.

George W.'s one exception was picking Dick Cheney, his dad's defense secretary, as his running mate. I knew and respected Dick and thought he was a very good pick. He was not seen as a Bush family loyalist in quite the same way I was, and was young enough to be considered more of George W.'s generation than his father's. Of course, he proved to be a good campaigner and a loyal and influential vice president.

I helped the campaign in modest ways, but quietly and for the most part privately. At different times, Don Evans, the governor's close friend, campaign chairman, and chief fund-raiser, and Joe Allbaugh—all six feet, four inches, and 275 pounds of him—came to see me in Houston to talk about organization and strategy. I also did a couple of small fund-raisers, one in Alaska.

What did I think about the campaign? Well, Bush-Cheney ran a good one. The only mistake, I think, was spending the last few days in California, which they really never had a chance of winning, instead of, say, Florida. But twenty-twenty hindsight is a luxury reserved for the aftermath of a campaign, not something that is ever available in real time.

Gore-Lieberman had a lot of trouble getting organized, but from the convention on it also did a pretty good job. Vice President Gore's biggest mistake, I thought, was in distancing himself too far from the president. Bill Clinton might have helped Gore win in a number of states, any one of which could have given him the electoral votes he needed to win.

In general, however, I was just a bystander in 2000. I told George W. Bush I would do what I could to help, but it would not have been good for him if I had had a major role in the campaign.

. . .

ON ELECTION DAY, November 7, 2000, Susan and I camped out in Austin's Four Seasons Hotel, along with Dick and Lynne Cheney and several hundred other friends and family of the candidates. Early that evening, Susan and I watched television in the crowded hotel ballroom. A while later, a few of us— including, I think, Jack and Joanne Kemp, Trent and Tricia Lott, and Bob and Betsy Teeter—joined the Cheneys in their suite. From the beginning, it was clear that it would be a long night.

Dick was bone weary. Even as his fate was being sorted out in election counting rooms across the nation, he kept nodding. "Go take a nap," we finally said, and he gave up and slipped away to his bedroom. A restless George W. Bush and his family, including his father, were gathered in the governor's mansion a short distance away to watch election results and prepare for what might come.

Florida was the make-or-break state. A few minutes before 8:00 P.M. Eastern time—7:00 P.M. in Austin—the networks called Florida for Al Gore. There were two problems with this. First, people were still voting in the panhandle section of Florida. Second, it was not an accurate call.

The projections came from the Voter News Service, a consortium of the commercial and cable networks that conducted exit polls in each state, then fed the information into a computer model for that state. In past years, the projections had almost always been right, but Florida 2000 proved to be an exception. The Bush campaign quickly issued a statement quarreling with the call, and by 10:00 P.M. Eastern time, all networks had backed down and put the state back in the undecided column.

Finally, at 2:16 A.M. Eastern time, Fox News Channel called Florida for Bush, and the other networks quickly followed. A few minutes later, Vice President Gore telephoned Governor Bush to concede. That was the traditional signal that it was all over but the shouting, so Susan and I went back to our room, got our stuff, and headed down to the hotel lobby. Buses were lined up to take guests to the bunting-draped podium near the state capitol where Governor Bush would accept Gore's concession and address his own supporters and the nation.

But it was raining like hell, I had a terrible cold, and all Susan and I had for cover was one dinky umbrella. As much as I wanted to see the speech, I told Susan I didn't want to stand in the rain, so we decided to go back up to our room and watch the festivities on television.

As everyone knows by now, there was no public concession. While Al Gore was being driven to a rally in Nashville for the speech, aides told him the Bush lead in Florida was down to a few thousand votes and falling. He quickly telephoned George W. to retract his earlier private concession. "Our campaign continues," Gore's campaign chairman told the waiting crowd. Shortly afterward, the networks backed down once again. Too close to call, they said, finally getting it right. Florida was still in play.

That was one twist of the road farther than my seventy-year-old, fever-ridden body was willing to travel, so I gave up, went to bed, and fell asleep. It was a little after 3:00 A.M. local time, I think.

When I awoke a few hours later that morning, I felt a little bit better, but Florida and the election were still up in the air. Susan and I packed and flew back to Houston, as originally scheduled. As we drove into town from Hobby Airport, we told our driver to drop me at the office, then take Susan home. And that's when the cell telephone in the car rang. It was Don Evans. "If the governor asked you to go to Florida to represent him in the vote recount, would you be available?"

SIXTEEN

"GOOD EVENING, MR. PRESIDENT-ELECT"

I WAS IN the Bush-Cheney headquarters in Tallahassee, Florida, late on the night of Tuesday, December 12, 2000, when the United States Supreme Court handed down its decision in *Bush v. Gore*. The offices were filled with lawyers and staff members who had worked by my side since early November in the dispute over Florida's electoral votes. We anxiously jumped from channel to channel as reporters struggled to read the opinion on the air and figure out what it meant. Meanwhile, our lawyers flipped through their faxed copies of the document. The answer hit us all about the same time. What it meant was that five heart-stopping, up-and-down weeks of legal and political conflict in Florida were over.

A few minutes later, Governor George W. Bush called me from Austin, Texas, and I answered with a smile.

"Good evening, Mr. President-Elect."

Around me, the room exploded in cheers.

At some point, Don Evans's cell phone rang. The governor's long-time friend and campaign chairman had sweated out the Supreme Court watch with me in Tallahassee. "It's Big Time," Don said. "He wants to talk to you."

"Big Time" was George W.'s running mate, Dick Cheney. He had won his nickname at a campaign rally a few months earlier when, unaware that their mikes were open, George W. had leaned over and whispered to him that a *New York Times* reporter in the crowd was an "asshole." "Yeah, big time," Cheney replied.

"Jim, congratulations," said the vice president–elect and an old friend of mine. "Only under your leadership could we have gone from a lead of 1,800 votes to a lead of 150 votes."[*]

On his call, Governor Bush thanked me for helping him in Florida. It was a team effort, I replied. In turn, I thanked him for his leadership and confidence in me.

A bit more than five weeks later, the president-elect again showed his gratitude by seating Susan and me in very prominent seats on the platform for his inauguration (and later in the president's box on the parade route). When we arrived for the swearing-in, Secret Service agents whom we knew from the Reagan and first Bush administrations shook our hands and escorted us to our places.

As Susan and I waited, Vice President Gore and Tipper descended the aisle to their front-row seats.

"Hello," Tipper said cheerily to Susan.

She acknowledged me somewhat more coolly perhaps. "Oh, hello."

"Hi, Jim. How are you?" Al said more evenly.

"Fine, thank you, Mr. Vice President," I responded.

President and Senator Clinton soon followed. He stopped on the way down, motioned me from my seat just off the aisle, and whispered, "You were good in Florida. Really good."

After the ceremony, he stopped again. "I told those people that if they continued to play by the Marquess of Queensberry rules, you were gonna beat their brains out," he said sotto voce.

---

[*]Robert Zelnick's book *Winning Florida: How the Bush Team Fought the Battle* helped refresh my memory about the election dispute. Another good source is *Deadlock: The Inside Story of America's Closest Election,* by the staff of the *Washington Post.* And for a deeper look at the legal issues along with some fine humor, see Judge Richard Posner's *Breaking the Deadlock.*

And thus in a couple of quick comments, he took a shot at the Gore camp, which had not used him in the campaign in the way he probably should have been used, and flattered me for being on the winning side. At the same time he implied that the reason his side lost was because it played by the rules in a way that our side did not.

With all due respect to the forty-second president, the two major reasons we won in Florida were actually much simpler. First, George W. Bush and Dick Cheney had more votes. They had more votes on election day, more votes when the dispute ended thirty-six days later, and more votes every day in between. And although this was legally irrelevant, Bush-Cheney also had more votes in the media recounts that followed.

Second, the law was on our side. I'll explain this in a moment. For now, just remember that we won every significant case in Florida at trial or on appeal. The purpose of my going to Florida was to *preserve* the Bush-Cheney victory, not to take it away from the other side. The idea that Florida was stolen is a fantasy that says more about the people who believe it than about what really happened.

But I'm getting ahead of myself. Let me back up and tell the story from the beginning—how and why I got involved, how the Bush-Cheney operation in Tallahassee was organized, why we fought the legal battles the way we did, how we ultimately prevailed, and what lessons were learned.

GOING TO FLORIDA was the last thing on my mind as I crawled out of bed in Austin, Texas, early Wednesday, November 8. When I went to sleep in the wee hours that morning, I didn't know who had won Tuesday's presidential election—George W. Bush or Al Gore. When I awoke, the race was still up in the air.

A few things were clear. For one, Al Gore had a national popular-vote majority that would eventually reach about 540,000 votes. With Florida, New Mexico, Wisconsin, Iowa, and Oregon still in limbo early Wednesday, however, neither candidate could claim victory where it mattered—in the Electoral College. Unless George W. picked up all the smaller states (and he didn't), whichever candidate took Florida's twenty-five electoral votes would be the next president. And Governor Bush led there by only 1,784 votes out of almost six million cast. Florida law mandated a statewide machine recount in races where the margin was less than one-half of one percent. This one certainly qualified, and the machines started retabulating the ballots early Wednesday.

Susan and I didn't see any reason to hang around Austin, so we flew home, as scheduled. At the same time, postelection battle plans for Florida were being laid in both Nashville and Austin, and the early advantage, we would soon learn, had already gone to Gore-Lieberman.

A team of about seventy experienced Democratic lawyers and political operatives lifted off from Nashville early that morning, headed to the Florida capital, Tallahassee. The Democrats had also done good research before November 7 on the election laws in Florida and other potential toss-up states, so when that plane hit the ground, the Gore team could come out swinging, not looking for the nearest legal library.

Before sunrise, the Bush campaign had also instructed its general counsel, Ben Ginsberg, to head for Tallahassee, but he was unable to get into the air until about 10:00 A.M. Ben had good contacts in the Florida bar and a good grasp of the state's election laws, but he was just one guy going into battle against a cadre.

Later that morning, the Democrats named Warren Christopher, seventy-five, to represent Gore-Lieberman in Florida. In many ways, it was a good move. He had served as President Clinton's first secretary of state. Before that, he had led the search that selected Bill Clinton's running mate, Al Gore. Now he was senior partner of the prestigious law firm of O'Melveny & Myers. Warren (or "Chris," as his friends call him) was a serious, capable, and trustworthy man who was seen to be "above politics"—instant gravitas in a double-breasted suit.

Chris is a real gentleman and fine public servant, and he has always treated me with perfect respect and courtesy. In 1993, for instance, he lent me an office at the State Department, along with full access to department files, classified and unclassified, as I was writing *The Politics of Diplomacy.*

The Democrats' appointment of Warren Christopher—a septuagenarian former secretary of state and a big-firm lawyer—to represent them in Tallahassee may have influenced the Bush camp's decision to ask me—a septuagenarian former secretary of state and a big-firm lawyer—to represent the Republicans. Tit for tat. The biggest difference between Chris and me was that he had not been a political animal in the same sense that I had. That's probably why Gore-Lieberman also sent campaign chairman Bill Daley of Chicago to Florida.

I first heard of the Christopher appointment when Don Evans called my car shortly after Susan and I had touched down in Houston. "We've been talking about you up here," he said, adding something like this: "If the governor asked you to go to Florida to represent him in the vote recount, would you be available?"

"Yes," I replied.

One reason for the request, I think, is that I fit the job description of what Bush-Cheney needed at that point: an experienced lawyer with extensive political and media-relations experience. Another factor, obviously, was my special relationship with the Bush family. Without George H. W. Bush, I would never have even dreamed of working in the White House or serving in the cabinet. *El Jefe* never asked me to help his son, but I owed it to my dear friend to try.

Another old friend, fellow Texan Bob Strauss, later tried to talk me out of taking the assignment. He's a Democrat, but I've never held that against him. He's a wonderful person and a brilliant political strategist.

"Jim," he said, "you're going to get hurt by this. Florida is going to be a tough legal and political brawl that will be very emotional with both sides. It could diminish your aura as a statesman."

What could I say? Florida was not the Middle East and fighting over vote recounts was not a high-level diplomatic mission, but in my view helping to preserve the integrity of a presidential election was plenty important. It certainly never once crossed my mind to say no. My aura as a statesman would just have to take its chances.

I also told Bob there was one other reason I wanted to help Governor Bush in Florida. I still hadn't forgotten the outlandish charges about the imaginary scandal, Iraqgate, that Al Gore had leveled against Bush 41 and me in 1992. (Susan often speaks of the need to be more forgiving. I confess falling short of her ideal here, but give me points for another virtue—honesty.)

Confirmation of my appointment came shortly after that first contact. I don't remember who called this time—I believe it was Governor Bush—but I do remember the message: please go to Florida ASAP!

The first thing I had to do was clear my calendar, including a long-planned hunting trip in Great Britain with George H. W. Bush. He went on to England, and one of my tasks while he was there was to take his daily calls, chew him out for having a good time while I worked, and brief him on what was happening in Florida.

I also tried to call Warren Christopher to arrange a meeting. I knew his executive assistant, Kathy Osborne, very well. She had once served as President Reagan's personal secretary. When I asked, however, she quite properly refused to tell me where Chris was. I later learned he had flown, or was flying, to Nashville to talk to Al Gore and his advisers, en route to Florida.

About 2:00 P.M., George W. Bush's campaign manager, Joe Allbaugh, arrived from Austin in a private jet the campaign had arranged. I boarded with the one suitcase Susan had packed for my trip. The plane quickly lifted off and set a course for Florida. Meanwhile the campaign announced to the press that I would represent Bush-Cheney in Florida. The purpose was to checkmate the Christopher announcement in the same news cycle.

JOE AND I ARRIVED in Tallahassee about 4:00 P.M. local time. Our hotel would be our home away from home for the next week and a half, after which we were evicted in favor of guests with longstanding reservations for the Florida–Florida State football game. In that city on that weekend, the Seminoles-Gators rivalry easily trumped a mere presidential election dispute. After we were kicked out of the hotel, we moved into apartments.

The first thing I needed to do was some serious "prior preparation to prevent poor performance," starting with an inventory of where our side stood. What did Florida law say? How many people did we need and how many did we already have? What other assets would we need?

I quickly hooked up with Ben Ginsberg, and we had our first sit-down with Florida Republicans Wednesday evening in the conference room of Al Cardenas, state GOP chairman. At the time, I didn't know Ben very well. I quickly learned, however, that he was a first-class party general counsel with good instincts, organizational skills, and contacts.

Only a handful of lawyers and political types attended that first meeting, including Barry Richard, a really good lawyer who happened to be a Democrat and whose expertise in Florida election law would prove indispensable, and Frank Jimenez, acting counsel to Florida Governor Jeb Bush, George W.'s younger brother.

Jeb had rightly recused himself from direct participation, as governor, in the dispute, but he was still available to us as an information source and a strategist. In the days to come, I would often seek his counsel.

All of us in that first meeting were acutely aware that the Democrats' head start in getting lawyers and other workers into the field had given them a big advantage. The Republican Party had put observers in place for the mandatory county-by-county statewide recount, but we did not have a full team of battle-ready attorneys, media people, and political types at our headquarters, as the other side did.

One bit of good news was that the early numbers in the mandatory recount didn't look too bad. The next day, however, several hundred votes evaporated. I began to think Bush-Cheney might fall behind in the mandatory recount before it ended, but we never did.

As I've said, we had two big advantages, both of which were immediately evident. One was being ahead in the vote count. It seems almost silly to have to remind people that elections are about votes and that the candidate with the most, wins. But in all the subsequent controversy about pregnant chads, voter intent, and all the rest, that simple point was constantly in danger of being lost. By the time the mandatory recount was over, our lead was down to 300 votes. Whether it was 300 votes or 300,000, however, the outcome would be the same. It would be enough to win.

The second big advantage was that the law was on our side. Given all the controversy that followed, this may be difficult to believe, but events proved that we were right. Once the mandatory recount was over, I don't think there was ever any serious doubt on either side that if Florida law as it existed on November 7 were followed to the letter, Bush-Cheney would be certified as the winners. The essence of the legal problem faced by the other side was how to prevent that from happening.

As the days wore on, we developed one other advantage—organization. It began at the top with Governor Bush. He delegated the day-to-day management of Florida to me, and we developed a strong chain of command under him.

I reported directly to the candidate, not to the campaign staff in Austin or to anyone else. There was never any question about that. After all, I had been around since George W. Bush was twelve or thirteen years old, had served as his father's closest political adviser and secretary of state, and had run several presidential campaigns.

In turn, I quickly set up my own brain trust in Tallahassee, featuring some of the usual suspects from my days in government—among them, Bob Zoellick to serve as my right-hand man on strategy and message, and Margaret Tutwiler to handle communications. There were important additions from the Bush-Cheney campaign, particularly Joe Allbaugh, and still others with whom I had worked in the Reagan or Bush 41 administrations, like John Bolton and Josh Bolten.

Each morning, I would have a private telephone conversation with George W. and Dick, just the two of them. No staffers were involved on either side. I passed along information and made recommendations about the major issues, but never bothered them with the small stuff. They listened, then made any decisions I needed made. After that, we generally had an open conference call with key staff members in both Tallahassee and Austin.

This is how I had conducted business in the White House, at Treasury, and at State—by dealing directly with the president, then acting on his personal authority to implement his decisions. Thus, when I spoke, I always spoke for the president and everyone knew it. True leaders are always good delegators. In a strong organization, that's the way it has to work, and that's the way it worked in Florida.

George W. had the ability to listen to advice, then make up his own mind what to do, and he was good at delegating. This was especially important in Florida because of the complex legal issues, the dozens of separate legal challenges around the state, and the fast pace of events. "Any questions you have about what's happening in Florida, I would ask you to refer those to Jim Baker," he told the press on November 10. "Secretary Baker is in charge of that process."

Al Gore, on the other hand, was apparently more of a micromanager. This may have served him well in Congress and when he was vice president, but it probably hurt him in Florida. It likely spread him too thin, distracted him with peripheral issues, and created competition within his own ranks for his time and attention.

One decision I suspect he would like to have back was replacing the respected constitutional scholar Larry Tribe at the eleventh hour with David Boies, a trial lawyer, for the final oral argument before the U.S. Supreme Court. This was exactly the sort of decision a principal— especially a principal who was not a lawyer—should have delegated, not made.

And speaking of lawyers, we may have started behind, but we soon built an instant law firm with an all-star staff, a physical base in Tallahassee, and, thanks to computers and other equipment installed by Joe Allbaugh, virtual support from sympathetic attorneys around the country. Some good lawyers simply showed up in Tallahassee looking to help. Among them were prominent Democrats or former Democrats such as Griffin Bell (President Carter's attorney general) and John Hill (former attorney general of Texas and chief justice of the Texas Supreme Court). But I recruited many others on the legal team.

With the possible exception of Ted Olson, the brilliant trial and appellate lawyer I tapped to argue Governor Bush's case in the U.S. Supreme Court, few readers probably remember (or ever knew) the names of these talented men and women.* Among many, many others, our team included Barry Richard (mentioned earlier); George Terwilliger, deputy attorney general in the first Bush administration; Washington attorney Michael Carvin; and Chicago trial lawyers Phil Beck and Fred Bartlit.

Several of my partners from Baker Botts also migrated to Florida during this period, notably Kirk Van Tine, who coordinated much of our legal research, and trial lawyers Daryl Bristow and Irv Terrell, each of whom handled major cases. (Terrell and Beck had each successfully gone head-to-head in litigation with David Boies, Gore's chief lawyer. I wanted them on our team to share the lessons they had learned in battling him.) Others were Bobby Burchfield, Marcos Jimenez, Ken Mehlman, Tim Flanigan, John Bridgeland, Ken Juster, Alex Azar, and Bill Kelley.

I had no problem getting all these people to sign on. My biggest problem was slotting them into the project in ways that would take full advantage of their talents. These were first-chair attorneys, top partners from some of the best firms in the country. Most dropped big cases to come to Florida and do whatever needed to be done, even work they might ordinarily have delegated to associates.

Every day we had to make tough calls. Do we contest this Gore

---

*Less than a year later, Ted's wife—a brilliant attorney and writer—Barbara Olson, died on the hijacked airliner that hit the Pentagon on September 11, 2001. What a great loss for him, their friends, and the nation.

move? Do we initiate this move for Bush-Cheney? Do we file in this court or that court? Our brilliant, competitive, and strong-willed lawyers often held different views on how to proceed and *who* would proceed (that is, handle the case). But it was out of this vigorous clash of opinions that we developed our successful legal strategies. Zelnick later quoted Ginsberg as saying, "This was the biggest group of egos not flexing their egos I've ever been associated with." For those five-plus weeks in Florida—if I may say so—I was privileged to serve as managing partner of what might have been the finest law firm in America.

If most people can't remember our lawyers, many surely remember the name of Gore's lead attorney, David Boies of New York, one of the nation's best trial lawyers and a genuine legal celebrity. He was no doubt assisted by a strong team, but he was spread pretty thin. Arguably, at least, handling most of the high-profile cases himself—in state and federal courts, and in trials and appeals—was too much for one person, no matter how talented.

Our usual approach, by contrast, was to send fresh players into every game, not to rely on one traveling superstar. Exceptions were Florida election-law expert Barry Richard, who represented us in several different state court contests, and Olson, who worked most of the federal cases. In general, however, our lawyers had narrow, specific assignments. Some wrote briefs for particular cases in federal court. Others argued one case or maybe one element of one case in state court. Big law firms are organized on the principle of division of labor, and that's how we organized our legal team in Florida.

I wrote no briefs and argued no cases myself. It had been a long time since I had practiced law at that level, and anyway I could not have competed with the exceptional talent around me. I did review some documents, ask questions, and occasionally suggest a line of legal argument, but my real job was to recruit, organize, and make assignments, then to listen to the debates on tactics and strategy and decide what we should do, subject always, of course, to the instructions of our client in Austin. To be done well, this work had to be handled by an experienced lawyer, not by the principals and certainly not by campaign advisers.

Florida is largely remembered as a legal battle, but in my opinion it was every bit as much a political battle, and we may have understood this point better than the other side. That's why we put so much effort into setting up a communications and press operation in Tallahassee, rather than relying solely on the campaign's existing (and excellent) press apparatus in Austin. It was vital to our ultimate success that we controlled both the messengers and the message on what was happening in Florida.

One of my first calls was to recruit Margaret Tutwiler as our press person in Tallahassee. She worked well with reporters and was simply the best person I knew at designing a communications strategy. She had done it for me at the White House, at Treasury, and at State, and now she would do it in Florida.

I resisted pressure to get overly involved in the daily televised battles of the talking heads. In part, I didn't want to use myself up. That's why we brought in a number of respected Republican surrogates— among them, Bob Dole, Christie Todd Whitman, Fred Thompson, Arlen Specter, and Marc Racicot—to communicate our daily messages to the press. Remember, too, that I was in Florida as a former secretary of state to put a patina of statesmanship on a political dispute. I didn't want to go out there every day as a sort of hired-gun pol, despite what some of the Bush-Cheney advisers in Austin might have wanted. Governor Bush, of course, was properly reserved for blockbuster statements to the nation, not for the daily give-and-take.

One surrogate we didn't get was Colin Powell. After the Democrats tried to throw out some overseas military ballots, we asked him to speak up for the right of our troops to have their votes counted, but he demurred. He was in line to be George W.'s secretary of state, and I think he wanted to stay above the fray.

I regret that he did not come to Florida. My own political work for Ronald Reagan and George H. W. Bush never did me any harm when it came to being confirmed by the Senate for cabinet posts, and it considerably improved my standing with the presidents I served. Coming to Florida might well have strengthened Colin's relationship with George W. Bush, which in turn might have helped him in the first-term battles for influence and power in the administration.

Another reason I resisted going out there every day, however, is that in dealing with the press, oftentimes less is more. I am not sure the Gore team understood this. They had too many people speaking for the campaign at the same time, not always with a common message. Their lawyers, in particular, were always ready to talk whenever a reporter stuck a microphone in their face. Good manners, perhaps, but not always good politics. By limiting my appearances, I was able to fill the room with reporters every time I called a press conference, which was fairly often. A couple were after midnight.

I think we were more disciplined. We coordinated our message and we coordinated our messengers. With rare exceptions, no one spoke to the press except me, the principals, and our surrogates, always with well-thought-out statements and talking points. This kept the press focused on the message we wanted to convey.

As we fought to maintain good order on the legal, political, and media battlefields, the GOP state headquarters building—recently named the George Bush Republican Center (after Bush 41)—was a scene of creative chaos. Lawyers and other workers had quickly overwhelmed the resources of our hosts. I had a nice office but some had to share space, sometimes in shifts. Many lawyers and legal assistants worked together in the conference room. Legal research, briefs, and other documents were stacked on the floors, and those stacks grew until no one quite remembered what was in them, then fell over. Extension cords snaked around corners and down halls in search of electricity for computers, fax machines, television sets, and copiers. And everywhere there were people—people working in every cranny of the building, people bumping into one another, people installing equipment, people clicking away on keyboards, and people talking, talking, talking. The intensity grew until we could bear no more, then it grew again.

. . .

BEFORE MY AIRPLANE ever hit the tarmac in Tallahassee, local Gore supporters had filed the first two lawsuits in Florida, demanding either a *revote*—a do-over—in Palm Beach County or a court-ordered reallocation of the votes. They blamed a badly designed butterfly ballot for confusing many would-be Gore voters.

These lawsuits were a joke. For one thing, there was no way to change the date of an election set by the U.S. Constitution. A local trial judge quickly and correctly threw the plaintiffs out of court. Still, the cases offered a near-perfect illustration of the dynamics of the Florida election dispute, with its unique interplay of public relations, politics, and law.

On day one, every network was carrying angry interviews about the butterfly ballots and other real or imagined voting problems. Some of this was genuine, I'm sure, but Democrats clearly orchestrated many of the protests. (In fairness, both sides organized rallies and protests.) The Democrats' purpose, I believe, was to delegitimize the Bush-Cheney victory and set the stage for intervention by the courts. Even though local Democrats, not the Gore campaign, filed the butterfly cases, Bill Daley, Warren Christopher, and others publicly embraced the charge that the Palm Beach County ballot was illegal. On Friday, November 10, I spoke about the butterfly ballot and, to use a phrase from an old lawyers' joke, I pounded the law.*

There's a rule of law to be followed in all elections. The state of Florida has established legal procedures to design, approve, publish, and if need be to protest ballots before the election. The [butterfly] ballot was designed by a Democratic elections supervisor. She ap-

---

*How do you win a case? When the law is on your side, pound the law; when the facts are on your side, pound the facts; and when neither the law nor the facts are on your side, pound the table. The other side was pounding the table, in my opinion. From November 10 onward, we pounded the law.

proved it. The Democratic Party did not question it before the election. This butterfly-type ballot was used in recent elections in the
same county and under the same rules and, again, the Democrats did
not complain.... Our lawyers have confirmed the legality of this ballot. And we have with us here today ... copies of the relevant Florida
statutes if you would like to have them.

The butterfly ballot cases illustrate what the rule of law is all
about, which is playing by the rules as they existed *before* the game was
played, then living with the results, good or bad. This is the same principle, by the way, that says you can't go to court to collect a debt if you
file your lawsuit after the deadline set by the statute of limitations. It
is unjust, in some sense, for a deadbeat debtor to get away without paying, but it would be an even greater injustice to change the rules after
the event. The law is full of deadlines and technicalities and procedures, and if we purport to live under the rule of law, we have no
choice but to respect them, even when they hurt us.

"Butterfly ballots" was a warm-up bout. The main event started on
Thursday, November 9, when Bill Daley announced that the Gore
campaign would request a hand count of ballots in Palm Beach County
and three others: Volusia, Miami-Dade, and Broward.*

Obviously, Al Gore didn't invite me to represent him in Florida or
to play Monday morning quarterback, but I will say this: his decision
to seek manual recounts in four heavily Democratic counties rather
than all sixty-seven counties was a big mistake. It undermined his otherwise effective public relations slogan—"count every vote"—and gave
us the moral high ground on that issue.

There was debate in our camp on how to respond. Some team
members believed we should call for hand recounts in pro-Bush counties or for a full statewide hand recount, but these folks, in my opinion,
were not seeing the big picture. First off, political strategists in the

---

*I later joked that after arriving in Florida, I learned that the state has sixty-three coun-
ties ... and four *re*counties!

state advised me that there weren't many places where we could expect to get a bounce. Secondly, I worried about the fact that most of those counting the ballots were Democrats. At the very least, there would be, as I put it to the press, "the opportunity for mischief." The final and most important reason for not seeking a recount, however, was that recounts are for losers, and we had won.

We were still ahead, unofficially, by 300 votes when the mandatory statewide machine recount ended on Friday, November 10, and my position was, "Hey, it's over." Even though two-thirds of the state elections supervisors were Democrats, I told reporters, Bush-Cheney had prevailed. All that was left was to count the overseas ballots, and they traditionally favored Republican candidates. "We will vigorously oppose the Gore campaign's efforts to keep recounting over and over until it happens to like the result," I said.

In answer to a question, I reminded reporters of another close race. "I'm particularly drawn back to the memory of 1976, when I was in the room and many, many people were arguing to President Ford that he should insist upon a recount, because he was only some seven thousand votes or so down in Ohio. . . . And he said, 'No. . . . That's not what would be good for the country.'"*

I'll come back in a moment to our legal efforts to block the recounts, but, as everyone knows, they went forward. Human vote counters began holding machine ballots up to the light, twisting in their seats, squinting, trying to read the minds of voters based on whether tiny rectangles of paper were dangling or hanging or dimpled or pregnant. There were absolutely no uniform standards for this process. At times, the rules changed in the middle of the counts. It was chaos from beginning to end—what we in Texas would call a "goat rope." To try to protect against the excesses of creative counting, we had senior

---

*My memory was a bit off. As noted in chapter one, a shift of fewer than 5,600 votes in Ohio would have moved the state to the Ford column, but we would also have needed to turn just under 3,700 votes in Hawaii.

people—including John Bolton and Frank Donatelli—sitting in the chad rooms for days and days.

This is where Katherine Harris, the elected secretary of state of Florida (and a Republican), became a familiar figure to America's television viewers. Each county was supposed to certify its results to her office on November 14, exactly one week after the election. With the hand recounts just getting under way, however, the four counties obviously could not meet that deadline. Under legal pressure, she announced on November 14 that Bush-Cheney led by 300 votes, but postponed formal certification to November 17, subject only to counting the overseas ballots and to the possible acceptance of late returns that could be legally justified. Two days later, however, the Florida Supreme Court ordered that the hand recounts could continue, pending its decision on whether they were legal. By then, Miami-Dade had simply given up, so we were down to three counties.

Shortly after arriving in Florida, Zoellick, Allbaugh, and I went to see Katherine Harris. She would soon be subjected to some vicious ad hominem attacks by both the Gore team and members of the press. Secretary Harris was obviously very bright, but I sensed that she was uneasy about the position into which she had been forced by circumstances, almost to the point of being paralyzed. She wanted to do what the law required, and we made the case that the law required her to certify the election at a specific time and in a specific manner, which basically meant sooner rather than later. For her own sake, we also advised her to get the best legal help she could, which she did. I understand that Gore representatives also visited her to make their case, as was perfectly appropriate.

The next stop was the Florida Supreme Court. By then, the absentee ballots had come in and the Bush-Cheney lead had grown to 930 votes. Oral arguments were set for November 20 and the opinion came down the next day. It was an outrageous piece of judicial overreaching. In complete disregard of the statutory law of Florida and of Article II, Section 1, of the United States Constitution ("Each State shall appoint, *in such Manner as the Legislature thereof may direct,* a Number of Electors . . . "), the court extended the deadline set by the legislature for the ongoing recounts to Sunday, November 26, twelve days after the deadline set by Florida statutes.

"For the first time since his arrival in Tallahassee," Robert Zelnick wrote later, Baker "looked his age as he read a statement attacking the court's decision." Absolutely. I was worn out, angry, and worried.

> Today, Florida's supreme court rewrote the legislature's statutory system, assumed the responsibilities of the executive branch, and sidestepped the opinion of the trial court as the finder of fact. Two weeks after the election, that court has changed the rules and invented a new system for counting the election results. One should not now be surprised if the Florida legislature seeks to affirm the original rules.

The court said it was guided by "the will of the people, not a hyper-technical reliance upon statutory provisions." That's the sort of lawyer talk that sounds impressive until you think about it. The best expression of "the will of the people" on this subject, after all, was the statute enacted by lawmakers elected by the people. And "hyper-technical reliance upon statutory provisions" is another name for what this court had just trampled into the dust—the rule of law. "It is simply not fair, ladies and gentlemen," I said, "to change the rules, either in the middle of the game or after the game has been played."

WHEN I WAS treasury secretary, I became friends with Lawton Chiles, the Democratic senator from Florida who chaired the Senate Budget Committee. We both loved to hunt wild turkeys. Our friendship continued after I left Washington in 1993, and we would sometimes hunt together at my ranch in Texas and at various places in Florida.

In 1994, Lawton was elected governor of Florida. He defeated Jeb

Bush, who was making his first run for the office. Lawton ran a tough campaign—many thought it was too negative—focused mostly on Social Security, which is a federal issue, not a state issue. After that, it wasn't particularly popular with the Bushes for anybody to be friends with Chiles, but the Chiles-Baker relationship had been struck up long before Jeb ran for governor, and it survived.

On one trip in Florida, Lawton and I were joined by his close friend Dexter Douglass, a silver-haired lawyer who served as the governor's general counsel. Dexter was a colorful humorist and lively conversationalist. In short order, I learned two important things about him. One was that he was a liberal Democrat, big time. The other was that one of his jobs was to recommend candidates to Lawton for appointment to the Florida Supreme Court. I think he may have recommended five of the seven justices on the court.

At the time, I didn't think any more about it. In November 2000, however, that memory helped shape the Bush-Cheney legal strategy, which was very, very simple. The only way to deal with the Florida Supreme Court, I believed, was to go over its head.

I told the Dexter Douglass story in the first meetings with my brain trust in Florida to help explain why I thought we needed to file a federal lawsuit. "If we don't get into federal court," I said, "we'll be as dead as a doornail."

Some of them argued with me. They thought Florida was a state issue and that the federal courts would be reluctant to intervene, but I insisted we try anyway. I also recommended that course to Governor Bush. He agreed, and on Saturday, November 11, Ted Olson filed our motion in U.S. District Court in Miami for an injunction to stop the manual recounts. We argued that the recounts violated both the due process and equal protection clauses of the Fourteenth Amendment because they gave too much latitude to the men and women who were counting the ballots and because all Florida voters were entitled to have their votes counted in the same way.

It's important to understand that our purpose in going to the federal courthouse was not to *overturn* the election. Our purpose, rather, was to *preserve* a lawful Bush-Cheney victory by stopping the election results from being changed by a subjective recount system without uniform standards, which we believed was both wrong and unconstitutional.

We took a lot of flak for filing the lawsuit, some of it from Republicans. I got a real earful, for instance, when I called my friend, former Missouri senator Jack Danforth, to ask him to be our lead counsel in federal court. Jack is well liked and well respected across the political spectrum and has a spotless reputation for integrity. He was a former Missouri attorney general, a man Dick Cheney had recommended as W's running mate, and an ordained Episcopalian priest. I thought he would lend instant stature to our federal case.

Jack was vacationing in Cancun when I asked him to sign on. Instead of a yes, I got a lecture, the essence of which was: if you go to court and lose, you're going to ruin Bush's career; he's young enough to run again sometime, but not if he's seen as having challenged a presidential election in court. When I reported this to Bush and Cheney in Austin, we decided to look elsewhere. That's when I recommended Ted Olson, who went on to do a superlative job for us in the federal courts, including two successful appeals to the U.S. Supreme Court.

Our first shot at the federal courts went nowhere. On November 13, a district judge ruled against us. Two days later we appealed to the 11th Circuit Court of Appeals, and on November 17 that court upheld the lower court. The recounts would continue.

These defeats didn't come as a surprise. The 11th Circuit said we had not exhausted our remedies in state courts and, with the recounts just beginning, had not demonstrated a substantial threat of irreparable injury. We were disappointed, of course, but our case had been dismissed without prejudice, which meant we still had a foot in the federal courthouse door.

Three days later, the Florida Supreme Court conducted oral arguments on the recount issue. This was the hearing that led to the November 21 opinion I have already described as outrageous. The first few seconds of the Gore-Lieberman oral arguments were fairly memorable to me.

"Mr. Chief Justice, members of the court, I'm here to introduce the speaker today who will argue the case for us, Mr. David Boies from the state of New York."

It was a routine introduction, except for one thing. The man who introduced Boies, who sat at the table with Boies, who was sometimes referred to as Boies's right-hand man, was none other than Dexter Douglass. He was introducing his new Yankee friend to the very justices he had helped place on the court. I felt like a stranger at somebody else's family reunion.

I've already said all I need to say about the Florida court's decision to extend the deadline for the recounts to November 26. I resisted the temptation back then to assign political motives to the seven justices, and I'll resist it now. I assume they honestly believed they were doing the right thing, which just happened to be what Gore-Lieberman wanted. What they really did by changing the rules in the middle of the game, however, was to give our side a new and stronger case for the U.S. Supreme Court. I quickly met with Ginsberg, Olson, Zoellick, Terwilliger, Carvin, and others to decide what to do next. Some of them were not optimistic that the Supreme Court would take an appeal of the Florida decision, and, in any event, estimated our odds of winning at no better than fifty-fifty. Maybe we should just keep going with the recount suit, some suggested, to avoid putting the high court in the posture of overruling a state court. The calendar was also a factor. There were only five days until the Florida Supreme Court's new deadline for certification. Was it realistic to expect the U.S. Supreme Court to grant our petition, hear arguments, and rule that quickly? If not, the recount would be over before a decision could be issued.

I listened, then decided we should go forward. For one thing, I liked our chances. For another, we simply needed to try in every way possible to get into federal court. Once again, Governor Bush gave us a green light, and on November 22, our lawyers asked the U.S. Supreme

Court to review the Florida Supreme Court's decision. The state court had violated a federal statute by changing the deadline for certifying the election, we argued. In doing so that court had also violated Article II of the U.S. Constitution, which gives state legislatures authority to determine how presidential electors are chosen. We also argued that the selective recounts and random counting rules violated the due process and equal protection clauses.

On November 24—to the surprise of many, including some of my colleagues—the high court agreed to hear our case. Now what? To paraphrase the famous Groucho Marx line about club membership, we now had to decide whether we wanted to have anything to do with a court that would have us. The November 26 deadline was now only two days away, and it was beginning to look as if we would still be ahead when the recounts were completed. What could a victory in the U.S. Supreme Court add to a certified victory at the ballot box? One word, I argued: *legitimacy*.

We presented Governor Bush with a memorandum listing "reasons for dropping the case" and "reasons for continuing the case." Among the reasons for dropping: "If we lose the case after eking out a narrow win in the vote count, Gore will be seen as scoring a big victory, which he will use to lend momentum and legitimacy to his contest challenges in Florida courts." Among the reasons for continuing: "A Supreme Court win might remove the basis for Gore's election contest. . . . Furthermore, as long as the case is pending, the Florida Supreme Court is likely to be more careful in contest proceedings."

Governor Bush quickly decided he wanted us to continue. Why? One word: *legitimacy*.

On November 26, Secretary of State Harris certified Bush-Cheney as the winner by 537 votes. In Tallahassee we drafted a speech for the governor to claim victory and call on Gore to end his fight. In Austin, however, the Bush team reportedly thought the language "too arrogant." Governor Bush delivered a kinder, gentler version. "Now that the votes are counted, it is time for the votes to count," he said.

In *Winning Florida*, here's how Zelnick describes my remarks to the press that same evening: "The speech may have been 'too arrogant' to be delivered by the next president of the United States, but, with a few modifications it seemed just right for a tough old political strategist slugging it out in Florida but wishing he were off somewhere abbreviating the lives of pheasants."

Unfortunately, Vice President Gore did not accept the certified results and concede. In a nationally televised speech on November 27, he vowed to press onward. In what surely was the one of the oddest remarks of the thirty-six-day dispute, the man who had asked for selective recounts in just four heavily Democratic counties said, "That is all we have asked since election day: a complete count of all the votes cast in Florida." We were all pretty tired by then, so maybe "complete count of all the votes" was just a slip of the tongue.

Certification changed the legal landscape entirely. George W. Bush had now officially won. From this moment, Gore-Lieberman were no longer *protesting* the election count; they were *contesting* a certified election and seeking to overturn it. This created two enormous problems for the Democrats. For one thing, the burden of proof would be much higher, requiring evidence of fraud or some other serious wrongdoing or of some monumental irregularity or inaccuracy significant enough to change the statewide results. The second problem was that the Florida Supreme Court's extension of the recount deadline to November 26 had chewed up so much time that there weren't many days left for the contest. Both camps and all courts were working on the assumption that the election had to be resolved by December 12 to meet a statutory federal "safe harbor" deadline for settling the names of Florida's electors.

The United States Supreme Court heard our case on December 1. Olson argued the case and did an excellent job. I stayed away. I had been in the Reagan and Bush administrations when some of the justices were appointed. My presence was unnecessary, and it could have been distracting. Some might even argue, inappropriate.

The next day, distinguished and folksy Circuit Judge N. Sanders

Sauls kicked off a three-day quickie trial in Leon County to hear the Gore contest. Boies gave it his best shot, but on December 4, Judge Sauls ruled against Gore-Lieberman on every issue, without exception. That same day, the U.S. Supreme Court vacated the Florida Supreme Court decision of November 21. And elsewhere, we were soon to win cases filed in Florida courts by the Democrats to challenge absentee ballots and overseas ballots. For a couple of days, Bush-Cheney was running the table.

But the Democrats still refused to concede, and once again the Florida Supreme Court saved their bacon. On December 8, the justices voted 4–3 to reverse Judge Sauls's decision and ordered something that Gore-Lieberman had not even asked for, a *statewide* manual recount of so-called undervotes—those ballots the machines registered as not having voted for any candidate for president. This decision will be reprinted in law books for decades to come as an example of what appellate courts are *not* supposed to do.

Wearily, wearily, wearily I trudged to the microphone to explain, yet again, that the Florida court had overstepped its boundaries, this time by (among many other things) overruling Judge Sauls's findings of fact that there was no evidence of fraud or other serious wrongdoing. Appellate Law 101 says appeals courts are supposed to deal with the law, not—except in rare instances—with the facts, which are settled in lower courts.

In a scorching dissent, Florida Chief Justice Charles Wells explained the true nature of this opinion. "The majority's decision to return this case to the [trial] court for a count of the undervotes from either Miami-Dade County or all counties has no foundation in the law of Florida as it existed on November 7, 2000, or at any time until the issuance of this opinion," he wrote.

Amen, brother. That's the sort of thing we had been saying since November.

"I have a deep and abiding concern that the prolonging of judicial process in this . . . contest propels this country and this state into an unprecedented and unnecessary constitutional crisis," Chief Justice Wells said.

There's no point in my saying much more about the decision, because the U.S. Supreme Court promptly stayed the Florida court's order, then vacated it in *Bush v. Gore,* the famous late-night decision of December 12. By a 7–2 vote, the high court held that the recount ordered by the Florida Supreme Court was unconstitutional because the lack of uniform counting rules violated the equal-protection clause of the U.S. Constitution. Let that sink in. Seven out of nine justices agreed with Bush-Cheney on the issue of constitutionality. Critics who say the case was "really 5–4" are talking about a second vote on a subsidiary matter, the remedy—what to do about the Florida Supreme Court's outrageous decision. Referring to December 12, the federal statutory safe harbor deadline, a majority of the court said, "That date is upon us, and there is no recount procedure in place under the State Supreme Court's order that comports with minimal constitutional standards."

It was over.

Yet again, the law was on our side. And yet again, we still had more votes than the other side—537 to be exact.*

The next day, I flew back to Houston and, despite some fairly serious fatigue, dropped by my office at Baker Botts. Dozens of lawyers and staffers flocked down to my end of the hall to welcome me home.

"Did you ever think you might lose?" someone asked.

"Every day I thought it was possible," I replied. "Every day."

---

*One subject I chose not to write much about in this chapter is the so-called "nuclear option." A very strong argument can be made that under the U.S. Constitution, the Florida legislature simply could have named a slate of electors and put an immediate end to ongoing court battles. There was a lot of talk about this possibility, and we did a fair amount of legal research on it. On December 12, the Florida House actually approved a slate of twenty-five pro-Bush electors, but the Senate never acted.

I don't think Governor Bush would have authorized us to try to win Florida's electors by legislative fiat rather than through the votes of the people of Florida. Having lost the popular vote by more than 500,000 votes, he understood very well how hard it would have been to govern if he won the White House that way.

. . .

FLORIDA WAS an unsettling experience for the American people. I hope we never have to go through anything like that again. It was equally unsettling to the world at large. As the legal battles dragged on, I received telephone calls from several present and former prime ministers and foreign ministers with whom I had worked as secretary of state. "What's happening to your country?" they asked. "Can't you even conduct an election?" In part this was simple curiosity, but there was also a whiff of anxiety about the uncertainty of who would be president of the sole remaining superpower.

"What's happening," I replied, "is that our system is working. This is a very emotional issue for the American people, but on both sides, I think, we are handling it with dignity and pursuant to the rule of law. And whatever else may be happening, we do not have tanks in the street." For a few callers, I added a zinger: "as might have been the case, were this to have happened in some other countries."

I meant what I said about dignity. In a dispute as important and contentious as Florida, it was inevitable, given human nature, that some things would be said outside the boundaries of civility and that other things would be done that, in hindsight, might have been done differently. What is striking, however, is how few those incidents were and how quickly they have faded from mind.

That tone was set early. Two days after the election, I met with Warren Christopher. As we touched gloves, neither of us suggested that a settlement could be negotiated. One candidate was bound to win and the other was bound to lose. There was no middle ground, even for experienced negotiators. But we agreed that the contest would be conducted in an honorable and dignified way on both sides. That's what both sides did, by and large, and I salute Chris and his colleagues. Al Gore's gracious concession speech deserves special acknowledgment. It helped our nation accept the legitimacy of the outcome.

One great benefit of having done things in the right way and in accordance with the rule of law—and it would have been the same for Al Gore, had he won—is that the American people were more willing to accept the outcome and move on. Some didn't, of course, but that was also inevitable, given the intensity of feelings on both sides.

Even the Florida Supreme Court finally had second thoughts about the process it set in motion. "Upon reflection," the court wrote in a little-noted December 22 opinion, "we conclude that the development of a specific, uniform standard to ensure equal application and to secure the fundamental right to vote throughout the State of Florida should be left to the body we believe best equipped to study and address it, the legislature."

A bit more of that sort of judicial restraint early on, and the Florida recount exercise would have unfolded very differently.

After all the visiting lawyers, political operatives, and reporters had packed up and gone home, two different media-sponsored organizations conducted statewide recounts of the Florida ballots. Here's what the *New York Times* reported on November 12, 2001:

> A comprehensive review of the uncounted Florida ballots from last year's presidential election reveals that George W. Bush would have won even if the United States Supreme Court had allowed the statewide manual recount of the votes that the Florida Supreme Court had ordered to go forward.

> Even under the strategy that Mr. Gore pursued at the beginning of the Florida standoff—filing suit to force hand recounts in four predominantly Democratic counties—Mr. Bush would have kept this lead, according to the ballot review conducted for a consortium of news organizations.

In a separate study, the *Miami Herald* and *USA Today* said that if the recount called for by the Florida Supreme Court's final opinion of December 8 had been implemented—the opinion the Supreme Court declared unconstitutional—Bush-Cheney would have widened their lead to more than 1,600 votes from 537 votes.

I'm sometimes asked if I think I tarnished my reputation by going into the trenches of the Florida election dispute. This is a way of suggesting that maybe Bob Strauss was right, that going to Florida had "diminished my aura as a statesman."

My answer is that Florida was a unique and historic event in the political life of our nation, and I'm proud to have been able to play a successful part in it. It was tough on both sides, but defending the rule of law and preserving a legitimate victory in a presidential election are important and satisfying tasks. Politics and public service are two sides of the same coin. There is nothing disreputable about doing politics if you do it with dignity and play by the rules. It is, after all, through politics that our leaders achieve the right to practice public policy or statesmanship.

One of the big lessons of Florida is that candidates must abide by the rules in place on election day. A corollary is that if you don't like those rules, you should try to change them before the next election. We can always do better next time. That's one reason I agreed to serve with former President Jimmy Carter in 2005 as cochair of a bipartisan Commission on Federal Election Reform. More on that in the next chapter.

Election 2000 also generated a lot of talk about doing away with the Electoral College and electing our presidents by popular vote. That will never happen, and it shouldn't. The Electoral College was part of the grand bargain by which the Founders induced the states to give up some of their sovereignty and become part of the United States. As part of that compromise, the small states won disproportionate influence in the U.S. Senate (each state, regardless of size, gets two senators) and in electing our presidents. The Founders wanted our presidents to have broad appeal among many states, not one-sided political majorities in a handful of big states. Even if you disagree with the theoretical and historical arguments, however, there is no practical way to get rid of the Electoral College. That would require a constitutional amendment ratified by a significant number of the small states, which ain't gonna happen.

The media also learned a few lessons in humility, thanks to their erroneous election-night calls on Florida. The call for Gore was made before the polls had even closed in the Florida panhandle, which is strong Republican territory. Most fair-minded people would agree that this hurt the Bush-Cheney ticket. Some potential voters simply stayed home after they heard the race in their state was over. Given the obvious importance of Florida in the Electoral College and the closeness of races in Iowa, New Mexico, Oregon, and Wisconsin—all within one percent—it is also reasonable to speculate that the early, erroneous call may have influenced the results in those states.

The media exercised more caution and restraint in the 2004 presidential election. Still, as memories fade and competitive pressures mount, it's fair to ask what we might do within the limits of the First Amendment to avoid adverse effects from early or erroneous reporting of results in future elections. The most obvious answer—to forbid journalists to call the races until all the polls have closed—is probably unconstitutional. One other possibility might be for the states to arrange polling schedules so that voting would end everywhere at the same time. But even that would not prevent early birds from calling the whole thing, based on exit polls, or prevent erroneous calls based on erroneous exit polls, as happened in 2000. It's a real conundrum. It may just boil down to hoping that journalists will recognize and embrace a special obligation on their part to let our elections play out naturally, without doing anything that would undermine the integrity of the process. It's the right thing to do, and they ought to do it.

We also need to keep a sense of perspective about Florida. Having a presidential election with more than 105 million ballots decided by fewer than a thousand votes in one state was a rare event that exposed flaws in our election laws and voting systems. We can certainly do better, and I think we will. But if that ever happens again, I suspect that no matter what reforms we have made, the losing side will find more than a thousand votes to complain about. No system is or ever will be perfect.

Finally, the biggest lesson of Florida was that the system worked. Despite all the turmoil, as I told the foreign leaders, there were no riots and no tanks in the streets. We Americans may take the peaceful transfer of power for granted, but measured against the standards of history, Florida testifies to the strength of our constitutional democracy and our faith in the rule of law.

THE BUSH-KERRY presidential race of 2004 was close, but not as close—thank heavens—as 2000. Still, when America went to bed on election night, Senator Kerry had not conceded. Whoever won Ohio would win the presidency. There was talk that the Democrats might protest the vote in that state, which the networks had called for Bush.

I was on the way to the dentist the next morning when I got a call from Andy Card, President Bush's White House chief of staff. My heart stopped. "Please, Andy," I thought, "don't ask me to go to Cleveland."

SEVENTEEN

"MR. PRESIDENT, THIS IS NOT THE FIRST TIME I'VE DONE THIS"

"MR. SECRETARY," asked Andy Card, "would you mind calling Vernon Jordan to see if he would encourage Senator Kerry to concede?"

I've known Andy since 1979 or 1980, when he signed up to help organize Massachusetts for George H. W. Bush's first presidential run. He was a Republican state legislator back then, still in his early thirties. Andy came to Washington in the mid-1980s and through hard work, telling it like it is, and fierce loyalty, climbed the ranks in the Reagan and Bush 41 White House staffs to become secretary of transportation.

In November 2004 he was White House chief of staff for President George W. Bush, the same office I once held for Presidents Reagan and Bush. I'd worked with him a lot over the years, admired him, and regarded him as a friend. He had a low-key style, but was very effective and had President Bush's full confidence. When his tenure in the office extended longer than my own four-plus years, I joked that he had taken my place as the longest-serving chief of staff in the past fifty years, except for Eisenhower's Sherman Adams (who resigned in disgrace) and Nixon's H. R. Haldeman (who ended up in prison).

I've also known Vernon Jordan a long time. He's a mover and shaker in Washington with close ties to the Democratic Party, a deep friendship with Bill Clinton, and a wonderful sense of humor. We both try not to treat our political adversaries as enemies. Right after Governor Clinton won the 1992 election, Vernon came to my house to start talks about the presidential transition. He and I are both past presidents of Washington's Alfalfa Club, the only function of which is to hold one dinner each year to poke fun at ourselves and our national leaders.

In September 2004, Vernon and I negotiated the terms of the Bush-Kerry and Cheney-Edwards debates. Both of us had experience at this, and our talks were amiable and efficient, done mostly by telephone. Going in, the biggest issue was how many debates to have. As always, however, almost all other details of the event were also in contention. Would the candidates sit or stand? Where would the podiums be located? Who would ask questions? Would the candidates be permitted to address each other? Would there be warning and stop lights to keep the candidates within their time limits? (Senator Kerry initially didn't want them. His fallback position was that the lights should not be visible to the television audience.)

I proposed the following to Vernon: "You're gung ho for three debates, and we would probably prefer two, since our candidate is president and has a lead in the polls. I'm absolutely convinced that we can say we'll do only two and won't have to pay a political price. But I want to know if your side would be willing to give us everything we want on format, subject matter, duration, warning lights, and so on, if the president were to agree to do three."

Vernon's first reply was, "Well, I don't know." But after we had feinted back and forth for several days, he said, "Yeah, we'd be willing to do that."

I proposed this idea in a meeting in the White House residence with the president, Karl Rove, and Karen Hughes. The president was not eager to do three debates, initially, and Karen favored just two.

President Clinton had given Bob Dole only two, which would have been good precedent for saying no to more. But Karl and I supported three if we could get everything else we wanted.

"Mr. President, this is not the first time I've done this," I said. "I remember times when I was darn glad my candidate had another debate to make up for a poor performance in an earlier one."

He listened, then agreed. "Okay, if we get everything we want on the other issues."

As it turned out, the third debate was President Bush's best performance. He hit a home run. But you never know in advance how these things will turn out. I thought our bargain was a good one, and it certainly worked out well this time, but it could have bitten us in the tail.

After Vernon and I had tied up all the loose ends, we repaired to the bar of New York's Waldorf-Astoria to seal the agreement with martinis. Our conversation drifted back to 2000. "It's too bad what happened in Florida," we agreed, perhaps for different reasons. Then we began to muse. What if either candidate, Bush or Kerry, lost the popular vote and also lost the electoral vote by a narrow margin? Would it be appropriate for him to ask for recounts in one or two states—other than the recounts mandated by state law—to try to reverse the outcome in the Electoral College? I didn't think that would be appropriate, nor did Vernon. At that point, of course, we were just two guys nursing our drinks, not representatives of our candidates.

Which brings me back to my telephone call from Andy Card.

It was Wednesday morning, November 3, 2004, the day after the presidential election. I was on my way to the dentist. To all appearances, Bush-Cheney had defeated Kerry-Edwards by healthy margins in both the popular and electoral votes. The networks had called the election for the GOP, and they were right this time. George W. wound up with 50.6 percent of the popular vote (Kerry took 48.1 percent) and 286 electoral votes to Kerry's 252.

On Wednesday morning, however, Senator Kerry had yet to concede. He had his eyes on Ohio and its twenty electoral votes. When the counting ended that morning, the president was leading there by about 136,000 votes. The senator was said to be holding out hope that uncounted provisional ballots could give him the Buckeye State, which in turn would give him the Electoral College and the presidency.

Provisional ballots are those cast by voters whose names do not appear on the registration rolls at the local polling stations—for example, because of an administrative error. The top state election official estimated the number as high as 175,000 (which later turned out to be about 20,000 too high). Under state law, it would be November 13 before these ballots had been verified and tallied. If Senator Kerry wanted to wait out that process before conceding, we were in for a long wait.

Andy Card was the public face of the Bush-Cheney campaign on Wednesday morning. "We are convinced that President Bush has won reelection with at least 286 electoral votes," he told supporters, but "President Bush decided to give Senator Kerry the respect of more time to reflect on the results of this election."

Andy's call to me to see if I would ask Vernon Jordan to encourage his candidate to concede was clear evidence that in politics as in diplomacy, there are back channels.

"Sure," I said, "I'll give him a call. It took a while to track Vernon down by telephone. When I reached him, he was on the eleventh tee at Augusta National Golf Club, home of the Masters tournament. He didn't say he would or would not talk to Senator Kerry, but my suspicion is that he either weighed in or was about to when the senator called President Bush to concede at about 11:00 A.M. Eastern time.

That concession was absolutely the right thing to do. Senator Kerry had lost the popular election by almost three million votes and Ohio—after the provisional and overseas ballots were counted—by almost 119,000. There was no plausible way for him to have reversed the outcome.

George W. Bush won the 2004 election for a number of reasons. In large part it was a referendum on his leadership in the aftermath of the terrorist attacks of September 11, 2001. I also believe the debates helped him, on balance. Another big reason was simply that our side did a much better job of organizing and getting our voters to the polls. Turnout was more than 122 million, up about 16 percent from 2000, and the sixty-two million votes cast for the president broke the prior record by about eleven million.

I certainly didn't see this coming. On election day, I was in Washington, D.C., for a board meeting of the Howard Hughes Medical Institute. When I arrived back in Houston that afternoon, I was given the results of several exit polls that didn't look good for the president. I mentioned my concerns to Margaret Tutwiler. She happened to talk to Lynne Cheney later that day, and before long Dick Cheney was on the telephone to let me know the exit polls were wrong, as indeed they turned out to be. The more things change . . .

I LEFT full-time public service in 1993 after working for three great American presidents—Ford, Reagan, and Bush 41—each a man of character and each of whom left our nation in far better shape than he found it. An unexpected pleasure of later years has been adding a fourth name to that list, although in a more limited role.

Early in his first administration, President George W. Bush asked me to let him know each time I came to Washington, and I do. When it's convenient for him (and it usually is), he asks that I drop by for a private visit at the White House. I usually stay about thirty to forty-five minutes. We discuss whatever is on his mind—sometimes foreign or economic policy, sometimes politics, sometimes personnel. He wants me to be candid and frank, and I am. This idea that he is overly sensitive to critical comment is not accurate, as far as I'm concerned. And despite what a lot of pundits may imagine, I always speak for myself, not as a conduit from the president's father or anyone else. Finally, what I learn in confidence in those visits to the Oval Office stays in the Oval Office.

On a couple of occasions I have been asked by the president, or by the vice president on the president's behalf, whether I would consider a full-time position in the administration. I know how demanding and all-consuming these kinds of jobs are, however, so my reply in each case was the same: "I am extremely honored by the suggestion, but at my age and stage of life I do not think this is something I should do." Discussing the details of these inquiries would break my rule about respecting presidential confidences.

In addition to negotiating the ground rules for the debates in the 2004 election, I have taken other special assignments at the president's request—a diplomatic mission to former Soviet Georgia, a mission to win forgiveness of Iraqi debt, and service as cochair of the Carter-Baker federal election reform commission. At the request of members of Congress and with the approval of the White House, I recently agreed to cochair a bipartisan study group to conduct a forward-looking assessment of the situation in Iraq. In addition, I led presidential delegations to the twenty-fifth anniversary commemoration of the Solidarity movement in Poland and events commemorating the tenth anniversary of the assassination of Israel's prime minister, Yitzhak Rabin.

EDUARD SHEVARDNADZE was foreign minister of the Soviet Union during most of my tenure as secretary of state. We worked side by side as the Berlin Wall fell, Germany was reunited, Eastern Europe and Central Asia were released from Soviet domination, and an international alliance formed to liberate Kuwait from Iraq. Thanks to Eduard, the Cold War ended more quickly, more peacefully, and in a more orderly fashion than it otherwise might have. For that, he will have an honored place in history.

When it was all over, he went home to Georgia—a small country bounded by Russia, the Black Sea, Turkey, Armenia, and Azerbaijan. His countrymen called him back there after their experiment with freedom dissolved into chaos and internal violence. The elegant and soft-spoken man known to his countrymen as "Grandfather" or the "Silver Fox" had a reputation for honesty and hard work, and, serving as acting chairman of the state council, he quickly restored a degree of stability. Three years later Georgia adopted a new constitution and elected Eduard president.

In one of my last acts as secretary of state, I flew to Georgia in 1992 to show support for my old friend. A civil war was still raging. I could hear gunfire from the government guesthouse where I stayed, which had been the home of Joseph Stalin's infamous KGB chief, Lavrenty Beria. Tens of thousands of Georgians rallied in Freedom Square, and my diplomatic security agents nearly swallowed their walkie-talkies when Eduard and I went down to address the crowd amid all the burned-out buildings. Things were more peaceful when I visited again as a private citizen in 1994.

The Shevardnadze years in Georgia were mixed, at best. At times the economy showed signs of life, but Eduard had to fight hard to pre-serve the territorial integrity of Georgia against tremendous pressure from Russia and other neighboring countries. Eduard never succeeded in eradicating corruption—a fight that, in a twist of history, he had be-gun as a Soviet apparatchik in the 1960s, also without much success.

In addition, an estimated 260,000 Georgians were driven out of their homes by violence in outlying regions, much of it sparked by ethnic discord. And thousands more, many of them well-educated young adults, fled to Europe to find work.

Through it all, Eduard was steadfastly pro-Western, and the United States reciprocated with economic aid, diplomatic support, and low-level military support. In 1997, he visited the United States (and the Baker Institute). "Georgia's future security," I wrote at the time, "is important to America's security" because Georgia occupied a strategic location between the vast oil and gas resources of the Caspian Sea and international markets in the West.

No wonder, then, that the United States cared what happened in Georgia's tumultuous parliamentary elections of November 2003 and the presidential election that would come early the next year. Liberal reformers had substantial political support for taking Georgia in a new direction, but they feared that irregularities that had been evident in past Georgian elections would deprive them of their victory.

That's when the White House and State Department asked me to visit my old friend to impress upon him how important it was that the elections be free and fair. To lend authority to the undertaking, I was appointed as a special presidential envoy (SPE), without salary or benefits. On the flight to Georgia in early July 2003 on one of the White House's Air Force jets, I worked out a set of election guidelines—we called it "Scorecard for Georgian Elections"—with my traveling team, Elizabeth Jones, assistant secretary of state for European and Eurasian affairs, Matt Bryza from the National Security Council and Julie Fisher, the State Department's desk officer for Georgia. We were joined on the ground by the U.S. ambassador, Richard Miles. Among other things, we called for equal access to the media, independent election observers, and most important, perhaps, the rejection of violence by all sides.

It was not pleasant to tell an old friend how to run his nation's business, and we knew that fair elections would not necessarily go his way. As always, however, Eduard was gracious and did the right thing. "America has been providing Georgia with invaluable assistance since the very first day of its independence," he would say later, "and therefore [has] the moral right to give us friendly advice." He quickly signed the guidelines, as did the opposition. As far as I know, Eduard's government implemented the guidelines, except in those provinces that were out of its control.

That November, exit polls showed that the opposition had won, but for several days the election commission refused to certify the results. Tens of thousands of Georgians took to the streets in what came to be known as the Rose Revolution. Just as he had done at the end of the Cold War, Eduard refused to use force to preserve the old order. He held out a few days, then, facing the inevitable, he resigned.

Less than a year later, he lost his beloved wife, Nanuli. They had been married fifty-three years. Today he is writing his memoir. I still have a big warm spot in my heart for this man and his family. I had told him many times, as a friend, that life after politics was good and that he should not stay too long. Sadly, I am afraid, that is what he did. But he will be treated well by history for his refusal to support the use of force to keep the empire together when he was foreign minister of the Soviet Union.

LESS THAN two weeks after the Shevardnadze resignation, President Bush announced that I had accepted another assignment as special presidential envoy, this one concerning Iraq. "Secretary Baker will report directly to me and will lead an effort to work with the world's governments at the highest levels, with international organizations, and with the Iraqis in seeking the restructuring and reduction of Iraq's official debt," the White House announced on December 5, 2003.

The first administration contact about this mission came from Condi Rice, then the president's national security adviser, in October 2003 while I was at my Wyoming ranch. Earlier that same year, the U.S.-led military coalition had invaded and occupied Iraq. A necessary first step in rebuilding the devastated country was to get rid of the billions of dollars of Iraq's debt to other countries.

Saddam Hussein's government had borrowed far more money from other governments—an estimated $120 billion or more—than the people of Iraq would ever be able to repay. Much of it went for tanks and missiles, billions more for palaces and luxuries for the governing elite. After debt repayment, no money would be left over for humanitarian relief or to rebuild schools, hospitals, utility systems, and other infrastructure. And a financially crippled Iraq, like the Weimar Republic after World War I, would almost certainly guarantee permanent instability in Iraq. One more point: from a U.S. perspective, every dollar of debt relief would potentially be one less dollar that

the American taxpayer might have to be asked to pay toward reconstruction.

My debt-relief mission covered only government-to-government
(or sovereign) debt, not the billions more that Iraq owed to private
companies or the reparations the Security Council had ordered Iraq to
pay Kuwait after the first Gulf War. The idea was that I would do a
reprise of my tin-cup tour in the fall of 1990, when I went from capital to capital soliciting pledges of financial support for a military campaign to liberate Kuwait. This time, however, I would be asking
governments to write off their Iraqi debts.

Condi suggested that I operate through the Treasury Department.
"For this to work," I replied, "I have to be seen as a representative of
the president." That meant that my office, if I had one, had to be in the
White House, that I needed to report directly to George W. Bush, not
to a cabinet officer, and that I should meet with prime ministers and
other foreign heads of government, not with their finance ministers.

All this was agreed to, and I was again appointed as special presidential envoy. This time, however, I was actually put on the roster of
the White House as its lowest-paid employee at one dollar per year,
before taxes. I also had to take a drug test, which, fortunately, I passed.
With me standing by in the Oval Office, the president then telephoned
Jacques Chirac, Gerhard Schroeder, and other government leaders
and asked them to see me.

The president and I also talked about strategy. I don't recall the exact words, but my main point was that this would be a delicate mission,
in view of the opposition of many creditor nations—France, Germany, and Russia in particular—to Operation Iraqi Freedom. There
was no reason to think they were in a mood to do us any favors.

"Regardless of our disappointment with the way we were treated
by longtime allies, however, we can't let that disappointment cloud our
judgment," I said. "These alliances have meant a lot to us through the
years, and now we're up against a situation where we need them if
we're going to rebuild Iraq. So I want to be able to go to them and say

that we're reaching out." The president agreed, and I later used this in my talking points with foreign leaders.

On Monday, December 15, an Air Force 757 from the fleet available to the White House picked me up in Houston for a four-day trip to France, Germany, Italy, Great Britain, and Russia. I was delighted to get one of the big birds, usually reserved for the vice president, the secretary of state, or the secretary of defense. It had excellent facilities for staff, communications, and most of all, sleep, that vital friend of the successful diplomat. Traveling with me were the indispensable Gary Edson, deputy assistant to the president for international economic affairs and deputy national security adviser; Larry Greenwood, deputy assistant secretary of state; Clay Lowery, deputy assistant secretary of the treasury; and Sean McCormack, press spokesman from the National Security Council, all of whom offered superb support.

Our strategy was simple. *The president values our historic alliance and is grateful that you have received me. Our countries have had disagreements about Iraq, but we are reaching out and asking you to help the Iraqi people rebuild their country. These debts can never be repaid. By forgiving them, we simply accept that reality and move on, which will lift a dark shadow from Iraq's future. What the president seeks is your agreement to the principle of a substantial reduction in your country's debt in Iraq. We also seek your commitment to settle this matter quickly, in 2004.*

One thing I would not do, however, is talk numbers. The details could be settled by finance ministries. My job was to create momentum by winning commitments on very generous *words* at the political level that would translate into very large *numbers* at the technical level.

My meetings with President Chirac and others went remarkably well. In a joint statement, France and Germany pledged "substantial" reductions in the debts owed them by Iraq and urged other nations to do the same. Great Britain and Italy, both coalition allies, also gave their support. Russia agreed to consider the matter. Later that month, Japan raised the bar by agreeing to forgive the "vast majority" of its debts. China refused to be pinned down publicly, but privately assured me of a "big, big reduction." On a later trip to the Middle East, Qatar and the United Arab Emirates quickly signed on. Because of special circumstances, however, Kuwait (reparations) and Saudi Arabia (a dispute over whether payments were loans or grants) did not come to terms, and last I heard negotiations with these two countries were still ongoing. I also talked to leaders of several other countries by telephone.

By December 2004, a year after we started, the Paris Club—a consortium of nineteen industrialized countries that have worked together since the 1950s to help over-indebted countries—had agreed to an across-the-board reduction of *a minimum of* 80 percent, which was a new record for that organization. (The previous high, I have been told, was 67 percent.) Some creditors wrote off even more. The United States, for instance, forgave every dollar Iraq owed us—$4.1 billion. If this was not the largest debt-relief operation in history for a single nation, it was certainly one of the largest. Iraq's finance minister, Adil Abd al-Mahdi, called it "the second liberation of Iraq." And from my point of view, it also demonstrated how much good the developed nations can accomplish when they work together.

As I was putting this book to bed in early 2006, another opportunity for service on Iraq came my way. I was asked to cochair a bipartisan study group on Iraq. Our assignment: to make a forward-looking assessment of the situation there. The group was formed at the urging of members of Congress, but the White House welcomed it and agreed to help with travel, access to documents, and other assistance. (Anyone who has read this far knows I would not have taken this assignment without White House approval.)

My cochair is former congressman Lee Hamilton, a Democrat, who chaired the House Foreign Affairs Committee. He now heads the Woodrow Wilson International Center for Scholars, which will assist with the project, along with the United States Institute of Peace, the

Baker Institute, the Center for Strategic and International Studies, and the Center for the Study of the Presidency.

I don't have any illusions about the difficulty of the task. My hope is that we can develop insights and advice that will be helpful to the administration and to Congress, and that will benefit our country. To me, this study group has much the same mission as the Social Security commission in 1983. That group worked out a bipartisan consensus on a set of commonsense policies that helped Congress and the administration put aside considerations of political advantage and do what was best for our country on a very difficult and contentious issue. My hope, my prayer, is that the Iraq Study Group can do something similar.

IN THE 2000 Florida presidential election recount dispute, I objected strenuously to changing the rules in the middle of the game, not to the idea that election reforms might be needed. But those reforms should come by legislative action between elections, I believed, not by letting courts rewrite the rules while the votes were being counted.

In late 2004 I was challenged to put up or shut up on election reform. The call came from Ken Mehlman, head of the Republican National Committee. After the 2000 election, a commission headed by former presidents Jimmy Carter and Gerald Ford had recommended a package of election-law changes, some of which were enacted by Congress in 2002. Now President Carter wanted a new bipartisan commission to push for additional reforms, and unfortunately, President Ford no longer traveled.

This was not something I was eager to do, but I told Ken I would consider it. The commission would be a private undertaking, not anything official, and we were winning elections, not losing them, so I wondered why the administration cared about it. "Because," Karl Rove told me later, "President Carter will find a Republican who will be willing to serve, and we want someone on our side who won't get rolled."

I still hadn't made up my mind in January 2005 when I attended a White House dinner in honor of George H. W. Bush and Barbara Bush's sixtieth wedding anniversary. President Bush 43 sort of settled the issue for me, however, when he pulled me aside and said, "Thanks for being willing to do this federal election reform commission with President Carter."

"You're welcome, Mr. President."

I'm glad I accepted. Working as cochair with President Carter turned out to be a pleasure. We have had our political and policy differences in the past, and I'm sure we'll have more in the future, but he's a man of integrity who deserves credit and respect for promoting free and fair elections around the world, personally and through his Carter Center. In 1990, for instance, he worked with our Republican administration in connection with the elections in Nicaragua that replaced Daniel Ortega with Violeta Chamorro, ending more than a decade of violent conflict in that Central American nation. But for President Carter's moral authority, I doubt that Ortega would have accepted the results and stepped down.

We held hearings at American University, the Baker Institute, and the Carter Center. I was concerned that the commission would turn into a philosophical debating society, then make a bunch of pie-in-the-sky recommendations. That didn't happen. The report came out in September 2005, and it was a good one.*

"Americans are losing confidence in the fairness of elections," President Carter and I wrote, "and while we do not face a crisis today, we need to address the problems . . ." Our goals were to improve the administration of our elections, enhance their integrity, and increase voter participation.

The commission had eighty-seven recommendations. The big four, I think, were asking voters to present driver's licenses or other

---

*My assistant on the project was John Williams, a former political reporter for the *Houston Chronicle*. His writing skills, practical experience covering elections, and hard work with the commission staff had a lot to do with how well things turned out.

photo IDs when they show up to vote, improving our system for registering voters, turning elections over to nonpartisan administrators, and requiring electronic voting machines to print paper records that can be audited. The commission also asked states to do more to register potential voters and to supply IDs without cost for people who lacked driver's licenses.

States should take responsibility for the accuracy and integrity of their voting lists, we said—local officials do it now—and all state lists should be linked together through a national computer, so a prospective voter would need to register only one time.

Other recommendations included four regional presidential primaries; a request that the media wait until voting ends in all forty-eight contiguous states before projecting the results anywhere; and the enfranchisement of ex-felons who have done their time, except registered sex offenders and those convicted of capital crimes. That last one was something I would not have proposed myself, but I accepted it as part of the overall package.

All in all, the Commission on Federal Election Reform turned out to be a positive experience—practical in its aspirations, bipartisan in its spirit and approach, successful in its outcome.

In 2005, President George W. Bush also asked me to lead the presidential delegation to the twenty-fifth anniversary commemoration of the Solidarity movement in Poland. What a pleasure it was to renew old acquaintances (Lech Walesa, Bronislaw Geremek, Václav Havel), to reflect on how the spirit of Solidarity had transformed Poland and was still at work in peaceful democratic movements like the Rose Revolution in Georgia, and to read to the assembled dignitaries President Bush's letter of greeting.

Later that year, I also led the presidential delegation to the ceremonies commemorating the tenth anniversary of the assassination of Israel's prime minister, Yitzhak Rabin. If anything, this event was even more emotional, because Yitzhak—architect of the Oslo accords, advocate of peace, Nobel laureate—was also my friend. The ceremony at his grave on Mount Herzl in Jerusalem reminded us all of what he had done and, even more, what he might have done if he had not been cut down.

I saw and visited with many acquaintances and colleagues from the old days—among them, Ariel Sharon, Ehud Olmert, David Levy, Benjamin Netanyahu, and Eytan Bentsur. I had dinner one evening with Olmert, Condi Rice, and Sharon. "Tell the prime minister," I joked to Ehud, "that this is the only time I've ever come to Israel and he has not announced the creation of a new settlement." Ehud translated my remark to Prime Minister Sharon, who smiled and replied in English: "That's because I've used that trick before."

The irony, of course, is that Sharon, who long resisted the peace process, had now become a peacemaker himself. How sad, then, that he would be disabled by a severe stroke two months later. Time's winged chariot . . .

EIGHTEEN

"A SINGLE BLUEBELL"

IT's A TRADITION in the news business to prepare obituaries for prominent people before the event, and reporters also like to get their interview stories ready ahead of time. That's why my office telephone lit up in early June 2004. Ronald Reagan had been ill for almost ten years. Now word had spread that it was just a matter of time before Nancy lost Ronnie and our nation lost one of its greatest presidents. Journalists wanted my memories of the man and reaction to his death. Hour by hour, the list of press inquiries grew, but I didn't return the calls. I had nothing to say. One of my rules, rarely violated, is not to give past-tense interviews about anyone who is still alive. To me, it seems inappropriate.*

President Reagan's illness had cut him off from his friends long before death took his body. For years, however, I had made a point of visiting Nancy most every time I was in Southern California. Seeing her,

---

*In the years before President Reagan's death, I put one or two retrospective interviews in the can, but only because Nancy approved of my doing so, along with others who had served the president.

even for a few minutes, was my way of communicating love and respect, and it always refreshed my spirit.

My last conversation with the president came three days before his
eighty-third birthday at a February 1994 gala in his honor. I don't recall what we talked about—probably just social chitchat—but he was
in great spirits. His political soul mate, Margaret Thatcher, spoke that
night, and he always delighted in her presence. "It is an honor and a joy
to be here with you to celebrate the forty-fourth anniversary of your
thirty-ninth birthday," she joked.

A bit more than eight months later, President Reagan supplied a
taped message for the groundbreaking ceremony of the Baker Institute.
In the excitement of the moment, I failed to notice what is now evident
to me. His speeches usually soared, even for routine events. On this
day, however, his words fluttered to the earth, never quite taking wing.

Exactly sixteen days later, on November 5, 1994, he announced that
he suffered from Alzheimer's. "At the moment, I feel just fine," he wrote,
but he understood the burden his family would bear. "I only wish there
was some way I could spare Nancy from this painful experience."

"When the Lord calls me home, whenever that may be," he concluded, "I will leave with the greatest love for this country of ours and
eternal optimism for its future. I now begin the journey that will lead
me into the sunset of my life."

On Saturday, June 5, 2004, Margaret Tutwiler telephoned to say
the president had passed away. He was ninety-three. I was deeply saddened, but I took consolation in knowing that his suffering, and
Nancy's, had ended, and that he was in a better place.

Now I could talk, so I went to my office at the Baker Institute and
gave interviews until nine or ten that night, then got up early the next
morning for a couple of Sunday talk shows. Each contact with reporters was coordinated through the White House, at its request.

I repeated the Reagan story to all who cared to hear it. "Restored
America's pride . . . made everybody feel good . . . completely without
guile . . . big-picture president . . . stuck to his principles . . . changed

the world." And Nancy "has handled these final difficult years with dignity and grace."

I also mentioned that the Washington of Ronald Reagan's time was a more civil place than today. Political adversaries then were not treated as personal enemies. The president could fight all day with Tip O'Neill over public policy, then sit down with him over drinks that evening and share a laugh.

Early Wednesday, June 9, Susan and I caught a ride to Washington with George and Barbara Bush on the White House airplane sent to fetch the forty-first president and his first lady. That afternoon, President Reagan's coffin arrived from California and was pulled slowly up Constitution Avenue to the U.S. Capitol on a horse-drawn caisson, followed by a riderless horse.

Shortly after George, Barbara, Susan, and I arrived in Washington, we went by the Capitol Rotunda to pay our respects. The flag-draped coffin—brightly spotlighted, framed by a military honor guard—rested alone in that vast space on the same catafalque (I am told) used for President Lincoln. In a ceremony there a few hours earlier, Vice President Dick Cheney had eulogized President Reagan as a gentle man— "If Ronald Reagan ever uttered a cynical, or cruel, or selfish word, the moment went unrecorded"—and a powerful figure in history—"It was the vision and will of Ronald Reagan that gave hope to the oppressed, shamed the oppressors, and ended an evil empire." As we walked down the steps of the Capitol afterward, I wept. My emotions were still in turmoil when Susan and I went to sleep that night in the Lincoln Bedroom, guests of the forty-third president.

As thousands of mourners streamed through the Rotunda to pay their respects the next day, Susan and I accompanied George 41 and Barbara on a visit to Nancy at Blair House. We said all the right things, I am sure, but the fact is that she comforted us more than we comforted her. Nancy was a source of strength for her Ronnie. And as she accompanied him to Washington one last time—and later back to California— her love and devotion were a source of strength for us all.

The agency in charge of state funerals is the Military District of Washington, a unit of the U.S. Army, which worked out the details with the family well ahead of time. Mike Deaver had coordinated much of the planning for Nancy. Everything was prearranged, tightly scripted, and beautifully done. The staging would have delighted the former actor, I think. He was playing a leading role in a vast national drama, this one about love, remembrance, and heroism, an old pro hitting his marks one last time.

On Friday, Susan and I traveled in the president's motorcade from the White House to the National Cathedral for the memorial service. We entered in a Secret Service "security package" after most others—including all former presidents except 41—had been seated, which was a bit embarrassing.

Former senator Jack Danforth, an ordained Episcopalian minister, officiated. The text of the homily for President Reagan was based on the Sermon on the Mount, "'You are the light of the world. A city set upon a hill cannot be hid,'" Jack said. "For him, America was the shining city on a hill."

George H. W. Bush delivered one of the eulogies. "As his vice president for eight years, I learned more from Ronald Reagan than from anyone I encountered in all my years of public life," he said. "I learned kindness [and] I also learned courage."

Margaret Thatcher, present for the funeral service but not well, spoke by prerecorded tape. While "others hoped, at best, for an uneasy cohabitation with the Soviet Union," she said, "he won the Cold War—not only without firing a shot, but also by inviting enemies out of their fortress and turning them into friends."

As the former British prime minister's distinctive voice filled the cathedral, she sat quietly, head bowed. In the chair immediately to her right was one of the friends she had in mind, Mikhail Gorbachev, invited (like her) as a special guest of the Reagan family.

"For the last years of his life, Ronnie's mind was clouded by illness," she said. "That cloud has now lifted. He is himself again—more himself than at any time on this earth. For we may be sure that the Big Fella Upstairs never forgets those who remember Him."

The outpouring of love and affection, and deep respect, for this former president—in the ceremonies and on the street—was overwhelming. His supporters had always loved him, but now everyone, including some of his old detractors, had come to realize something that those of us who worked with him knew about his character, his integrity, and his performance as president.

Even members of the media, many of whom had abhorred his policies, could never bring themselves to dislike him as a person. And now that he was gone, many journalists and commentators, to their credit, admitted the obvious—that he had changed the nation and the world for the better.

I've had a lot to say, pro and con, about the impact of television on American politics and public life, but an event like this one demonstrates the power of the medium to unite our country around shared experiences, this time in celebrating the life of a great president and mourning his passing.

I owe my career in politics and public service to my friend George H. W. Bush, but I also owe it to President Reagan. Who else would have had the confidence, the comfort in his own judgment, to hire the campaign chairman for two political rivals as White House chief of staff? How was I fortunate enough to serve this wonderful man for eight years? My life was forever changed by his one generous decision to invite me into his administration, and I tried every day to be worthy of that honor. I loved him dearly.

That's one of the things I told Nancy at Blair House the day before. After everyone else had said their goodbyes, I lingered a bit. "Nancy, I want to tell you one more time," I said, "how appreciative I am for having had the opportunity to serve the president."

"We're very grateful," she replied, my hands in hers, "for what you did for us."

I left the room in tears.

. . .

AFTER THE memorial service, I waited for my ride in a group at the side entrance of National Cathedral, along with President Carter and Rosalynn, President and Senator Clinton, Senator Kerry, and others. I think George and Barbara were there, too. I was talking with Rosalynn when someone grabbed me from behind, turned me around, and gave me a big hug and kiss. My osculatory partner was none other than Teresa Heinz Kerry, wife of the presumptive Democratic nominee for president. She and her first husband, Senator John Heinz, were friends of Susan's and mine before his death in a 1991 air crash. This was the first time we had seen her in years, and she was as vibrant as ever. Although he didn't kiss me, John Kerry was also very friendly. I didn't know the incident had been caught on camera until my friends kidded me about it later.

After the ceremony, George, Barbara, Susan, and I rushed back to Houston. Forty-one was turning eighty, and a long-planned party for him was scheduled for Saturday night in Minute Maid Park. The next day, he went skydiving over the Bush Library in College Station, Texas—a stunt that made me wonder whether he was aching for his own funeral!

A FRIEND later told me he was fascinated by the aftermath of President Reagan's funeral. Cameras followed some dignitaries as they left the cathedral, and he was struck by the sight of former national leaders and world leaders setting off down the sidewalk by themselves, without fanfare, destined in all likelihood to fade into the crowd.

I was not surprised by this. When I was President Reagan's chief of staff back in the early eighties, I saw my counterpart from a former administration walking down Pennsylvania Avenue. Once he had been at the center of American public life. This day, however, he was by himself—no reporters, no security, no trappings of power—just a solitary man, unnoticed, alone with his thoughts. Ever after, that mental picture served to remind me of the impermanence of power and place.

Three things helped me stay grounded during my years in the spotlight—my family, my friends, and my faith. I've talked about my family throughout the book, and will return to that subject. But for my friends, of course—and in particular George H. W. Bush, but also Gerald Ford, Rog Morton, Dick Cheney, Stu Spencer, Mike Deaver, and Bob Teeter—most of this book would have been blank pages. I have only alluded, however, to the role of faith, and I want to say more about this.

I had been a churchgoer and a regular participant in small-group worship, but the first time I spoke openly about my faith was at the National Prayer Breakfast in 1990. Of all the speeches I've ever given, the transcript for this one is the most requested.

Many believe faith is more difficult for those in public life. For me, at least, the exact opposite was true. Living in the centrifuge of politics encouraged, even demanded, spiritual growth. That life was certainly exciting and, in many ways, satisfying. But power can also be intoxicating and addictive. "Power tends to corrupt, and absolute power corrupts absolutely," Lord Acton said, and I think that's true. I've felt the temptation myself, and it's unsettling.

In addition, temporal power is fleeting. I cleaned out my desk in January 1993 and became a private citizen. Like the lonely chief of staff I had spotted on Pennsylvania Avenue so many years before, all my titles now had "former" in front of them. As my public prominence diminished, I also discovered that I could stand on busy street corners and walk through airports without being recognized. This was liberating in a way, but also—truth be told—disquieting.

Power has its satisfactions, but inner security and the deepest kind of personal fulfillment are not among them. It is only through a relationship with God, not by our actions here on earth, that life has real meaning. And for me, at least, a life of faith does not come easily. I have to work at it.

One blessing of faith is that you can see God's handiwork in the events of your life. When I was secretary of state, for instance, a great revolution swept Eastern Europe and the former Soviet Union. As the Berlin Wall fell, dictators were toppled, the Soviet Union collapsed, and communism was consigned to President Reagan's "ash heap of history," it was hard not to see the profound influence of the religious beliefs of those who were freed from tyranny. I do not discount the role of human agency or the powerful economic and political causes of this revolution, but I believe it also had a spiritual source.

I'll never forget my September 1989 meetings in Wyoming with former Soviet Foreign Minister Eduard Shevardnadze. He and I ended our very productive round of negotiations with an exchange of gifts. I gave him cowboy boots. He gave me an enamel picture of Jesus teaching the people. "You see, even we communists are changing our worldview," he said.

He was right. Communism had denied the very existence of God and treated individuals as servants of the state, but the political revolution that swept Eastern Europe and the former Soviet Union brought with it a resurgence of faith. Individuals were affirmed as children of God, each equally worthy of respect, free to choose, and responsible for their choices.

Václav Havel, then president of Czechoslovakia, said his country's democratic revolution was a moral event, restoring the faith, compassion, humility, and forgiveness that communism had opposed. It was no accident that the churches of Eastern Europe played such an important part in these political changes. Despite decades of oppression, the people of God maintained their integrity as custodians of the faith and guardians of the dignity of individual men and women.

There was a lesson for the United States in these events. Lech Walesa, the hero of a free Poland, once said, "Americans were drifting away from spiritual values as they become richer." "Sooner or later," he said, "we will have to go back to our fundamental values, back to God, the truth, the truth which is God." This is a useful reminder, I believe, that the great political experiment of the United States was, and continues to be, a great spiritual experiment as well. President Kennedy had this in mind, I think, when he closed his inaugural address with these words: "here on earth God's work must truly be our own."

MY INSTINCT as a young man was to go it alone. I loved my friends, but I was slow to accept their help in getting through life. If you were strong enough, if you prepared carefully enough, and if you worked hard enough, I believed, you could do it all yourself. Self-reliance meant never admitting you needed help. If you suffered pain, you endured it. If you had problems, you solved them.

The truth, however, is that we can't do it alone. We need each other. Friends are especially important in times of personal distress. I've written about how I lost my first wife, Mary Stuart, to cancer when she was only thirty-eight. My friends helped save my life. They were there with me at her bedside during the last days. There to help our four boys—heartbroken, scared, confused. And there to stand with Susan and me as we put two families together at a very difficult time in the lives of our seven children.

My public career was a monument to the friendships I made along the way. I also developed close relationships with many of the young people who worked with me. We formed a team, and their judgment, creativity, hard work, and loyalty were responsible for much of what we accomplished together. That's why I have mentioned so many of them in this book, and I wish there was room to mention many others. In the end, however, we do not choose our friends because of what they can do for us. They are the people we love and trust, and whose company we enjoy.

MY OTHER ANCHOR has always been my family. My mother, Bonner Means Baker, taught me—by precept and example—many of the values that have guided me. I will always treasure her memory. That's why I dedicated my first book, in part, "to my wonderful mother, whose love and support gave me wings to fly."

The other dedication went to "my great-grandfather, my grandfather, and my father, the three generations of James Addison Bakers whose belief in God, integrity, and hard work gave me a remarkable heritage that inspired me." It's hard to explain what it means to carry the same name as such accomplished men. From childhood, I was simply expected to succeed. I was also given the love and support to allow me to do well in life. Without this legacy, I doubt that I would have ever had the education, the experiences, or the confidence my public life demanded.

I'm not sure I did as well for my own children as my father and grandfather did for me. I loved them all dearly, but when they were young I worked hard in my big-firm law practice and left most of the child-rearing to Mary Stuart. We were a happy family, but I wish I had spent more time with the boys.

One of the biggest mistakes in my life was not telling them how ill their mother was. Another was surprising them three years later with my marriage to Susan. My four and Susan's three knew one another beforehand, so that helped with the blending, but it was a rough time for all of them—losing one parent through death or divorce, dealing with the disloyalty (from a child's perspective) of the remaining parent's remarriage, then sharing that parent's attention with other children.

The family name that was such an asset to me sometimes proved to be a burden for my children. They were the fifth generation of a distinguished family, with a father whose name was often in the newspapers. It was natural for them to wonder, I suspect, whether their best would ever be good enough. "Why can't we just be a normal family?" one child wondered aloud.

Some in our family struggled with alcohol and drug abuse during their teen and early adult years. We had the resources, thank God, to help them find the treatment they needed, and we are very proud of how they have put their problems behind them.

It was Susan who ran the car pools to four different schools and countless after-school activities, bought the groceries, kept the chart in the kitchen to determine which teenager got the station wagon on which night, and explained why Daddy wasn't home. The way I knew it was time to get up many mornings was when I heard the *whack, whack* of her knees hitting the floor to pray for our family.

The joy of my life is that those prayers were answered. When our family gathered for Thanksgiving about eight or ten years ago, I asked everyone to say in one sentence what they were thankful for. "I'm thankful," one of my sons said, "that my parents didn't give up on me." I want to say to our children—for the world to hear—how thankful and proud I am to be their father and stepfather.

In MID-MAY of 2002, I found myself tromping through the woods of northwestern Alabama with a group of distant cousins I had never met before. They were descendants of Mary Jane Baker, a sister of the first James Addison Baker, who had married a James Carroll and produced a large family that still has its roots around Florence, Alabama. We came into a small opening that showed evidence of a lot of fresh work with axes and weed trimmers, and there—amid thirteen small American flags pushed into the ground to decorate the site for my visit—I saw the gravestone of our common great-great-grandfather, Elijah Baker, 1792–1845. Hunters had recently found it, and my cousins had reclaimed it from the encroaching forest.

Later that day, I told this story in a commencement speech at the University of North Alabama in Florence. "We are all embedded in history," I told the graduates. "It shapes us. It defines our opportunities. And it challenges us."

The first James Addison Baker and four brothers left Alabama in the early 1850s and planted themselves in Huntsville, Texas. James

Baker's first wife had died early, and he was probably looking for a fresh start. He soon met and married Rowena Crawford, the principal of the Huntsville (Texas) Female Academy, and that's how my Baker ancestors wound up in Texas.

It's an interesting story, one I have heard repeated all my life. My family scrapbooks contain old handwritten genealogies that trace our history back to Elijah Baker (and trace some branches even further back), but I've never really been much of a genealogy buff myself. What I take from family history is the idea that we did not invent ourselves. The past lives in us and we are, individually and as a nation, the beneficiaries of untold generations of love and toil and sacrifice. It is our responsibility, in turn, to pass on these same values to future generations.

In *The Politics of Diplomacy,* I wrote that President George H. W. Bush characterized our friendship "as a big brother–little brother relationship." "I think that's a fairly accurate description," I said in the book, "and one that I consider quite a compliment."

Well, according to genealogist William Addams Reitwiesner, George and I are not brothers; we're long-lost cousins. Reitwiesner makes this claim on a Web site—"Ancestry of George W. Bush"—that my staff ran across while doing research for this book. The site traces the Bush family history to colonial America and beyond. At the end of his genealogical database, Reitwiesner reports that two of George's remote ancestors are also mine—Richard Cocke and Mary Aston. They lived in Henrico County, Virginia, in the 1600s. One son (Richard, Jr.) was George's ancient grandpa, and another (William) was mine.

I've always been suspicious of far-out claims of kinship and there's no way for me to judge the accuracy of Reitwiesner's work, other than to say that the bottom of his twelve-generation chart of my ancestry is consistent with Baker family records. My staff asked him about his sources, and he said two of Captain James A. Baker's sisters (my great-aunts) had joined the Daughters of the American Revolution, "and their lines take Mr. Baker back to pre-revolutionary Caroline County, Virginia. From there," he said, "it's trivially easy to make the connection to the Cockes and Astons that the Bushes descend from."

Is it true, then, that I am a distant cousin of my close friend, my tennis partner, the man who led me into politics and public service? All I can say is that the Bush-Baker family connection is such a perfect story that I plan to believe it until someone proves it ain't so. Maybe I'll drop *Jefe* and start saying *cousin.**

It rained on the cold November day in 2004 that I was supposed to give an outdoor speech in the Oakwood Cemetery in Huntsville, Texas. That's where my great-grandfather, the first James Addison Baker, is buried, along with his friend Sam Houston, the general who won Texas independence, served as its first president, then—after annexation—as U.S. senator and governor. The Texas Historical Commission had authorized a marker for my great-grandfather's grave, and I was invited to attend the ceremony to install the marker and say a few words.

Susan and I got out of our car and started walking to the cemetery under a dripping umbrella, when we were stopped by a very tall, attractive gentleman, who approached from the other direction. I had never seen him before.

"How do you do, sir?" he said, extending his hand. "My name is James Baker."

---

*I am less confident in, but intrigued by, the possibility that I also share common ancestry with Thomas Jefferson. In reviewing the Bush-Baker connection, my researcher (who is not a genealogist) noticed that one branch of my ancestral family, the Blands, traced back to Richard Bland and Elizabeth Randolph. This is something my family has known, or at least claimed, for many years. My researcher said it appeared plausible to him that Elizabeth Randolph was the daughter of William Randolph and Mary Isham, Thomas Jefferson's maternal grandparents. If it's true, the sixty-first secretary of state would be a distant cousin of the first one.

"That's interesting," I said, playing along. "My name is James Baker, too."

"I know," he replied. "I have followed your career for a long time. I'm your cousin."

His name was James Otis Baker. Though born nearby, he had lived most of his life in Los Angeles. He quickly introduced me to his brother, Wendell Baker, who still lived in Huntsville.

I wasn't sure whether to take them seriously, but they seemed genuine in their assertion of kinship. In my remarks a few minutes later, I introduced my children and other relatives who were present at the event. Then, not quite knowing if I myself were serious, I introduced my "just-discovered cousins."

James Otis and Wendell Baker—handsome African-American men—smiled as the crowd turned to identify them.

Afterward, a woman warned me to be careful. "That Wendell Baker is an agitator," she whispered.

"WHAT ARE these called?"

It was Sunday, July 3, 2005, and I was driving through the woods just southwest of Huntsville with my newfound cousins, James Otis, eighty-six, and Wendell, eighty-two. Out the window, I spotted a beautiful flower.

"They're called bluebells," Wendell said.

"May I pick one?"

"Pick as many as you want."

Jesse Baker was James's and Wendell's father, and their family still owned the sandy-soiled acreage and the old home place—off "Baker Road"—where Jesse and his wife, Fannie Willis, had farmed and reared their children. Jesse's father was Andy Baker, my grandfather's first cousin. Andy had had a relationship with an African-American woman named Emma Curtis, which made James and Wendell my third cousins.

They had told me about Andy and Jesse that rainy day the preceding November when I first met them, but they mistakenly thought "Andy" was a nickname for Robert Baker, a brother of my grandfather. They also invited me to attend the biennial reunion of Jesse Baker's descendants. I accepted, and that's how I came to be riding through the woods with them on a hot Sunday afternoon in July, eight months later.

Susan and I had arrived at Wendell's home about an hour earlier, along with two of our sons, John and Mike, and Mike's daughter Mary. (Some of my Houston Baker cousins showed up later.) It was a lovely brick residence on a large green lot shaded by towering pines. The living room walls were covered with scores of family pictures—formal portraits, wedding pictures, graduation shots—including one of a smiling Jesse Baker in a suit, tie, and hat. It was similar in style to the photographs of my grandfather when he was young.

I had had the family connection researched, and I explained what I had learned to James Otis and Wendell. "Your great-grandfather was Gabriel Baker," I told them. "Judge James Addison Baker and Gabriel were sons of Elijah Baker, whose grave I saw when I went to speak at a graduation ceremony at the University of North Alabama in 2002. My great-great-grandfather, Elijah, was also your great-great-grandfather."

Gabriel had a son named Andy, I said. He was born in 1864, one year before the Civil War ended, and he would have been about twenty-three when Jesse was born in 1887. According to research done by Dr. Bernadette Pruitt, a history professor at Sam Houston State University, Andy acknowledged his son, wanted him to have the Baker name, and (by one account, which Wendell disputes) helped provide for Jesse until adulthood. (I have no way of knowing who is right about the question of support, but I hope Andy did that.)

When he grew up, Jesse farmed cotton and vegetables with mule-drawn plows, bought and sold land, and cut pulpwood and timber, James Otis and Wendell told me. "Everybody worked for my dad in the summer. He'd buy the land just to get the trees off it. And if he ran out of money, the bank wouldn't bounce his check."

Jesse had eleven sons and daughters, they told me. One was Herbert, who married a beautiful woman named Mackie. As a boy, I actually knew her. She worked for my grandfather, Captain Baker, and lived with her husband in Houston in a house behind the Captain's residence. The Houston Bakers "didn't know who she was," Wendell said. "We laughed about it."

My grandfather might well have known about Jesse because Andy is buried in the same cemetery plot with Captain Baker, who was his cousin. I don't know whether Mackie's employment was merely a coincidence or happened because she was married to a grandson of Andy Baker. One thing's for sure, however: no one ever told me or others of my generation of Houston cousins anything about this other branch of our family.

At the reunion, I couldn't help thinking about how much things had changed since my grandfather's day, and for the better. In the early 1890s, Captain Baker and other Houston leaders wrote a charter to establish what is now Rice University as a first-class institute for the "white inhabitants of Houston and Texas." That kind of overt discrimination seems foreign to us now, but it was standard back then and evidently what the founder, William Marsh Rice, dictated. University trustees went to court in 1963 and got the racial restrictions eliminated.

Wendell and Jesse told me with pride about their accomplished family and in-laws. Teacher. Lawyer. Judge. Social worker. Entrepreneur. Health inspector. First African-American deputy sheriff in Harris County. Mathematician. Jazz prodigy. Network budget officer. Vice president at Disney–ABC Television Group. Marriage to a son of James Lawson, the intellectual architect of the nonviolent civil rights movement. (Lawson "is the guy who got Mandela out of prison and he is the one who taught Dr. King the power of nonviolence," Wendell said.)

As for Wendell's being an agitator—"and a troublemaker, too," he added cheerfully—that stemmed from civil rights work, including the registration of black voters throughout East Texas in the early 1960s and the peaceful racial integration of Sam Houston State University.

Wendell explained his motivation this way: "I said to myself, 'I have served in the army to defend America.' I said, 'We've been good citizens. We're taxpayers. We're a productive family. Hell, I'm not going to take it.'"

One of his most fascinating stories was how he helped lead a movement in 1961 to throw African-American support to Republican senatorial candidate John Tower. Conservative Anglo Democrats had locked African Americans and Mexican Americans out of the party, according to Wendell, and anointed a candidate he and other minority leaders regarded as a racist.

"Boy, we wiped 'em out. We put John Tower in there," he said. And afterward, "calling Tower was just like calling my brother. He'd pick up the phone and say, 'What do you want?' We got blacks appointed to all sorts of offices."

I told Wendell and James Otis about having the support of several African American leaders, including Barbara Jordan and Mickey Leland, when I ran for attorney general as a Republican against a conservative Democrat in 1978. "Barbara Jordan," Wendell said wistfully. "She understood."

Wendell then passed around a copy of his book, *If Not Me, Who? What One Man Accomplished in His Battle for Equality*. It's a fascinating read, including an appendix at the end filled with his aphorisms. "Make changes, but use the system to do it." "Compromise, but never when you get nothing." "Results count; excuses don't!"

In telling these political yarns, Wendell and I were not ignoring the likelihood that we had spent most of our political careers on different sides of many important issues. We were just doing what we should have done, which was to start our relationship on the basis of what we had in common, not what we might disagree about. At our ages, we'll probably never get around to the other stuff anyway, and it doesn't much matter whether we do. We did our part. The rest belongs to younger generations.

James Otis sat quietly while his younger brother told political stories, interjecting only once that I should have run for president. "I'll
tell you, you did a good job," he said. "You know how to go and talk to
people. You straightened out things."

On the way to the reunion, I had stopped by the family cemetery
in Houston and copied the inscription off Andy Baker's gravestone. I
now read it to his grandchildren. "They who knew him best will bless
his name and keep his memory dear while life shall last." He never
married, I told them. Jesse was his only child.

The reunion itself was wonderful. It was held a mile or so away at
the home of one of Wendell's sons, Bruce, in and around a beautiful
hardwood-shaded home down the hill from the main road. Out front,
he displayed an old disk harrow, a symbol of his family's heritage.

When I arrived, barbeque was sizzling on big cookers, kids were
running everywhere, and probably 150 relatives were swapping stories
and studying a large board that displayed their family history. James
Otis and Wendell introduced me to their sister, Leola. They were the
last living children of Jesse Baker.

The day brought a swirl of emotions. A year ago, this branch of my
family was unknown to me. Now Susan and I were being accepted
with open arms and sweet spirits. I was profoundly moved by this experience and pleased to have had the opportunity to learn about them
and to reminisce with them about our mutual great-great-grandfather.

James Otis quietly shared memories of his beloved wife with Susan.
Baker relatives came by, one by one, to shake hands, explain how they
fit into the family, and welcome us. We posed for group photographs.
Jokes were told. Children ran past, kicking up dust and wondering who
these old people were. In these ways, two families acknowledged and
embraced each other, becoming one family, quietly and happily.

Reverend Chris Bell, a great-grandchild of Jesse Baker, blessed the
meal. "Holy Father," he said, "thank you for another opportunity for
fun and fellowship, and for all those who have come such a long
way. . . . Bless this food, Father God, that it would be a nourishment to
our bodies. In the name of Jesus, Amen."

Our hosts pushed us to the head of the line, and Susan and I stacked our plates with brisket, sausage, ribs, potato salad, beans, tomatoes, onions, and sliced bread. Then we went inside Bruce's home to enjoy our feast. In her lovely strawberry blond hair, Susan wore a single bluebell.

EPILOGUE

Work Hard, Study... and Keep Out of Politics! hit the bookstores on October 5, 2006, and I hit the road that same day to promote the book. Over the next few weeks, I participated in more than seventy radio, television, and print interviews, speeches, and book signings.

I sat down with Charlie Rose, Jim Lehrer, Diane Sawyer, Jon Stewart, and many others. With a few exceptions, they asked me not about my decades-long friendship with George H. W. Bush. Nor about the collapse of the Soviet Union. Nor about Reaganomics, tax policy, nor even how Republicans won the controversial Florida 2000 recount battle.

They asked about Iraq.

This was understandable. Three and one-half years after the invasion, American soldiers were still fighting in the streets of Baghdad and in other towns and cities across the country. Just over a month after the book was published, concern over Iraq tipped the 2006 midterm elections to the Democrats. And sixty-two days after the book came out—a pure accident of timing—the bipartisan Iraq Study Group (the ISG) published its long-awaited recommendations about the way forward for U.S. policy in Iraq.

I was cochairman of the group and when I showed up to discuss the book, my interviewers had the choice of chatting up a seventy-six-year-old guest about his memories of three decades in politics and public service—ancient history in today's bang, bang media environment—or about Iraq, the hottest issue in a hot political season.

The ISG report was still being drafted while I was on the road, and our group had studiously attempted to stay off the media's radar screen. If our internal discussions went public, we believed, we would be lobbied by partisans, our positions might harden before we had heard all the evidence, and our freedom of action might be narrowed. We also believed a low profile would lower expectations about our project. There truly was no magic bullet to solve all the problems in Iraq, we agreed, and we didn't want to build up expectations that we could not meet.

Lowering expectations is a time-honored tradition in Washington, and the ISG had done a good job of it. Some newspapers published short articles about our first meeting in March. Another round of perfunctory stories greeted our return from a September fact-finding mission to Baghdad. About all we said at the follow-up press conference was that we were still working. Until October, at least, the media had largely ignored the ISG, and that was fine with us.

Another principle the ISG followed—besides lowering expectations—was to look forward, not backward. Was the 2003 invasion good policy or a mistake? Had the occupation of Iraq been handled well or badly? Those issues belonged to politicians, voters, and, ultimately, historians. We were not going to be Monday-morning quarterbacks. For better or worse, the United States and its allies had invaded and occupied Iraq, and things weren't going well. Those were the facts. Now what?

The group also agreed that we could be effective only if we developed a unanimous bipartisan consensus. That's why the group had equal cochairmen—me, a Republican, and Lee Hamilton, a leading voice among Democrats on foreign policy issues—and equal numbers of Republican and Democratic members. And that's also why we worked hard to develop a plan that every member could support. Just as a unanimous Supreme Court decision usually commands greater respect than a 5–4 decision, we believed that the ISG had a better chance of influencing policy if we all stood together on every recommendation.

We also agreed not to release our report until after the November midterm congressional elections. But waiting was not easy. In late spring, conditions in Iraq were deteriorating, and some members wanted to issue an interim report that summer. On reflection, however, we agreed to wait until near the end of the year. For one thing, we needed the time for research. For another, we wanted to stay out of the political debate in the run-up to the election. That approach, we believed, would increase the chances that our report would be accepted by both sides.

When we finally issued the report in early December, it was the first—and so far, remains the only—truly bipartisan plan for U.S. policy in Iraq. I'm proud of our unanimity, and I'm also proud that the report was so well received by policy-makers and the public. I only wish we had been more successful at lowering expectations, because the media buildup made it difficult for President Bush to accept all of our recommendations. And my book tour, sadly, contributed to that media buildup.

When I was asked about Iraq during the book tour, I largely repeated what I had said in this memoir. (See chapter thirteen.) Yes, administration turf battles had hurt the planning and implementation of war policy. Yes, the Department of Defense had made some "costly mistakes" in its conduct of the war and its administration of occupied Iraq.

After the first Gulf War in 1991, I told interviewers, I was often asked why, after liberating Kuwait, the U.S.-led coalition had left Saddam Hussein in power. I answered that neither our allies nor the United Nations had signed on for regime change. Furthermore, we believed at the time that to remove Saddam from power would have forced us to occupy all of Iraq and would have exposed us to sectarian violence—exactly what happened in the aftermath of the 2003 invasion. Why hadn't we marched on Baghdad and taken Saddam out? "Nobody asks me that question anymore," I said.

But I also reminded interviewers that in 2003 virtually everyone—including the French, the Russians, and a majority of congressional Democrats—believed Saddam possessed weapons of mass destruction. Furthermore, Saddam had violated UN resolutions for twelve years, and regime change in Iraq had been U.S. policy since the Clinton administration. In the post-9/11 environment, American patience with Saddam finally ran out.

In the same interviews, however, I also urged a broader diplomatic effort to bring peace to the region, including direct talks with Iran and Syria. "It took me fifteen visits to Syria before I could persuade President Hafez Assad to change years of policy and come to the table at the Madrid Conference to negotiate with Israel," I said. "Talking with your enemies is not appeasement—not a sign of weakness—provided it is done in the right way."

I was speaking for myself, of course, not the Iraq Study Group, but my interviews made news and clearly ratcheted up expectations for the ISG. Then the hype started.

After the Democrats' midterm election victory, Don Rumsfeld resigned as secretary of defense, and President Bush nominated the very able Bob Gates to replace him. Gates was a friend and a former CIA director for President Bush 41. He was also someone I had recruited as a member of the Iraq Study Group, though he quickly and properly resigned after his nomination. The next thing I knew, I was on the cover of *Newsweek* with Lee Hamilton, and pundits were noisily suggesting that President Bush was being forced to seek help from his father's advisers.

We released *The Iraq Study Group Report: The Way Forward—A New Approach* on December 6, 2006. Unfortunately, it had already largely been debated in print and on the airwaves, based on fragmentary leaked reports (some erroneous) of what it was expected to say. Still, more than 120 news outlets showed up at our 11 A.M. news conference, and all major television networks, including cable, broadcast large portions of the event live.

Four hours before the press conference, President Bush graciously met in the Cabinet Room of the White House with all ten ISG members and told us that he genuinely appreciated our willingness to undertake the effort. He already knew what was in our report, however, because a day earlier, with the consent of the group members, I had briefed him. The president thanked us for our service and listened carefully, but in the days that followed, press reports said he was cool to our proposals.

The president subsequently said that he wanted to move the Iraq issue toward the positions we recommended in our report. But I understand his reluctance to do so initially. A president governs best from a position of strength, and the press buildup for the ISG report—including the "father knows best" and the "administration is subcontracting out its foreign policy" analysis—had put him in a position where acceptance could have been seen as giving in to pressure from the media and political rivals. Furthermore, early and erroneous press reports had misinterpreted the very conditional March 2008 goals in our report as a firm deadline for a withdrawal of U.S. combat troops.

Although the president may have been slow to accept all of the ISG's recommendations, he fully supported the process. The Iraq Study Group was the brainchild of Frank Wolf, a Republican congressman from Virginia. In the fall of 2005, he concluded that a bipartisan commission might offer the best hope of developing a way forward in Iraq that could be embraced by the president, Congress, and the public. He first kicked the idea around with respected think tanks, then suggested Lee Hamilton and me as cochairs of the group.*

---

*The think tanks were the United States Institute for Peace (headed by Dick Solomon), the Center for the Study of the Presidency (David Abshire), the Center for Strategic and International Studies (John Hamre), and the Baker Institute for Public Policy at Rice University (Ed Djerejian). These four institutions served as sponsors for the project. Congress authorized the ISG on March 15, 2006, and two months later funded our project with $1 million.

Lee is a former Democratic congressman from Indiana who now heads the Woodrow Wilson International Center for Scholars. He is an able, respected, and dedicated former public servant. Secretary of State Condoleezza Rice also called me about the project and said the administration would like me to cochair it.

Before I accepted, however, I met with President Bush and asked if he really wanted me to serve. I did this out of personal loyalty to him and his family, out of respect for the office, and for an important practical reason: the project had little chance of success if he opposed it. I also did not want to appear to be somehow undercutting his authority on the issue that had come to define his presidency. Being commander in chief is difficult enough without having "friends" publicly second-guess your policies.

Lee and I each selected four other panel members. We wanted strong, successful men and women who had earned the public's trust and respect, and whose presence would lend credibility to the project. We also wanted participants who would work for nothing except personal satisfaction. ISG members were to receive no compensation.*

After panel members were selected, we organized the project and formed staff working groups.† Foreign policy analysts and Iraq experts

---

*I picked former Supreme Court associate justice Sandra Day O'Connor, former Wyoming senator Alan Simpson, former New York City mayor Rudy Giuliani, and former CIA director Bob Gates. Rudy later resigned when he saw that he could not attend to his responsibilities at the ISG while ramping up a presidential campaign. He was replaced by former U.S. attorney general Ed Meese, an old pal from our days in the first Reagan administration. As mentioned, Gates also left the panel when he was asked to serve as secretary of defense. He was replaced by former secretary of state Larry Eagleburger, a savvy and trusted colleague of mine in the Bush 41 administration. Lee selected an equally distinguished group: former Virginia governor and senator Chuck Robb, former congressman and Clinton chief of staff Leon Panetta, former National Urban League head and Clinton adviser Vernon Jordan, and former secretary of defense Bill Perry.

† Key to our project were Dick Solomon, Dan Serwer, Paul Hughes, and others at the United States Institute for Peace, which provided logistical and scholarly support. Ambassador Ed Djerejian, founding director of the Baker Institute for Public Policy, served as a senior adviser, along with Chris Kojm, former deputy executive director of the 9/11 Commission. My policy aide, John Williams, and Lee's aide, Benjamin Rhodes, served as special assistants to the group. All played essential roles.

were recruited to help answer four big questions. How should Iraq be governed (the political development group)? How should street-level and national security be established and maintained (the military and security group)? How should the economy be rebuilt (economy and reconstruction)? And what should be the regional and geopolitical role of Iraq (strategic environment)?

We then picked the brains of roughly 170 U.S., Iraqi, and foreign military experts, government officials, scholars, journalists, and representatives of other countries. These included President Bush, Vice President Cheney, former president Clinton, Iraqi leaders Jalal Talabani and Nouri al-Maliki, active and retired generals Abizaid, Casey, and Zinni, former secretary of state Colin Powell, *New York Times* columnist Tom Friedman, and journalist George Packer. With the approval of the president, we also talked quietly with representatives of Syria and Iran.

But printed staff reports and oral testimony were not enough. We wanted to see the reality on the ground. In late August, seven of us boarded a C-130 in Kuwait and flew to Baghdad. We spent four days there and talked to U.S. and Iraqi government officials, U.S. and Iraqi military leaders, Iraqi religious representatives, and others.

Toward the end of our interviews in Baghdad, we began brainstorming, a process that continued after we returned home. How about a rapid withdrawal of all U.S. troops from Iraq? No, that would create a power vacuum that could lead to catastrophe. What about sending upward of 100,000 more combat troops to Iraq? Probably not; the American public wanted to see more soldiers, sailors, and airmen coming home, not a massive buildup. And anyway, we had nowhere near that number of combat personnel available.

What about a phased withdrawal? Political realities probably demanded that we make a serious effort to see if there could be some reduction in U.S. combat forces. In the meantime, we all agreed that it was important for the Iraqi government to start taking care of its own security. It might be possible to achieve both objectives—putting more responsibility on Iraqis for their own security and reducing the number of U.S. troops—if the primary mission of the U.S. military in Iraq was changed from one of refereeing sectarian violence to one of training and supporting Iraqi forces to maintain security. This approach seemed workable.

The devil, as always, was in the details. When study group member Bill Perry proposed a timetable for withdrawing U.S. combat brigades, I balked. Naming a date certain should be left to the commander in chief, I argued.

This was our most difficult issue. If we had reached an impasse—with some favoring a hard deadline and some opposing one—our report would have been weakened, perhaps fatally. But with suggestions from other members and Bill's willingness to consider alternatives, we crafted language that all could support—a specific recommendation that the United States seek to complete the training and equipping of the Iraqi military by the first quarter of 2008.* The recommendation was qualified with two general statements: "as additional Iraqi brigades are being deployed" and "subject to unexpected developments in the security situation on the ground." If those two very broad conditions were met, all U.S. combat brigades "could"—not "would" or "should"—be out of Iraq by the first quarter of 2008 except those required to advise, train, equip, and support the Iraqi army, protect all coalition security and military forces in Iraq, and conduct counterterrorism operations in Iraq.

In other words, we set a very conditional goal, not a timetable, for partial U.S. withdrawal, and we recognized that substantial U.S. forces would have to remain in Iraq and the region after the first quarter of 2008.

There were other differences along the way, though none that seriously threatened our unanimity. One point that I insisted go into the report was in response to the idea of dividing Iraq into three semi-autonomous regions—one for the Shia, one for the Sunni, and one for

---

*This date of the first quarter of 2008 for completion of training and equipping of Iraqi forces was based on the estimate General George Casey made on October 24, 2006. At that time, and at the time of the release of our report, he was the U.S. and coalition commander on the ground in Iraq.

the Kurds. That plan was being promoted by Senator Joe Biden and Leslie Gelb of the Council on Foreign Relations. Unfortunately, Iraq's population does not divide neatly into three regions, which would make it difficult or impossible to craft acceptable boundary lines, particularly between Sunni and Shia, and especially in the larger cities. The group agreed that a quick breakup might trigger mass population shifts, the collapse of an already unstable Iraqi security force, and ethnic cleansing, among other problems. Instead of merely saying no, however, we took a pragmatic approach. If events were to move irreversibly in this direction, the report said, the United States should undertake to manage the situation to ameliorate the human consequences, contain the spread of violence, and minimize regional instability.

After months of discussions, negotiations, and tedious word editing, we finally reached agreement in late November. Our executive summary began with these sober words: "The situation in Iraq is grave and deteriorating. There is no path that can guarantee success, but the prospects can be improved."

This is not the place to summarize the entire report, which was well received by the American people and was number one on the nonfiction best-seller lists for eight or nine weeks. If you want details, you can buy a copy at bookstores or download a free copy on the Internet. (Search for "Iraq Study Group Report.")

Broadly, the report argued that two approaches were needed to help restore stability in Iraq—an external approach and an internal one.

Externally, the ISG believed that Iraq cannot be addressed in isolation from other major conflicts and unresolved issues in the region. Accordingly, the "United States should immediately launch a new diplomatic offensive to build an international consensus for stability in Iraq and the region. This diplomatic effort should include every country with an interest in avoiding a chaotic Iraq," specifically including Iran and Syria. We also said the United States should deal directly and more aggressively with the Arab-Israeli conflict, which contributes greatly to regional instability.

As for the internal approach, we believed that the most important questions about Iraq's future are the responsibility of the Iraqis. "The United States must adjust its role in Iraq to encourage the Iraqi people to take control of their own destiny," we wrote. More specifically, we said, the Iraqis needed to increase the number and quality of their army brigades. The primary mission of U.S. forces in Iraq should evolve to one of supporting the Iraqi army.

But the report also said that our military presence would still need to be "sufficiently robust" to train, equip, and support Iraqi forces, provide political reassurance to the Iraqi government, confront al Qaeda and other terrorist organizations, deter even more interference in Iraq by Syria and Iran, and diminish the prospects of a regional war. Though we did not include in the report any estimate of the number of U.S. troops that would remain in Iraq, we informally discussed a figure between 80,000 and 100,000.

Finally, the ISG report recommended a carrot-and-stick approach. If the Iraqi government demonstrated political will and made progress toward national reconciliation, security, and governance, the United States should continue its support, we wrote. But if the Iraqis failed to make "substantial progress" in these areas, "the United States should reduce its military, political, or economic support for the Iraqi government."

Not everyone agreed with our recommendations, of course. The strongest criticism, no surprise, came from the far right and the far left.

I am not sure how thoroughly the critics read the report. One frequently overlooked section said the ISG "could support a short-term redeployment or surge of American combat forces to stabilize Baghdad, or to speed up the training and equipping mission, if the U.S. commander in Iraq determines that such steps would be effective."

In all but name, this endorsed the troop surge to quell sectarian violence that the administration announced just after our report was published. The ISG believed that stability in Baghdad was a key to stability in all of Iraq, and that more troops might be needed to provide such stability. I made that point during testimony before the Senate Armed Services Committee in late January 2007. I testified then, and believe now, that General David Petraeus's surge deserved a chance at success. And I was pleased when he returned to Congress eight months later to report that the surge appeared to have reduced levels of violence throughout Iraq. Sadly, the Iraqi government failed to match the security progress on the ground with equal political progress on national reconciliation.

Our report certainly changed the terms of the debate about Iraq, and in some ways it changed U.S. policy. As I have noted, the president said publicly that he wanted to move toward the recommendations of the ISG report, and he has begun to implement many of those recommendations. He has started low-level discussions with both Syria and Iran, for instance, and ramped up Arab-Israeli talks during the recent conference in Annapolis, Maryland. He has also taken a firmer stance with Iraqi officials, cajoling and pressuring them to meet benchmarks on reconciliation, oil-revenue sharing, and other hard political issues. On May 24, 2007, he told reporters at a Rose Garden news conference that he would "like to see us in a different configuration at some point in time in Iraq." When asked if he had a Plan B, the president responded: "Actually, I would call that a plan recommended by Baker-Hamilton, so that would be a Plan B-H."

In September 2007, President Bush reported to the American people. Echoing earlier congressional testimony by General Petraeus and Ambassador Ryan Crocker, the president gave an upbeat assessment of the post-surge security situation in Iraq. By July 2008, he said, five of twenty combat brigades would be brought home from Iraq—roughly equivalent to the 30,000 troops that were "surged" into Iraq during the spring and summer of 2007. And starting in December 2007, administration officials said, the U.S. military would move toward the more limited mission of supporting Iraqi forces and confronting al Qaeda. These steps are generally consistent with ISG recommendations.

Our country remains deeply divided on Iraq. We continue to see pitched battles in Congress over policy and funding for the war. In general, however, it seems to me that the administration's steps along the path laid out by the Iraq Study Group, including the surge, have lowered the temperature of the debate for now. That's not to say that it won't remain a contentious topic as we head into the presidential campaign season.

The situation in Iraq, however, remains fragile. No matter what the United States does, things may still go badly. Even if things go well, American troops will probably remain in Iraq for many years to help maintain peace in a country that is crucial to Middle East stability. The Iraq Study Group understood these realities when it wrote its report. Even if all seventy-nine of our recommendations were followed, it would still be a long time before all of our troops come home.

In presenting our report we earned the respect of the vast majority of the American people, many of whom believed that the ISG spoke truth to power.* We also changed the terms of the debate by showing that when men and women of goodwill put their minds to it, bipartisan consensus is achievable. The real question, we said, is not what may have gone wrong in the past, but what we can do to make it go right in the future.

I'VE HAD OTHER projects since *Work Hard* was published. One of the most intensive was chairing an independent investigation of the culture of safety in the U.S. refinery operations of BP, the giant international energy company. An explosion at the company's Texas City

---

*My participation in the Iraq Study Group did not, as some have suggested, bruise my relationship with President George W. Bush. Three months after the report was released, the president sent me a handwritten letter saying that he had read *Work Hard* and liked the memoir. "What I enjoyed most," the president wrote me, "was reliving history through the eyes of one of our nation's most accomplished and successful public servants. Perhaps the book would be better titled—Baker: A Man Who Did It All—with Class."

refinery in March 2005 had killed 15 workers and injured 170 more. The U.S. Chemical Safety and Hazard Investigation Board asked BP to engage a panel of outsiders to review plant safety issues, and I was asked to head the group.

The refining industry is inherently dangerous, and every company owes it to its workers and the communities near its refineries to make workplace safety a top priority. I accepted the assignment only after John Browne, then the company's chairman, said he understood that our group would let the "chips fall where they may," that he expected nothing less, and that BP would cooperate fully.

Our panel was greeted with some skepticism. Could we be trusted to report fully and fairly about—and to criticize—the company that had appointed us? By the time we finished our review, however, that skepticism had largely faded. We traveled to all five BP refineries in the United States, reviewed thousands of documents, and interviewed hundreds of employees.

One thing we learned was that BP had a false sense of confidence about safety. For years, company officials had treated good "personal safety" records as evidence that its refineries were safe. But there is a difference between "personal safety"—the prevention of slip-and-falls and other routine accidents—and "process safety"—the hardware and procedures necessary to move crude oil and refined products through complex refinery processes without incident. A fall may break an arm or a leg, or even lead to the death of a worker. A process safety failure—as BP learned the hard way—can trigger an explosion or other catastrophic event that imperils many workers and others. Our panel identified significant process-safety concerns at each of BP's five refineries and recommended ways to correct them.

Our report was released in January 2007, and BP has pledged to implement our recommendations. The company hired one panel member to help monitor the company's progress. Another safety panel member agreed to help advise Bob Malone, the new chairman and president of BP America, on safety issues. In the meantime, other companies have directed their managers and workers to read the report.

In early 2007, I signed up to cochair with former secretary of state Warren Christopher a new bipartisan group, the National War Powers Commission.* Our mission is to study how the Constitution allocates the power to start, conduct, and end wars. From the first days of the Republic, these questions have proved difficult. They are even more problematic after the Cold War, Korea, Vietnam, the two Gulf Wars, and our ongoing conflict against stateless terrorist organizations. These days, the very definition of war is sometimes unclear. Yet what could be more important than a decision—in the words of the Declaration of Independence—to pledge our lives, our fortunes, and our sacred honor to armed conflict? The commission takes its responsibilities seriously, and we hope to provide useful advice on these difficult issues.

President Gerald Ford died on December 26, 2006, shortly after *Work Hard* was published. I can't say much more about his honor, his grace, his decency, his integrity, and his importance to U.S. history than I have already said in this book. After his death, however, his stature was all the more evident. Time had swept away the controversies and confusions engendered by the pardon of Richard Nixon and revealed how fortunate, even blessed, our nation was by Gerald Ford's presence in the White House.

---

*Like me, Christopher, President Clinton's first secretary of state, is one of the usual suspects who gets rounded up for this sort of public service project. After working against Chris during the 2000 presidential recount battle—he represented Democrat Al Gore and I represented George W. Bush—it is nice to be working alongside him on this project. Other commission members are Ed Meese, Lee Hamilton, former senator Slade Gorton, former U.S. trade representative Carla Hills, former secretary of the army John Marsh, former chief judge of the D.C. Circuit Abner Mikva, former commander in chief of the U.S. Atlantic Fleet Paul Reason, former national security adviser Brent Scowcroft, Anne-Marie Slaughter, dean of Princeton University's Woodrow Wilson School of Public and International Affairs, and Strobe Talbott, president of the Brookings Institution. Our sponsor is the Miller Center of Public Policy at the University of Virginia. Other partners include the James A. Baker III Institute for Public Policy at Rice University, the Freeman Spogli Institute for International Studies at Stanford University, Stanford Law School, the University of Virginia School of Law, and the William & Mary School of Law.

He personified all that is good about America. He was comfortable with himself, popular among friends on both sides of the aisle, admired and respected (even loved by his staff), and quietly effective as a leader. Armed with common sense and a solid work ethic, both rooted in his midwestern values, he calmly did whatever needed to be done. His funeral was as simple and dignified as his life. I was privileged to serve as an honorary pallbearer, along with Dick Cheney, Bob Dole, Don Rumsfeld, Henry Kissinger, Brent Scowcroft, and Alan Greenspan. Former presidents Carter and Bush each delivered remembrances.

In August 2007 I lost another friend, also prominent in the pages of this book, when Mike Deaver succumbed to pancreatic cancer. At Mike's memorial service, I recalled that President Reagan had restored our nation's spirit, revitalized our nation's economy, and hastened the end of the Cold War. And Mike—often dismissed as a mere "media maestro"—helped him accomplish all these great things. He did it by linking the Great Communicator's powerful words with equally powerful images. This permitted Americans to experience the emotions associated with Reagan's ideas, to see that the president's words had meaning far beyond the headlines, and to trust the president enough to follow his leadership.

Mike was a friend to all, I said, but more than just a friend to President Reagan and Nancy, whom he served so loyally. Mike once wrote that he loved and respected Ronald Reagan as a second father. Naturally someone asked the president if he saw Mike as a son. "No, not really," the president replied. "More a brother." They were that close.

Mike also had a wonderful sense of humor. Who can forget the meeting after one cabinet officer had complained about guerrilla warfare by the White House staff? There in the Rose Garden right outside the cabinet room windows was Mike Deaver ... bouncing around in a gorilla suit.

And in January 2008, Dick Darman lost a heroic battle with acute myelogenous leukemia. Dick's fierce dedication to his country helped make him an outstanding public servant. He served four consecutive

U.S. presidents, starting with President Nixon and President Ford. He then worked with me when I was chief of staff and secretary of the treasury for President Reagan. Later, as budget director in the cabinet of President George H. W. Bush, his efforts contributed to the economic growth of the 1990s and the balanced budget late in that decade.

Always the tireless advocate, Dick was better at directing traffic at the intersection of policy and politics than anyone I ever saw. What critics sometimes dismissed as "Darmanesque" strategies were, in most cases, brilliant strategies. The proof is that they worked. Dick was a consummate detail man, but he never lost sight of the forest for the trees. He was the very best at condensing complex information and arguments into precise and straightforward policy options and recommendations.

I always respected and appreciated Dick's unvarnished perspective and crystal clear analysis. I hate to think where I would have been in my own public career without Dick Darman.

I'VE BEEN BUSY in the year since *Work Hard* was published, but I've also had time to reflect, especially about my country and its role on the world stage.

I was fortunate to have been born and raised in one of the greatest countries that mankind has ever witnessed. That's simply the way I feel—without reservation. My conviction has more to do with how we Americans operate than what we achieve—although our technological, industrial, and economic accomplishments are enormously inspiring. There is a deeper side to us.

The United States has a track record—from rebuilding Western Europe and East Asia after World War II to peacefully concluding the Cold War—of exercising power in ways that advance the human condition. Of course, as all nations do, we also advance our own self-interest, sometimes in ways that anger others. No country is perfect.

But on balance, the United States has proved itself to be a powerful force for good in world affairs. Indeed, America rightly views itself as the chief engine of economic growth and the historic champion of democratic values around the world. We are a unique country and people.

In recent months, I have been speaking about how the United States can use its uniquely preeminent position in global affairs today to help build a better world in the twenty-first century. My speech is a collection of useful principles for policy-makers, a distillation of my observations and experiences in international relations. I call the speech "The Case for Pragmatic Idealism." In February 2007 I presented it at the fifth Kissinger Lecture on Foreign Policy and International Relations at the Library of Congress. Not long afterward Henry Kissinger, my predecessor at the State Department, my friend, and the éminence grise of American foreign policy, sent me a note in which he said my speech was "substantially superb" and "timely," and suggesting that it be published.* Perhaps a good way to end this epilogue is to summarize what I said in that speech.

By any standard, the United States is the preeminent power in world affairs. Our influence is perhaps most obvious in the military arena. The defeat of the Taliban and the overthrow of Saddam Hussein clearly demonstrated our unparalleled ability to project decisive force across vast distances. Our military services are the best armed, best trained, and best led in the world. No other countries even begin to approach our capabilities, nor will they for decades to come.

We are also an economic powerhouse, we still wield immense diplomatic influence, and we represent an ideology—free-market democracy—without a serious global rival. That model is clearly not triumphant everywhere, but the trend over recent decades has unmistakably been in the direction of democracy and free markets.

---

*I followed Henry's advice. The full text of an article based on that speech appeared in *The National Interest Online* on August 29, 2007, under the title, "The Big Ten: The Case for Pragmatic Idealism." It can be found at http://www.nationalinterest.org/Article.aspx?id=15370. The text that follows this note is largely quoted and paraphrased from that article.

In sum, no country or group of countries can challenge our international preeminence. This may change as China, India, and other potential rivals loom larger on the world stage. But for now and the foreseeable future, the United States is the only true global power.

Our country is best served, I believe, when its foreign policy is not limited to the conflicting ideologies of either "realism" or "idealism." Instead, we should use the best elements of both. We are a practical people who are less interested in ideological purity than in solving problems.

"Pragmatic idealism," while firmly grounded in values, appreciates the complexity of the real world—a world of hard choices and painful trade-offs. This is the real world in which we must live, decide, and act. The first step in practicing pragmatic idealism is to be comfortable with using our power. We have no alternative. If the United States does not exercise power, others will. This was true before September 11, 2001. It is even more true today as we face the global challenges of international terrorism and the proliferation of weapons of mass destruction. Other countries depend on our leadership. This is most obviously true of our allies in Western Europe, Asia, and elsewhere, but even less friendly countries often seek our engagement.

We need to recognize, however, that even U.S. power is limited. We cannot be the policeman for the world. Powerful as we are, we cannot solve every problem. Iraq, for instance, has shown a limit of our military strength.

Our power is limited in other areas as well. As strong as our economy may be, we still need the cooperation of others in expanding trade and investment, and coordinating macroeconomic policy. The same is true in diplomacy, where our influence can be constrained when we are unable to convince others to join us.

When necessary, we must be prepared to go it alone. It is almost always preferable to work with others, of course, but others cannot be permitted to constrain our freedom of action when our vital interests are at stake.

But we must also appreciate the importance of allies. It is no coincidence that the three great global conflicts of the twentieth century—World War I, World War II, and the Cold War—were won by coalitions. Partners allow us to spread the human and financial costs of a joint foreign policy initiative. In the Gulf War of 1991, for instance, a military coalition of the United States, Britain, France, many Arab nations, and others was bolstered by financial support from Gulf Arab states, Japan, and Germany and a number of other Western European governments.

We must also remember to use all means at our disposal—military, political, and economic. As circumstances dictate, we need to be prepared to use both formal institutions, such as NATO and the United Nations, and informal arrangements, such as ad hoc coalitions.

We need to recognize and accept that the United States must sometimes deal with authoritarian regimes. In a "perfect world," we could perhaps work only with other democracies. Unfortunately, this is not a perfect world. And there is absolutely no sign that it will become one anytime soon.

The most striking example of this was America's alliance with Stalin's Soviet Union during World War II. Although the Soviet Union was one of the most murderous regimes in history, we had little alternative given the immediate and deadly threat posed by Nazi Germany. Later, during the Cold War, we made common cause with authoritarian regimes in Latin America, Asia, and elsewhere. Even today, our allies in the conflict with terrorist groups include countries in the Middle East and central Asia that bear scant resemblance to "Jeffersonian democracies." I cannot pretend that this is a satisfying state of affairs. But there is simply no alternative to it.

We should be prepared to change course if necessary. Consistency, of course, is an important element of foreign policy. It permits us to move beyond crisis management and facilitates the development of long-term strategies. Consistency can also foster stability by reassuring allies and setting down clear markers for potential adversaries.

When events change, however, we must be prepared to change with them. The rise of Mikhail Gorbachev in the Soviet Union, for instance, marked a dramatic shift in the worldview of the Soviet leadership. It was only right, therefore, that Washington should reach out to Moscow in ways unimaginable just years before.

We must also be prepared to talk with our enemies. I don't say this because talking is inherently a good thing (although there is something to be said for maintaining a bilateral dialogue to avoid misunderstanding and missteps). Instead, the fundamental reason we should be prepared to speak to our enemies is that it is in our interest to do so. This is why we maintained an embassy in Moscow throughout the Cold War. And this is why even so staunch an anticommunist as President Reagan was prepared to negotiate with the Soviets. Talking to hostile states—Moscow during the Cold War or Damascus today—is not appeasement. It was and is good foreign policy.

Values are important, but they are not the only thing. Promoting democracy and free markets is rightly central to U.S. foreign policy. A freer, more prosperous world is better for Americans and people everywhere. But we cannot be deluded into thinking that progress toward democracy and free markets is either inevitable or without its own strains.

Of course we should support free markets and democracy, but this support cannot be the beginning and end of our foreign policy. We should not underestimate the difficulties countries sometimes face as they embark on the path to reform. And we should remember that "stability" is not a dirty word in the conduct of foreign policy.

Finally, we must always be aware that domestic support is vital to successful foreign policy. The will of the American people is the final arbiter of foreign policy in our democracy. Generating and sustaining domestic support for a foreign policy is in every way as important as the policy itself. Without that support, policies may be repudiated at the polls. Worse, the public may become disenchanted with foreign engagement in general and turn toward isolationism.

The case for pragmatic idealism is based on an optimistic view of man, tempered by our knowledge of human imperfection. It promises no easy answers or quick fixes. But I am convinced that it offers our surest guide and best hope for navigating our great country safely though this precarious period of opportunity and risk in world affairs.

J.A.B.
February 2008

"Item One on Our Agenda Was the Dollar"

WHEN I RESIGNED from Treasury in 1988, my letter to the president said three of his second-term economic initiatives "will be widely judged to have lasting significance." One, of course, was tax reform. Another was a new system of multilateral economic policy coordination we set in motion. And the third was a free-trade agreement between Canada and the United States. I've described the tax reform battle in chapter ten. Now I want to say a few words about the other two items on that list, international economic policy coordination and the trade agreement with Canada. I'll also discuss Black Monday, that day in October 1987 when the stock market fell 508 points. I want to write about these issues because today we face many of the same challenges to U.S. and world prosperity that confronted us in 1985–1988. Our answers to those problems then, I think, hold important lessons for what might be done today.

The first of these subjects, international economic policy coordination, is a good-government catchphrase that, unfortunately, causes some people's eyes to glaze over. It shouldn't. The failure to understand its importance caused U.S. policymakers to pull up the drawbridges after World War I. We tried to insulate America from economic problems elsewhere in the world and keep whatever growth we could generate to ourselves. But those policies did exactly the opposite of what we had hoped. International trade and capital transfers dried up, and with them, economic growth. The isolationism and protectionism of that era actually helped cause the Great Depression and arguably set the stage for World War II. In other words, we got it wrong.

After World War II, however, we got it right. Victorious in war once again, the United States decided not to try to go it alone. Instead, we would cooperate to rebuild postwar economies. Under our leadership, forty-four nations signed the Bretton Woods agreements in 1944, setting up the International Monetary Fund and the World Bank. The dollar was pegged to gold and other world currencies were pegged to the dollar. Soon thereafter, the General Agreement on Tariffs and Trade (GATT) was put in place to promote free trade. These agreements provided a foundation for postwar global prosperity.

I wasn't worried about another Great Depression when I took my oath of office in February 1985. The Reagan tax cuts and the Fed's successful war on inflation—down 10 points since 1980—had set the American economy afire. As the U.S. economy grew, so did the world economy. What concerned me was how to *maintain* this prosperity in the face of unsustainable, and growing, global economic imbalances. We confronted an overvalued dollar, measured against other currencies, and a trade imbalance that favored the Japanese, Germans, and other trading partners at the expense of U.S. manufacturers and exporters. These two economic problems, in turn, had created a big political problem—a protectionist fever in Congress that grew hotter each time Honda or Mercedes won another customer from the Big Three or another pop economist wrote about the inevitable triumph of Japan, Inc. Would we return to the failed go-it-alone policies of the post–World War I era? Dick Darman (at the time, deputy treasury secretary) and I quickly concluded that the best way—and perhaps the only way—to solve these problems was to work more closely with the finance ministers and central bankers of other major economies.

Item one on our agenda was the dollar. For years, relative world currency values had been set by the market. Sometimes they fluctuated wildly on the foreign exchanges. This made it difficult for governments, companies, and investors to make long-range plans. A business could do everything right, then be ruined by a sudden overnight move in exchange rates. And the disparity between the strong dollar and weak foreign currencies gave foreign competitors a big advantage over companies in the United States. This contributed to our growing trade deficit and sparked demands for high tariffs, import quotas, and other protectionist measures.

An analogy may help explain the problem. In the early days of our nation's history, we had a multitude of currencies—paper issued by the Continental Congress, bills printed by the states, notes from private banks, even foreign bills and coins. Shopkeepers had to be mathematical geniuses to price a loaf of bread. The dollar eventually prevailed, thanks in no small part to the work of Alexander Hamilton. We now have a single national currency that makes it easy to buy, sell, and invest in markets from Maine to California, with perfect confidence in the medium of exchange and with no internal currency risk.

While there is no practical way to establish a global currency to provide the same benefits worldwide—and I was not advocating doing so—we knew we could move in that direction if we could stabilize the relative values of the major national currencies. The only way to achieve that stability, however, would be to coordinate the underlying economic fundamentals of the countries that issued these currencies. And doing that would require, in turn, a process for macroeconomic policy coordination among those countries. That *process* is what we created, beginning with the Plaza Accord in 1985.*

---

*A good account of this can be found in *Managing the Dollar: From the Plaza to the Louvre,* by Yoichi Funabashi.

The first Reagan administration's policy toward the dollar was invariably described by commentators as "benign neglect"—letting our currency wander where it will. I'm not sure that's a fair description, but, fair or not, the problem wasn't nearly as acute from 1981–1984 as in 1985. To win White House support to change this policy, we adopted a top-down strategy. There is truly only one decision-maker in the executive branch of the U.S. government, so all we needed was an okay from the president. To make sure we got it, however, I would have to sell Don Regan on the idea. Remember, he and I had traded jobs. His focus now as White House chief of staff, rather than treasury secretary, was more political and less economic. He agreed that we had to find a way to beat back the protectionist sentiment in Congress and that our plan offered the best way to do that. The president liked the idea as well, and with his approval we were in a position to go forward without telling anyone else. And we didn't. A leak would have destroyed or diminished the effectiveness of what we were planning.

Of course, we also needed the support of Federal Reserve Board Chairman Paul Volcker. At one of our regular weekly meetings, I told him what we were considering. He had been on record since early 1985 in favor of correcting the overvalued dollar, so he liked the idea, but he questioned whether I would be able to get the administration to change its dollar policy in such a fundamental way. He was strongly of the view, which I shared, that the dollar's decline must be orderly, not precipitous.

Treasury then made quiet contacts with the finance ministries of the four other major currency countries—Germany, Japan, the UK, and France. On first hearing about what we were considering they too were skeptics, but as the summer of 1985 wore on, they began to realize that we were serious. Our leverage with them was that if we didn't act first, the protectionists in Congress would throw up trade barriers. Auto makers and other industries were pounding the desks at the White House, Treasury, and Congress, demanding that something be done to save them from foreign competition, and Congress was listening. By late summer, top foreign economic officials had begun to see that we were serious.

To our great relief, news of these quiet contacts never leaked. On our side, we kept the circle very tight—the president and his chief of staff, the Fed chairman and his top assistant, and at Treasury, Darman, David Mulford (assistant secretary for international affairs), Margaret Tutwiler (assistant secretary for public affairs), and me. Our foreign counterparts evidently did the same. All that was needed now was a face-to-face meeting of the finance ministers and central bank governors of the five countries to agree on the actions to be taken by each toward coordinating their underlying economic policies.

That came on September 22, 1985, in the Gold Room of New York's lovely old Plaza Hotel. All participants had managed to arrive secretly in New York for the Sunday afternoon meeting. We picked that day because financial markets would be closed. We didn't tell the press until the meeting was under way. (Once alerted, they showed up in droves. The room was packed.) By the end of the day, we had agreed on what came to be known as the Plaza Accord. The public communiqué described the risks to the world economy in these words:

> The U.S. current account deficit together with other factors is now contributing to protectionist pressures which, if not resisted, could lead to mutually destructive retaliation with serious damage to the world economy: world trade would shrink, real growth rates could even turn negative, unemployment would rise still higher, and debt-burdened countries would be unable to secure the export earnings they vitally need.

Ministers and governors "stand ready to cooperate more closely to encourage" exchange-rate adjustments, the communiqué said. And in a masterful use of understatement, it added that "exchange rates should play a role in adjusting external imbalances." The word "intervention" was never used, but in a separate document, a "nonpaper" that was not made public, participants agreed to sell dollars and buy other currencies to adjust the relative values of the currencies—that is, to lower the value of the dollar against other currencies.

The results were spectacular. Despite strong resistance from traders, the dollar dropped against other currencies, quickly and substantially, but in an orderly way. In his January 1986 state of the union address, President Reagan signaled our satisfaction with the Plaza Accord and our commitment to continue working with our trading partners to stabilize exchange rates.

Plaza was about more than just currency adjustments. It also established the principle (and for a while, at least, the practice) of multilateral economic policy coordination. Among other things, the United States undertook to control the fiscal deficit, Japan agreed to stimulate domestic demand and open its borders to more imports, Germany said it would reduce the size of its public sector and remove "rigidities" (read, "excessive regulations") that inhibited the labor and capital markets, and all signatories promised to fight protectionism.

Critics say the United States later reneged on its deficit-reduction pledge. All I can say is that we made the promise in good faith and did our best to implement it. In December the president signed the Gramm-Rudman-Hollings Act, which slowed the rate of growth of federal spending. Other signatory countries also fell short on their commitments. What was important, however, is that we were all trying to coordinate our policies. Each country was subject to political constraints that made it difficult to put all the desirable policies fully into practice. Just because implementation of the Plaza Accord was not perfect, however, does not mean that the agreement itself was not good. It was clearly successful in forestalling potential protectionist legislation in Congress.

In early 1986, Treasury even pushed for international coordination of monetary policy to drive down interest rates. Central bankers resisted. They didn't want finance ministers, mere politicians, telling them what to do. Some understandings were reached, however, and interest rates began to fall as central bankers responded to calls for coordinated action.

In time, concerns grew that the dollar might have fallen too far. This led to the Louvre Accord of February 22, 1987. While Plaza was a onetime agreement to deal with a specific set of circumstances, Louvre was more ambitious. It aimed to *institutionalize* the process of coordination of economic policies to stabilize world currencies within an agreed, but unpublished, set of ranges. Like Plaza, it worked. Deputy finance ministers began to meet monthly, finance ministers less frequently, to work out common policies, and the dollar headed north. By the fall of 1987, I publicly referred to the possibility of looking at "a basket of commodities, including gold," to stabilize our currencies on the basis of what economists called "purchasing power parity."

The effects of macroeconomic policy adjustments often are not visible for many months. By 1987, however, the U.S. current account deficit—which the Plaza communiqué had cited as evidence of trouble in the global economic system—had begun to fall. In 1991, it reached zero. Talk in Congress about erecting trade barriers never completely died away, but it subsided. The Reagan economic boom continued, and the world economy grew with it.

Multilateral coordination of economic policy is very difficult politically for all countries involved, but that is no reason not to make the effort. After I left Treasury in 1988, the process continued of its own momentum for a short time, then fell dormant. In President Clinton's second term, Robert Rubin briefly revived it to deal, successfully, with the East Asian economic crises. Otherwise, and sadly, the process largely ended with the Reagan administration.

The need for aggressive economic policy coordination today is, if anything, more acute now than in 1985. The U.S. current account deficit that worried us so much in 1985 was only 2.7 percent of GDP. In 2005, it reached 6.4 percent. Even China is starting to bid for high-profile U.S. assets—shades of "Japan, Inc."—and, all too predictably, protectionist sentiments are strong and growing in Congress. The U.S.

current account deficit together with other factors is now contributing to protectionist pressures which, if not resisted, could lead to mutually destructive retaliation with serious damage to the world economy: world trade would shrink, real growth rates could even turn negative, unemployment would rise still higher, and debt-burdened countries would be unable to secure the export earnings they vitally need.*

Furthermore, the United States is now, for the first time, about to start paying debt service on its net investment debt position. In other words, for the first time we have less total U.S. investment abroad than foreign investment here. If something isn't done, that net debt service—payable to China, Japan, and other creditor countries—will approach $200 billion a year in another couple of years.

There are only two ways out of this problem, as I see it. One is through the mechanism of a U.S. recession, which would come at a terrible cost to both the U.S. and global economies, and is, of course, unacceptable. The other is through another round of aggressive international economic policy coordination, which could over time reduce imbalances. Unfortunately, the prospects for coordination now are not good. The United States today has a policy, not quite "benign neglect," of hoping the dollar will fall, but not saying or doing much about it. Our trading partners appear to be less interested in currency stability than in maintaining their trading advantages against the United States. Also, they generally view the dollar as too weak, not too strong—exactly the reverse of 1985. Finally, there is widespread resistance in Europe and elsewhere to following U.S. leadership on many issues. This is not a happy picture. We should not be indifferent to these risks to the global economy, nor should our trading partners.

THE THIRD MAJOR economic accomplishment of President Reagan's second term, after tax reform and international economic policy

---

*In case you didn't catch it, I lifted this sentence word for word from the twenty-one-year-old Plaza Accord. Sadly, it is even more true today than it was then.

coordination to defeat protectionism and stabilize exchange rates, was the Canada–United States Free Trade Agreement. It went into effect on January 1, 1989, and removed many trade barriers between the United States and its largest trading partner. More important, perhaps, it served as a model for the North American Free Trade Agreement (NAFTA), which went into effect five years later and made Mexico, Canada, and the United States the world's largest trading bloc.*

The catalyst for the agreement with Canada was the election of a conservative government headed by Brian Mulroney in 1984. Like President Reagan, he passionately believed in free trade and had the political courage in the face of significant domestic opposition to try to erase tariffs and other barriers to the movement of goods between Canada and the United States. The ultimate agreement was a testament to the vision, courage, and political will of these two great leaders.

Trade liberalization is as close to accepted gospel as anything in economics. It holds that free trade between any two countries makes both more prosperous, even if one is dominant in all sectors. Politically, however, free trade is always a tough sale. The reason is that the benefits are diffuse (everybody shares to some extent in the general increase in prosperity), but the costs are specific and painful (some industries and labor groups invariably suffer when import tariffs and quotas are removed). Beneficiaries of trade liberalization are usually quiet, but victims scream and politicians listen, which makes it easy to rail against free trade (as Ross Perot did in the 1992 presidential election). That's why efforts to liberalize the world trading system through the General Agreement on Tariffs and Trade (GATT) and, later, the World Trade Organization (WTO) have stretched over many decades. Countries impatient with this slow pace have independently formed regional trade blocs, such as the European Community (forerunner of the European Union) or signed bilateral trade agreements, such as the one Prime Minister Mulroney and President Reagan wanted.

---

*Two good references are *Free Trade: Risks and Rewards,* edited by L. Ian MacDonald, and *Building a Partnership: The Canada–United States Free Trade Agreement,* edited by Mordechai Kreinin.

The agreement almost didn't happen. Negotiations were protracted, painful, and more than once on the verge of complete collapse. Initial talks began in 1984 while I was still White House chief of staff and went on for years. Still, with just days to go before the midnight, October 3, 1987, deadline for submission to Congress, no agreement was in sight.

The deadline was set under "fast-track" legislation that authorized the negotiations. If we met the deadline, Congress would have to vote up or down on the agreement as a whole and not pick it apart with amendments. If we missed it, however, the agreement was as good as dead.

As the deadline approached, President Reagan asked me to take over as point man for U.S. negotiators and gave me a simple mandate: if a deal is at all possible, get it! With only two days left, I telephoned Derek Burney, Mulroney's chief of staff, with a plan for resuming negotiations. "This was a critical move in itself," Burney wrote later. "We knew we needed someone like Baker to make it happen."

The next day we started through the agreement, point by point, in a high-level meeting in the Treasury conference room. I was ably assisted throughout these negotiations by Peter McPherson, who by then had replaced Dick Darman as deputy secretary of the treasury. (Peter later served as president of Michigan State University.) I have participated in many negotiations in my career, but few that compared in complexity and contentiousness with these. There was a lot of thunder and lightning as old controversies were fought one last time and new ones brought to the table. Meanwhile, teams of lawyers in another building were sweating over language to satisfy Canada's biggest sticking point—a mechanism to enforce the agreement. In the last hours before the deadline, Burney and I worked out the final details in my office.

Successful negotiation requires a sense of political limits. For this agreement, that meant sensitivity to the political dynamics in both Canada and the United States, two democracies where interest groups are varied and vocal, and power is divided and diffuse. I spent a lot of time gauging congressional opinion and cultivating bipartisan support from friends of free trade on Capitol Hill. I also had to educate myself on the political constraints faced by the Canadians. For instance, it was a no-no in Canada to give up trade and investment barriers designed to protect their culture against Americanization. The principle was okay with us, but to the Canadians, "culture" was a very elastic concept. It seemed that whatever they wanted to protect, they called culture. I finally told them, more for effect than anything, "Fine, okay, let me tell you what is cultural in the United States—automobiles!" That seemed to encourage them to become less elastic about what was culture and what wasn't. Even today, however, Canadians are still "protected" from seeing too many American movies or sitcoms on television.

Getting the agreement ratified in the U.S. Congress was no picnic, but the Canadian ratification fight almost brought down Mulroney's government. National elections were called in 1988, and only after his party won could we be certain that our deal would stick.

One thing that I will never forget about President Reagan is his political courage in going on the offensive on trade and investment liberalization. Remember that at the same time we were seeking to knock down trade barriers with Canada, powerful protectionists in Congress were threatening punitive legislation against our major trading partners. Instead of playing defense, however, President Reagan snatched the ball and ran the other way. We turned the debate from narrow questions of advantage for one industry or another and from near-xenophobic attacks on our trading partners to broader questions of our national interest.

The agreement was a huge success. Trade between Canada and the United States more than doubled in the decade after it went into effect. The result: higher economic growth, more jobs, and better wages in both countries.

The deal with Canada also prepared the way for NAFTA, a trade agreement that today covers more than 425 million people. After

George Bush 41 became president in 1989, he worked with Prime Minister Mulroney and Mexico's President Carlos Salinas to bring Mexico into the trade zone. Negotiations went more quickly this time, primarily because of the lessons learned in the Canadian round. President Bush signed the agreement in December 1992. "We've committed ourselves to a better future for our children and for generations yet unborn," he said.

The next administration inherited the task of winning congressional ratification. I salute President Clinton for having the political courage to do so, despite strong opposition from labor unions and other constituencies within his own party. On November 2, 1993, fifteen days before Congress would vote NAFTA up or down, he organized a bipartisan show of support for the trade pact in the White House East Room. I attended, along with former president Carter, five other former secretaries of state, five other former treasury secretaries, eight Nobel laureates, and Paul Volcker. Former presidents Bush, Ford, and Reagan issued statements of support. (As I said, trade liberalization is as close to accepted gospel as anything in economics.) In my remarks to the distinguished attendees that day, I said, "Our task . . . is to persuade Americans that they have nothing to fear from NAFTA . . . Working together on a bipartisan basis, we must expose the fact-fudging, the fearmongering, the prophets of protectionism who are playing on the doubts of the American people." The House passed NAFTA by 234–200 and the Senate by 61–38, with Republicans providing more votes than Democrats.

Over the past decade, NAFTA has been a resounding success. Trade among the three signatory countries has more than doubled. The economies of Mexico and Canada have grown more than 30 percent and the economy of the United States has grown about 40 percent. Wages and productivity are up in all three countries. The strong U.S. economic expansion of the 1990s owes a great deal to NAFTA, I think, and the trade pact clearly helped Mexico weather a currency crisis, consolidate free-market reforms, and strengthen its democracy.

What we still lack, however, is the long-dreamed-of FTAA—Free Trade Area for the Americas—uniting South, Central, and North America in one trade zone. Immediately after NAFTA went into effect, prospects looked good. President Clinton convened the first Summit of the Americas in Miami in December 1994 to announce plans for "a free trade area that stretches from Alaska to Argentina." It would be in place by 2005, he said. More than thirty heads of state from Latin America endorsed the plan, then went home to wait, expectantly, for negotiations to begin.

What President Clinton lacked, however, was the same fast-track authority from Congress that had made it possible for Presidents Reagan and Bush to put in place the two earlier trade agreements. He could have gotten that authority in 1995. Unfortunately, however, he waited until 1997 to ask for it. By then, opposition within his own party had hardened. Lacking critical support from Democrats, President Clinton became the first president since President Ford to be turned down on a fast-track vote. He tried again in 1998, but seemingly not wholeheartedly. His personal troubles had erupted earlier that year. The House would vote on an impeachment resolution later that year and he apparently hesitated to alienate fellow Democrats in the run-up to the midterm elections.

President Clinton's decision not to go for fast-track authority in 1995 was arguably the biggest mistake of his presidency. Why? Because nothing would have done more for economic growth for all the countries of this hemisphere, including the United States, than to have been part of a free trade agreement for the Americas. And the opportunity we had to get there at that time was lost. Now Asians and Europeans are cutting free trade agreements with many countries of South America while Uncle Whiskers is left sitting on the sidelines. This is a real tragedy.

George W. Bush has resumed the movement toward hemispheric trade liberalization with the Central America–Dominican Republic Free Trade Agreement of 2005. My former adviser, Robert Zoellick, queued up that project as U.S. trade representative in the forty-third president's first term. In the absence of real progress on liberalization of world and hemispheric trade, he also won bilateral free-trade agreements with a number of U.S. trading partners, including Morocco and Australia. We've also signed deals recently with Chile, Peru, and Colombia. Unfortunately, however, the all-important FTAA is still just a dream, not a reality.

As I have said, the U.S. economy exploded into a frenzy of growth under President Reagan, thanks to tax cuts, tax reform, free trade, and stabilization of the dollar. There were some dark days along the way, however. One came on "Black Monday," October 19, 1987.

In all my years of public service before then, I had never taken a real boondoggle overseas trip. Things were going so well in 1987, however, that I decided to do just that when the king of Sweden, Carl Gustaf, invited me to hunt elk with him.*

I was scheduled to depart for Stockholm on Sunday, October 18. Signs of trouble appeared the week before, although I didn't regard them as particularly serious at the time. From the end of 1984 through the late-August peak in 1987, the Dow Jones Industrial Average had gained a stunning 127 percent. Since then, it had been drifting down. The Wednesday before I left, the downtrend accelerated as bad trade figures set Congress to talking about protectionism.

On Thursday, I tried to calm the market in a press briefing at the White House. We weren't about to go into a recession, I said, but I complained about the plans of the Bundesbank (Germany's equivalent of our Federal Reserve) to hike interest rates. On Friday, the market declined again.

Before my Sunday departure, I appeared on *Meet the Press.* Again I criticized the Bundesbank. "We will not sit back in this country and

---

*What the Swedes call "elk," we call "moose."

watch surplus countries jack up interest rates and squeeze growth worldwide on the expectation that the United States somehow will follow by raising its interest rates," I said. Then I boarded a plane and flew to Europe, visions of majestic Swedish elk playing in my head.

When I landed, my official host, the Swedish minister for finance, Kjell-Olof Feldt, met me at the foot of the stairs. His face was white as a snowcapped glacier on a mountain peak, and he could hardly speak. "The market closed down five!" he said. I was puzzled. What's wrong with a five-point drop in the market? "No, no!" he said. "Five hundred!"*

The Dow Jones Industrial Average had dropped 508 points in one excruciating day, losing about 22 percent to close at 1738, the second-biggest one-day percentage decline in history. I went to my room in the government guesthouse for visiting dignitaries and started working the phones. I don't remember all the details, but I quickly learned that my Treasury staff had frantically been trying to reach me. I also called the White House to get a briefing from former senator Howard Baker, who had succeeded Don Regan as chief of staff. I also talked to officials at Treasury and the finance ministers of Germany, Japan, the UK, and—if I'm not mistaken—France. This was a global crisis, I was told, and we had to consider the possibility that it was just beginning. After spending the entire night on the telephone, I flew to London the next morning and caught the Concorde home.

Back in Washington, I went straight to a meeting in my office at Treasury with Alan Greenspan, Howard Baker, George Gould (our under secretary for domestic finance), Robert Zoellick (Gould's assistant at the time), and others. By then, it appeared that the markets were beginning to stabilize, but we couldn't be sure they wouldn't drop again. The most important thing, we decided, was to reassure investors. John Phelan, who headed the New York Stock Exchange at the time, did a great job by instituting emergency procedures to let trading resume without

---

*Almost the same thing happened to Alan Greenspan when he landed in Dallas to deliver a speech. Over the summer, he had succeeded Paul Volcker as Fed chairman. Alan immediately hopped a plane back to Washington.

getting out of control. We all agreed that it was important to inject huge amounts of liquidity into the system, and this is exactly what Alan then did and would continue to do. Alan also issued a statement that affirmed the Fed's "readiness to serve as a source of liquidity to support the economic and financial system." This permitted investors to borrow to cover their positions, which prevented a cascading series of defaults that could have brought down banks and investment houses. In addition, the president issued a statement to reassure the public.

There was one more aftershock—an 8 percent drop on October 26— then the crisis ended almost as precipitously as it had begun, with little impact on either exchange rates or long-term economic growth. It hurt a lot of people, clearly, and raised disturbing thoughts about where the economy might be headed. Despite Black Monday, however, the Dow Jones ended 1987 with a 2 percent *gain* for the year, then went on to post solid gains in eleven of the next twelve years.

I'm not sure why Black Monday occurred and won't try to speculate. The president appointed former New Jersey senator Nicholas Brady to head a task force to investigate the meltdown. At the time, he headed Dillon Read, a prominent Wall Street firm, and he later succeeded me as treasury secretary. The task force report in January 1988 mentioned several contributing factors, including overvaluation of the market, a negative investor psychology that took root the preceding week, concern about our fiscal and trade deficits, worries about protectionist legislation and antitakeover legislation (Ways and Means had just okayed a bill to eliminate the tax deduction for interest on borrowed money in corporate takeovers), automatic program trading by computers in the big investment houses, the failure of market specialists to serve as buyers of last resort for securities they managed, and capacity problems at the exchanges (they simply couldn't handle the flood of sell orders).

The report also mentioned my remarks to the press about Germany and exchange rates. I still have difficulty believing my remarks contributed to the sell-off, and I absolutely don't believe they triggered it. What I said then wasn't substantially different from other statements I had made to the press. Still, if I had it to do over, I wouldn't say the same thing. One lesson I learned at Treasury is that even the most innocent remarks about the dollar or other economic issues could provoke investors to buy or sell, almost blindly, in response.

A number of market reforms were installed after Black Monday, including restrictions on program trading and "circuit breakers" to halt trading and allow investors to cool off after significant drops in the market. They seem to have helped. In addition, I believe our ongoing efforts to stabilize the dollar probably prevented the crisis from being worse. While the dollar lost value during this period, it did so in an orderly way and did not plunge with the securities market. I think this helped restore confidence. We've had several other significant one-day sell-offs—including two 500-plus-point drops in the late 1990s and two 600-plus drops in the early 2000s, one of which came on the day the market reopened after 9/11—but nothing like 1987, as a percentage of total market value.

The big lessons, I think, are that we survived that dark day, that it didn't trigger a depression (or, for that matter, a recession), that the economy was healthy and kept growing without significant damage, and that the market recovered and prospered as investor confidence returned.

P.S. I never did see the king of Sweden, much less an elk.

ACKNOWLEDGMENTS

Writing a book—I learned with *The Politics of Diplomacy* and relearned with *Work Hard, Study . . . and Keep Out of Politics!*—is a team sport, especially for someone whose writing career was long on contracts, diplomatic statements, and points lists, and short on writing for a general audience.

My quarterback was collaborator Steve Fiffer. Steve is a professional writer and editor with fourteen other books to his credit. He researched my story from public sources and my files, interviewed me for hours, and churned out first drafts that I then edited into my own voice. He may be a Baby Boomer, a Yankee (by way of Evanston, Illinois), and a Democrat, but he did an honest and very fine job for his client, a septuagenarian Texas Republican. And one of the great pleasures of working on the book was getting to know Steve and his wife, novelist Sharon Fiffer.

My second collaborator was my former policy assistant and speechwriter, Darrell Hancock. Darrell originally authored first drafts of many of the later chapters of this book and helped research and fact-check the entire manuscript. Without his expertise, judgment, advice, and talent, this book would not have happened.

Neil Nyren at Putnam did his usual expert job of editing and was particularly generous in his understanding of my inability to complete the work as rapidly as I had originally agreed.

And of course, my editor in chief was Susan, never shy about telling me when I got something wrong, ever helpful in suggesting ways to improve the book.

Margaret Tutwiler offered invaluable advice, as usual, including reading drafts of chapters for accuracy and refreshing my memory of events.

I was fortunate that Dick Darman was willing to review parts of the manuscript and help me in confirming facts and reminding me of things that I had forgotten. My great friend Otis Carney, a talented and prolific writer himself, reviewed much of the manuscript and offered many helpful suggestions, in spite of the fact that he was ill with terminal cancer.

Many people consented to be interviewed by my collaborators, beginning with President George H. W. Bush and including Robert Mosbacher, Stuart Spencer, Peter McPherson, Gary Edson, Preston Moore, Caron Jackson, Peter Roussel, Frank Donatelli, Anna Theofilopoulou, and James and Wendell Baker.

My researchers and I also relied on a number of fine books, magazine articles, and newspaper accounts of my years in politics and public service, many of which are mentioned in the book.

A number of people constantly encouraged me to write this book—too many to mention here. The recurring theme of their arguments was: you've written about your State Department experiences as a statesman, but you've also had other experiences in public service and in politics that very few other people have had; you need to write about those. Susan was one who encouraged me to write. Another was David Paton, my college roommate and lifelong friend. Two others were Ed Djerejian, founding director of the Baker Institute, and his wife, Françoise, who also assisted Steve and Darrell in accessing my files and in selecting photographs for the book.

My staff—Charlotte Cheadle, John Williams, and Catherine Duke of Baker Botts—contributed in ways too numerous to mention. So, too, did Joe Barnes of the Baker Institute.

Others who were helpful were my attorney Bob Barnett, and Dan Linke and Dan Santamaria of Princeton University's Seeley G. Mudd Manuscript Library, where my political and public service papers are stored. I also received valuable assistance from Fannie Richard, Wendell Baker, Jr., Wistar Morris of the Miller Center of Public Affairs, Maggie Cryer, formerly with the Baker Institute, and researchers Anne Hong, Alexandra Joseph, Cornelia van Amerongen, Marina Powell, and Jessica McBride.

Every memoirist is, I suppose, faced with the question of whether to kiss and tell. For me, the answer was easy: I would not violate the principles by which I gained and held the trust of Gerald Ford, George H. W. Bush, Ronald Reagan, George W. Bush, and many others, and by which I served them. I love and respect the presidents I served, and anyone who thinks James Addison Baker, III, might turn on them in his old age must have another James Addison Baker, III, in mind.

Many quotations in the book came from my memory, not from a written record. (Most quotations in *The Politics of Diplomacy*, by contrast, came from detailed transcripts and notes taken by State Department stenographers.) Although some quotations in this book may not be word for word, I believe all of them convey the substance of what was said.

To the trout, quail, and turkeys whose lives were spared because I had to work on this book when I might otherwise have been in the field or on the stream, go forth and multiply. I'll be back.

Finally, everyone says this, but I certainly mean it: Credit those I have mentioned above for their help in keeping errors out of this book, and blame me for those that may have slipped through my defenses. They are, I assure you, unintentional.

INDEX